Freedom of Information Handbook

SECOND EDITION

Other titles available from Law Society Publishing:

Company Law Handbook
Stephen Griffin

Data Protection Handbook
General Editor: Peter Carey

Drafting Confidentiality Agreements (Second Edition)
Mark Anderson and Simon Keevey-Kothari

Execution of Documents: A Practical Guide
Mark Anderson and Victor Warner

Insolvency Law Handbook (Second Edition)
Vernon Dennis

Intellectual Property Law Handbook
Bird & Bird, Edited by Lorna Brazell

All books from Law Society Publishing can be ordered through good bookshops or direct from our distributors, Prolog, by telephone 0870 850 1422 or email **lawsociety@prolog.uk.com**. Please confirm the price before ordering.

For further information or a catalogue, please contact our editorial and marketing office by email **publishing@lawsociety.co.uk**.

FREEDOM OF INFORMATION HANDBOOK

SECOND EDITION

General Editors: Peter Carey and Marcus Turle

The Law Society

© Law Society 2008

ISBN 978-1-85328-654-4

First published in 2006
This second edition published in 2008 by the Law Society
113 Chancery Lane, London WC2A 1PL

Typeset by IDSUK (DataConnection) Ltd
Printed in the United Kingdom by Hobbs the Printers Ltd, Totton, Hampshire

The paper used for the text pages of this book is FSC certified. FSC
(The Forest Stewardship Council) is an international network to promote responsible
management of the world's forests.

Printed on totally chlorine-free paper.

Contents

About the editors and contributors

EDITORS

Peter Carey is a Consultant Solicitor with Charles Russell in London, where he is Head of the Information Law Team. After gaining a Masters degree in International Business Law in the United States in 1993, Peter spent six years as a Senior Lecturer at the College of Law, the UK's leading legal education provider. Peter has established a reputation as one of the UK's leading data protection and privacy experts. He has written the UK's leading book on data protection (*Data Protection: a practical guide to UK and EU law*, Oxford University Press) and is the editor of the journal, *Privacy & Data Protection*. Peter advises commercial organisations of varying sizes on all aspects of information law compliance. His clients include a major water utility, several charities, a global telecommunications services provider, one of the world's largest medical data suppliers, local authorities and several e-commerce companies.

Marcus Turle is a Partner at Field Fisher Waterhouse LLP and a founder member of FFW's Privacy and Information Law Group. Marcus is a technology lawyer whose practice focuses on outsourcing, procurement and cutting edge IT projects, but he also specialises in the legal regulation of information. This includes freedom of information, data protection, information security, confidentiality and human rights. Marcus has worked closely with central and local government on freedom of information, including advising on the information law aspects of the national DNA database and the government's proposed national identity card scheme. He also advises banks, consultancy firms and the health sector. Marcus edits *Freedom of Information* (**www.foij.com**), the only legal journal dedicated to this area, and he is General Editor of *Data Protection Laws of the World* (Sweet & Maxwell), a two-volume looseleaf covering data protection in over 60 jurisdictions. He is also a visiting lecturer on the Northumbria University Information Rights LLM. Marcus would like to thank Jennifer Martin, trainee solicitor at Field Fisher Waterhouse LLP, for her invaluable research and assistance in updating the two chapters covering the Freedom of Information Act 2000 exemptions.

CONTRIBUTORS

Patricia Barratt graduated from Jesus College, Cambridge with a degree in Classics in 1984 before working for a Greek law firm in Piraeus for several years. She trained in law at Chancery Lane College of Law, and qualified as a solicitor with Clifford Chance in 1991. In 1992 she joined Clifford Chance's newly established Public Policy Group, headed by Richard Thomas, the current Information Commissioner. She has extensive experience of advising on all aspects of parliamentary and public policy related work with particular expertise in parliamentary procedure, freedom of information and standards of conduct in public life, including advice on corruption and political donations. She travels regularly to Brussels for meetings of the European Services Forum Policy Committee, a pan-European organisation representing the interests of the services industry. She also sits on the Law Society's GATS working group, and is on the Editorial Board of the *Freedom of Information* journal, to which she is a regular contributor. She has spoken frequently on freedom of information, and is the co-author of the Clifford Chance guide to the Freedom of Information Act.

Carolyn Bigg is an Assistant Solicitor at Charles Russell LLP, specialising in technology and information law, with particular expertise in IT and communications procurement agreements, outsourcings and managed service agreements. She is a member of Charles Russell's dedicated freedom of information and data protection teams. Carolyn advises a number of companies and not-for-profit organisations on data protection law and practice, in particular in the field of e-commerce, as well as several public authorities and private contractors on the impact of the Freedom of Information Act 2000. Carolyn was educated at Gonville and Caius College, Cambridge and qualified as a solicitor in 2003. She has contributed articles on various aspects of information law to a number of publications.

Jeremy Ison is a commercial litigator at Clifford Chance, where he qualified in 1997. He has handled corporate disputes in a range of industries, representing airlines, banks, energy suppliers and apparel manufacturers, among others. In addition, much of his work has a media slant and he advises both claimants and defendants pre- and post-publication in relation to libel and contempt. Formerly the editor of *Media Law Review*, co-published by Clifford Chance and the Periodical Publishers Association, he has also authored several articles on defamation and freedom of information. His regulatory experience includes a secondment to the Broadcasting Standards Commission where he worked on fairness and privacy cases, and he has brought and defended complaints for clients before several content regulators, such as the Advertising Standards Authority. Aside from public authorities, Jeremy has advised both information seekers and third parties wishing to protect their information on FOI issues.

Brian Jones joined Herbert Smith as a consultant in 2000 following a career in which he taught administrative law and environmental law at a number of universities in the UK and in Australia. Between 1994 and 2000 he was Professor of Environmental Liability at De Montfort University in Leicester. He has published extensively in both subject areas: his most recent book being a co-authored work on *Environmental Liabilities* (Shaw and Sons, 2004). He was involved in the late 1990s in several consultancy projects, advising governments in EU accession countries about requirements for harmonisation with EU environmental law. Since 1992 he has been editor of the bi-monthly professional journal *Environmental Liability*. He was recently appointed an Honorary Professor in the Department of Law, University of Wales, Aberystwyth. Brian works closely within Herbert Smith with the environmental law, planning law, public law and IP groups. He is a member of the editorial board of the *Freedom of Information* journal.

Keith Mathieson is a partner specialising in media law at London solicitors Reynolds Porter Chamberlain. He has taken a close interest in the new freedom of information legislation and its application to the media. RPC is well known for its representation of media organisations in the defence of libel and other claims. Its clients include national and regional newspaper publishers, magazine publishers, book publishers, broadcasters, independent production companies, journalists and media liability insurers. As well as advice on freedom of information issues, Keith's practice encompasses all legal aspects of free speech, including defamation, copyright, privacy and reporting restrictions. Keith is a member of the Editorial Board of the *Freedom of Information* journal.

Christopher Rees is a Partner at Herbert Smith LLP where he specialises in Technology work. He has 30 years' experience of the IT industry and advises on all types of IT-related issues. His practice covers system supply, outsourcing, M&A and corporate transactions for IT-centred businesses, privacy and FOI, and internet-related issues of all kinds. He has acted for numerous overseas technology companies in buying and selling assets in the UK and elsewhere around the world and for clients in High Court litigation and in ICC arbitration. He acts for both buyers and sellers of technology in order to retain a balanced view of transactions and to facilitate the resolution of disputes. Christopher is a leading commentator in the developing field of information law. He is a regular writer and lecturer on the subject in specialist journals and at international conferences. He is Chairman of the Computer and Database Committee of the International Bar Association. Christopher has been ranked in the top three of the world's IT lawyers in the two last surveys conducted by Euromoney (Euromoney, 'Best of the Best').

Andrew Sharpe is a Partner at Charles Russell LLP, practising information technology, intellectual property and telecommunications law. Andrew has lectured widely on freedom of information and data protection law, including conducting tailored training onsite at clients' premises. He has advised companies, public authorities and not-for-profit organisations on all aspects of data protection, freedom of information and communications legislation. He has written on data protection and privacy issues for *Privacy & Data Protection* and also on issues relating to the new freedom of information regime for the *Freedom of Information* journal.

Prior to qualifying as a solicitor in 1999, Andrew was a Royal Air Force engineering officer. He was one of the first Data Protection Officers in the RAF, responsible for the introduction of data protection operating procedures and compliance upon the introduction of RAF data protection policies under the Data Protection Act 1984.

Hugh Tomlinson QC is a founder member of Matrix Chambers with a wide-ranging practice covering media and information, commercial law, human rights, civil liberties and public law. He is a well known author and lecturer. His books include the leading practitioner's work on human rights, *The Law of Human Rights* (Oxford University Press, 2nd Edition, 2008) (with Richard Clayton) and, as editor, *Privacy and the Media: The Developing Law* (Matrix, 2002). He regularly acts as a Council of Europe expert on media and privacy issues. Hugh is a member of the Editorial Board of the *Freedom of Information* journal.

Antony White QC of Matrix Chambers practises in media and information law, commercial law and arbitration, employment law and public law. He appeared for the claimant in *Naomi Campbell* v. *MGN Ltd* [2003] QB 633 (CA) and [2004] 2 AC 457 (HL) which was the first successful High Court claim against a media defendant under the Data Protection Act 1998. He has appeared in several leading cases in the area of privacy/data protection/breach of confidence, and before the Information Tribunal in FOIA appeals. He is the co-author of *Privacy and the Media* (Matrix, 2002) and the author of the Privacy section of *Bullen & Leake & Jacob's Precedents of Pleadings* (16th edn, 2008).

Foreword

Open government is good government. The traditional culture of unnecessary secrecy is starting to erode.

The Freedom of Information Act 2000 and the Environmental Information Regulations 2004 have now been fully in force for more than three years. Already their effects have been deeply felt throughout the whole of the public sector and in many parts of the private sector too. Freedom of information has become part of the fabric of UK public life. Every day newspapers at national, regional and local level carry stories including the words '… disclosed this week under the Freedom of Information Act'.

There has been a strong public appetite for using the so-called Right to Know, with high volumes of requests. There is no central record, but it is likely that some 300,000 or more were requests made to public authorities over the first three years. Certainly, my office – the ICO – has received over 7,000 complaints and has closed over 6,000 of these. This includes over 750 formal Decision Notices, most upholding at least part of the complaint. Many complaints raise complex and difficult issues, often engaging public interest considerations, and require detailed and careful evaluation. The range of subject matter is astonishing – covering almost every aspect of public life in this country. There has been a steep learning curve for everyone, with much boundary-testing which still continues.

Although our tightly limited resources have prevented some cases being closed as fast we would like, we hope that we are earning wide respect for our decisions. These decisions, strengthened by the growing number of appeal decisions from the Information Tribunal, should help public authorities and requesters alike to get an ever-fuller understanding about how the law should work in practice.

This book will further help the processes of awareness and understanding. Written by legal professionals with expertise in freedom of information, it seeks to draw together the various threads of legislation, guidance, decisions and experience. Intended as a practical handbook for practitioners, I am sure this new edition will continue to provide an invaluable tool for navigating this important new regime.

Richard Thomas
UK Information Commissioner
February 2008

Abbreviations

ACAS	Advisory, Conciliation and Arbitration Service
BERR	Department for Business Enterprise and Regulatory Reform
BIU	Bank's Inquiry Unit
CCC	criminal conviction certificate
CPR	Civil Procedure Rules 1998
CRB	Criminal Records Bureau
CRC	criminal record certificate
DCA	Department for Constitutional Affairs
DCMS	Department for Culture, Media and Sport
DfES	Department for Education and Skills
DMI	Development and Maintenance Initiative (of the ICO)
DPA	Data Protection Act 1998
DWP	Department for Work and Pensions
ECRC	enhanced criminal record certificate
EIR	Environmental Information Regulations
FCO	Foreign and Commonwealth Office
FOI	freedom of information
FOIA	Freedom of Information Act 2000
FSA	Financial Services Authority
GCHQ	Government Communications Headquarters
GRO	General Registry Office
HFEA	Human Fertilisation and Embryology Act 1990
HMSO	Her Majesty's Stationery Office (now OPSI)
IAR	Information Asset Register
ICO	Information Commissioner's Office
LLP	legal professional privilege
LSLO	Legal Secretariat to the Law Officers
MoJ	Ministry of Justice
MoU	Memorandum of Understanding
NAO	National Audit Office
NDPB	non-departmental public body

OFT	Office of Fair Trading
OPSI	Office of Public Sector Information
PCA	Parliamentary Commissioner for Administration (also known as the Parliamentary Ombudsman)
PSI	public sector information
TULRCA	Trade Union and Labour Relations (Consolidation) Act 1992
UKTI	UK Trade & Investment
VFM Reports	Value for Money Reports

Table of cases

Table of statutes

Table of statutory instruments

Table of treaties, conventions and European legislation

TREATIES AND CONVENTIONS

EUROPEAN LEGISLATION

CHAPTER 1

Introduction and background to the law

Patricia Barratt, Clifford Chance LLP

1.1 INTRODUCTION

How much do individual MPs claim in expenses and what for? How viable did the Treasury think the government's ID card scheme was? What advice did Gordon Brown receive when deciding to abolish dividend tax credits? And who did Tony Blair as Prime Minister invite to dinner? The list of questions that requesters have received answers to under the Freedom of Information Act 2000 (FOIA) is endless and highly political. Since information is power, it is hardly surprising that so many people have made use of the new right of access to information, with over 200,000 requests in less than three years since that right came into being. The press, in particular, has enjoyed a bonanza of politically embarrassing freedom of information disclosures.

The FOIA undoubtedly has a political side, but it has also a very real practical application for a very large number of people, and not just those who work in the 115,000 public authorities to which the Act applies. Public sector expenditure, not just that of central government, has attracted unprecedented scrutiny as a result of the Act, with private sector contractors also deeply affected. Grant funding, planning permission applications, development plans, government-compiled statistics, lobbying efforts, public procurement details, departmental meeting minutes, public service contracts – these are all potentially accessible under the Act.

It could be argued that a number of different developments made the Act almost inevitable. Perhaps the most influential of these is the creation and growth of the internet. With such a huge range of information from all sources already easily accessible to anyone using the internet, and with few, if any, effective mechanisms for blocking the dissemination of information via that route, a government seeking to protect information that others want is frequently going to be fighting a losing battle. The *Spycatcher* case (*AG* v. *Guardian Newspapers (No.2)* [1990] AC 109) had already shown the limits of the government's power to restrain publication of information, but the internet multiplies this problem to the nth degree with websites accessible from anywhere in the world and publication immediate. Also, with information access regimes becoming increasingly common in other countries, the UK was on the back foot in terms of international legal comparators. Sweden, famously, has had a form of freedom of information legislation in place since 1776. New Zealand has had a freedom of information act since 1962, the United States since 1966 (strengthened in 1982), Australia since 1982 and Ireland since 1997.

1.2   THE CODE OF PRACTICE ON ACCESS TO GOVERNMENT INFORMATION

The Conservative government, resisting calls for legislation, introduced the voluntary Code of Practice on Access to Government Information ('the Code') in April 1994 (revised in January 1997), since then often described as one of government's best kept secrets. It fell under the remit of the Parliamentary Commissioner and only applied to organisations under her jurisdiction. This meant that any complaints about how requests were dealt with under the Code had to be approached in the same way as other complaints about, for example, maladministration by government departments – in other words, via a Member of Parliament. This cumbersome mechanism, coupled with the lack of real powers on the part of the Parliamentary Commissioner, kept the number of requests under the Code down, and its influence on public sector culture minimal, save within a few better informed and more progressive central government departments.

Decisions of the Ombudsman, as the Parliamentary Commissioner is also known, were, however, useful, at least in the early days, because the UK Information Commissioner had said he would expect to have regard to decisions of the Ombudsman. (Readers are referred to the practical journal, *Freedom of Information*, as an excellent resource for keeping up to date with developments – **www.foij.com**.)

The Code came into force on 4 April 1994 (and was revised in 1997), setting out common standards applicable to all government departments responding to requests for disclosure of information, new procedures enabling those requesting the information to seek internal review of decisions not to disclose, and a new mechanism for external review of such decisions by the Parliamentary Ombudsman.

In the opening paragraph of the Code, under the heading 'Purpose', it clearly stated that: 'The approach to release of information should in all cases be based on the assumption that information should be released except where disclosure would not be in the public interest, as specified in Part II of this Code.' A number of MPs later argued for the inclusion of such an assumption – a presumption in favour of disclosure – on the face of the Act. However, amendments to this effect were rejected by the government.

The Code also set out three aims:

- to improve policy-making and the democratic process by extending access to the facts and analyses which provide the basis for the consideration of proposed policy;

2

- to protect the interests of individuals and companies by ensuring that reasons are given for administrative decisions, except where there is statutory authority or established convention to the contrary; and
- to support and extend the principles of public service established under the Citizen's Charter.

However, the aims are immediately qualified by the need:

- to maintain high standards of care in ensuring the privacy of personal and commercially confidential information; and
- to preserve confidentiality where disclosure would not be in the public interest or would breach personal privacy or the confidences of a third party, in accordance with statutory requirements and Part II of the Code.

The main concerns of the private sector and businesses providing information to government under commercial contracts, grant applications, or other submissions, were therefore explicitly addressed, to some extent, the focus of the Code resting squarely on releasing genuinely official information, rather than simply information held by officials.

As part of this voluntary regime, the Chancellor of the Duchy of Lancaster undertook to report annually on the progress of the Code. In his report (*Open Government: Code of Practice on Access to Government Information, 1995 Report*) on the first full year of the Code's operation, 1995, he said that 1,353 requests for information had been recorded for that year (compared to over 7,000 requests recorded for the first three months of the operation of the FOIA). Code requests were narrowly defined as requests that specifically mentioned the Code; those for which a charge or standard fee was imposed; or those in respect of which information had been refused under one or more of the exemptions set out in the Code.

The Code only applied to those government departments and bodies which fell within the jurisdiction of the Parliamentary Commissioner (these are set out in Sched.2 to the Parliamentary Commissioner Act 1967). The Code provided that complaints about the way in which a request had been handled should be made first to the department or body concerned. Only after this should the complaint be referred, via an MP, to the Ombudsman. Guidance on this internal review stage, contained in the Guidance on Interpretation of the Code (2nd edition, Part I, para.72), recommended that internal reviews should be a 'single stage process', though this advice has clearly not been followed by a number of public authorities which have set up two-tier, and in some cases, three-tier FOIA appeal procedures. Further:

The aim should be to ensure that the applicant has been fairly treated under the provisions of the Code, that any exemptions have been properly applied and that charges are reasonably and consistently applied. It is good practice for such review to be conducted by someone not involved in the original decision.

3

The Code, thought by many to give superior rights of access to information than the Act, nevertheless suffered from a lack of profile, poor enforcement mechanisms and a limited application. It was made obsolete on 1 January 2005 when the FOIA right of access was finally introduced, four years after the Act was passed.

1.2.1 Lessons to be learned from the Code

Decisions on the application of the Code made by the Parliamentary Commissioner are only precedents insofar as the Information Commissioner chooses to follow them. From a legal point of view they are not binding. There are differences in wording between the exemptions in the Code and the exemptions in the Act which further limit the usefulness of Code decisions as precedents. Nevertheless, the Information Commissioner initially indicated that he expected all public authorities to take decisions of the Parliamentary Commissioner into account when making decisions on disclosure of requests for information.

> In a UK context, it will also be important to consider any decisions made by the Parliamentary Ombudsman when considering complaints under the Open Government Code. Although the Code is not statutory and applies to a much smaller number of public authorities, the public interest test applied by the Ombudsman is identical to that required under the Act. Summaries of cases considered by the Ombudsman under the Code can be found on the Ombudsman's website (at **www.ombudsman.org.uk/pca/document/aoi03nj/index.htm**).
>
> (Information Commissioner's Office, Freedom of Information Awareness
> Guidance No.3, The Public Interest Test)

Public authorities must therefore be familiar with these decisions, and those requesting information may also find valuable material there to substantiate their arguments for or against disclosure.

The Parliamentary Ombudsman published regular reports summarising her investigations into complaints under the Code. Her last annual report on Code investigations (*Access to Official Information: Investigations Completed July 2003–June 2004*, HC 701), published in June 2004, contained decisions on a range of issues, from briefings for Ministers, meetings between Ministers and trade associations, a National Audit Office report, information about the awarding of a contract and the publication of a Ministerial Direction. A further report, looking at more than 10 years of the operation of the Code, was published in June 2005. To reiterate, the Information Commissioner may choose not to follow these decisions but there is likely to be considerable adverse criticism of any decision which appears to row back from the position under the non-statutory Code.

The first reported case (A.21/03) in the 2004 report makes very interesting reading. It dealt with a request made to the Cabinet Office (and 17 other government departments) on 6 and 10 June 2002 for details of any contact between Ministers and representatives of a particular trade association since a specified date and in particular, the number of meetings that had taken place, the number of letters exchanged and the number of representations made by Ministers on behalf of the trade association to other parties.

Only one department provided the information requested: the Department for Culture, Media and Sport (DCMS) replied that there had been no contact between departmental Ministers and the trade association, and that Ministers had made no representations on behalf of the trade association. Eleven departments, including the Cabinet Office, refused to supply the information requested. The Cabinet Office (on 12 September 2002, three months after the request) claimed that the information was exempt under Exemptions 7(b) and 13 of the Code: that the release of the information sought would harm the proper and efficient conduct of the department and would constitute an unwarranted disclosure of commercial confidences which would harm the competitive position of a third party. (These exemptions correspond roughly to the exemptions set out in ss.36 and 43 respectively of the FOIA.) They also considered that the public interest in disclosure did not outweigh the harm which would result from such disclosure. This reply drew on central guidance issued by the Lord Chancellor's Department (as it was then) on 13 August 2002 to the effect that departments should regard information relating to contact between Ministers and officials and representatives of outside organisations as exempt under the Code, based on the application of the exemptions mentioned above.

When the applicant asked for an internal review of the refusal to disclose, further central guidance was issued confirming that it should not be the normal practice to release details of meetings with outside interests, and the refusal to disclose was repeated.

The applicant appealed to the Ombudsman, who found that the stated exemptions did not apply, and that the Cabinet Office was not justified in withholding the information requested. She recommended that the Permanent Secretary supply the information and issue revised guidance to the Department for Constitutional Affairs to enable it to advise the other departments to whom requests for release of information had been addressed. The Ombudsman also criticised the Cabinet Office for the way in which it had dealt with the request (the officials had failed to locate and identify the information requested before deciding whether to disclose it), and for delays in providing information to the Ombudsman's office.

The Cabinet Office confirmed that it would now provide the information requested to the applicant. This decision is of direct relevance to the request made under the FOIA by the *Guardian* newspaper to the DCMS, for information about meetings between Ministers, officials, and representatives of the gaming industry prior to the introduction of the Gambling Bill into

Parliament. The public interest test (a slightly different test under the Code than under the Act) was not engaged in the Ombudsman's case because she held that the exemptions could not apply. The DCMS, in this case, released the information under the FOIA, leading to media criticisms of improper behaviour.

In other reported investigations, the Ombudsman recommended that background briefings for Parliamentary Questions should be released, but agreed that they could be edited so as to omit opinions and advice the disclosure of which might harm the frankness and candour of internal discussion (Exemption 2 under the Code, s.35 of the FOIA).

Interestingly, the Ombudsman was also asked to adjudicate on the Cabinet Office's refusal to supply copies of all documents drawn up by the Attorney General giving advice on the legality of military intervention in Iraq. The Ombudsman found that Exemption 4(d) of the Code relating to legal professional privilege (s.42 of the FOIA) applied and that the refusal to disclose the information requested was justified. She noted that the exemption in the Code was an absolute exemption and therefore she did not have to consider the public interest in disclosure. This, of course, is in direct contrast with the position under the FOIA, since the s.42 exemption is subject to the public interest test. In a Decision Notice (Ref. FS50062881), the Information Commissioner found that, since the Attorney General's advice dated 7 March 2003 was already in the public domain following a partial leak in April 2005, it was not necessary for him to consider that part of the request.

Other investigations included in the report deal with:

- the Ministry of Defence's refusal to provide information about accidents involving nuclear weapons;
- a refusal by the Department for Education and Skills to provide information about a decision to discontinue a procurement exercise relating to the electronic registration of schools;
- a refusal by the Foreign and Commonwealth Office and the Department of Trade and Industry to provide reasons why a company's application for funding under the Export Market Research Scheme had been refused;
- the Department of Health's refusal to provide information about the award of a contract to supply a stock of smallpox vaccine;
- a refusal by the Higher Education Funding Council for England to provide information about issues of financial probity and corporate governance;
- the Department of Trade and Industry's refusal to release a Ministerial Direction; and
- HM Treasury's refusal to provide details of external meetings attended by the Chancellor of the Exchequer, Treasury Ministers and special advisers.

1.3   HISTORY AND DEVELOPMENT OF THE LEGISLATION

Despite the existence of the Code, there was still strong pressure to introduce a statutory regime enabling access to public sector information. The Labour Manifesto in 1997, promising such a regime, said:

> Unnecessary secrecy in government leads to arrogance in government and defective policy decisions. The Scott Report on arms to Iraq revealed Conservative abuses of power. We are pledged to a Freedom of Information Act, leading to more open government, and an independent National Statistical Service.
>
> (New Labour, *Because Britain Deserves Better*
> Labour Party Manifesto 1997, M/029/97)

Further, in December of the same year, the newly elected Labour government presented a White Paper (*Your Right to Know – The Government's Proposals for a Freedom of Information Act*, Cm 3818, December 1997) to Parliament, setting out radical proposals for a new statutory right to obtain information from public authorities.

In introducing the White Paper, the Prime Minister said that 'The traditional culture of secrecy will only be broken down by giving people in the United Kingdom the legal right to know' (Cm 3818, Preface). (The soundbite would not, of course, be so effective if one were to add 'subject to 23 legal exemptions and over 400 statutory bars'.)

The White Paper was considered by a House of Commons Select Committee, which welcomed the proposals, and a report (*Third Report of the Select Committee on Public Administration: Your Right to Know – The Government's Proposals for a Freedom of Information Act*, HC (1997–98) 398-I) published in May 1998, said that a Freedom of Information Act would 'help to begin to change for good the secretive culture of the public service'. The report, in addition to making 44 recommendations and observations, also found the proposals for increased access to information, if implemented in their White Paper form, would have three purposes and effects. They would:

- make it easier for members of the public to find out what information government holds about themselves;
- make it easier for politicians, journalists and members of the public to hold the government to account by making government cover-ups more difficult; and
- make it easier for members of the public to participate in an informed way in the discussion of policy issues, and improve the quality of government decision-making because those drafting policy advice know that they must be able, ultimately, to defend their reasoning before public opinion.

The White Paper was followed by a consultation paper (*Freedom of Information: Consultation on draft legislation*, May 1999, Cm 4355) containing a draft Freedom of Information Bill, which was subject to pre-legislative scrutiny by committees of both Houses of Parliament, as well as to public consultation. The House of Commons Select Committee on Public Administration welcomed the draft Bill, but warned of 'serious deficiencies which, if not remedied, will undermine the potential' (House of Commons Select Committee on Public Administration, *Freedom of Information Draft Bill*, Third Report of Session 1998–99, 570-I, published 29 July 1999). Among its specific recommendations for remedying these deficiencies, it called for a purpose clause with a clear presumption in favour of disclosure on the face of the Bill, for the public interest in disclosing information to be balanced against the harm in so doing, for the right of access to apply as broadly as possible and exemptions drawn as narrowly as possible with a more demanding harm test, and for enforceable rights of access to information.

The House of Lords Committee looking at it said that the single most important amendment required to the draft Bill was one which would give the Information Commissioner 'a public interest override power in clause 44 to overrule a ministerial decision under clause 14, and to order disclosure' (House of Lords Select Committee, *Draft Freedom of Information Bill – First Report*, HL97, published 27 July 1999). It also called for the Long Title of the Bill to be amended from the neutral 'make provision about the disclosure of information' to the purposive 'facilitate the disclosure of information'.

After this very long lead-in period, with examination from no fewer than three parliamentary committees, the Bill was finally introduced into the House of Commons on 18 November 1999, though not to universal acclaim. Critics of the Bill argued that the proposals had been significantly watered down since the draft Bill, and complained that the views of the committees had not been taken on board sufficiently. Once the Act had received Royal Assent on 20 November 2000, there was further criticism of the long delay in implementing it, despite the Lord Chancellor's announcement:

> The Act will be fully implemented by January 2005, 11 months before the timetable set out in the Act itself. The publication scheme provisions will be implemented first, on a rolling programme, starting with central government in November 2002. . . . the individual right of access to information held by all public authorities, including government departments, will be implemented in January 2005.

1.4   THE COURTS AND ACCESS TO INFORMATION

As recently as 1989, the Official Secrets Act 1911 prevented government officials or contractors from revealing any information learned in the course of carrying out their duty to any person unless authorised. The comprehensive nature of this prohibition – which applied to any information regardless of whether there was any justification for protection against disclosure or not – was gradually eroded by a series of court cases. In *R.* v. *Peter Anthony Galvin* (1988) 86 Cr App R 85 the Court of Appeal was asked to decide whether documents already in the public domain should be excluded from the parameters of the prohibition. Although the court found that the wording of the legislation would not permit this interpretation, it found that no breach of the prohibition had occurred because the document in question had been so widely distributed that there had been implied authorisation for those in possession of it to use it as they saw fit. In 1990, the House of Lords (*AG* v. *Guardian Newspapers (No.2)* [1990] AC 109, the '*Spycatcher* case') held that an injunction would only be granted where the Crown could show that disclosure of the material in question would be likely to damage the public interest. Since the information (in the form of a book, *Spycatcher*) was already published worldwide and therefore no longer secret, the courts would not grant a continuing injunction against disclosure.

A new Official Secrets Act replaced the 1911 statute in 1989, and restricted the prohibition against disclosure to information about security, defence, international relations and law enforcement.

At the same time, the continually growing power of the courts to look at administrative decision-making through judicial review proceedings, meant that the relevant decision-making bodies were forced to disclose to the courts background information relevant to the decision-making process. Fairness in the exercise of administrative powers, Lord Mustill said (*R.* v. *Secretary of State for the Home Department, ex p. Doody* [1994] 1 AC 531) required that those affected by decisions should be informed of the matters relevant to the decision and be given the opportunity to make representations.

Case law on the tort of breach of confidence, vital to an application of the s.41 exemption in the FOIA for information provided in confidence, also continues to develop from the statement of basic principles set out in the landmark case of *Coco* v. *AN Clark Engineers Ltd* [1969] RPC 41. This will be explored further in **Chapter 4** dealing with exemptions.

1.5 FREEDOM OF INFORMATION IN OTHER JURISDICTIONS

The Information Commissioner has said he will consider decisions from other jurisdictions that have freedom of information laws, and will aim to remain in line with them as far as reasonably possible (though this, of course, imports no obligation on him to do so in any particular circumstance). This opens up a huge resource of potential precedents for anyone making decisions on access requests or seeking disclosure. Clearly, the decisions are more likely to be influential if the underlying legislation is similar to the FOIA. Decisions in the United States, Ireland, Canada, Australia and New Zealand are therefore likely to be the most influential in this regard due to the closer similarities in the legislation itself, as well as the common language.

Many other jurisdictions have legislation on access to information. The Foreign and Commonwealth Office published a table[1] in 2004 with an alphabetical list of 53 countries that have such legislation, from Albania to Zimbabwe. Thirty other countries were said to be in the process of introducing access to information legislation and the number is now said to be over 70. The oldest legislation (in Sweden) dates back over 200 years, whilst many other countries have adopted legislation within the last decade. In addition, there are various freedom of information laws and codes which apply to international organisations or political groupings. A variety of factors has led to their introduction, including the creation of the Information Society and the expansion of the internet, pressure from the international community, the transition of countries to democracy, public demand following campaigns by civil society, and political scandals relating to health and the environment.

While ostensibly sharing a common goal of improving public access to information held by public bodies, the codes vary widely in their content and approach as well as in their effectiveness. There follows a discussion of some of the typical features of access to information regimes and consideration of how they are dealt with in different jurisdictions. This whistle-stop tour of global freedom of information laws does not aim to be comprehensive, but rather to identify a few areas of agreement and of disagreement.

1.5.1   Bodies to which freedom of information applies

Since the drive for freedom of information springs from a desire to improve transparency and accountability in government, it is clear that the legislation must apply to government bodies. Depending on the type of government, this may include local or regional government. The courts, legislative assemblies and the security and intelligence services are normally exempt from application of the legislation.

US legislation only applies to organisations that are controlled by the federal government. State governments, municipal corporations, the courts and Congress are not subject to the regime (though all of the states have their own disclosure legislation). In Canada, the right to information applies to records 'under the control' of a 'government institution'. Irish legislation, like the FOIA, lists bodies to which it applies in a Schedule to the Act: the list includes local authorities, health boards, government departments and other public sector organisations, but does not extend to voluntary hospitals, schools, universities, the police force, a range of government agencies, and commercial state-funded enterprises.

The South African law, the Promotion of Access to Information Act 2000, goes further in providing a right for individuals and government bodies to obtain information from private sector entities where this is necessary to enforce people's rights – a separate Part of the Act is entitled 'Access to Records of Private Bodies'. The UK legislation, of course, gives the Secretary of State the power to designate certain private sector entities as public authorities for the purposes of the FOIA. This power has not yet been used but the Ministry of Justice has published a consultation ('Freedom of Information Act 2000: Designation of additional public authorities', 25 October 2007) with a view to such designation.

1.5.2 The right of access

The right of access is frequently to 'information', but sometimes to 'documents' or 'records'. Where documents are specified, these are sometimes defined to include mechanical or electronic records. The use of the term 'information', as in the FOIA, is thought to be more flexible. Often, requests must be made in writing and a response deadline of 20 or 30 days is common, though there are usually provisions enabling the deadline to be extended in given circumstances.

1.5.3 Proactive publication

Another common feature of freedom of information legislation is a requirement that government agencies publish information or documents proactively. This is reflected in the UK legislation in the duty on public authorities to maintain Publication Schemes. In the United States, each agency must publish a large amount of agency-specific information, including a description of the organisation of the agency, the internal reports of the agency, its regulations for reviewing information that it holds, statements of the general methods or agency procedures, and other sources of data that could be useful to the public.

The Indian regime includes a requirement that public bodies publish information on their structure and duties, relevant facts concerning important decisions and policies, reasons for their decisions to those affected by such decisions, and background facts prior to initiation of projects.

In Ireland, public bodies are required to publish information relating to their structure, functions, duties, descriptions of records, and the internal rules, procedures, practices, guidelines and interpretations of the agency.

1.5.4 Exemptions

Not surprisingly, very similar exemptions are found in many of the access to information laws. In some cases certain exemptions are mandatory, i.e. prohibitions on disclosure, in contrast with the FOIA where exemptions, whether they are absolute or qualified, are to be applied at the discretion of the authority to which the request is addressed (with the exception of the exemption for statutory bars).

The most common exemptions concern the protection of national security and international relationships, personal privacy, commercial confidentiality, law enforcement and public order, information received in confidence and internal discussions. Privacy, protecting internal decision-making, and national security tend to attract the highest level of protection. The United States has an unusual exemption covering geological or geophysical information, including information about wells and, in the wake of 9/11, created new exemptions, for 'critical infrastructure information', and all information held by the Office of Homeland Security.

It is common for a harm test to be incorporated into the exemptions, i.e. that the information is only exempt if harm, or substantial harm, would result from disclosure. Many laws include a public interest test requiring the public interest in withholding the information to be balanced against the public interest in disclosure.

1.5.5 Charging

The level of fees charged for requests is a critical factor in the effectiveness of any freedom of information regime. Where fees are too high, access to information is placed outside the reach of ordinary people. US charging provisions distinguish between requests for educational or journalistic purposes, and those for commercial purposes. Agencies may charge commercial interests 'reasonable standard charges' in respect of their costs of searching for, reproducing and reviewing the information requested. Requests for educational or journalistic purposes attract only duplication fees. Where requests fall outside these two categories, reasonable standard charges may be made for document search and duplication. Documents are to be provided at no charge, or at a reduced charge:

> if disclosure of the information is in the public interest because it is likely to contribute significantly to public understanding of the operations or activities of the government and is not primarily in the commercial interest of the requester
> (Freedom of Information Act 1966, s.552(a)(4)(A)(iii))

Ireland amended its freedom of information charging regime (the Freedom of Information (Amendment) Act 2003) to allow the government to impose fees for requests and appeals. The Irish Information Commissioner, Emily O'Reilly, in a report (Irish Information Commissioner, *Review of the Operation of the Freedom of Information (Amendment) Act 2003*, June 2004) into the impact of the charges for making freedom of information requests introduced by the Minister for Finance in July 2003, found that overall usage of the Act had fallen by over 50 per cent while requests for non-personal information had declined by 75 per cent.

Japanese law provides for a request fee and a disclosure fee, which must be within the limit of actual expenses and in accordance with government regulations. These fees may be reduced or waived in cases of economic hardship or for other 'special reasons'.

12

Unlike the UK, some countries impose charges for appealing refusals. The Irish legislation now provides for payment of €75 in respect of internal reviews and €150 for reviews by the Information Commissioner.

Recent proposals in the UK to amend the fees regime were abandoned (in an announcement by Prime Minister Gordon Brown, on 25 October 2007) following widespread opposition and allegations that the proposals were politically driven.

1.5.6 Third party rights

There has been considerable criticism of the FOIA for its failure to provide rights for third parties whose interests are affected by the disclosure of information. Many access to information laws require the public body to which the request has been made to notify third parties, and to give them the right to make representations. The United States is the best known example, though in fact no right of action is afforded by the Freedom of Information Act – a more general right, which would permit an affected third party to bring an action to prevent disclosure, is provided by the Administrative Procedure Act 1946 (see *Chrysler Corp* v. *Brown*, US Supreme Court 441 US 281 (1979)).

The South African legislation requires the public authority to 'take all reasonable steps to inform a third party to whom or which the record relates of the request' within 21 days. The third party has a statutory right to make written or oral representations as to why the request should be refused, and the public authority is under an obligation to give 'due regard to any representations made by a third party' (the Promotion of Access to Information Act 2000).

In Japan, a public body which has received a request for certain types of information (as specified) must notify the third party concerned and give him an opportunity to provide a written opinion, before making a decision to disclose (unless the third person's whereabouts are unknown). If the third party opposes disclosure, the public body, when making a decision to disclose, must immediately notify him in writing of the decision to disclose being made, the reason for it, and the date of implementation of disclosure, which must be at least two weeks later (the Law Concerning Access to Information held by Administrative Organs 1999, Art.13).

Canada also provides statutory rights for third parties to be notified of an intended decision to disclose specified information, to be given the opportunity to make representations and to be notified of the public body's decision on disclosure following consideration of the representations. The third party may apply to the Federal Court of Canada to seek an order against disclosure.

1.5.7 Appeals and enforcement

In most jurisdictions, where a decision by a public body on disclosure of information is challenged the first step will be an internal review by the public body concerned. If the results of the review are still unsatisfactory to the applicant, there will usually be a right to appeal the internal review decision to a third party. In the best enforcement regimes this will usually be an independent Information Commissioner or Ombudsman.

The Canadian Information Commissioner receives complaints and can investigate and issue recommendations but does not have the power to issue binding orders. He, or the applicant, can seek review of a refusal to disclose in the Federal Court of Canada. In Ireland, the Office of the Information Commissioner is able to make binding decisions which can be appealed on a point of law. The Ministry of Justice has the power to issue certificates preventing the release of information.

Japan has an Information Disclosure Review Board within the Cabinet Office, consisting of 12 members approved by both Houses. Cases are referred to the Board by the head of the body that has made the decision under dispute. Decisions of the Board may be appealed to the courts. In South Africa, the Human Rights Commission oversees the functioning of the Act, earlier proposals to create an Open Democracy Commission and specialised information courts having failed to make it to the statute book. While this has advantages in placing access to information alongside human rights enforcement, the Commission has reported that its work on information rights is hampered by a lack of funding.

The United States lacks a central regulator of information rights, the district courts having exclusive jurisdiction in relation to decisions under the Freedom of Information Act. The courts will normally consider all the issues of the case and will look at the procedures followed by the agency in trying to locate the requested information, but have no power to order disclosure where an exemption applies. Each of the individual states has legislation on access to government records, and some states also have information commissions which review decisions.

In most countries there is a final level of appeal to the national courts.

1.5.8   Application in the United Kingdom

Within the UK, the FOIA applies to England, Wales and Northern Ireland. Separate legislation in Scotland (the Freedom of Information (Scotland) Act 2002) applies to public authorities that operate solely in, or with regard to, Scotland, and is enforced by a separate Scottish Information Commissioner. Likewise, the Scottish Executive has issued its own Code of Practice on Access to Scottish Executive Information. The Scottish legislation is very similar, but not identical, to the FOIA, and is not specifically addressed in this publication. Further divergence between the two regimes may develop as a result of differences in approach by the two Information Commissioners.

1.6 OTHER UK LEGISLATION ON ACCESS TO INFORMATION

Probably the most significant pieces of UK legislation in this area, prior to the FOIA, were the Data Protection Acts of 1984 and 1998 (these implemented Council Directive (EC) 95/46 on the protection of individuals with regard to the processing of personal data and on the free movement of such data). Although one of the main purposes of data protection legislation is the antithesis of freedom of information – to protect information and keep it confidential – the data protection legislation also introduced an important right for individuals to have access to information held about themselves, initially in the form of electronically processed data, but extended by the 1998 Act to apply also to non-electronic records that are held in a structured form. **Chapter 8** looks more closely at the data protection legislation and how it interacts with the FOIA, but the basic rule is simple enough to understand (if not to apply): information to which the Data Protection Act applies will be exempt from disclosure under the FOIA. Anyone receiving a request for information must therefore be able to determine whether the information is personal information and whether disclosure of the information would contravene any of the eight data protection principles (governing the use of personal information, as set out in the Data Protection Act 1998).

Also of importance are the Environmental Information Regulations. Originally introduced in 1992, these Regulations, SI 1992/3240, which also implement an EU Directive (EU Directive 2003/4/EC on public access to environmental information), provide access to information about the environment held by public bodies. Lacking any effective enforcement mechanism, and not widely publicised, they did not have a significant impact, but revised Regulations (Environmental Information Regulations 2004, SI 2004/3391), brought into force on the same date as the FOIA, on 1 January 2005, and also enforced by the Information Commissioner, have enjoyed a higher profile. The definition of 'environmental information' for the purposes of the Regulations is very wide, and includes elements of the environment, such as land, water, biological organisms, etc., as well as measures and activities which affect these, and information on the state of human health and safety. If information falls within the remit of the Environmental Information Regulations, then a request for such information must be treated in accordance with the procedures set out in the Regulations, and not in the FOIA. Just to make life more difficult, the exemptions in the Regulations are similar to, but by no means the same as, the exemptions in the FOIA. The similarities and differences between these two parallel regimes have caused some confusion. The Regulations are dealt with in more detail in **Chapter 9**.

In addition to these major pieces of legislation, there is a patchwork of smaller pieces of legislation which has, over the past decade, incrementally improved public access to official records. A number of these were drafted by the Campaign for Freedom of Information, and started life as Private Members' Bills. Where there exists a separate statutory right to information, it is likely that the s.21 exemption in the FOIA (for information reasonably accessible otherwise than by an access request) will apply.

One of these statutory rights was introduced by the Local Government (Access to Information) Act 1985, which amended the Local Government Act 1972 (by inserting Part VA) to provide rights of access to council meetings, reports and papers. (Limited rights existed previously in the form of the Public Bodies (Admission to Meetings) Act 1960.) There are specific exemptions for a number of types of personal information, as well as for contractual terms, and expenditure in relation to contracts for the acquisition of property or the supply of goods and services.

The Access to Personal Files Act 1987 (now repealed) gave the public the right to see manually held social work and housing records about themselves. The Access to Medical Reports Act 1988 provided the right for applicants to see reports produced about them by doctors for an employer or insurance company. The Access to Health Records 1990 provided wider access to information on individuals' medical records, though this was largely superseded by the Data Protection Act 1998.

The Environment and Safety Information Act 1988 gives people the right to see enforcement notices issued following breaches of environmental protection legislation.

1.7   THE INFORMATION COMMISSIONER – ENFORCING THE REGIME

Chapter 10 examines closely the legal enforcement mechanisms of the FOIA. This short section does not aim to duplicate that, but attempts rather to look at the policy approach the Information Commissioner is taking vis-à-vis its dealings with government departments.

The approach was set out, to a large extent, in an agreement in February 2005, when the Department for Constitutional Affairs (DCA) (as it was then) and the Information Commissioner signed a Memorandum of Understanding[2] (MoU), the stated purpose being 'to promote good standards of co-operation between Departments and the Commissioner'. Following criticism of the content of this MoU in the press, the Information Commissioner, writing in the *Guardian* (Media, Letters, 4 April 2005) denied that it skewed the complaint process in the government's favour, and said that the key commitment in the MoU was that government departments provide all relevant information in relation to a valid complaint swiftly. He confirmed that, in relation to relevant information, the MoU 'sets out a number of corresponding undertakings from my office – such as keeping it secure and not disclosing it improperly to others'.

The signing of the MoU followed in the footsteps of the Parliamentary Ombudsman. In an attempt to address 'a lack of knowledge within departments about the Code, unacceptable delays in responding to my Office and, in some cases, a lack of cooperation with my investigations', the Ombudsman had initiated discussion with the Cabinet Office and the DCA resulting in a MoU, published by the Cabinet office on 22 July 2003. This MoU[3] (the 'PCA MoU') set out timescales and procedures departments were expected to adhere to in their dealings with the Ombudsman. In particular, departments were required to:

- respond in full within three weeks of receipt of the Ombudsman's statement of complaint;
- reply to the draft investigation report within three weeks;
- contact the PCA as soon as possible if these timescales were not going to be met;
- provide all relevant papers as quickly as possible; and
- avoid citing new exemptions following receipt of the draft report.

While the majority of commitments specified in the PCA MoU are ones entered into by government departments, the Ombudsman in turn stresses that she will not disclose the information provided to her by the department, and that the decision on whether or not to disclose the information remains that of the department. Although she may use background information supplied to her in her report, she 'will only identify officials or disclose information which would otherwise be exempt under the Code (such as internal advice or consultation) to the extent that it is necessary to do so to make sense of the investigations or conclusions'.

The commitments in the MoU entered into by the Information Commissioner with the DCA are far more extensive. There must be a suspicion that, rather than being a tool to increase acceptance by, and cooperation with, public bodies in their duties in relation to access to information, as the PCA MoU undoubtedly was, it was instead driven by a realisation on the part of the DCA that the Information Commissioner himself is subject to the freedom of information regime and could be asked to disclose information he holds. Under the provisions of the Act, he would have to decide whether any exemptions applied, and whether there was a public interest in disclosure. There is a statutory prohibition on disclosure by the Information Commissioner or his staff of any information obtained by them for the purposes of the Act, and which 'relates to an identified or identifiable individual or business' (Data Protection Act 1998, s.59), unless the disclosure is made with 'lawful authority'. There will be lawful authority for a disclosure which is, among other things, 'necessary in the public interest'. These provisions appear to leave the Information Commissioner a considerable amount of discretion.

The Information Commissioner undertakes in the MoU to:

- contact the relevant department when he receives an application under s.50 of the FOIA, as soon as practicable and in any event within 10 working days;
- provide the department with details of the complainant's application;
- request all relevant information and invite comment; and
- aim to establish a single channel of communication.

He also agrees not (normally) to serve an Information Notice under s.51 of the FOIA on any government department unless he believes that relevant information is being withheld from him or that there has been undue delay in providing the information requested, and to inform the department in advance where he does intend to serve an Information Notice.

These are administrative matters designed to make enforcement of the Act a cooperative, rather than a confrontational, act. This cooperative approach is further enhanced by the obligations entered into by the Information Commissioner in relation to the disclosure of information provided to him. While the PCA MoU mentions in passing the fact that the Ombudsman will not disclose information provided to her, the MoU contains nine numbered paragraphs (9–17) headed 'Obligations in relation to information provided in accordance with this MoU', which set out a range of procedures designed to protect information provided.

Paragraph 9 states that the Commissioner:

will not disclose to the Complainant or to any third party any information provided to him by a government department either under the terms of this MoU, or as a result of serving a notice under section 50 or 51 of the FOI Act unless:

- the Department consents to the disclosure, or
- subject to paragraph 26, all appeal proceedings have been exhausted.

While the Information Commissioner's position is undoubtedly different from that of public authorities holding information provided to them from private sector companies, the MoU does make a strong contrast with the guidance issued to government departments, which are told not to accept such provisions from private sector companies. The statutory Code of Practice[4] states, at para.26:

It is highly recommended that public authorities take appropriate steps to ensure that such third parties, and those who supply public authorities with information, are aware of the public authority's duty to comply with the Freedom of Information Act, and that therefore information will have to be disclosed upon request unless an exemption applies.

Further, at paras.34 and 35:

Where there is good reason, as recognised by the terms of the exemption provisions of the Act, to include non-disclosure provisions in a contract, public authorities should consider the desirability where possible of making express provision in the contract identifying the information which should not be disclosed and the reasons for confidentiality. Consideration may also be given to including provision in contracts as to when consultation with third parties will be necessary or appropriate before the information is disclosed.

Similar considerations will apply to the offering or acceptance of confidentiality obligations by public authorities in non-contractual circumstances. There will be circumstances in which such obligations will be an appropriate part of the acquisition of information from third parties and will be protected by the terms of the exemption provisions of the Act. But again, it will be important that both the public authority and the third party are aware of the limits placed by the Act on the enforceability of expectations of confidentiality, and for authorities to ensure that such expectations are created only where to do so is consistent with their obligations under the Act.

Clearly (and not unreasonably), government departments want certainty that if they provide information to the Information Commissioner he will not then disclose it in response to a request under the Act. In some other jurisdictions, the prohibition on disclosure of information provided as part of an investigation into whether such information should be disclosed or not by the Information Commissioner's counterpart is more stringent – in Japan a sentence of one year's hard labour could be the penalty for such disclosure.

Government departments undertake to:

- provide all relevant information as quickly as possible and in any event within 20 working days of being contacted by the Information Commissioner, unless otherwise agreed;
- provide any additional relevant information subsequently requested by the Information Commissioner as quickly as possible and in any event within 10 working days;
- provide all information requested including any redacted information; and
- inform the Information Commissioner, giving reasons, where they are not able to provide the information within the time periods.

It is, however, most unlikely that the Information Commissioner would ever be minded to disclose information provided to him in the context of an investigation. There are clearly a number of exemptions which would almost certainly apply to any information held by the Commissioner, including ss.30, 31, 36 and 41. The MoU also contains a get-out clause, stating that 'nothing in this MoU shall operate to restrict or otherwise inhibit the exercise of the Commissioner's or Department's powers and duties under the FOI Act or the EIRs'.

Perhaps then, the significance of this MoU will be as a precedent for agreements between private sector companies and public authorities, given that it has been created by the two authorities with lead responsibility for implementing and enforcing the Act. The Information Commissioner has indeed publicly stated that he hopes public authorities will follow the approach taken in the MoU.

1.8   FREEDOM OF INFORMATION – THE FUTURE

FOI in the UK is still in its infancy, though the huge number of requests made annually to public authorities demonstrates its immediate popular appeal. Perhaps a direct measure of its success has been a number of recent attempts to limit its scope. A notorious Private Member's Bill (the innocuously named Freedom of Information (Amendment) Bill) introduced in the House of Commons in December 2006, sought to exclude Parliament altogether from the FOI regime. Although the Bill managed to pass through all stages in the Commons, it failed to find a sponsor in the House of Lords, perhaps as a result of mounting public indignation. There was also widespread opposition to proposals by the Ministry of Justice to amend the FOI fees regime. The effect of these proposals, now abandoned, would have been to make it easier for public authorities to refuse politically sensitive requests and to handicap the media, FOI campaigners and other multiple requesters.

There have also been moves in other jurisdictions to increase limitations on access to information, most obviously in the United States as a direct consequence of the terrorist attacks of 11 September 2001. The Department of Homeland Security, created in response to these attacks, has a blanket Freedom of Information Act exception for everything it produces, whether it involves national security or not. There is also a new exception for 'protection of voluntarily shared critical infrastructure information'. The Ashcroft Memorandum (Memorandum for Heads of all Federal Departments and Agencies from John Ashcroft, Attorney General, 12 October 2001), issued a month after the 2001 attacks, also marked a cultural change in the administration's approach to FOI, changing the presumption from one of openness, to one of protection:

> As you know, the Department of Justice and this Administration are committed to full compliance with the Freedom of Information Act (FOIA) 5 U.S.C. §552 (2000). It is only through a well-informed citizenry that the leaders of our nation remain accountable to the governed and the American people can be assured that neither fraud nor government waste is concealed.
>
> The Department of Justice and this Administration are equally committed to protecting other fundamental values that are held by our society. Among them are safeguarding our national security, enhancing the effectiveness of our law enforcement agencies, protecting sensitive business information and, not least, preserving personal privacy . . . I encourage your agency to carefully consider the protection of all such values and interests when making the disclosure determinations under the FOIA.

It is essential to reach the correct balance in any FOI regime between the rights of the public to have access to public sector information in the interests of accountability and transparency, and the need to protect sensitive information, disclosure of which could be damaging to either the public interest, or to legitimate private sector concerns. The FOIA has already brought about a radical change in the law and practice on access to government information, but whether the correct balance has been achieved will only be revealed over time, and through a continuous dialogue between all the many players involved – the information applicants (including the media), public authority decision-makers, third party information providers, Ministry of Justice officials responsible for issuing guidance, Ministers with the right to veto release, the Information Commissioner's Office, the Information Tribunal and the courts.

1.9 KEEPING UP TO DATE WITH DEVELOPMENTS

Readers are referred to the practical journal *Freedom of Information*, as an excellent resource for keeping up to date with developments as they happen – **www.foij.com**.

NOTES

1   Appendix C, *Freedom of Information – Getting it Right*, Issue 3, September 2004. It states that the information is taken from David Banisar: *Global Survey: Freedom of Information and Access to Government Record Laws Around the World* (at **www.freedominfo.org**).
2   *Memorandum of Understanding (MoU) between the Secretary of State for Constitutional Affairs (on behalf of government Departments) and the Information Commissioner, on co-operation between government Departments and the Information Commissioner in relation to sections 50 and 51 of the Freedom of Information Act 2000 (the 'FOI Act') (including ss.50 and 51 as applied, as amended, by Regulation 18 of the Environmental Information Regulations 2004)*, signed 24 February 2005.
3   *Memorandum of Understanding on co-operation between government Departments and the Parliamentary Commissioner for Administration of the Code of Practice on Access to Government Information*, Cabinet Office, Propriety and Ethics Team, July 2003.
4   Code of Practice (FOIA, s.45), Guidance to public authorities as to the practice which it would be desirable for them to follow in connection with the discharge of their functions under Part I of the Freedom of Information Act 2000.

CHAPTER 2

Publication Schemes

Patricia Barratt, Clifford Chance LLP

Section 19

(1) A publication scheme must:

  (a) specify classes of information that the public authority publishes or intends to publish;

  (b) specify the manner in which information of each class is, or is intended to be, published; and

  (c) specify whether the material is, or is intended to be, available to the public free of charge or on payment.

. . .

(3) In adopting or reviewing a publication scheme, a public authority shall have regard to the public interest in allowing public access to information held by the authority and in the publication of reasons for decisions made by the public authority.

Publication Schemes could certainly prove to be a powerful vehicle for greater openness, depending on how much public authorities choose to include in them.
(House of Commons Select Committee on Public Administration in the report on its pre-legislative scrutiny of the draft Bill: *Freedom of Information Draft Bill*, Third Report of Session 1998–99, 570-I, published 29 July 1999)

2.1 BACKGROUND

Publication Schemes – called 'a sort of Cinderella' by Richard Thomas, the Information Commissioner, in his evidence to a Parliamentary Select Committee[1] – are an often overlooked element of the freedom of information regime. Requesters and practitioners, and certainly the media, focus on the requests for information under s.1 of the Freedom of Information Act 2000 (FOIA), and the nature of the exemptions. This ignores the fact that all public authorities are now legally required to publish information proactively and that a great deal of valuable information is available directly through Publication Schemes. However, there are a number of reasons why they are outshone by their more forward sister. They were brought in in waves (see below), before the main s.1 access right, and without the publicity surrounding the s.1 right. Also, the FOIA's requirements in relation to Publication Schemes are stated in very generalised terms. So, while there are specified classes of information which are entirely removed from the ambit of the FOIA by absolute exemption (e.g. all information directly or indirectly supplied by, or relating to, bodies dealing with security matters (s.23), or information contained in court records (s.32)), there are no specified classes of information which must be included in a Publication Scheme. Some may say this is a deliberately inclusive approach: everything must go in, apart from that which is exempt. Others, more cynical, might argue that this lack of even basic minimum content requirements means that the schemes are meaningless.

For public authorities subject to the FOIA, and for those seeking information under the FOIA, however, Publication Schemes are likely to be the starting point. The staged way in which the FOIA was implemented means that public authorities were required to produce and maintain a Publication Scheme a considerable time (up to two years) before requests under the FOIA could be made. This will therefore have been most authorities' first experience of the new regime. The old Code on Access to Government Information (Code of Practice on Access to Government Information, second edition, 1997) included a voluntary commitment on the part of central government departments and the public bodies which were signatories to make certain types of information available. This information included the facts and analysis of the facts behind major policy proposals and decisions, explanatory material on departments' dealings with the public (including rules, procedures, internal guidance to officials and administrative manuals), reasons for administrative decisions, and information about the operation of public services, though it was subject to the exemptions set out in Part II of the Code. There was no structural framework to the provision of this information and only limited enforcement capability: those seeking information would generally begin by making a request in writing to the relevant authority.

Under the FOIA, however, the first port of call should be the authority's Publication Scheme, and its public website. Any information accessible through the Publication Scheme, or the authority's website, is automatically exempt from disclosure by the authority in response to requests (see below). While the authority does not have to supply the information requested by way of a s.1 request, because of the duty to provide advice and assistance (s.16) it should ensure that the requester knows how to, and is able to, access the information. Guidance from the Information Commissioner's Office (ICO) states that although inclusion of information in a Publication Scheme will mean it does not have to provide that information in response to a s.1 request, 'it would still be necessary for the authority to direct the requester to its Publication Scheme' (*Publication Schemes, Guidance and Methodology*, ICO, April 2003, para.5.8).

23

2.2   IMPLEMENTING THE PUBLICATION SCHEME PROVISIONS

To facilitate processing of submissions by the ICO, the provisions relating to Publication Schemes were brought into force a considerable time before the main right of access, and implementation of these provisions was staggered according to the type of public authority, with central government departments the first to jump (or to be pushed). The Information Commissioner published a table showing three dates for each type of authority: the date from which he would accept submissions, the final deadline for submission of the Publication Scheme, and the date by which public authorities were required to have adopted and be operating an approved Publication Scheme. From this date, public authorities were required to make the information contained in their Publication Schemes available to the public in accordance with the terms of the schemes. Table 2.1 below includes a further column for the date on which the Information Commissioner's approval expires.

Publication Schemes are initially approved for a period of four years (although the Information Commissioner reserves the right to vary this for particular Publication Schemes, if appropriate). The ICO has since announced that the deadline for re-approval for all sectors will be June–December 2008.

Table 2.1   Publication Scheme dates

Sector	Submissions accepted from	Final deadline for submissions	Scheme must be active by	Approval expires *
Central government	1 July 2002	30 September 2002	30 November 2002	30 November 2006
Local government	1 October 2002	31 December 2002	28 February 2003	28 February 2007
Police and Prosecuting bodies	1 February 2003	30 April 2003	30 June 2003	30 June 2007
Health Service	1 June 2003	31 August 2003	31 October 2003	31 October 2007
Education (except for maintained nursery schools), remaining NDPBs and publicly owned companies	1 October 2003	31 December 2003	29 February 2004	29 February 2008
Other public authorities and maintained nursery schools	1 February 2004	30 April 2004	30 June 2004	30 June 2008

* The ICO has extended the deadline for re-approval of all sectors to June–December 2008.

2.3 WHAT IS A PUBLICATION SCHEME?

Section 19 of the FOIA requires all public authorities to whom the FOIA applies to 'adopt and maintain' a Publication Scheme, which must be approved by the Information Commissioner. The Publication Scheme must set out the classes of information that the authority publishes, or that it intends to publish, and the manner in which it publishes each class of information. It must also state whether the information is freely available or whether there is a charge. In adopting a scheme, the public authority must have regard to the public interest in allowing public access to information held by the authority, and the publication of reasons for decisions made by the authority.

Described, more prosaically, by the ICO as 'a guide detailing types of information which are to be made routinely available' (*Publication Schemes: Approval documentation*, April 2003) the purpose of the schemes 'is to ensure a significant amount of information is easily and routinely available'. They are also intended 'to encourage organisations to publish more information proactively and to develop a greater culture of openness'.

The Publication Scheme provisions mirror similar requirements set out in the information access laws of a number of other jurisdictions, including the United States, Australia and New Zealand. In the United States, the relevant provisions are known as the 'reading room' requirement (Freedom of Information Act 1966, s.552(a)(2)), and they require public bodies subject to the US 1966 Act to publish information falling within specified categories, including rules of procedure and a description of all forms and papers produced, as well as statements of policy and legal rules of general applicability. Amendments to the US 1966 Act introduced the electronic reading room concept, requiring records created after 1 November 1996 to be made available by electronic means, as well as records released in response to a request which 'the agency determines have become or are likely to become the subject of a subsequent request for substantially the same records'. The Canadian Access to Information Act 1982 requires the designated Minister to publish a bulletin, updated at least once a year, containing 'a description of all classes of records under the control of each government institution in sufficient detail to facilitate the exercise of the right of access under [the] Act'. In New Zealand, under comparable provisions contained in the Official Information Act 1982 (s.20), the Ministry of Justice is required to publish a separate list for each department and organisation subject to the 1982 Act, a general description of the categories of documents held by it, a description of the manuals containing policies by which decisions are made, as well as the name of the officer to whom requests for information should be sent. Specified documents are publicly available as of right. Irish legislation (the Freedom of Information Act 1977) requires each public body to prepare and publish a reference book giving a description of the classes of records held by it, including the rules, procedures, etc. used by the body for the purposes of any enactment or scheme administered by it, as well as any details that might be reasonably necessary in order to exercise the right of access.

2.4 CLASSES

As described above, many access to information laws require public authorities to publish lists consisting of classes or categories of information that are publicly available. It is also usual for such legislation to contain some indication of what that means in practice, by specifying types of documents or records that must be included. The UK legislation provides no such indication, the only requirement being that the authority has regard to the public interest in allowing access to information and in publishing reasons for decisions.

The White Paper, *Your Right to Know*, harbinger of the FOIA, stated that:

> Experience overseas consistently shows the importance of changing the culture through requiring active disclosure, so that public authorities get used to making information publicly available in the normal course of their activities. This helps to ensure that FOI does not simply become a potentially confrontational arrangement under which nothing is released unless someone specifically asks for it.
>
> We believe it is important that further impetus is given to the pro-active release of information. So, the Act will impose duties upon public authorities to make certain information publicly available, as a matter of course. These requirements will be consistent with the other provisions of the Act – including its harm and public interest tests. They will be broadly along the lines of those in the Code of Practice, namely:
>
> - facts and analysis which the government considers important in framing major policy proposals and decisions;
> - explanatory material on dealings with the public;
> - reasons for administrative decisions to those affected by them;
> - operational information about how public services are run, how much they cost, targets set, expected standards and results, and complaints procedure.
>
> (*Your Right to Know, the Government's proposals for a Freedom of Information Act*, Cm 3818, 11 December 1997 (paras.2.17 and 2.18))

However, this requirement to publish specified types of information was not reflected in the draft Bill. The House of Commons Select Committee on Public Administration in the report on its pre-legislative scrutiny of the draft Bill argued in favour of a clearer definition of classes, and for the inclusion, on the face of the FOIA, of a requirement to publish internal guidance:

> Good schemes might provide, for example, for the publication of departmental manuals, rules and internal guidance . . ., the routine publication of government contracts (contract price, unit prices, performance standards), and the publication of all information which has been the subject of previous Freedom of Information requests.
>
> We recommend that the obligation to publish information be strengthened in the Bill. It should specify more clearly the type of information that authorities will

be required to publish. In particular authorities should be obliged to publish internal manuals and guidance as a matter of statutory duty.

(House of Commons Select Committee on Public Administration, *Freedom of Information Draft Bill*, Third Report of Session 1998–99, HC 570-I, published 29 July 1999 (paras.46 and 47))

There was a further attempt[2] to amend the Bill as it went through Parliament so as to require all public authorities to publish (subject to applicable exemptions):

any manuals, instructions, precedents and guidelines used by the officers or employees of the authority, for the purpose of –

(a) interpreting any enactment, or
(b) administering any scheme for which the authority is responsible, and to make adequate reference to the existence of such information in its publication scheme.

(House of Commons Standing Committee B, 6th sitting, 20 January 2000, Part I)

This was intended broadly to replicate wording in the Open Government Code, which required authorities:

to publish or otherwise make available, as soon as practicable after the Code becomes operational, explanatory material on departments' dealings with the public (including such rules, procedures, internal guidance to officials and similar administrative manuals as will assist better understanding of departmental action in dealing with the public) except where publication could prejudice any matter which should properly be kept confidential under Part II [the Exemptions] of the Code.

(Code of Practice on Access to Government Information, 2nd edition, 1997)

It was also claimed that such a provision was present 'in every English language freedom of information law throughout the world' (House of Commons Standing Committee B, 6th sitting, 20 January 2000, Part I.).

The government resisted the amendment, however, on the basis that, while it might be an appropriate requirement for some public authorities, the reach of the legislation was much broader than that of the Code, and included many very small entities, such as doctors' surgeries and dental practices for whom such a requirement could be overly burdensome, and inappropriate. Although a number of ways round this problem were suggested, the government maintained its position that the best way to regulate Publication Schemes was to require authorities to have their scheme approved by the Information Commissioner, or adopt a Model Publication Scheme.

What is meant by 'classes' is therefore left, to some extent, to the interpretation of the individual authority. But only to some extent, because of the requirement that each scheme be approved by the Information Commissioner, who is also able to approve Model Publication Schemes (see below). The Information Commissioner said that he did not intend to be prescriptive with regard to the description of classes, but that it was important that the way in which classes are described has 'meaning both for those seeking to obtain information from the authority and those within the authority responsible for creating and managing information' (*Publication Schemes, Guidance and Methodology*, Information Commissioner's Office, April 2003, First section, Guidance, paras.6.2 and 6.3). The classes must be relevant to each particular authority or type of authority, but must not be determined by authorities 'according to their own internal needs or historical filing systems, where these would not support the principle of "reasonable accessibility" for the purposes of the Act' (para.6.5).

The ICO recommends that public authorities consider whether consultation with relevant users or user groups might be helpful in identifying or developing classes of information for inclusion in the Publication Scheme. Public bodies are warned not to restrict the content of their Publication Scheme to information about the services they provide, but are specifically told to include information about their own internal structures, at least in outline, information about their decision-making processes and information about how key appointments are made, in order to fulfil their obligations under s.19(3)(b).

Since all information falling within the classes listed in the Publication Scheme must be published, it is tempting for public authorities to define the classes very narrowly, or to exclude particular types of classes entirely, in order to avoid the situation where the classes might be held to include information which would otherwise be exempt. The Information Commissioner has said he would not support such a restrictive approach (*Publication Schemes, Guidance and Methodology* (above) para.6.8).

To avoid the problem of including exempt information, the Information Commissioner recommends that the description of a class should be set out 'in such a way that it excludes information which might be covered by an exemption. . . . The requirement to publish information in accordance with the scheme . . .', it goes on to say, '. . . can therefore be met by the public authority because the exempt information has never fallen within the ambit of the scheme'.

The Financial Services Authority's (FSA) Publication Scheme includes a good example of a class – 'Dear CEO' letters – the extent of which is restricted by a note, so that the FSA can retain discretion over which letters are to be published.

Class D10	Dear CEO letters
This class comprises	Selected letters sent by the FSA to the chief executives of groups of regulated firms, where the FSA has judged that open publication is consistent with its objectives.
Note	This class does not include letters where the FSA judges that disclosure would unnecessarily damage market confidence.

28

Where the public authority holds a lot of information which would be covered by exemptions, the ICO recommends that it states this in its Publication Scheme, and should outline the nature of the exempt information it holds and the exemption that applies. The Office of Fair Trading (OFT) follows this advice, with a separate section in its Publication Scheme devoted to setting out all the exemptions that may apply, as well as its position on the exemption most relevant to it (s.44 – where there is a statutory bar on disclosure). The section headed 'What we may not disclose', states:

> The Act sets out exemptions to the right of access for certain types of information. Information on these exemptions is available on the Information Commissioner's website **www.informationcommissioner.gov.uk/eventual.aspx?id=6452**

The OFT will rely on these exemptions where, for example:

1. There is a statutory bar on disclosure or disclosure would be incompatible with a European Community obligation or constitute contempt of court (an absolute exemption – section 44). Part 9 of the Enterprise Act 2002 prohibits certain authorities, including the OFT, from disclosing information which is not in the public domain and relates to the affairs of an individual or the business of any undertaking and is obtained in the course of carrying out certain of their statutory functions. It is a criminal offence to disclose such information in circumstances where disclosure is not permitted by Part 9 of the Enterprise Act. Disclosure of such information is permitted in certain limited circumstances. **We will not normally be able to disclose details of complaints about a particular trader for instance.**

    There are certain circumstances when we are permitted to disclose information despite the Part 9 restriction:

    *   with the consent of all those concerned;
    *   to help either our statutory functions or those of another enforcer or public body;
    *   for the purpose of a Community obligation; or
    *   to help investigations leading to criminal proceedings (or certain kinds of civil or criminal proceedings if disclosure is to an overseas public authority).

2. The information has been obtained from any other person or public authority where disclosure would constitute an actionable breach of confidence (an absolute exemption – section 41).
3. We consider disclosure is not in the public interest and a qualified exemption applies. The following are qualified exemptions under the Act:

    a) the OFT intends to publish the information and it is reasonable to withhold it until it is published (section 22)
    b) disclosure may be prejudicial to the economic interests of the UK or any part of the UK or the financial interest of any government body (section 29)
    c) disclosure would be prejudicial to someone's commercial interests (section 43)
    d) information is held for purposes of a criminal investigation or criminal proceedings (section 30)
    e) information is held for the purpose of an investigation (including non-criminal investigations) or criminal proceedings and relates to the obtaining of information from a confidential source (section 30(2))

f) disclosure would be likely to prejudice specified matters such as the prevention and detection of crime, the administration of justice and the exercise by the OFT of its functions for any purpose specified in section 31(2) such as:

- investigations to find out whether any person has complied with the law or
- is responsible for any conduct which is improper
- or for checking whether regulatory action is justified (section 31)

g) information relates to policy formulation or development and ministerial communications. We will consider whether disclosure is in the public interest (section 35)

h) the information would or would be likely to prejudice the effective conduct of public affairs (section 36).

4. The information is personal data related to an individual and disclosure to a third party would contravene the Data Protection Act (section 40).

The Information Commissioner's Guidance on Publication Schemes advises public authorities to make it clear where exemptions might apply to information falling within a class. For example, the class 'staff policies' would be likely to include the Staff Handbook:

> Whereas the majority of the handbook might be information that can easily be made public, it may well contain some exempt information. The amount of information that would be exempt may be very limited and so it would be unhelpful to exclude the whole book from the class. The Commissioner intends to adopt an approach that would allow a scheme to accommodate such a situation. Although considering in advance whether an exemption might apply to material covered by their scheme may mean extra work at this stage, there are clearly long-term savings to be gained by the authority, once the right of access becomes available.
>
> (*Freedom of Information Act 2000: Preparing for Implementation, Publication Schemes: A Practical Guide: Part I 'Classes'*, April 2003, paras.4.4 and 4.5)

The important point is that where a class includes information from documents that also contain exempt information this is made clear when defining that class. Hence the definition of 'staff policies' given above may be refined as follows:

> internal policies which collectively establish the procedures that should be followed and conduct that is expected by members of the authority's staff in the performance of their duties. Some of the material in this class is derived from documents which we consider to contain exempt information. Where this occurs the material will clearly show where information has been withheld and explain what exemption has been applied and why. Typically information may be withheld if its release would compromise the health and safety of staff or national security.

It is interesting to note also the approach of the now defunct Department for Constitutional Affairs (DCA) to this issue in dealing with the inclusion of decisions of the Information Commissioner within its Publication Scheme:

Class:	Decisions.
Definition:	Decisions of the Information Commissioner in relation to the Freedom of Information Act and Data Protection Act 1998, in relation to the Department for Constitutional Affairs. Some of the material in this class is derived from documents that we consider to contain exempt material. Where this occurs the material will clearly show where information has been withheld and explain what exemption has been applied and why. Typically information may be withheld if it constitutes personal data.
Format available:	Hard copy from DCA.

The Publication Scheme, at the time of writing (September 2007), is available on the archived DCA website, but not yet available on the new Ministry of Justice (MoJ) website. The MoJ took over responsibility for policy on freedom of information in May 2007.

MoJ Guidance, while stressing these should not be considered as recommended classes of information sets out some kinds of information which all departments and non-departmental public bodies (NDPBs) should consider for inclusion in their Publication Schemes (*Freedom of Information Act 2000 – Publication Schemes: Central Government and Non-Departmental Public Body Guidance*, July 2002). These are:

1. *Guidance to staff* – including rules, procedures, internal guidance to officials and similar administrative manuals that assist better understanding of the organisation's interaction in dealing with the public, plus internal guidance to officials on implementing/operating the FOIA, the Environmental Information Regulations (EIR) and the Data Protection Act 1998 (DPA).
2. *Background to policy* – facts and analysis of the facts the government considers relevant and important in framing major policy proposals and decisions.
3. *Management information* – full information about how public services are run, how much they cost, who is in charge and what complaints and redress procedures are available; full and, where possible, comparable information about what services are being provided, what targets are set, what standards of service are expected and the results achieved. Information about the mission, objectives and functions of the authority; organisation of the authority; information about board meetings ('This may include the agendas and minutes of the meetings and associated papers or summaries where appropriate'); targets for standards of service and financial performance as well as results achieved and comparable information; sources of income and how effectively money is raised and spent.
4. *Public consultation* – the guidance advises authorities to follow the Cabinet Office guidelines on consultation. 'Responses submitted in confidence should have that confidence respected if the information submitted is properly confidential'.

5. *Departmental circulars* – it is probable that some circulars should be included.
6. *Information placed in the Libraries of the Houses of Parliament* – departments and NDPBs are advised to consider whether these should be included.
7. *Decisions* – including decisions of the ICO relating to the organisation, decisions of other bodies relating to the organisation and decisions made by the department where the decision affects a significant number of interested parties, or where it sets a precedent or is likely to have ramifications for the future handling of similar cases. The guidance uses as an example the Charity Commission, which, it says, is making more information available in relation to its decisions, particularly when there is considerable public interest.
8. *Speeches* – keynote speeches by Ministers and senior officials should be made available.
9. *Legislation and related information* – the legal framework within which the public authority operates including a description of the relationship between the legislation and the department's structure and functions; details of legislation or Codes of Practice that give rights of access to information; texts of international treaties, conventions and agreements should be accessible if not provided elsewhere.
10. *Procurement, grants, loans and guarantees* – departments and NDPBs are encouraged to be as open as possible when considering making available information in relation to procurement, grants, loans and guarantees. In particular, the publication of procurement and supplier policies should be considered for publication as should the details of contracts awarded. Departments and NDPBs should also consider the provision of information on specific projects including notification of bidding opportunities, decision criteria, contract performance standards, results of regular performance reviews, and results achieved where appropriate. They should also consider including information on the awarding of grants, loans and the provision of guarantees, as well as background information on schemes they administer; an account of how grants have been dispensed under a particular scheme, including overall funds dispensed, and an assessment of the benefit of the scheme in terms of its objectives should be considered. The publication of details of guarantees such as the recipient, purpose and amount should be considered, subject to protecting legitimate personal and commercial confidentiality.
11. *Information required to be published under other legislation* – in particular information accessible under the EIR, Environmental Impact Assessments and Departmental Sustainable Development Strategies where appropriate.
12. *Research reports; risk and impact assessments, etc.* – appropriate guidance on the publication of scientific research from the Office of Science and

Technology and on risk assessment should be followed when considering the content of a Publication Scheme. Regulatory impact assessments are also likely to be accessible.

13. *Information disclosed under the FOIA* – if of general interest should be included.

Despite its non-prescriptive approach to classes, the ICO has issued a guide to classes – *Freedom of Information Act 2000: Preparing for Implementation, Publication Schemes: A Practical Guide: Part I 'Classes'*, Information Commissioner's Office (April 2003) – augmenting the guidance already issued in *Guidance and Methodology and Approval Documentation*. Among the aims of the guide was 'to help clarify what a class of information is and some of the considerations a public authority should take into account when constructing or defining classes' (para.3.1). A definition suggested by responses to the Information Commissioner's consultation on schemes was 'a group of information having one or more common characteristics'. Perhaps the most obvious interpretation would be categories such as minutes of meetings, consultation documents, internal guidance notes or staff policies. The ICO uses as its main example a sectoral heading, 'Recruitment', saying:

> if a public authority chose to use 'recruitment' as a class of information then the expectation would be that all information held in connection with the recruitment process would be available through the publication scheme. This would clearly not be appropriate, not least because much of the information that might fall under that heading would be personal data held on application forms, the disclosure of which may breach the Data Protection Act 1998.

It suggests breaking down 'Recruitment' into separate classes, such as vacancies, induction and job descriptions, with a further definition of each class, including any limitations or potential exemptions.

2.5   APPROVAL BY THE INFORMATION COMMISSIONER

'The judgment about what is appropriate in an individual Publication Scheme is a matter not for the Government but for the Information Commissioner', said a Home Office Minister, David Lock, during the passage of the Bill through Parliament.[3]

All Publication Schemes must be approved by the Information Commissioner, and the ICO produced guidance on how to obtain approval: *Freedom of Information Act 2000: Preparing for Implementation, Publication Schemes: Approval Documentation*, Information Commissioner's Office (April 2003). The public authority must submit two documents: a Publication Scheme text document and a completed approval questionnaire. These can be submitted in hard copy, or electronically. There is a different process where authorities wish to adopt a Model Publication Scheme.

The Information Commissioner set out specifications which he said must be clearly identifiable in the Publication Scheme and which must be set out in the text document:

1. *Information about the identity of the public authority operating the scheme, including a brief description of the authority's responsibilities and an explanation of the purpose and aims of the scheme:*

   - Full title of the public authority operating the publication scheme.
   - Job title at senior level that contains responsibility for the scheme on behalf of the organisation.
   - Job title and name of the individual with responsibility for maintaining the scheme on a day to day basis.
   - A list of all agencies, if applicable, contained within the publication scheme along with clearly and easily identifiable access routes and information relating the agencies.
   - Statement explaining the purpose and aims of a publication scheme (this can either be the ICO's own standard statement, or a statement drafted by the authority for its own purposes – the ICO's standard statement is reproduced below).

2. *Classes of information the public authority publishes, or intends to publish:*

   - List and definitions of all classes of information contained within the scheme, in an easily identifiable manner.
   - List of all classes which are to be published at a later date, with timescales, and reasons for delays.
   - Any classes that could contain information which may be subject to exemptions should be clearly identified as such and the reasons given.
   - Overview of approach used in determining which classes are to be included.

3. *Manner in which the information of each class will be, or is intended to be, published:*

   - For each class a list of formats available and from where that information can be obtained.

4. *Whether the material is, or is intended to be, available to the public free of charge or on payment:*

   - Indication of whether a class includes chargeable material (this relates to charges for materials available within the publication scheme, not charges made for individual access requests made under section 1, FOIA).

The ICO's standard statement as to the purpose of the publication scheme – which authorities may use as a component of their response to Question 1 – is as follows:

The Freedom of Information Act 2000 (FOIA) received Royal Assent on 30 November 2000. It gives a general right of access to all types of recorded information held by public authorities, sets out exemptions from that right and places a number of obligations on public authorities. A 'public authority' is defined in FOIA, and includes but is not restricted to, central and local government, non-departmental public bodies (NDPBs), the police, prosecuting bodies, the health service, and schools, nurseries, colleges and universities. The general right of access to the information held by a public authority is provided for under section 1 of the Act. Any person wishing to exercise this right, which will not come into force until January 2005, will have to make a written request to the public authority. Any person who makes such a request must be informed whether the public authority holds that information and, subject to exemptions, supplied with that information.

However, the Act provides another mechanism for gaining access to information. Every public authority is required to adopt and maintain a publication scheme. A publication scheme is a guide detailing types of information which are to be made routinely available. This guide should provide the public with a simple means of obtaining information and reduce the need for public authorities to respond to requests made under section 1.

A publication scheme must set out the classes of information contained within the scheme, the manner in which the information is intended to be published, and whether or not a charge will be made for the information. The purpose of a scheme is to ensure a significant amount of information is easily and routinely available. Schemes are intended to encourage organisations to publish more information proactively and to develop a greater culture of openness.

Once a public authority has prepared a scheme and approval for the scheme has been given by the Information Commissioner, the scheme is adopted by the public authority. On adopting a publication scheme the public authority is committed to making the information contained within the scheme routinely accessible, and to reviewing the scheme periodically.

The approval questionnaire asked the following questions, in order to assess a public authority's compliance with the FOIA s.19(3) and, in particular, whether the scheme has regard to the public interest:

(1) What exercises, consultations and initiatives did you carry out in order to assess what information is of public interest and so should be included in your publication scheme? Please give specific details.

(2) How does your scheme provide access to records of the decisions taken by your authority together with the information upon which those decisions were based and the decision making process? Please give specific examples.

(3) Have you considered frequently asked questions and specific areas of interest when determining your classes of information? Please give specific details.

(4) Have you made information available within your scheme that has not previously been made available under other information regimes? If yes, please give details of new information. If no, please give reasons why no new information is to be made available.

(5) Have you decided not to include in your scheme any information which has been made available by you in the past? If yes, please give specific details.

(6) What steps have been taken to produce your publication scheme in alternative formats and languages so that it is accessible to individuals with disabilities, those who do not have English as their first language or those in disadvantaged communities? Please give specific examples.

With some 115,000 public authorities now subject to the FOIA, according to government pronouncements, the ICO clearly had a mountainous task, even taking into account the staggered introduction of the requirement to adopt Publication Schemes and the existence of Model Schemes.

In giving evidence before a Select Committee, the Deputy Information Commissioner said that:

given the size of the task, it was not possible for us to cross check each and every instance of that [whether the Scheme put information into the public domain that was not there before]. The way we approached the approval of publication schemes was very much getting all public authorities, if you like, on to a first base.

(House of Commons Constitutional Affairs Committee, *Freedom of Information Act 2000 – progress towards implementation*, First Report of Session 2004–05, HC 79-II, published 7 December 2004)

The Parliamentary Select Committee highlighted this in its report:

However, the sheer number of schemes approved in the time available meant that these schemes were apparently assessed in terms of their form, not their content. That is, the ICO staff did not have time to check what the publication schemes actually contained, but rather how they were structured.

(House of Commons Constitutional Affairs Committee, *Freedom of Information Act 2000 – progress towards implementation*, First Report of Session 2004–05, HC 79-I, 7 December 2004)

Approval is normally for a period of four years, though the Information Commissioner has the power to approve schemes for a different period and may also revoke his approval (see below).

2.6 MODEL PUBLICATION SCHEMES

To cut out duplication and to spare small public authorities the burden of devising a Publication Scheme from scratch, the FOIA permits the use of Model Publication Schemes. The ICO has indicated that Model Publication Schemes are appropriate where 'a large number of public authorities all perform very similar functions' (Information Commissioner's Guidance Note, attached to the Model Publication Scheme for Acute Trusts). Section 20 provides that the Information Commissioner may approve Model Publication Schemes for public authorities falling within particular classes. The Model Publication Schemes may be drafted by the Information Commissioner, or by 'other persons'. If there is a Model Publication Scheme for a particular class, then a public authority which falls within that class and which adopts the Model Publication Scheme does not need to get the approval of the Information Commissioner for its scheme. If the public authority has changed the Model Publication Scheme, however, then it will need to get the approval of the Information Commissioner in relation to those changes. If the Information Commissioner refuses to approve a proposed Model Publication Scheme, on the application of any person he must give a statement of reasons for his refusal to the applicant. Similarly, if the Information Commissioner refuses to approve any modifications that a public authority has made to the Model Publication Scheme, he must give a statement of reasons for his refusal to the public authority.

The Information Commissioner may provide that his approval of a Model Publication Scheme expires at the end of a specified period (s.20(3)). He also has the power to revoke his approval for a Model Publication Scheme though he must issue a notice of revocation giving a six-months notice period before the approval is revoked. The notice must include a statement of the Information Commissioner's reasons for revoking the approval.

The Information Commissioner has approved Model Publication Schemes for classes of public authorities in a number of sectors including local government, the health sector and education. In local government there are Model schemes for District Drainage Commissioners, Fire Authorities, Internal Drainage Boards, Parish and Town and Community Councils, Parish Meetings, Passenger Transport Authorities and Port Health Authorities. In the health sector there are Model Publication Schemes for Acute Trusts, Ambulance Trusts, Community Health Councils, Dentists, GPs, Health and Social Services Boards, Mental Health Trusts, Opticians and Optometrists, Pharmacists, Primary Care Trusts, Strategic Health Authorities and Trust Agencies and Councils (NI). In some cases there are different Model Schemes for Wales, Northern Ireland and England (Scotland, of course, is subject to its own, different, legislation on access to information).

Although there is no legal requirement for authorities adopting a Model Scheme to make any submission to the ICO, in practice it is common for some kind of notification to be made. Under some of the Model Schemes the public authority is requested to complete a Declaration Form and submit it to the Information Commissioner with contact details of the person responsible for maintaining the Publication Scheme and who should be contacted if any issues arise. The Declaration Form for Acute Trusts, for example, includes the statement that the signatory has adopted the relevant Model Publication Scheme and an indication as to whether the Trust is adopting an additional Optional Class for Archive Deposit.

The Model Publication Schemes in the healthcare sector were developed by the NHS FOI Project Board, which also produced guidance notes outlining the information that is expected under each heading. The other Model Schemes were developed by representative bodies in the relevant sector.

Approval is time limited. For example, public authorities in the health sector were required to have adopted approved Publication Schemes by 31 October 2003. The Information Commissioner's approval of the Model Schemes was for a four-year period from that date, expiring on 31 October 2007. However, as above, the ICO has extended the deadline for re-approval of all sectors to June–December 2008.

Guidance from the ICO on Model Publication Schemes points out that, in order to fulfil its obligations under the FOIA, a public authority needs to do more than simply sign and return the Declaration Form (Information Commissioner's Guidance Note, attached to the Model Publication Scheme for Acute Trusts). It must also make the Publication Scheme available and must publish information in accordance with it. It has a further obligation to review the Scheme on a regular basis.

2.7   ACCESSING PUBLICATION SCHEMES

In addition to the statutory requirement that all public authorities maintain and adopt a Publication Scheme, each public authority is also required to 'publish its Publication Scheme in such manner as it thinks fit' (s.19(4)). There was some debate over this wording as the Bill passed through Parliament, one MP identifying this as a dangerous loophole.[4] Continuing, Mr Maclennan MP pointed out that this wording leaves the manner of publication of an authority's Publication Scheme entirely up to the authority, with no provision for review by the Information Commissioner:

> An authority could publish its scheme in an obscure form, which could make it extremely difficult to inspect. There could be a single copy, which could be held in the office of a chief executive and made available for perusal only by appointment and at an unacceptably high cost.

The Minister (Mr Mike O'Brien, then Parliamentary Under Secretary of State for the Home Department) responded by saying that a requirement to have the Information Commissioner's approval for the manner of publication would be unnecessary since:

> It is in the authority's interest to publish the scheme and make it widely available, as one of the scheme's effects would be to reduce the number of requests under clause 1 and reduce the burden on the authority.

The Minister also thought that making the manner of publication subject to the ICO's approval would be unnecessarily bureaucratic and entail considerably more work for the Information Commissioner.

Although the Information Commissioner does not have statutory authority over the manner of publication, he has stated his view, as follows:

> Web access is not sufficiently universal to render it the sole means by which a scheme is delivered. Though a scheme may be intended to supply information primarily on the Internet, a hard copy must exist for those who do not have Web access. The hard copy guide must explain how to access information, and procedures should be in place to facilitate requests for information by phone and mail. A hard copy guide does not need to replicate all of the Web content; it does not need to list every document in the scheme, but it should give a clear description of how the scheme is structured, and state where documents covered by the scheme can be accessed.
>
> Due attention must be paid to making the scheme accessible to people with disabilities. The guide should be available to all who request it and, in normal circumstances, authorities should not charge users for copies of it. It may also be appropriate to have the hard copy scheme placed in, or distributed to, a range of outlets according to the nature of the authority, in order to demonstrate openness.
>
> (*Publication Schemes, Guidance and Methodology*, Information Commissioner's Office, April 2003, Second section, Methodology, paras.6.4 and 6.5)

Many Publication Schemes are easily accessible online. A dedicated NHS website, for example, lists over 4,000 Publication Schemes with direct links to the individual Schemes (see **www.foi.nhs.uk/practice**). Public authorities will frequently have a direct link to the Publication Scheme from their home page.

Good Publication Schemes should include details of how to access information where the applicant has special requirements, for example, by offering to make the information available, where possible, in a variety of formats such as Braille, audio, or in a language other than English. The Metropolitan Police Publication Scheme, for example, states it is available in Arabic, Bengali, Chinese, Greek, Gujarati, Hindi, Punjabi, Serbian, Turkish and Urdu.

Information which falls within one of the classes in a Publication Scheme does not have to be directly accessible from the Publication Scheme, and does not have to have been published already. For example, an authority may include as a class: Minutes of Committee X. It will then be required to publish all minutes of Committee X but may, as a matter of policy, publish such minutes after a specified period, whether that be one day or three months. The Scheme should also spell out how long the information in each class will be kept in accordance with the authority's policy on retention of documents.

2.7.1 Principle of reasonable accessibility

There is no obligation on public authorities to provide information in response to a s.1 request where the information is 'reasonably accessible to the applicant' by other means (FOIA, s.21). The FOIA specifies that information may be reasonably accessible even where the information is not freely available but is subject to a charge. It also specifically provides that this exemption (which is an absolute exemption) does apply where the information is available in accordance with the authority's Publication Scheme. If a payment is required this must be specified in, or determined in accordance with, the Scheme.

In some cases, however, the fact that payment is required may result in the information not being reasonably accessible. Guidance issued by the Information Commissioner suggests, for example, that where a public authority is asked for information contained in its annual report, or other long report, it may not be reasonable to require the applicant to purchase a copy of the report if the request is only for a small amount of the information contained in it (Freedom of Information Act Awareness Guidance No.6, *Information Reasonably Accessible to the Applicant by Other Means.*).

2.8 CHARGING FOR INFORMATION IN PUBLICATION SCHEMES

The fact that information falls within a class of information in a public authority's Publication Scheme means that the public authority is committed to publishing that information, but does not mean that the information must be made available without charge. Indeed, the FOIA requires public authorities to spell out in the Publication Scheme which information is available free of charge, and which information is subject to charges. There are no provisions regulating how much public authorities may charge for information under the Publication Scheme – the Freedom of Information and Data Protection (Appropriate Limit and Fees) Regulations 2004, SI 2004/3244 only apply to requests made under the s.1 access right, and not to information provided under a Publication Scheme.

However, the FOIA does not give public authorities the power to charge for providing information outside the fees regime set up for s.1 access requests. If a public authority were to attempt to charge for information where statutory authority did not exist, that authority could be acting ultra vires. There may be situations in which a public authority has the power to charge but only on a cost recovery basis, whereas in other cases there may be authority to make a specified profit margin.

Within the FOIA regime, the only sanction available in the case of public authorities which attempt to overcharge for information contained in the Publication Scheme is the nuclear option of revocation of approval by the Information Commissioner, though doubtless there would be a dialogue prior to such a step being taken.

The ICO's guidance to completing the Model Publication Scheme for Acute Trusts states:

> Much of the information covered by the model schemes will be available at no charge. However where charges are to be levied in respect of the provision of information, this needs to be indicated to scheme users by the inclusion of the £ sign within the relevant class. The circumstances in which charges may be levied are set out in the model scheme.
> (Information Commissioner's Guidance Note, attached to the Model Publication Scheme for Acute Trusts)

The Model Scheme itself says:

> For the most part, we will charge you only for hard copies or copying onto media (e.g. CD-ROM). Some information is available free, but for others there may be a charge. The charges will vary according to how information is made available. Charges are as follows:
>
> a) Via the Trust's website – free of charge, although any charges for Internet service provider and personal printing costs would have to be met by the individual.
>   For those without Internet access, a single print-out as on the website would be available by post from . . . or by personal application at Trust Headquarters . . . However, requests for multiple printouts, or for archived copies of documents which are no longer accessible or available on the web, may attract a charge for the retrieval, photocopy, postage etc. We will let you know the cost and charges that will have to be paid in advance. We will not provide printouts of other organisations' websites.

b)   Leaflets and brochures – free of charge for leaflets or booklets on, for example, services we offer to the public. A list is available from . . .
c)   'Glossy' or other bound paper copies, or in some cases a CD Rom, video or other mediums, are charged for as in our publication lists available from . . .
d)   E-mail – will be free of charge unless it says otherwise.

The charges will be reviewed regularly.

There is a separate paragraph dealing with Crown copyright.

Ordnance Survey, which publishes a vast quantity of commercial information, has similar wording; the section on Crown copyright and reuse of information is included under the Fees heading:

The printed hard copy items in the publication scheme are free unless otherwise stated and can be ordered from the General Enquiries Helpdesk, Ordnance Survey, Romsey Road, Southampton, SO16 4GU, phone: 08456 05 05 05, fax 023 8079 2615 or by personal application at the same address. Send your request to them, giving the full title of the publication and stock code number (see publications table).

The other items in the scheme are electronic documents in, for example, Word or .pdf, and can be downloaded free of charge from the web site.

To read .pdf documents you will need Adobe® Acrobat Reader®, which is free and available from Adobe.

Requests for multiple printouts, or for archived copies of documents that are no longer available on the web, will attract a charge for the cost of retrieval, photocopy, postage and so on. We would let you know this at the time of your request (the charge would be payable in advance).

Glossy or other bound paper copies, or in some cases a CD-ROM, video or other mediums, are charged as in our publication list available from General Enquiries Helpdesk (address as detailed above).

If you wish to reuse or reproduce our publications, for example, commercially or for circulation for education and similar purposes, you will in most cases need to apply for a copyright licence for this. Ordnance Survey is a Crown body and our information is subject to Crown copyright administered by Her Majesty's Stationery Office [now Office of Public Sector Information (OPSI)]. For HMSO [now OPSI] Guidance Notes on a range of copyright issues, see the [OPSI] website or write to Intellectual Property and Legal Department, Ordnance Survey, Romsey Road, Southampton, SO16 4GU.

The Department for Business Enterprise and Regulatory Reform (BERR) makes it clear that it will follow Treasury Guidance on charges (*Charges for Information: When and How – Guidance for Government Departments and other Crown Bodies*) where it makes a standing charge for a publication. It also points out that BERR, its Agencies and UK Trade & Investment (UKTI) operate a number of Schemes providing information, as part of a paid service, derived from a range of sources held by BERR, its Agencies or UKTI as well as information not already held in recorded form.

Much of the material listed on the BERR's Publication Scheme is freely available on the internet. Other material listed is available on subscription, e.g. under 'Bidding Opportunities' it states:

Class	Bidding opportunities for contracts to be awarded through EC procurement procedures: • Nature of contract • Evaluation criteria • Period of contract
Format available	Hard copy, web pages – 'Official Journal of the European Communities' and 'Government Oppportunities' (you will need to subscribe).
Available from	Hard copy: Procurement Unit Department of Trade and Industry [sic] Room 354 1 Victoria Street London SW1H 0ET Tel: 020 7215 5741 Fax: 020 7215 5746 Online: EU contract notices Invitations to tender Official Journal of the European Communities – Tenders Electronic Daily (TED) http://ted.europa.eu
Cost	Subscription

Similarly, publications such as 'Quarterly Building Price and Costs Indices', and 'Monthly Statistics of Building Materials & Components' are included in the Publication Scheme, clearly marked 'cost priced'.

The fact that information is only available from a subscription service, or on payment of the cost price, does not preclude that information from being included in the Publication Scheme.

Guidance from the Information Commissioner's Office on charges under Publication Schemes states that the level of charges made by a public authority for the provision of information in its Publication Scheme should be 'compatible with the principle of promoting public access to the information held by public authorities' (Awareness Guidance, *Charging under Publication Schemes*, October 2003). It also points out that the general public will easily be able to compare charging regimes across similar organisations.

While the guidance warns public authorities against including information in a Publication Scheme with the intention of charging for information that was previously provided free, it recognises that the public authority may be entitled to reserve the right to levy a charge as a concomitant of its assumption of a legal commitment to provide access in place of a previous policy of providing information on a purely discretionary basis.

2.9 PUBLICATION SCHEMES FOR COMPANIES DESIGNATED UNDER S.5

The government was reported to have said that it would start the process of designating companies under s.5 after the general election and once the new Parliament was sitting. A company may be designated under s.5 if it:

(a) appears to the Secretary of State to exercise functions of a public nature, or
(b) is providing under a contract made with a public authority any service whose provision is a function of that authority.

There is no provision in the FOIA for any derogation from the effect of ss.19 and 20 and therefore designated companies will also have to adopt and maintain a Publication Scheme, whether bespoke or model, which will have to be approved by the Information Commissioner. The designation will only relate to the functions performed by the company which are public functions and, similarly, the company's Publication Scheme will only need to list classes of information relevant to those functions. No company has been designated under s.5 as yet, though the Ministry of Justice is currently consulting on such designations.

2.10 THE INFORMATION ASSET REGISTER AND THE PUBLIC SECTOR INFORMATION DIRECTIVE

Derived from a consultation exercise into Crown copyright (and announced in the White Paper, *The Future Management of Crown Copyright*, Cm 4300, 1999), the idea of an Information Asset Register (IAR) was intended to be a one-stop shop for potential re-users of government-generated or government-held information.

In practical terms, it is an online catalogue of unpublished information resources, accessible to anyone with internet access, on **www.opsi.gov.uk/iar**. It is supposed to contain details of all information held by all government departments and other Crown bodies, focusing on unpublished information.

Anyone searching the register should, however, expect mixed results. A general search on the word 'regulation', for example, threw up a surprisingly low number of results – only 40 – among them a record entitled 'Rats in the Sewer Working Group', a collection of minutes of meetings, discussion papers etc., another called 'Instructions to staff on interpreting the Weeds Act 1959', as well as already published 'Value for Money (VFM) Reports' by the National Audit Office. Other searches suggest that a high number of records are in fact pieces of legislation, which of course should already be published.

The development of the IAR has been supported by the Public Sector Information Directive ('the Directive'), implemented in the UK by the Re-use of Public Sector Information Regulations 2005, SI 2005/1515, which introduced a statutory obligation on public sector bodies to provide access to details about reusable information held by the public sector. A recital to the Directive claims:

Public sector information is an important primary material for digital content products and services and will become an even more important content resource with the development of wireless content services. Broad cross-border geographical coverage will also be essential in this context. Wider possibilities of re-using public sector information should inter alia allow European companies to exploit its potential and contribute to economic growth and job creation.
(Recital 5, Directive 2003/98/EC of the European Parliament and of the Council of 17 November 2003 on the reuse of public sector information)

Article 9 provides for the creation of information asset lists:

Practical arrangements

Member States shall ensure that practical arrangements are in place that facilitate the search for documents available for reuse, such as assets lists, accessible preferably online, of main documents, and portal sites that are linked to decentralized assets lists.

The Regulations implement this Article by requiring public sector bodies to ensure that a list of significant documents available for re-use is made available to the public, preferably by electronic means and, as far as reasonably practicable, with an electronic search capability.

The main thrust of the Directive is to ensure that, where public sector information is available for re-use, it is made available on terms that are fair, reasonable and not anti-competitive. It does not require any information actually to be made available for re-use, and even the requirement on the creation of asset lists is sufficiently vague and non-prescriptive to allow considerable room for manœuvre.

Nevertheless, while the Public Sector Information Directive could be seen as less ambitious than the Information Asset Register initiative which pre-dated it, in terms of what it requires of the Asset Register, it does at least put a voluntary policy initiative onto a statutory footing.

An OPSI Guidance Note, *Information Asset Register and Freedom of Information – a co-ordinated response to information access* (revised 9 May 2004), is intended to explain how the IAR, and specifically departmental IARs, 'should contribute usefully to Freedom of Information Publication Schemes and the broader management of information requests under FOI'.

Government departments are required to produce both a freedom of information Publication Scheme for the purposes of the FOIA and an Information Asset Register for the purposes of the public sector information regime (PSI). The guidance says that information that departments have left out of their Publication Scheme because, for example, it could not be made widely available without considerable cost, or there is thought to be limited interest in it, 'should already be included in departmental IARs, which detail information that may be of interest, yet is not published' (para.15). The guidance also states that the existence of the IAR will make it simpler for departments to identify where information requested is held and so will facilitate the management of information requests, whether or not covered by the FOIA or the EIR.

The main area of overlap, therefore, between the two regimes, is the respective requirements to produce a list of information held by the public authority, albeit according to differing criteria. It is clear that it would not be possible to combine the two information schemes, although there have been calls to do so, in order to avoid duplication of effort. Publication Schemes are intended to be a means of making more information available proactively and, in most cases, free of charge. The IAR is, however, a Scheme to facilitate the commercial reuse of public sector information. Despite OPSI's cheerleader tones, the divergent aims of these two Schemes give rise to a tension and even, potentially, a conflict of interest between them. This tension is perhaps more apparent in the underlying principles than will be the case in practice: requests for access to information under the PSI will typically be in relation to large collections of information as opposed to the much more targeted requests for discrete 'bits' of information which would be appropriate under the FOIA. Further, the PSI entails no obligation to supply the information requested, unlike the statutory obligation under the FOIA to provide information unless subject to an exemption. The other major difference is that information requested under the PSI is intended for re-use, while information accessed under the FOIA, including by way of Publication Schemes, will generally be subject to restrictions on re-use.

2.11   REVIEW OF PUBLICATION SCHEMES

Each public authority is required (under s.19(1)(c)) to review its Publication Scheme 'from time to time'.

The best Publication Schemes, of course, change on a daily basis, with new material being added. The then Lord Chancellor, Lord Falconer, announced in December 2004 that where information disclosed in response to an access request was likely to be of wider interest, then it should be published simultaneously online. Some departments, for example, the Foreign and Commonwealth Office (FCO), provide a separate link from their website for such information, the FCO's link being called 'Released Documents' (see **www.fco.gov.uk/foi**). This link is also directly accessible from the FCO Publication Scheme.

The review requirement is not, however, merely a requirement to update the Publication Scheme so as to give access to the most recent components of a specified class. Rather it is a requirement to consider whether the nature of the classes and the structure of the Scheme are still appropriate, taking into consideration the public interest both in allowing access to information held by the authority, and in the publication of reasons for decisions made by the authority.

Where any changes are made to a Publication Scheme as a result of a review (or otherwise) these must be notified to the Information Commissioner. His approval will be required where it is proposed to remove classes of information.

A survey carried out by the ICO in relation to the experience of local authorities and freedom of information found that 'Formal reviews of the Publication Schemes have been reported by the majority of local authorities in England, with most conducting them on a six monthly or annual basis' (Information Commissioner, *Freedom of Information Act 2000 Survey Findings: Principal Local Authorities*, February 2004).

A further finding was that:

> Local authorities have approached the task of developing and reviewing publication schemes in the right spirit, although some may need to think of more regular reviews particularly in the light of patterns of individual requests for information.

The survey also found that local authorities engaging in best practice carried out a review of their Publication Schemes every six months.

A number of Publication Schemes make no mention of the review process, failing even to mention the statutory requirement (including the ICO's Publication Scheme). Table 2.2 shows some different approaches to the review requirement adopted by a random sample of 10 public authorities, selected to present a spread of different categories of authorities. The fact that some Publication Schemes make no reference to a review does not, of course, mean that no review mechanism exists. The findings are as at October 2007 and are the result of an examination of the Publication Schemes only.

In his evidence to the Select Committee on Constitutional Affairs,[5] the Information Commissioner said 'We have plans to put pressure on selected public authorities to upgrade their publication schemes'. He did not say which authorities he had in mind, but if he expected to implement these plans before the expiry of the four-year period, i.e. outside the formal approval procedure, then it is likely that he expected the upgrading to take place within the review process. From a first base position, then, authorities are encouraged by the Information Commissioner to improve the availability of information under their Publication Schemes as part of the ongoing review process required by the FOIA.

Some of the findings of the ICO's Development and Maintenance Initiative (DMI) (reported in the Development and Maintenance Initiative Advisory Panel Newsletter: May 2007) on Publication Schemes are discouraging. It highlighted as key messages that: 'The maintenance of schemes is haphazard. This is compounded by the current approval process which does not encourage or support systematic maintenance' and 'Public awareness of schemes is low, and members of the public find some schemes difficult to use'.

46

Table 2.2 Public authority Publication Scheme review policies

Public authority	Review policy
Metropolitan Police Service	*Reviewing and Updating the Publication Scheme* New material will be added to the Scheme regularly and brought to the attention of users on the Internet through the What's New Page We are committed to expanding the amount of information in this Scheme and ensuring that you can find it easily.
Bank of England	We are currently in the process of formally renewing the scheme.
Worcestershire Primary Care Trust	Date: 2 August 2007 Revision Date: 1 October 2007
Wigan Council	Wigan's Council's publication scheme is currently under review. We expect this review to be completed by the end of January 2007.
Office of Communications	*Approval and review* The scheme was approved by the Information Commissioner for a period of four years until 29 February 2008. The scheme will therefore be formerly [sic] reviewed in February 2008. Our website is updated daily and we will regularly review the scheme to ensure it is up to date and provides as much information as possible.
Royal Mail Group	We will continue to update the material shown in the Annex to this scheme [the classes of information] and review it annually, or as directed by the Information Commissioner.
Environment Agency	The statutory requirement to maintain and develop the Scheme means that we must take stock of what information we make available and what, in the public (and therefore environmental) interest we intend to make available in the future . . . We shall publish information in accordance with the scheme, and shall monitor and review its operation in order to develop the scheme in the light of public comment and feedback.
Lancashire Combined Fire Authority and Lancashire Fire and Rescue Service	The Publication Scheme is a 'living' document and will be updated on a regular basis.
Peak District National Park Authority	This publication scheme is part of an ongoing process aimed at improving the openness and accessibility of the National Park Authority.
Kingston University London	No reference.

2.12   ENFORCEMENT

The obligation to adopt, maintain and review Publication Schemes is a statutory duty on the public authorities who are subject to the FOIA. Failure to do so is a matter, in the first instance, for the Information Commissioner. He has stated that his policy is to secure compliance by a process of educating and advising public authorities. However, where compliance cannot be achieved by this informal route he will consider exercising his formal enforcement powers set out under ss.50–6 of the FOIA. Where the ICO is satisfied that a public authority has failed to comply with any of the requirements of the FOIA, including the requirements on Publication Schemes, it may serve an Enforcement Notice requiring the authority to comply. If the public authority fails to comply with the Enforcement Notice the ICO may certify that fact in writing to the High Court. The court may then deal with the public authority as if it had committed a contempt of court. The procedures for enforcement are set out in much more detail in **Chapter 10** on enforcement, but it is worth noting that the Information Commissioner's very first foray into enforcement of the FOIA was in relation to Publication Schemes.

When the relevant deadlines for submission of Publication Schemes had passed, a small minority of public bodies had not established Publication Schemes. One of these was Allerdale Borough Council, which was required to submit its Scheme to the Information Commissioner for approval by 31 December 2002, and to have the Scheme active by 28 February 2003. The Information Commissioner therefore served a Preliminary Enforcement Notice (which warns the authority that legal action will be taken if the problem is not resolved). The Information Commissioner has indicated that he would expect this notice to be effective in resolving the problem in a majority of cases, his experience being that most public bodies are keen to cooperate and that delays in setting up a Publication Scheme were usually due to administrative problems rather than to any reluctance to implement the legislation. However, Allerdale, alone of the bodies on whom Preliminary Enforcement Notices were served, did not respond to the notice.

The Information Commissioner then took enforcement proceedings against the Chief Executive Officer of Allerdale Borough Council for contempt of court, with the aim, the ICO has said, of seeking compliance, rather than of punishing. The Information Commissioner believed that Allerdale would immediately comply once proceedings were served. However, the Council failed to respond to the claim form and to a number of letters, and no one from the authority appeared at the Directions Hearing. Nothing was heard from Allerdale until the day of the actual hearing.

The case was transferred from Macclesfield County Court to Chester Crown Court because of the statutory requirement in the FOIA (s.54) that proceedings must be before a High Court judge. The case is unreported but the ICO has indicated that, on the day of the hearing (in spring 2004), a representative from Allerdale Council explained that it had now implemented a Publication Scheme. The judge therefore dismissed the case. No explanation was given for the delay, or indeed the earlier failure to respond.

Lessons were learned from the case, though: the Information Commissioner had issued proceedings against the CEO of Allerdale Council, rather than the Council itself. This issue was raised by Allerdale at the last minute at the hearing and it was eventually agreed by all parties that the FOIA required the Information Commissioner to initiate proceedings against the Council directly and not against the CEO in person. However, this procedural irregularity had no direct bearing on the result of the case. Moreover, if Allerdale had not established a Publication Scheme by the day of the hearing then the Information Commissioner would no doubt have requested that the claim form be amended so that proceedings were issued against the Council.

There have been just two Decision Notices by the ICO with direct bearing on Publication Schemes. The first, issued on 29 March 2007 (FS50135471), involved a request for minutes of a specific Council Management Committee meeting. The public authority in question (Brockhampton Group Parish Council) had adopted the Model Publication Scheme for Parish, Town and Community Councils, which had been approved by the Information Commissioner and endorsed by the National Association of Local Councils. This includes under the heading 'CORE CLASSES OF INFORMATION':

1) COUNCIL INTERNAL PRACTICE AND PROCEDURE

Minutes of council, committee and sub-committee meetings – limited to the last 2 years.

The Council refused to supply the minutes even though, at the time the request was made, they fell within the two-year stipulated period. When pressed by the Commissioner, the Council wrote (six months after the initial request) to the requester accusing him of 'pursuing a continual vexatious, repeated and time wasting process to obtain copies of minutes over two years old', and continuing to refuse to supply the minutes.

The ICO considered the question of whether the request was vexatious. He found that the fact that the minutes were listed in the Model Publication Scheme demonstrated that there was 'inherent value in the information requested'. The Council's contention that the request was vexatious could not therefore be justified on the ground that the request clearly had no serious purpose or value (the ICO considered other grounds also). The Commissioner, unsurprisingly, found that the Council was in breach of s.19(1)(b), in that the information in its Publication Scheme should have been available, and ordered the Council to supply the information requested. In a fascinating aside, the Council claimed that the requester already had a copy of the requested minutes and that they had a witness prepared to make a statement to that effect. The Commissioner replied that even if such a statement was provided, the ICO would not necessarily find in the Council's favour. This is surprising, since evidence that a requester already had in his possession information he was requesting seems like prima facie evidence of vexatiousness, one of the key issues at stake.

In the second case, Argoed Community Council refused to supply a requester with a copy of its standing orders. Not only were the standing orders listed in the Council's Publication Scheme, but there is, moreover, a statutory obligation on all local authorities to supply a copy of their constitution (including their standing orders) to any person who requests a copy, on payment of a reasonable fee (Local Government Act 2000, s.37). Initially, the Council seems just to have ignored the request and it was only after the intervention of the Information Commissioner that it issued a refusal notice citing s.21 and referring the requester to the National Association of Local Councils or One Voice Wales for a copy of the orders. The requester had also requested a copy of the Council's FOI Publication Scheme; this was not mentioned in the refusal notice but was eventually provided to the requester. Following further correspondence, the Council agreed that the standing orders were not reasonably accessible through the organisations mentioned and agreed to provide a copy to the requester on payment of a small fee, and the issue of a disclaimer. The requester again involved the ICO to complain about the way his request was being handled and to ask the Commissioner to consider whether it was appropriate for the Council to insist on a signed disclaimer before supplying the standing orders. The disclaimer required the requester to use the document for the purposes of information only for himself and not to reproduce or transmit in any form or by any means any part of the orders without prior permission from the Council.

In its Decision Notice, issued on 29 August 2007 (FS50142974), the ICO found that, technically, the information was exempt from disclosure under s.21 because it was reasonably accessible to the applicant via its Publication Scheme (though not through the bodies to which the Council had referred the requester), though it went on to say 'in any case [it] would have been required to provide the information'. It found the Council in breach of FOIA, s.1(1)(a) (the duty to inform a requester whether the public authority holds the information requested), as well as s.19(1)(b) (the duty to publish information in accordance with the authority's Publication Scheme). Though not strictly relevant to Publication Schemes, the most interesting of the ICO's findings in this case was that 'whilst public authorities can place restrictions on the end use of information, they cannot use these restrictions as a pre-condition of supply'. Exactly how the restrictions are to be placed or enforced in the absence of such a mechanism is not explored. Since there was, in any case, a clear statutory duty on the authority to supply the orders, this was more of a red herring. Perhaps a solution to this problem (for the public authority) would be to specify in the Publication Scheme that certain classes of information would only be made available on the issue of a disclaimer. In the same way as fees cannot be charged for information disclosed following an FOI request, except in line with the Fees Regulations, but information listed in the Publication Scheme can be charged for, there would seem to be no legal bar to requiring a disclaimer before releasing information in a Publication Scheme. It would of course be dependent on the approval of the ICO of the Scheme.

The cases do not involve abstruse legal analysis. They simply confirm what public authorities and others should already know, that a public authority must publish documents included in a Publication Scheme in accordance with the Scheme and that the ICO will enforce the obligations which a public authority enters into when adopting a Publication Scheme.

The Information Commissioner's role in the shaping of the still-developing FOI regime remains critical. If Publication Schemes are still the Cinderella of the FOI regime, only the Information Commissioner has the magic wand to make a dazzling transformation.

NOTES

1 House of Commons Constitutional Affairs Committee, *Freedom of Information Act 2000 – progress towards implementation*, First Report of Session 2004–05, HC 79-II, published 7 December 2004.
2 Amendment No.65 tabled by Mr Maclennan MP, Standing Committee B (Pt 8), 20 January 2000.
3 Standing Committee B, Part 2, col.189, 20 January 2000.
4 Mr Maclennan MP, Standing Committee B (Pt 7), 6th sitting, 20 January 2000, Part I.
5 House of Commons Constitutional Affairs Committee, *Freedom of Information Act 2000 – progress towards implementation*, First Report of Session 2004–05, HC 79-II, published 7 December 2004.

CHAPTER 3

The right of access

Andrew Sharpe and Carolyn Bigg, Charles Russell LLP

3.1   INTRODUCTION

The Freedom of Information Act 2000 (FOIA) sparked an unprecedented level of awareness amongst the media and the public about accessing documentation and information held about them, their community and about local and national issues and causes. Using the FOIA to access information is now common practice for investigative journalists,[1] as well as for individuals and lobbying groups. However, unlike in other jurisdictions, use of the FOIA by businesses for commercial use (e.g. regarding business opportunities within the public sector) has been slow.[2]

This chapter aims to provide practical guidance first to members of the public as to how to make an effective request for information under the FOIA, and secondly to public authorities on how to respond to requests for information under the FOIA. Broadly we will consider the formalities and practicalities of making and responding to requests for information, as well as the type of information that is available by means of the public's right of access under the FOIA.

An individual's right of access to information in fact goes far wider than that prescribed under the FOIA. While interest since 1 January 2005 has naturally focused on rights granted under the FOIA, there are also a number of other statutory rights of access to certain information. These may in fact prove more relevant and useful to an individual in obtaining a required piece of information, particularly as certain of these rights are to information held by private individuals and organisations. In addition, a public authority may need to deal with a request for information asking for mixed types of information.

Accordingly, in addition to considering rights of access under the FOIA, in this chapter we will also consider an individual's right of access to information under the Data Protection Act 1998 and we will also refer to the Environmental Information Regulations 2004 (EIR) (which are covered in more detail in **Chapter 9**) and some other statutory rights of access to information (which include rights to medical and educational records and financial information relating to companies).

The FOIA was intended to enhance, rather than replace, existing information regimes. Indeed, information is exempted from disclosure under the FOIA if it is available to applicants by other means (s.21). Therefore, an individual may only be able to access information by means of these other statutory rights.

3.1.1 Initial considerations for an individual wishing to make a request for information

The first consideration in relation to any request for information should be: 'Under what statutory access right should I make my request?' The answer will depend on:

- *the nature and focus of the information desired:* we have identified below the type of information that may be disclosed under each statutory regime; and
- *the organisation that holds the desired information:* certain information rights only oblige public authorities to disclose information, whereas others apply equally to public and private bodies. We have identified below to whom each statutory right of access applies.

3.1.2 Initial considerations for a public authority responding to a request for information

Equally on receipt of a request for information a public authority's first consideration must be: 'What is the nature of the information requested?' The answer to this question will identify the statutory access regime under which the public authority must respond to that request. We have identified in this chapter the type of information that may be disclosable under each statutory regime, together with the costs and formality involved in responding to each type of request.

If a request for information comprises a mix of environmental information, personal information relating to the individual requesting the information and other information, then a public authority must separate out the requests and deal with each element separately under the Environmental Information Regulations (EIR), the Data Protection Act 1998 (DPA) and the FOIA as appropriate.

The following flowchart at Figure 3.1 provides a useful summary to both applicants and public authorities (or other bodies to whom requests for information may be made under the various statutory access regimes) as to which regime should be applied to specific requests for information.

The flowchart at Figure 3.2 (see p.73) provides a process for a public authority or others to follow when dealing with a request for personal data (and see **3.3.1** for an explanation of the defined terms used in the flowchart).

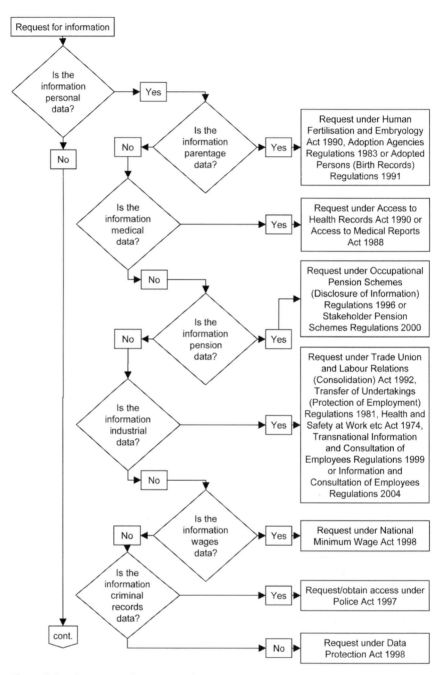

Figure 3.1   Summary of access regimes

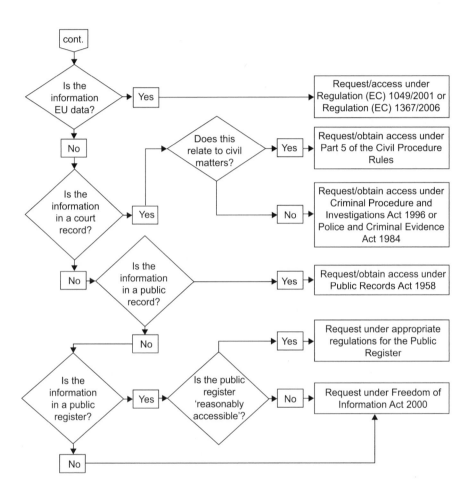

Key:

EU data   means data held by the European Union institutions.

court record   means a document or evidence from records of Court (FOIA, s.32(1) and (2)).

public record   means a record within the definition at FOIA, s.84.

public register   means a register within the definition at FOIA, s.21(2)(b), and 'reasonably
                   accessible' for the purposes for Public Registers is defined at FOIA, s.21(1) and
                   (2)(a).

Figure 3.1   Summary of access regimes – *cont.*

3.2 FREEDOM OF INFORMATION ACT 2000

3.2.1 What information can be accessed?

The FOIA provides a right of access to the general public to information held by public authorities. The information is disclosable via Publication Schemes and requests for information (subject to a number of important exemptions).

Any information in the possession of, or held on behalf of, a public authority (as defined) is potentially disclosable under the FOIA regime, provided it is held for the purpose and interest of the public authority and is held at the time of the request. Information held by public authorities will comprise information created (solely or partly) by or on behalf of the public authority but also may include information received from third parties, regardless of whether or not that third party was aware that such information may be disclosable under the FOIA. This could include information provided to a public authority by a private sector body, such as correspondence from a private contractor providing services to a public authority, or information about individuals, such as education and benefits records. Whether or not information licensed to a public authority constitutes information 'held' will depend on the scope of the licence (see *Mr G Marlow* v. *Information Commissioner*, 1 June 2006 and 31 August 2006 (EA/2005/0031)).

Guidance has been given by the Information Tribunal as to whether electronic records supposedly deleted by public authorities, but which are stored on back-up files or servers, are considered to be 'held' by public authorities (see *Mr P Harper* v. *Information Commissioner and Royal Mail Group plc*, 15 November 2005 (EA/2005/0001)). Electronic records are often still accessible even if deleted from a computer. A public authority must consider the extent to which the information has been deleted, whether it can be recovered, and by what means. If the public authority can simply retrieve the information from a computer's 'recycle bin', hard drive or back-up tapes, then the public authority will normally be expected to do this to comply with an information request. However, if retrieving or restoring the deleted information (e.g. restoring the computer back to its previous state) would involve specialist staff or software or will involve a significant cost exceeding the limit for complying with a FOIA request (see **3.2.2**), then the public authority may use this as a reason for not complying with the request.

The Information Tribunal has decided that 'held' can be construed as 'have they got it' in layperson's terms: i.e. a document may be 'held' on the balance of evidence available even if it is lost and cannot be located and there is no record of deletion. The s.12 cost limits 'serve as a guillotine' generally to prevent a search for information becoming too onerous on a public authority (see *Mr P Quinn* v. *Information Commissioner and the Home Office*, 15 November 2006 (EA/2005/0010), paras.50, 52 and 53). Nevertheless, good practice suggests that if previously missing information is subsequently found, a public authority should inform an applicant (see *Mr P Quinn* v. *Information Commissioner*, 15 November 2006 (EA/2005/0010), para.65; and *Mr A Campsie* v. *Information Commissioner*, 16 April 2007 (EA/2006/0052), para.24).

The Information Tribunal has also given useful guidance on the extent to which information is 'held' when the specific information requested is not held by the public authority, but the raw data that forms the 'building blocks' from which the requested information could be calculated is held (see *Mr M L Johnson* v. *Information Commissioner and the Ministry of Justice*, 13 July 2007 (EA/2006/0085)).

Information is potentially disclosable regardless of the format of the information (FOIA, s.84) (for example, whether it is electronically stored, a hard copy, an audio recording[3] or a graph), and includes handwritten notes, opinions and historical data. It is important to bear in mind that, unlike access regimes in other jurisdictions, the FOIA provides a right of access to information rather than to documentation (see *Mr N Ingle* v. *Information Commissioner*, 29 June 2007 (EA/2007/0023), para.7). Therefore, while a specific document, or part thereof, may be exempt from disclosure, some or all of the information contained within that document may be disclosable, perhaps by way of a summary or by redacting the remainder of the document. The FOIA also only covers information that is recorded (see *Mr N Ingle* v. *Information Commissioner*, 29 June 2007 (EA/2007/0023), para.7; and FOIA, s.84). Therefore, information which may be in the knowledge of an employee of a public authority, but which is not, or is no longer, recorded in a permanent form will not be disclosable. The FOIA is also not concerned about the quality of the information held by a public authority for the relevant purpose (see *Mr E Simmons* v. *Information Commissioner*, 16 December 2005 (EA/2005/0003), para.23), nor does it 'give a right to the requester to get the information he or she thinks he should receive' (see *Mr T Prior* v. *Information Commissioner*, 27 April 2006 (EA/2005/0017), para.21); the concern is simply whether or not the requested information is held and potentially disclosable (see *Mr N Ingle* v. *Information Commissioner*, 29 June 2007 (EA/2007/0023), para.8 – 'no obligation . . . to create a record where none exists'; and *Mr ML Johnson* v. *Information Commissioner and the Ministry of Justice*, 13 July 2007 (EA/2006/0085), para.45 – 'the purpose of the Act is . . . not to require public authorities to undertake research to create new information').

Certain information is excluded or exempted from disclosure under the FOIA:

- personal data about the applicant, disclosure of which is covered by the access regime under the DPA (see **3.3**);
- environmental information, which is disclosable under the EIR (see **3.4**);
- information which is because of its subject matter or nature subject to an exemption under Part II of the FOIA. These exemptions are considered in detail in **Chapters 4** and **5**. For example, information is exempted from disclosure under the FOIA if it is available to applicants by other means

(FOIA, s.21), as is information which is intended for future publication by the public authority (FOIA, s.22); and

- there are a number of procedural limitations on disclosure set out in Part I of the FOIA, which are discussed in **3.2.4**.

A number of existing Acts of Parliament have been amended so as to permit disclosure of information under the FOIA that would otherwise have been prohibited or restricted (Freedom of Information (Removal and Relaxation of Statutory Prohibitions on Disclosure of Information) Order 2004, SI 2004/3363). However, decisions of the Information Tribunal have highlighted that there are still some statutory restrictions in other legislation which prohibit disclosure notwithstanding FOIA rights of access.[4]

Publication Schemes

The first port of call for any potential applicant under the FOIA should be a public authority's Publication Scheme. Any individual, company or other organisation may request a copy of the information included within a Publication Scheme (FOIA, s.19).

As described in **Chapter 2**, a variety of information, and particularly frequently requested information, is increasingly available via public authorities' Publication Schemes. The advantages to a potential applicant of making use of this resource are:

- the information will be quickly and easily accessible (as Publication Schemes must be), often on the public authority's website;
- the information will often be available via the Publication Scheme free of charge (the Publication Scheme should set out whether or not the public authority is going to charge to provide a copy of the information). It is clear that the Information Commissioner will assist complainants who are denied information that is included in a Publication Scheme, even if the costs of providing the requested information potentially exceed the appropriate limit (see **3.2.3** below);[5] and
- public authorities are under no obligation to provide information in response to an information request where that information is already available under the authority's Publication Scheme (FOIA, s.21). Therefore, checking the Publication Scheme first may save the need to go through the process of submitting an information request.

Information requests

The general principle of the FOIA is that any person making a request for information to a public authority is entitled (subject to a number of exceptions and exemptions):

(a) to be informed in writing by the public authority whether or not it holds information of the description specified in the request; and

(b) if it does hold the information, to have that information communicated to him (FOIA, s.1(1)).

We have set out in the next section practical guidance to enable a potential applicant to make a request for information under the FOIA, and in **3.2.4** we consider how, and when, the public authority should respond to the information request.

3.2.2 The request

Who can make an information request?

A request can be made by any individual, partnership, unincorporated body or company, whether or not they are UK national or resident, and regardless of the purpose of the application.

To whom can a request be made?

The FOIA grants a right of access to individuals to information held by or on behalf of a public authority, both as defined in the FOIA (ss.3(1) and (2)).

The definition of public authorities in the FOIA includes public bodies listed in Sched.1 to the FOIA (as amended by various secondary legislation (ss.3(1)(a)(i) and 4)), certain authorities designated by the Secretary of State for Justice (ss.3(1)(a)(ii) and 5)[6] and all companies that are 'publicly owned' (FOIA, s.3(1)(b); 'publicly owned' is as defined in FOIA, s.6). For example, this definition will encompass central government and local authorities, the Houses of Parliament,[7] NHS trusts and health authorities, schools and other educational institutions, the police and the armed forces, as well as executive agencies. As the number of public authorities caught by the FOIA is continuously expanding, it is advisable to check the consolidated list of public authorities maintained by the Ministry of Justice (MoJ) and its guidance on FOIA public authorities (**www.foi.gov.uk/yourrights/publicauthorities.htm**). Some of the bodies listed may only be caught by the FOIA in relation to certain information (for example, the BBC is liable to disclose all information except that held for the purpose of journalism, art or literature). Wholly-owned subsidiaries of bodies which are caught only in relation to particular information are not public authorities for the purposes of the FOIA (s.6(1)(b)(ii)).[8]

Unlike other rights of access, information requests cannot be submitted to organisations in the private sector, even if they perform public functions. However, the Prime Minister announced in a speech on 25 October 2007 that the government intends to widen the definition of 'public authority' to include private organisations that perform a public function; the formal consultation commenced by the MoJ as a result closed on 1 February 2008

(*Freedom of Information Act 2000: Designation of additional public authorities*, Ministry of Justice, CP 27/07 dated 25 October 2007).

Information requests should be addressed to the relevant public authority which the potential applicant believes holds the desired information, either where the public authority has the information in its own possession, or where the information is held for that public authority by another person (FOIA, s.3(2)). The reasons for which a public authority holds information will be relevant, as information which is merely held on behalf of a third party (for example, for preservation or security reasons), where the public authority itself has no interest in the information, will not be disclosable under the FOIA. This will obviously depend on the circumstances in question but, for example, information belonging to a Minister about party political matters, or a purely personal email sent by an employee of a public authority, which are stored on the authority's computer system will not be deemed to be held by the public authority for the purposes of the FOIA.

Formality of the request?

(i) *Legal formality:* The information request must be made in writing, which includes requests by letter, fax or email, and must include details of the name and address of the applicant (FOIA, s.8(1)(a), (b) and (2)). The request should also describe in as much detail as possible the required information (FOIA, s.8(1)(c)).

(ii) *Practical guidance on how to make a request more effective:*

- Provide contact details, or else the public authority cannot respond to, and indeed is not required under the FOIA to deal with, the request. There is, however, no restriction on a pseudonym, generic email address or PO Box being used.
- Requests may be submitted in English or Welsh. If requests are made in other foreign languages, the public authority may ask the applicant to resubmit the request in English or Welsh; otherwise, the public authority is not obliged under the FOIA to respond to a request in other languages.
- A public authority must provide assistance to enable a written request to be submitted if an applicant is unable to do so (see 'Advice and assistance' later in this section). Some public authorities may also provide standard request forms to assist an applicant to make a request.
- Explain the nature and scope of the information desired as clearly as possible. It will be easier for a public authority to respond to a request which focuses on the particular information sought, rather than a general request for information on a wider topic. Therefore, if possible, refer to a specific document containing the information (for example, a report or minutes of a meeting); otherwise, give examples of the type

of documentation that may include the information or an indication of when the information may have been originally documented.[9]

- The request need not refer expressly to the FOIA, but mentioning this in a request may assist the public authority in identifying and responding appropriately.
- If the information is required urgently, ask the public authority to respond in a shorter timescale than that prescribed in the FOIA (see **3.2.4**). Although the public authority is not obliged to respond quicker than 20 working days from the day after the date of receipt of the request, the Code of Practice suggests it is good practice for the authority to try to respond promptly (*Freedom of Information Act Awareness Guidance No.11*, ICO, para.1), which may be within a quicker timescale.
- An applicant is entitled to request that the information be provided in a convenient form or format, but bear in mind that this should be reasonable (see **3.2.4**). Note also that requesting a particular form or format should not be used as a way of avoiding paying for published information.
- An applicant does not have to disclose why he or she wants the information, even if asked by the public authority. This principle was confirmed by the Information Tribunal in *Dr C T Husbands* v. *Information Commissioner (preliminary decision)*, 16 February 2007 (EA/2006/0048), which agreed with the view that 'the motive of the person making a request for information ought to be irrelevant' (para.19). The FOIA is 'applicant and motive blind' (see *S* v. *Information Commissioner and the General Register Office*, 9 May 2007 (EA/2006/0030), para.19).
- Public authorities may refuse to answer a request altogether on the grounds that it is repetitious or vexatious (i.e. does not have any genuine or serious value or intention, is designed to be disruptive, cause annoyance or harassment, or is manifestly unreasonable) (FOIA, s.14; Access Code of Practice Part II at para.15; and *Freedom of Information Act Awareness Guidance No.22*, ICO, para.2. See also **3.2.4** 'Dealing with a request – initial considerations'). Otherwise, a public authority should treat requests made as part of an organised campaign in the same way as individual requests.
- Ensure that the information requested is not already available as part of the public authority's Publication Scheme – this will save time and effort. In any event the public authority need not respond in these circumstances (see **3.2.1**). Information that is requested repeatedly is likely to have been included in the authority's Publication Scheme.
- It may be sensible to submit a separate request for more controversial information or older materials which are likely to have been stored away. This way a public authority should be able to provide more

straightforward data promptly and can deal separately with the more problematic request.

To whom should the request be sent?

Requests for information under the FOIA can be made to any employee (or agent) of a public authority. However, directing requests to the appropriate person or department within a public authority is likely to bring a quicker and more focused response.

Each public authority (and certainly larger public authorities) should have appointed a nominated officer to deal with, and to advise on, requests for information under the FOIA. A public authority should publish its procedures for dealing with requests for information (or for assistance), including details of an address, email address and telephone number of the person to whom requests for information should be directed (Access Code of Practice Part II, para.5). If this information is not easily available, it is recommended that a request for information is sent to the relevant public authority's head of legal or to the relevant head of the public authority (for example, the Minister or head of the executive agency or local authority), so as to ensure that the request reaches the appropriate person without undue delay.

If an information request is made to an authority that holds the information on behalf of another public authority, the recipient public authority may either decide to deal with the request in consultation with the authority that actually holds the information, or may redirect the request as soon as possible to the originating authority, bearing in mind its duty to provide reasonable assistance and advice to applicants (Access Code of Practice Part III, paras.16–24).

Advice and assistance

A public authority is obliged to provide advice and assistance to applicants, and to those considering making a request for information, so far as it is reasonable to do so (pursuant to its responsibilities under FOIA, s.16(1)), and in accordance with the Codes of Practice (see **3.2.4**) (FOIA, s.16(2) and Foreword to the Access Code of Practice, para.13).

The duty to provide assistance is wide-ranging and covers all stages of making and responding to a request, including the type of information that may be accessed under the FOIA, how to formulate a clear and focused request, other sources of the information desired, and the progress of a submitted request. There is 'nothing to prevent an authority volunteering advice and assistance: an applicant does not have to ask for it' (see *Dr C Lamb* v. *Information Commissioner*, 16 November 2005 (EA/2006/0046), para.2).

Public authorities should be prepared to explain why they are asking for additional information in relation to a request or proposed request (Access Code of Practice Part II, para.9). The key is for a public authority to be flexible and to provide appropriate advice and assistance in the circumstances having liaised with the applicant (Access Code of Practice Part II, para.7 and *Freedom of Information Act Awareness Guidance No.23*, ICO, para.1. See also *Mr Christopher Bellamy* v. *Information Commissioner and the Secretary of State for Trade and Industry*, 3 April 2006 (EA/2005/0023), para.40, in which the Information Tribunal 'endorses the general desirability that requests for information be treated with as much practical assistance as possible'). The public authority should not ask why the applicant or potential applicant is requesting the information, although an applicant is free to disclose this information (*Freedom of Information Act Awareness Guidance No.23*, ICO, para.2).

Other than a public authority's right to request further information from an applicant in order to locate and/or identify information requested (where an extension of time for responding to the request is available – see **3.2.4** 'Timescale for response') (FOIA, ss.1(3) and 10(6)), a public authority will not be entitled to an extension to the standard 20 working day response period to provide all other advice and assistance once a request has been made.

The advice and assistance must be provided free of charge (unless it is provided as part of clarification of a request for information already submitted, in which case fees may be chargeable as set out in **3.2.3**), and should be provided in any appropriate or reasonable media or format. Public authorities should also be aware of their obligations under other Acts of Parliament (such as disability and race discrimination legislation and Welsh language legislation) when providing advice and assistance (Foreword to the Access Code of Practice, para.14). Any employee of a public authority may provide advice and assistance. It is good practice for a record of the advice or assistance to be kept by the public authority, in case it is later queried.

3.2.3 Fees

Publication Schemes

A public authority's Publication Scheme should state whether or not the authority will charge to provide a copy of information made available as part of the Scheme (FOIA, s.19(2)(c)). If a charge is payable, the amount of the charge should also be stated within the Scheme. VAT will be payable on any fees charged for information made available under a public authority's Publication Scheme (see former Department for Constitutional Affairs' *Guidance on the Application of the Freedom of Information and Data Protection (Appropriate Limit and Fees) Regulations 2004*, para.6).

Information requests

Fees chargeable under the FOIA are subject to an 'appropriate limit' (FOIA, s.12). This has been defined by subsequent secondary legislation (the

Freedom of Information and Data Protection (Appropriate Limit and Fees) Regulations 2004, SI 2004/3244 ('the Fees Regulations'), made pursuant to FOIA, ss.9(4) and 12(4)), and fees will not be charged for FOIA information requests as long as the public authority will spend less than £450 in complying with the request, or £600 in the case of requests to central government departments (Fees Regulations, reg.3). Therefore, public authorities must comply with any requests that fall within these limits free of charge, although they may charge applicants for disbursements incurred in providing the information (for example, photocopying or postage costs) if it is reasonable to do so (see former Department for Constitutional Affairs' *Guidance on the Application of the Freedom of Information and Data Protection (Appropriate Limit and Fees) Regulations 2004*, para.3.4).

If a public authority estimates that it will spend more than these prescribed amounts, it need not comply with an information request (FOIA, ss.12(1) and (2)), and must generally notify the applicant of this (FOIA, s.17(5); any such notice should also give details of the public authority's FOIA complaints policy, and the applicant's right to appeal to the Information Commissioner under FOIA, s.17(7)). However, it may offer to do so if the applicant first pays the relevant cost (or even free of charge, at the authority's discretion) (FOIA, s.13). The information as to the cost payable should be provided to the applicant in a fees notice (FOIA, s.9(1)). The amount of fees payable must be subject to a maximum, specified in the fees notice (FOIA, ss.9(4)(b) and 13(2)), which should be calculated in accordance with the Fees Regulations (Fees Regulations, reg.7; FOIA, s.9(4)(c)). If an applicant refuses to pay any notified charge, or if the cost of complying with a request is likely to be high, a public authority should consider whether it can make available any information that may be of interest to the applicant free of charge or for a lesser fee (Access Code of Practice Part II paras.13 and 14 and *Freedom of Information Act Awareness Guidance No.23*, ICO, para.14).

The Fees Regulations provide guidance for public authorities in estimating the likely cost of compliance with any information request (Fees Regulations, regs.4, 5 and 6; pursuant to FOIA, ss.9(3) and 12(5)). The costs to be taken into account are limited to those which the public authority reasonably expects to incur in undertaking certain specified activities in response to the request, namely determining whether the information is held, locating and retrieving the information, and extracting the information from other documents. The public authority cannot take into account any costs incurred in considering whether the exemptions apply to the information (see former Department for Constitutional Affairs' *Guidance on the Application of the Freedom of Information and Data Protection (Appropriate Limit and Fees) Regulations 2004*, para.2.3). VAT will not be payable on the amount of any fees if the public authority is the only possible source of the information requested (para.6).

The former Department for Constitutional Affairs (DCA) conducted an extended consultation exercise on a revised Fees Regulation in 2007, but the proposals were opposed by a majority of respondents to the consultation, with the result that the MoJ withdrew the proposals.[10]

3.2.4 The response

A public authority should have in place a system to ensure the efficient processing of, and advising on, requests for information submitted under the FOIA. While any employee of a public authority can respond to a request for information, public authorities are advised to nominate an officer to deal with these requests. Nonetheless, public authorities are also advised to ensure that staff who deal with members of the public, or who provide information as part of their role, can identify information requests and are familiar with the requirements of the FOIA and other good practice guidance (*Freedom of Information Act Awareness Guidance No.23*, ICO, para.5; and Foreword to the Access Code of Practice, para.15).

The former DCA published two codes of practice ('the Codes of Practice') (pursuant to its then responsibilities under FOIA, ss.45 and 46), which provide guidance to public authorities:

- on desirable practice in discharging their functions under Part I of the FOIA ('the Access Code of Practice') (the former Secretary of State for Constitutional Affairs' Code of Practice on the discharge of public authorities' functions under Part I of the FOIA issued under FOIA, s.45); and
- in relation to records management (the former Lord Chancellor's Code of Practice on the management of records issued under FOIA, s.46).

The Codes are available at **www.foi.gov.uk/codepafunc.pdf** and **www.foi.gov.uk/codemanrec.pdf** respectively. The Information Commissioner (pursuant to his powers under FOIA, ss.47 and 48) has also published a number of guidance notes (available on the ICO website: **www.ico.gov.uk**), to assist public authorities in dealing with various aspects of the FOIA. The former DCA also published a number of useful guidance notes for practitioners, covering procedural matters as well as advice on how to handle specific types of requests, which continue to be available on the MoJ website (**www.foi.gov.uk** and **www.justice.gov.uk**).

Dealing with a request – initial considerations

It is recommended that a public authority acknowledges receipt of all requests received (or at least those that cannot fully and quickly be responded to), to inform applicants that the request is being dealt with and also as means of keeping track of the progress of compliance with the request (*Freedom of Information Act Awareness Guidance No.11*, ICO, para.3). All requests should

65

also as a matter of course be logged by a public authority on receipt for monitoring purposes (see former DCA's Procedural Guide, Chapter 6).

On receipt of a request for information the public authority must:

- *Consider whether a request for information is reasonable (not vexatious):* Public authorities may refuse to answer requests altogether on the grounds that they are repetitious or vexatious (see **3.2.2**) (FOIA, s.14). There have been a number of appeals to the Information Commissioner against public authorities citing s.14 as a reason to refuse requests, with the result that the Information Commissioner has regularly updated his guidance on repetitious or vexatious requests (see Awareness Guidance No.22, currently version 3 dated 23 July 2007). The Information Tribunal has commented that: 'There is no statutory definition for the term vexatious and its normal use is to describe activity that is likely to cause distress or irritation, literally to vex a person to whom it is directed' (see *Mr V Ahilathirunayagam* v. *Information Commissioner and London Metropolitan University*, 20 June 2007 (EA/2006/0070), para.32.i; in that case, the FOIA request was held to be vexatious). Note that there is a difference between a truly vexatious request, which is exempt, and a request simply phrased in subjective, accusatorial or objectionable language, to which a public authority must respond (see *Mr E A Barber* v. *Information Commissioner*, 11 November 2005 (EA/2005/0004)).

- *Consider whether the request is specific enough for the public authority to respond to it:* If a request does not describe the information desired in sufficient detail, a public authority may ask for further information or clarification to enable it to respond to the request. If the public authority requests further information from the applicant in order to identify and locate the information requested, the time limit for compliance (see 'Timescale for response' below) will not commence unless and until the date the further information is received from the applicant (FOIA, ss.1(3) and 10(6)).

  Where a public authority decides that a request is potentially voluminous (and so may exceed the appropriate limit) it must ask the applicant as soon as possible to focus the request, and must assist the applicant in doing this (*Freedom of Information Act Awareness Guidance No.11*, ICO, para.4). However, if the information request is not ambiguous, but just potentially time-consuming and expensive, the public authority will still have to respond within the time limit for compliance (see below) from the day following receipt of the information request.

  If, once initial assistance has been provided, the applicant is still unable to describe the information requested, or focus the request, in a way that would enable a public authority to identify and locate it, a public authority is not expected to seek further clarification and should just disclose what it can and then explain in a refusal letter why it cannot take the request further.

- *Determine whether or not it holds the information requested:* This is considered in **3.2.1** and **3.2.2**.
- *Consultation with third parties:* As a matter of good practice, a public authority should notify or even consult with third parties related to, or with an interest in, the information requested, as to disclosure or whether any exemptions apply, and whether additional explanatory materials should accompany the information to be disclosed (Access Code of Practice, Part IV, paras.25–30). However, in most circumstances the views of such third parties are not ultimately binding on the public authority.
- *Estimate whether or not a charge is payable:* If the cost of responding to a request is estimated to be less than the appropriate limit, the public authority must comply with the request. If the cost is likely to be higher than the appropriate limit, it need not comply with the information request or may choose to do so either free of charge or on payment of a fee by the applicant (see **3.2.3**).

Nature of response

If, having taken into account the initial considerations, a public authority is required to deal with the information request, the general principle of the FOIA is that any person making a request for information to a public authority is entitled:

(a) to be informed in writing by the public authority whether or not it holds information of the description specified in the request (the duty to confirm or deny) (FOIA, s.1(1)(a) and (6)); and

(b) if that is the case, to have that information communicated to him (FOIA, s.1(1)(b)),

in each case in the timescale set out in 'Timescale for response', and in the format set out in 'Format for response', both later in this section.

However, each of these rights to information is subject to a number of exceptions and exemptions (see **3.2.1** and **Chapters 4** and **5**) (FOIA, s.2). If a public authority relies on an exemption under the FOIA so as either not to confirm or deny to an applicant whether it has the requested information or so as not to disclose to an applicant information that it has confirmed that it holds, the public authority must explain this in a refusal notice (as set out in 'Format for response' later in this section).

Timescale for response

As a general rule, public authorities have 20 working days from the day after the date of receipt to comply with a request for information (FOIA, ss.10(1) and (6)), and must respond promptly, which may mean a shorter response time if the information is easily accessible (*Freedom of Information Act Awareness Guidance No.11*, ICO, para.1).

Where a fee is payable under a fees notice, the time limit for compliance will not restart until the fee has been paid (FOIA, s.10(2)) and, if it is not paid within three months of the date of the fees notice, the public authority may assume that the applicant no longer wants the information (FOIA, s.9(2)).

Where it is reasonable to do so, a public authority may inform an applicant that it requires an extension to the 20 working day standard response time in order to consider the public interest test in relation to a qualified exemption (FOIA, s.10(3)) (for details of the public interest test see **Chapter 5**). The public authority should give the applicant written notice of the anticipated additional time required (FOIA, s.17(2)) (the estimated time must be reasonable and justifiable). Any non-exempt information, or any refusal of a request where information is subject to an absolute exemption, must still be disclosed within the initial 20 working days. Public authorities should nevertheless aim to respond within the initial 20 working days even where the public interest test is to be considered (*Freedom of Information Act Awareness Guidance No.11*, ICO, para.7).

Subsequent secondary legislation (Freedom of Information (Time for Compliance with Request) Regulations 2004, SI 2004/3364 ('the Time Regulations'), made pursuant to FOIA, s.10(4) and (5)), which also came into effect on 1 January 2005, also allows public authorities in certain circumstances a longer maximum period of time than is normally provided to comply with information requests:

- where the information is held outside the UK a public authority must respond to the request within 60 working days following the date of receipt of the request (Time Regulations, reg.6);
- information requests to a public records office in relation to information wholly or partly contained in a public record (i.e. information transferred to the National Archives by another public authority) must be complied with within 30 working days following the date of receipt of the request (Time Regulations, reg.4);
- where the information must be obtained from a member of the armed forces on active operation, a public authority must apply to the Information Commissioner for an extension of time (which will normally be no more than 60 working days following the date of receipt of the request) and must then respond within the specified time (Time Regulations, reg.5); and
- information requests to the governing body of a maintained school or a maintained nursery school must be complied with within 60 working days following the date of receipt or the 20th working day following the date of receipt, disregarding any working day which is not a school day, whichever is the earlier (Time Regulations, reg.3).

However, in each of these circumstances, the extension of time granted to public authorities to comply is subject to the overriding obligation to comply promptly with all information requests.

The period of time within which a public authority must respond to a request for information commences on the day after the date of receipt of the request for information. In effect, this is the date that the request is received by any person within or on behalf of the public authority, and not necessarily the date when the request is received by the authority's nominated FOIA officer or the appropriate person for dealing with the request. Therefore, the public authority should ensure that it has in place an adequate system to ensure that all requests for information are promptly identified and passed to the relevant FOIA officer (or appropriate person) as quickly as possible. It is also good practice to ensure that there is a back-up system to deal with requests in the event that the nominated officer, or any other addressee of a request for information, is absent.

If the public authority requests further information from the applicant in order to identify and locate the requested information, the time limit for compliance will not commence unless and until the date the further information is received from the applicant (FOIA, ss.1(3) and 10(6)).

If a request has been transferred from, or referred by, another public authority, the request will be deemed to be received by the public authority on the date that it actually receives the transferred request (i.e. ignoring the period of time in which the transferring public authority received and considered the request) (Access Code of Practice Part III, para.22).

Format for response

A response either confirming or denying that a public authority has the information requested should be in writing and, provided it is reasonable, in the format requested by the applicant. In considering whether or not it is reasonable to comply with the applicant's requested format, the public authority must consider all the relevant circumstances, including the cost (FOIA, s.11(2)). If it is unreasonable, the public authority must state why, and provide the confirmation or denial in a format that is reasonable in the circumstances (FOIA, ss.11(3) and (4)).

Where the applicant has specified that he would like the information to be made available in a preferred form or format, the information should be made available in that form or format (for example, in electronic or hard copy, large print, Braille, audio version, database, in Welsh, as a summary or digest, or alternatively an opportunity to inspect the original) (FOIA, s.11(1)) unless:

- the information is already:

  - publicly available (for example, if the information is already made available as part of the public authority's Publication Scheme); and
  - easily accessible to the applicant in another form or format (taking into account, for example, whether the applicant has access to the

internet, the applicant's location, mobility and any disability, and also considering whether the applicant would have to pay for any alternative means of accessing the information); or

- it is unreasonable in the circumstances for the public authority to make the information available in the requested form or format (FOIA, ss.11(3) and (4)). For example, if the amount of work required to provide the information in the form or format requested would be excessive, or if creating the specified form or format may damage the original document.

However, note a decision of the Information Commissioner, which indicated that (in that particular case) the offer or provision of copies of the requested information, where the applicant had requested sight of the information, was not sufficient (Decision Notice FS50069396 (Cyngor Cymved Llandysul) dated 1 March 2006).

It may be sensible for public authorities to contact the applicant to determine whether the proposed alternative form or format is appropriate to them, especially if the cost of providing their preferred format is likely to be expensive, and also to explain the options available for providing the information.

The FOIA provides a right of access to information, not to documentation and so only part of a document may be disclosable, with the remainder of the document redacted, or else only extracts or a summary of the document need be provided.

Any notice either confirming or denying whether the public authority holds the requested information should also give details of the public authority's FOIA complaints policy, and the applicant's right to appeal to the Information Commissioner (FOIA, s.17(7)). Any disclosure of information should also give this information.

If a public authority relies on an exemption or a procedural limitation under the FOIA so as either to refuse to confirm or deny to an applicant whether it has the requested information, or to disclose information to an applicant that it has confirmed that it holds, the public authority must explain this in a written notice to the applicant. The written notice must specify the exemptions or limitations relied upon and the reason(s) why it believes the exemption or limitation applies (FOIA, s.17(1)). If the public authority has applied the public interest test in relation to qualified exemptions, the written notice should also state the public authority's reasons for the public interest in non-disclosure outweighing the public interest in disclosure (FOIA, s.17(3)). The duty to give reasons in these circumstances, however, will not apply if this itself would involve disclosure of exempt information (FOIA, s.17(4)).

Any notice of refusal either to confirm or deny and/or to disclose information should also give details of the public authority's FOIA complaints policy, and the applicant's right to appeal to the Information Commissioner (FOIA, s.17(7)).

3.2.5   What if not satisfied with a response?

Chapter 10 considers the procedure for making complaints to a public authority under the FOIA, and the appeals process to the Information Commissioner
if such complaints are not handled to the applicant's satisfaction.

3.3   PERSONAL INFORMATION

Under the FOIA, access to personal information by the subject to the information is subject to an absolute exemption (see **Chapter 4**) (FOIA, ss.2 and
40). This section, therefore, summarises how a person may obtain access to
information about himself or herself.

3.3.1   Data Protection Act 1998[11]

Background

The DPA essentially regulates the processing of 'personal data', which is
given a particular meaning at s.1(1) of the DPA. However, despite being in
effect since 24 October 1998, the scope of this definition continues to
cause problems. These problems most commonly occur when a processor of
personal data has to deal with a request for that personal data and other
information to which the subject of that data has a right. In particular, the
landmark case of *Durant* v. *Financial Services Authority* [2003] EWCA Civ
1746 was a case arising out of a challenge to a processor of personal data and
its unwillingness to disclose data relating to an individual who had made a request for that information under the DPA. The case has determined what is
meant by 'relevant filing system', which, as described below, is an important
component of the personal data definition.

As a result of the difficulties in interpreting what is meant by 'personal
data', the Information Commissioner has published revised guidelines on
determining what is personal data.[12]

What information can be accessed?

'Personal data' is any information on a living individual (the 'data subject' as
defined in the DPA) which is stored by reference to a unique identifier that can
be matched back to the data subject by the processor of the data, where those
data are of a private or biographical nature and are:

- contained in computerised records; or
- manual data held in a relevant filing system, where a 'relevant filing
  system' is one that allows a user of the system readily to find and process
  any particular personal data on the data subject; or

71

- in the case of public authorities (as defined in the FOIA), any other manual records.

The DPA provides, at s.7, a right of access to the applicant to personal data processed relating to him or her and certain other information relating to the processing of those personal data, subject to a number of important exemptions listed in Part 4 of the DPA ('non-disclosable data' for the flowchart at Figure 3.2), such as the total exemption from s.7 where processing is for the purposes of national security (DPA, s.28), or subject to parliamentary privilege (DPA, s.35A), or is information available by or under enactment (DPA, s.34). The introduction of all manual records within the scope of personal data for public authorities (as defined in the FOIA, s.68) (DPA, s.1(1)(e)), and amendments introduced by the FOIA, have required some rather specific exemptions to cover certain public authorities' manual data. For example, manual data not held in a relevant filing system relating to the appointments or removals, pay, discipline, superannuation or other personnel matters of any person in relation to service in any of the armed forces or any office or employment under the Crown or any authority are exempt from s.7 (DPA, s.33A(2)), as are personal data in relation to negotiations between a public authority and the applicant (DPA, s.37 and Sched.7, para.7), and personal data processed for the purposes of management forecasting or management planning of the public authority (DPA, s.37 and Sched.7, para.5) (all being 'exempt manual data' for the flowchart at Figure 3.2).

Some of the exemptions from s.7 are only partial, such as the exemptions to the obligation to disclose certain types of personal data relating to social work, health and education,[13] which in general exempt disclosure of the personal data where the disclosure would cause serious harm to the physical or mental health or condition of the applicant or any other person.

Certain other individuals have a right to access personal data of which they are not the direct data subjects, being principally those with parental responsibility or some similar authority to conduct the affairs of another, such as guardians or trustees appointed under the Mental Health Act 1983.

The DPA includes as a total exemption disclosures of information that is available to the public by or under another enactment (other than the FOIA) (DPA, s.34 mirroring FOIA, s.21). These other enactments are considered in **3.3.2**.

The request

A request can be made by any individual or, in the case of a child, a parent or guardian or any other person with parental responsibility for that child (see Children Act 1989, s.3), whether or not they are UK or EU citizen or resident, and regardless of the purpose of the application. The DPA does not state at what age a child can exercise his or her rights under the DPA, and so the common law on the capacity of the child as ruled by the House of Lords in

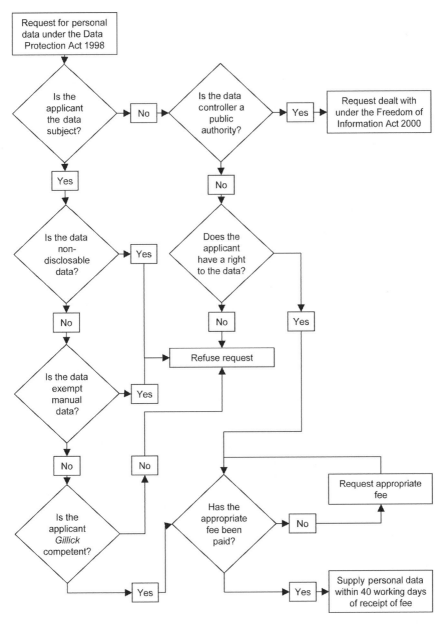

Figure 3.2 Data protection access

Gillick v. *West Norfolk and Wisbech Area Health Authority* [1986] AC 112 has to be considered (this case concerned capacity of a child to consent to medical treatment, but the subsequent test of maturity and understanding, or '*Gillick* competence' test, can be applied to other situations).

The DPA grants a right of access to individuals to information 'processed' by a 'data controller', both as defined in the DPA. 'Processing' is given a wide definition in the DPA, including merely holding the relevant personal data. A 'data controller' is the person who determines how any particular personal data are to be processed. Therefore, persons who only process data as directed by a third party (or 'data processors' as they are confusingly defined in the DPA) need not respond to the access request, but may merely refer the request to the proper data controller.

The subject access request must be made in writing, which includes requests by letter, fax or email. The request can be refused until the appropriate fee is paid to the data controller. In addition, the data controller can refer back to the data subject if the request is not made in sufficient detail to enable the data controller to identify the personal data the controller may or may not be processing.

As with all requests discussed in this chapter, the applicant for the information, here being personal data, will have a greater chance of succeeding if the request is as specific as possible. In general the courts, in determining whether a holder of information properly exercised its obligations under the relevant statutory regime, are not willing to support the use of the relevant regime for general applications of 'fishing expeditions'. (See *Durant* v. *Financial Services Authority* [2003] EWCA Civ 1746, [2004] FSR 573, *Johnson* v. *Medical Defence Union* [2004] EWHC 2509 (Ch) and *Smith* v. *Lloyds TSB Bank plc* [2005] EWHC 246 (Ch).)

There is no legal requirement for the request to be sent to any particular individual or officer of a data controller. However, if the data controller is notified to the ICO, then the notification details in the Public Register (accessible online at **www.ico.gov.uk**) will include the contact details for the data controller's data protection contact. Where the data subject has received a fair processing notice, then this may have given the contact details of the data controller's data protection representative, if there is/was one. Otherwise a request could be sent for the attention of the Data Protection Officer at the data controller.

Fees

The DPA provides that a data controller is entitled to charge for responding to a subject access requests, subject to certain limits (Data Protection (Subject Access) (Fees and Miscellaneous Provisions) Regulations 2000, SI 2000/191 as amended). Data subjects making standard subject access requests may only be charged a maximum of £10, but this can rise to £50 for access to certain medical and education records (these are defined terms in DPA, s.1(1) and Sched.6).

The response

The Information Commissioner has published a number of useful guidance and practice notes, to assist data controllers in dealing with subject access requests (see **www.ico.gov.uk/eventual.aspx?id=87**).

Under DPA, s.7 a data controller of any personal data must reply to an applicant with the following information, unless an exemption applies in respect of some or all of the following:

- whether personal data of which that applicant is the data subject are being processed by or on behalf of that data controller;
- if that is the case, a description of:
  - the personal data of which that individual is the data subject;
  - the purposes for which they are being or are to be processed;
  - the recipients or classes of recipients to whom they are or may be disclosed;
  - the information constituting any personal data of which that individual is the data subject;
  - any information available to the data controller as to the source of those data; and
  - where the processing by automatic means of personal data of which that individual is the data subject for the purpose of evaluating matters relating to him such as, for example, his performance at work, his creditworthiness, his reliability or his conduct, has constituted or is likely to constitute the sole basis for any decision significantly affecting him, the logic involved in that decision taking.

Data controllers have 40 working days in nearly all cases to comply with a subject access request (DPA, s.7(10)). The time limit for compliance will not commence until any fee payable in connection with the information request has been paid (DPA, s.7(2)(b)).

Provided the disclosure by the data controller complies with the requirements of DPA, s.7, then there is no prescribed format for any disclosures under the DPA.

What if not satisfied with a response?

The data subject has rights under DPA, s.7 to apply to a court to obtain a court order ordering disclosure by the data controller. Alternatively, the data subject can at any time lodge a complaint with the Information Commissioner, who may then use his powers to commence an investigation under the DPA to request of the data controller its reasons for not fulfilling the subject access request. Failure to respond or an inadequate response to the Information Commissioner may lead to further enforcement steps being taken by the Information Commissioner under the DPA.

3.3.2 Other access to personal information

Parentage data

For the purposes of the flowchart in Figure 3.1, 'parentage data' means data relating to the parentage of an applicant or other person under the Human Fertilisation and Embryology Act 1990 (HFEA) or under the Adoption Act 1976.

Access under the HFEA is as follows. The Human Fertilisation and Embryology Authority maintains a register of information relating to:

- the provision of treatment services (as defined in the HFEA) for any identifiable individuals so treated;
- the keeping of gametes of any identifiable individuals or of an embryo taken from any identifiable woman; or
- details of any identifiable individual who was or may have been born as a result of the provision of treatment services (HFEA, s.31).

Any person aged 18 or over may, by notice to the Human Fertilisation and Embryology Authority, make a request for any information held by the Authority on him or her, which the Authority must disclose if the person was or may have been born as a result of treatment services (HFEA, s.31(4)). The information must include information as to the true genetic parents of the applicant, where requested. Up until 1 April 2005, the Authority could not be required to give information on the identity of any gametes donor or persons from whom an embryo had been taken. However, such information will be disclosable to any persons born as a result of treatment services provided on or after this date (Human Fertilisation and Embryology Authority (Disclosure of Donor Information) Regulations 2004, SI 2004/1511, reg.2(3)).

In addition, a person under 18 may, by notice to the Authority, inform it of a person the applicant wishes to marry (the 'intended spouse' in the terms of the HFEA) and request that the Authority confirm that the applicant and the intended spouse are not or not likely to be related. Before responding, the Authority must ensure that the minor has had the opportunity to receive proper counselling about the implications of the Authority complying with the request.

Some of the information relating to treatment services will be held by persons licensed under the HFEA to provide the treatment services. Provisions are included in the HFEA to place restrictions on such licensed persons from disclosing this type of registrable information, with the notable exception of information disclosed on an application for access to health records (HFEA, s.33).

Access under the Adoption Act 1976 is as follows. This continues to apply in respect of information concerning persons adopted before 30 December 2005. As soon as an adoption agency has made an adoption order, it must disclose whatever information it considers appropriate about the adopted child to the adopters, charging them to share this information with the child when appropriate, but no later than the child's 18th birthday (Adoption Agencies Regulations 1983, SI 1983/1964, reg.13A).

In addition, the agency must provide access to its records to certain persons, as set out in the appropriate regulations, including a child's guardian or reporting officer for the purposes of the guardian or officer discharging their statutory duties (Adoption Agencies Regulations 1983, SI 1983/1964, reg.15).

For persons adopted on or after 30 December 2005, the procedures under the Adoption and Children Act 2002 apply (ss.56–65). The procedures define a special class of adoption related data, 'protected information' (Adoption and Children Act 2002, s.54) and include regulations on the disclosure of this protected information (Disclosure of Adoption Information (Post-Commencement Adoptions) Regulations 2005, SI 2005/888; and Disclosure of Adoption Information (Post-Commencement Adoptions) (Wales) Regulations 2005, SI 2005/2689).

Birth records must be obtained via the relevant adoption agency, which will obtain the official birth record from the Registrar General and forward it to the adoptee, subject to the regulations on the provision of counselling.[14]

Having obtained information to enable their birth parents or blood relatives to be traced, adopted persons had no method before 1989 of knowing whether those parents or relatives would welcome contact. For this reason, the Registrar General maintains a register, the Adoption Contact Register. However, this register is not open to inspection or access. Each of the adopted persons who want to contact their birth parents or relatives or those parents or relatives must apply to be included in the register. If the Registrar General discovers a match between the parties, he must forward the relevant contact details to the adopted person where the parent or relative has indicated that contact will be welcome; no information is forwarded to the parent or relative other than the knowledge that their details have been so forwarded (Adoption Act 1976, s.51A).

Medical data

For the purposes of the flowchart in Figure 3.1, 'medical data' means information contained in 'medical reports', as that term is defined in the Access to Medical Reports Act 1988, and data making up a 'health record', as defined in the Access to Health Records Act 1990.

Access under the Access to Medical Reports Act 1988 is as follows. Any person may obtain a copy of a medical report on him or her, which is or has been supplied for employment or insurance purposes by a medical practitioner (Access to Medical Reports Act 1988, s.2). A third party can, for purposes connected with employment or insurance, obtain a medical report only with the consent of the data subject, who can insist that a copy of the report be provided to him or her before it is disclosed to the third party (Access to

Medical Reports Act 1988, ss.3 and 4). However, the medical practitioner can withhold the report where its disclosure would be likely to cause serious harm to the physical or mental health of the data subject or any others; would indicate the practitioner's intentions in respect of the data subject; or would reveal the identity of a third party who has supplied information for the medical report, unless that third party has consented to the disclosure (Access to Medical Reports Act, s.7).

Access under the Access to Health Records Act 1990 is as follows. Certain representatives of a patient may make an application in writing for the patient's health records to the holder of the record (Access to Health Records Act 1990, s.3). A 'health record' is defined as information relating to the physical or mental health of a patient made by or on behalf of the health professional (as defined in the DPA) in connection with the care of the patient, other than information to which the patient is, or could be but for an exemption, entitled to access under the DPA. However, only those parts of the record made on or after 1 November 1991 are subject to the right of access, together with such earlier parts of the record as are necessary to make the parts made on or after 1 November 1991 intelligible (Access to Health Records Act 1990, ss.1(1), 5(1), 11 and 12(2)). However, an exemption to disclosure of the same nature as for medical reports, described above, may apply (Access to Health Records Act 1990, s.5(1)).

Persons other than the patient who can obtain access to a health record include:

- a person authorised in writing by the patient (Access to Health Records Act 1990, s.3(1));
- in England and Wales, a person having parental responsibility for the patient where that patient is a child and disclosure is in the patient's best interests, provided that if the patient is *Gillick* competent in the opinion of the holder of the health record and the patient has not consented to such access, it must be refused (Access to Health Records Act 1990, ss.4 and 5);
- a person appointed by a court to manage the affairs of a patient incapable to manage them (appointed by a Court of Protection under the Mental Health Act 1983 and the Court of Protection Rules 2001, SI 2001/824 (as amended)); or
- where the patient has died, the patient's personal representatives or any person who may have a claim arising out of the patient's death (Access to Health Records Act 1990, s.3(1)).

However, the holder of the records can withhold information that in the holder's opinion the patient would not have expected to have been disclosed (Access to Health Records Act 1990, s.5(3)).

Disclosure of the health records must be made within 21 days of a request, where the records were created within 40 days of the request, or otherwise within 40 days. If any part of the record is unintelligible without an explanation, this must also be given with the disclosure. The cost of making of copies and postage costs can be charged to the applicant (Access to Health Records Act 1990, s.3(2)).

Pension data

Trustees of certain occupational pension schemes have a number of statutory duties in respect of obtaining accounts audited by auditors to the schemes, the auditors' statements and valuations by an actuary of the assets and liabilities of the schemes, together with the actuary's statement concerning such aspects of the valuation as prescribed in the relevant regulations (Pensions Act 1995, s.41; the Occupational Pension Schemes (Disclosure of Information) Regulations 1996, SI 1996/1655 (as amended); and the Stakeholder Pension Schemes Regulations 2000, SI 2000/1403 (as amended)). The trustees are required to make copies of these documents available to members and prospective members of the scheme and their spouses, persons connected with the application of the scheme and qualifying or prospectively qualifying for its benefits or, independent trade unions recognised for the purposes of collective bargaining in relation to members or prospective members of the scheme. Any of these persons can apply for a copy of the latest documents, free of charge, which must be supplied with two months of the request (Occupational Pension Scheme (Disclosure of Information) Regulations 1996, SI 1996/1655, regs.6(1) and (2); and Stakeholder Pension Schemes Regulations 2000, SI 2000/1403 (as amended), reg.18).

Industrial data

For the purposes of the flowchart in Figure 3.1, 'industrial data' means information disclosable to trade union representatives under the Trade Union and Labour Relations (Consolidation) Act 1992 (TULRCA), the Health and Safety at Work etc. Act 1974 or equivalent employees' representatives under either the regulations implementing the EC Council Directive on the establishment of European Works Councils or the Information and Consultation Framework Directive.

Access under TULRCA is as follows. Employers who recognise independent trade unions for the purposes of collective bargaining have certain statutory duties to disclose to the representatives of the relevant unions on their request information relating to all stages of the collective bargaining and which is information without which the representatives would be materially impeded in carrying on the collective bargaining or which good industrial relations practice would dictate should be disclosed for the purposes of collective bargaining (TULRCA, s.181). Pursuant to its powers under TULRCA, the Advisory, Conciliation and Arbitration Service (ACAS) has produced a Code of Practice on Disclosure of Information to Trade Unions for

Collective Bargaining Purposes, which sets out the types of information a union representative should expect, under the headings pay and benefits, conditions of service, manpower, performance and financial: the Employment Protection Code of Practice (Disclosure of Information) Order 1998, SI 1998/45. As may be expected, the employer's duty to disclose is qualified: the employer is not required to disclose information, for example, which would cause substantial injury to its undertaking for reasons other than its effect on the collective bargaining.

A trade union can complain to the Central Arbitration Committee if it believes an employer has failed to disclose to its representatives that which it is required to disclose in accordance with these statutory requirements. Ultimately, the Central Arbitration Committee has the power to impose terms and conditions of employment on recalcitrant employers (TULRCA, ss.183–5).

Access under the Health and Safety at Work etc. Act 1974 is as follows. Employers have a statutory duty under the Health and Safety at Work etc. Act 1974 to allow trade union appointed safety representatives on reasonable notice to inspect and take copies of any document relevant to the workplace that the employer is required to keep by any statutory provision, except a document consisting of a health record of an identifiable individual (Health and Safety at Work etc. Act 1974, s.2; and Safety Representatives and Safety Committees Regulations 1977, SI 1977/500 (as amended)).

Access under the Transnational Information and Consultation of Employees Regulations 1999, SI 1999/3323 is as follows. The regulations implement in the UK the EC Directive on the establishment of European Works Councils for the right to information and consultation of employees in Community-wide undertakings (Transnational Information and Consultation of Employees Regulations 1999, SI 1999/3323 (as amended), implementing EC Council Directive 94/45). Whilst the regulations do not provide employees or their representatives express rights to demand information, by triggering the establishment of a European Works Council, the employees gain indirect rights to information. (This is triggered by a written request of at least 100 employees or their representatives in at least two undertakings or establishments in at least two different member states, where the undertaking has at least 1,000 employees with at least 150 in two or more member states.) If any information is not provided by the central management of the relevant undertaking on the grounds that it is confidential or exempt (as it would seriously harm the functioning of or would be prejudicial to the undertaking or group of undertakings concerned), the European Works Council can appeal to the Central Arbitration Committee for a declaration as to whether the information was properly withheld or an order for the disclosure of the information or relevant document.

Access under the Information and Consultation of Employees Regulations 2004, SI 2004/3426 (as amended) is similar. The 2004 regulations implement in the UK the EC Directive 2002/14/EC of the European Parliament and of the Council of 11 March 2002 establishing a general framework for informing and consulting employees in the European Community. Once lower employee number thresholds are crossed, the 2004 regulations trigger the requirement for an information and consultation negotiated agreement, under which employees gain indirect rights to information, including information concerning the development of the undertaking's activities and economic situation and the consequent effect on employment. (This is triggered by a single or a number of written request from at least 10 per cent of the employees in the relevant undertaking subject to a minimum of 15 or maximum of 2,500 employees, in undertakings that have at least 100 employees (from 6 April 2007) or 50 employees (from 6 April 2008).) The 2004 regulations also provide that the employees' representatives can appeal to the Central Arbitration Committee for a declaration as to whether any information was properly withheld or an order for the disclosure of the information or relevant document.

Wages data

Employers have a statutory duty to maintain records in the prescribed form in connection with the National Minimum Wage Act 1998 (National Minimum Wage Act 1998, s.9; and National Minimum Wage Regulations 1999, SI 1999/584 (as amended)). A worker may require his or her employer upon written request to produce the relevant records and may inspect those records and copy any part of them, where the worker believes on reasonable grounds that he or she is or may be being, or has or may have been, remunerated at less than the national minimum wage rate and for the purposes of establishing the actual position. The employer must comply within a reasonable time, not being longer than 14 days unless agreed between the worker and the employer.

If an employer does not allow access to records, the worker may make a complaint to an employment tribunal. If the worker's complaint is in time (within three months of the expiry of the 14 days referred to above) and the tribunal finds that the worker's underpayment complaints are well founded, then it can award the worker a sum equal to 80 times the hourly rate of the national minimum wage at the date of the award for the underpaid hours.

Criminal records data

Applicants are able to apply to the Criminal Records Bureau (CRB) for access to criminal records for employment purposes under the provisions of the Police Act 1997 (PA). The CRB provides applicants with either a criminal record certificate (CRC) or an enhanced criminal record certificate (ECRC), subject to the relevant fee (£31 for CRC, £36 for ECRC and nil for volunteers (Police Act 1997

(Criminal Records) Regulations 2002, SI 2002/233, as amended, reg.4)). In due course the CRB will also issue criminal conviction certificates (CCCs).

CCCs will be issued to any individual making an application (PA, s.112(1) – not yet in force) and will set out details of every conviction of the applicant which is recorded in police records or states there is no conviction, as defined in the Rehabilitation of Offenders Act 1974, other than a spent conviction.

CRCs give details of every relevant matter recorded in central police records against the applicant, or states that there is no such matter, and details whether the applicant is on the Sexual Offenders Register pursuant to the Sexual Offences Act 2003 (PA, s.113(3)). A 'relevant matter' means a conviction within the meaning of the Rehabilitation of Offenders Act 1974, including a spent conviction, and a police caution (PA, s.113(5)). An application must be countersigned by a person registered on a list maintained by the Secretary of State (PA, s.120(1), (4) and (5)) and be accompanied by a statement by the registered person that the certificate is required for an 'exempted question' in respect of an applicant seeking paid or voluntary work or training in an occupation which is exempt from the Rehabilitation of Offenders Act 1974 (PA, s.113(2) and (3)). (An exempted question is a question in relation to which the Rehabilitation of Offenders Act 1974, s.4(2)(a) or (b) (effect of rehabilitation) has been excluded by order of the Secretary of State under the Rehabilitation of Offenders Act 1974, s.4(4) (Police Act 1997, s.113(4)).) A copy of the certificate will be issued directly to the registered person countersigning the application (PA, s.113(4)).

The Secretary of State may issue an ECRC giving details of a CRC, but also providing additional relevant information on an applicant held by chief police officers of local police forces, including relevant non-conviction information (PA, s.113B(1)–(5)).[15] The additional information may concern offences which the applicant is suspected of committing, even though his responsibility has not been and cannot be proved. The information must, however, be information which the chief constable is of the opinion might be relevant to a position which involves regularly caring for, training, supervising or being in sole charge of persons under 18 or vulnerable persons aged 18 or over. An application must be countersigned by a registered person and submitted with a statement that the certificate is required for an exempted question asked in the course of considering the applicant for certain positions, including paid or voluntary work or training in a position whose normal duties include regularly caring for, training, supervising, or being in sole charge of children under 18 years of age or vulnerable adults (Police Act 1997 (Criminal Records) Regulations 2002, reg.5A). The certificate will be sent to the registered person together with any additional information the chief officer believes ought to be included (PA, s.113B(8)).

Provisions are included in the PA for the inclusion of suitability information relating to children and/or vulnerable adults, where the relevant application is accompanied by a suitability statement from the registered person (PA, ss.113C–113F).

An applicant can apply for a new certificate if the information it contains is inaccurate (PA, s.117). It is an offence for a person, with intent to deceive, to make a false certificate, to alter a certificate, to use a certificate which relates to another person in a way which suggests that it relates to himself or herself, or allow a certificate which relates to him or her to be used by another person in a way which suggests that it relates to that other person (PA, s.123(1)).

3.4 ENVIRONMENTAL INFORMATION

The EIR (made under powers set out in (i) FOIA, s.74; and (ii) the European Communities Act 1972) also came into force on 1 January 2005 (EIR, reg.1), and broadly grants rights of access to environmental information held by or on behalf of public authorities (including some non-public bodies carrying out a public function). 'Environmental information' (which is defined widely by EIR, reg.2(1)) is exempted from disclosure under the FOIA, s.39. Therefore, requests for such information, and consideration as to whether or not such information must be disclosed or withheld, must be made under the EIR. Other statutory provisions provide more limited rights of access to environmental information, but the wider right of access provided by the EIR takes precedence (Guidance to the EIR Code of Practice, para.3.11).

Chapter 9 considers the rights of access granted by the EIR, and how to make and respond to a request for environmental information. It is worth noting that, while the right of access to environmental information and the procedures for making and responding to requests for environmental information under the EIR are similar to those provided by the FOIA, there are some key differences, which are highlighted in **Chapter 9**.

3.5 OTHER STATUTORY RIGHTS OF ACCESS TO PUBLIC AUTHORITY INFORMATION

It should not be forgotten that there are numerous other statutory regimes that give the public rights of access to information held by public authorities. Information available under other Acts of Parliament include, for example:

- public records held at the National Archives (under the Public Records Act 1958);
- registration records relating to rights over land held by local authorities and HM Land Registry (under the Commons Registration Act 1965, Land Charges Act 1972, Local Land Charges Act 1975 and Land Registration Act 2002);
- records of registered intellectual property rights (under the Registered Designs Act 1949, Patents Act 1977 and Trade Marks Act 1994);

- records relating to incorporated companies (under the Companies Act 2006); and
- records regarding licensed premises (under the Licensing Act 2003).

Such legislation may prescribe the form for any requests and the form and timescales for the public authority response, and may include an appeals procedure, which varies from those provided by the FOIA. There is also a great deal of information that is available to the public upon inspection of the relevant records, such as the indices kept for the registrations of births, marriages and deaths in England and Wales kept by the Registrar General or superintendent or other registrars.[16] Access to these inspection-only records can be made under the FOIA.

3.6 ACCESS TO INFORMATION HELD BY EUROPEAN UNION INSTITUTIONS

In addition to information held by public authorities, the European Commission has a track record of ensuring that wherever possible, all European Union information is readily available to citizens of the Union.

The key document to prescribe access to European Union information is Regulation (EC) 1049/2001 regarding public access to European Parliament, Council and Commission documents (OJ L 145/43 31.05.2001). Under the Regulation, the European Parliament, Council and Commission are required to provide the widest possible access to documents held by them (including documents received by them) in all areas of activity of the European Union. As with the FOIA, however, there are a number of exceptions that permit the institutions to refuse access (Regulation (EC) 1049/2001, Art.4). The Regulation expressly states that it is without prejudice to copyright in any document, so that an applicant's right to reproduce or exploit released documents may be limited (Regulation (EC) 1049/2001, Art.16). For political documents the Regulation includes a public interest test in familiar terms. Each of the institutions has also put in place institution-specific procedures detailing their policies and practices for granting public access to their documents.[17]

In a parallel with the UK's later introduction of the EIR, Regulation (EC) 1367/2006 addressing access to environmental information (OJ L 264/13 25.09.2006) came into effect on 28 June 2007. As with the EIR, the definition within the Regulation of 'environmental information' is broad (Regulation (EC) 1367/2006 Art.2(d) – identical wording to EIR, reg.2(1)). There is also a presumption of disclosure, with Regulation (EC) 1367/2006 stating that there is an overriding public interest in disclosure where the information requested relates to emissions into the environment.

The European Commission published a Green Paper on these regulations (COM(2007) 185 final 18.04.2007) in 2007. Although the consultation period expired on 18 July 2007, no formal reform proposals have yet been published.

3.7 CONCLUSION

While the FOIA has certainly widened the scope of information made available to the public, additional rights of access to information available under other statutory regimes should also be considered.

It should be noted that there is a distinction between receiving information from public authorities (and other organisations, depending on the relevant statutory regime) and the re-use of that information by the person that requested it. The statutory rights of access to information discussed in this chapter do not automatically grant recipients of information the right to reproduce or re-use documentation supplied under these statutory regimes, and certainly not in a way that would infringe copyright (Draft Guidance to the EIR Code of Practice, para.6.35). Normal rules governing re-use of copyright works still apply, which means that charges may be applied for the re-use of the materials provided in addition to the fees paid (or payable) for the supply of the materials. The EU Directive 2003/98/EC of the European Parliament and of the Council on the re-use of public sector information was implemented in the UK on 1 July 2005; the Re-use of Public Sector Information Regulations 2005, SI 2005/1515 introduced a framework within which members of the public and organisations may request a licence to re-use documents held by a 'public sector body' (subject to certain exemptions) but also entitles the affected public authorities (as not all FOIA public authorities are caught by the re-use regime) to charge for the re-use of documentation provided to the public.

NOTES

1   See, for example, the FOIA stories published by the BBC at **http://news.bbc.co.uk/ 1/hi/in_depth/uk/2006/foi/default.stm** or the *Guardian* newspaper at **http://politics. guardian.co.uk/foi**.

2   For example, see the UCL Department of Political Science Constitution Unit study *FOIA 2000 and local government in 2006: The experience of authorities in England, Northern Ireland & Wales*, September 2007.

3   For example, the Information Tribunal held that a tape recording of court proceedings is a 'document' for the purpose of ss.32(1), commenting 'since that term is broadly construed in an age offering so many recording media . . . Transcripts of tapes are analogous to copy documents' (*Mr A Mitchell* v. *Information Commissioner*, 19 October 2005 (EA/2005/0002), paragraph 21).

4   See *Mr N Slann* v. *Information Commissioner and Financial Services Authority*, 11 July 2006 (EA/2005/0019), which concerned a prohibition under the Financial Services and Markets Act 2000; *Mr M J Dey* v. *Information Commissioner and Office of Fair Trading*, 16 April 2007 (EA/2006/0057), where provisions of the Enterprise Act 2002 imposed a prohibition on disclosure; and *Mr L Meunier* v. *Information Commissioner and National Savings and Investments*, 5 June 2007 (EA/2006/0059), where provisions of the Premium Savings Bond Regulations 1972 also meant that the FOIA, s.44 exemption applied.

5 See the Information Commissioner's Decision Notices: (i) Brockhampton Group Parish Council, Decision Notice FS50135471 dated 23 March 2007; and (ii) Argoed Community Council, Decision Notice FS50142974 dated 29 August 2007.

6 FOIA functions of the Lord Chancellor were first transferred to the Secretary of State for Constitutional Affairs (Order 4 of the Secretary of State for Constitutional Affairs Order 2003, SI 2007/1887) and then subsequently were transferred to the Secretary of State for Justice with effect from 22 August 2007 (Order 7 of the Secretary of State for Justice Order 2007, SI 2128/2007).

7 This is notwithstanding the attempted Private Member's Bill in summer 2007 to exclude the Houses of Parliament from elements of the FOIA regime. Despite being approved initially by the House of Commons (in a vote greeted with horror in the national press), the Bill was ultimately killed by the House of Lords.

8 For example, the BBC's trading subsidiaries – see Information Commissioner's Decision Notice FS50082246 dated 30 May 2007.

9 The Information Tribunal noted that 'the subject matter of the information must be set out and described as precisely as possible' (see *Dr C Lamb* v. *Information Commissioner*, 16 November 2006 (EA/2006/0046), para.3). That case highlighted, in the Tribunal's words, 'the danger in not alerting a complainant to the need to specify his request at the earliest possible reasonable opportunity' where a request is unclear (para.19).

10 *Draft Freedom of Information and Data Protection (Appropriate Limit and Fees) Regulations 2007* – DCA Consultation Paper 28/06 dated 14 December 2006, and *Supplementary Paper: Consultation on the Draft Freedom of Information and Data Protection (Appropriate Limit and Fees Regulations) 2007*. Confirmation that the proposals were withdrawn at: *Draft Freedom of Information and Data Protection (Appropriate Limit and Fees) Regulations 2007 – Response to Consultation*, Ministry of Justice, CP(R) 28/06 dated 25 October 2007.

11 This section gives a summary of the data subject access regime in the Data Protection Act 1998. For a full analysis of the data subject access provisions, see the sister publication to this book, Peter Carey (ed.), *Data Protection Handbook*, Law Society Publishing, 2004.

12 *Data Protection Technical Guidance – Determining what is personal data*, v1.0 dated 21 August 2007.

13 DPA, s.30, as detailed in the relevant orders (the Data Protection (Subject Access Modifications) (Social Work) Order 2000, as amended, the Data Protection (Subject Access Modifications) (Health) Order 2000 and the Data Protection (Subject Access Modifications) (Education) Order 2000).

14 Adoption and Children Act 2002, s.79(5) and Part 6 of the relevant Access to Information (Post-Commencement) Regulations 2005, SI 2005/588 or Adoption and Children Act 2002, s.79(5) and Part 6 of the relevant Access to Information (Post-Commencement) (Wales) Regulations 2005, SI 2005/2689, with counselling provisions at Part 5.

15 In *R (on the application of X)* v. *Chief Constable of West Midlands* [2004] EWCA Civ 1068, a decision by a chief constable under s.115 of the Police Act 1997 to disclose information that a prospective social worker had been charged with an offence of indecent exposure (even though the Crown Prosecution Service offered no evidence on those charges at trial) was not overruled by the Court of Appeal. The Court of Appeal held that there was no presumption against disclosure in a s.115 case.

16 Births and Deaths Registration Act 1953, ss.30–32; and Marriage Act 1949, ss.64 and 65; and see the range of online information available from National Archives at **www.nationalarchives.gov.uk**.

17 The Commission's procedures require requests to be sent by mail, fax or email to the Secretariat-General of the Commission or to the relevant Directorate-General or department, with a charge of €0.10 per page plus carriage costs being charged for documents over 20 pages long (Commission Decision dated 5 December 2001 – OJ L 345/94 29.12.2001).

The Council requires requests to be sent by post, fax or email to the Secretary-General of the Council or High Representative, to whom the authority to set charges for producing and sending copies of documents is delegated (Council Decision 13465/01 dated 22 November 2001 to amend the Council's Rules of Procedure – special email address is access@consilium.eu.int).

The European Parliament delegates access matters to the Secretary-General of the Parliament, with a charge of €10 plus €0.03 per page for producing copies of documents over 20 pages (subject to revision by the Secretary-General). The Bureau of the European Parliament deals with confirmatory applications it receives (European Parliament Bureau Decision on Public Access to European Parliament Documents 2001/C 374/01, OJ C 374/1 29.12.2001, and see Rule 97 of the Rules of Procedure of the European Parliament).

CHAPTER 4

The absolute exemptions

Marcus Turle, Field Fisher Waterhouse LLP

4.1 INTRODUCTION

As we have seen, the Freedom of Information Act 2000 (FOIA) establishes a new statutory right of access to information held by more than 100,000 public authorities across England, Wales and Northern Ireland. The right is retrospective, applies to all information regardless of format, provenance or right of use, and is available to anyone, anywhere in the world.

Importantly, however, while the entitlement to information under the FOIA is very wide, it is not unlimited. The law recognises that certain areas of government need to retain a measure of secrecy and that freedom of information imposes an administrative burden which, beyond a certain point, should justifiably be limited. It also seeks to balance the legitimate interests of those whose commercial and confidential information merits protection. A person making a request is therefore not entitled to have any information whatsoever – the FOIA confers a general right to know, but with exemptions. There are 23 exemptions within the FOIA, each of which overrides the duty to disclose information in certain circumstances. In effect, the exemptions represent particular interests for which Parliament deemed it expedient to grant dispensation.

Responsibility for ensuring that the exemptions are properly used lies with the Information Commissioner, whose office acts as both police and judge for freedom of information, investigating and adjudicating on complaints brought by FOIA applicants. (FOIA requestors are effectively compelled to lodge complaints with the Commissioner rather than take matters into their own hands, by virtue of s.56 of the FOIA which precludes civil claims against public authorities for damages.) FOIA, s.50 entitles anyone dissatisfied with a public authority's response to a request to complain, and there are no procedural requirements for doing so and no fee. On receipt of a complaint the Commissioner is obliged to investigate it, provided the complainant has already exhausted the authority's internal complaints process. Importantly, a complainant is not at risk over costs if the complaint is unsuccessful, so there is no downside to bringing an appeal.

If the Commissioner dismisses an appeal it is then open to the applicant to appeal to the Information Tribunal. Again, there is no fee and the only procedural requirement is the submission of a simple form, available from the Tribunal's website (see **www.informationtribunal.gov.uk**). Even at Tribunal proceedings, the circumstances in which costs can be awarded against an unsuccessful appellant are limited (see **Chapter 10** for a detailed explanation of the Tribunal's role in the enforcement process).

There is a further right of appeal to the High Court against a decision of the Information Tribunal, but only on a point of law. Only at this stage will an appellant be faced with the procedural complexities of litigation and the risk of having to pay the other party's costs if the appeal fails. Taken as whole, therefore, the FOIA regime is very appeal-friendly. It provides no disincentive to challenging public authorities who refuse to disclose information and it is clear from the number brought since 2005 that applicants have done so willingly.

Moreover, a review of Information Commissioner Decision Notices and Tribunal judgments indicates that both bodies will readily order disclosure in the absence of compelling evidence justifying the use of exemptions. Commentary and analysis of all the exemptions is set out below, and in **Chapter 5**, with references to Information Commissioner Decision Notices and Tribunal judgments where relevant.

Readers wishing to keep fully up to date with information on the latest cases in the Information Tribunal and decisions of the Commissioner are referred to the practical journal, *Freedom of Information* (**www.foij.com**).

4.2   THIRD PARTY INFORMATION

As the FOIA applies to all information which a public authority holds regardless of its provenance, the question arises: what about information originating outside the authority itself? Authorities will hold a large amount of information in the form of correspondence, contracts, invoices, tenders, technical data and all sorts of other material which was authored or otherwise provided by external organisations, but which will still be FOIA-accessible by virtue of being held in the authority's files. This should be of particular concern for anyone in the private sector doing business with government.

In effect, the law pre-1 January 2005 is now turned on its head. Much information which the law might then have protected will now be open to public scrutiny. What is more, the FOIA neither imposes an obligation on public authorities to notify or to consult third parties before disclosing information relating to them, nor does it provide any statutory mechanism for preventing disclosure. Assessment of the exemptions, and the decision whether or not to apply them, is entirely at the discretion of the public authority. (Part VII of the Lord Chancellor's Code of Practice issued under FOIA, s.45 makes it clear that consultation is good practice, but there is no requirement to consult.) Some suppliers may try to protect themselves using contractual provisions which require the customer to notify and consult before disclosing, but since the buck stops with the authority regardless of what the contract says, most will be reluctant to accept any contractual provisions which attempt to fetter their FOIA processes (unless, presumably, the supplier is prepared to give a properly compensating indemnity).

This leaves suppliers with limited options. Any pre-emptive challenge to an authority's application of the FOIA will be contingent on the supplier knowing a request has been made. The best advice to suppliers must therefore be to do everything to ensure their customers tell them when a request comes in. Suppliers can try putting contractual obligations on customers to this effect, but the key to risk management will be a close working relationship between the supplier's and the customer's teams. Customer liaison should be geared to ensuring the customer's information handling process functions to meet its own legal obligations, but also allows the supplier to mitigate the risk of sensitive information finding its way into the public domain. If there is disagreement over a document, then the ultimate sanction for the supplier would be an injunction preventing disclosure.

Without some kind of early warning system, customers will simply disclose information without the supplier knowing. In this case, there are only really two ways to go: either the supplier takes it on the chin, or it can sue for damages on the ground the information was disclosed unlawfully. This, of course, is a long way short of satisfactory, not least because litigation carries uncertainty of outcome, and further cost.

4.3   TYPES OF EXEMPTION

There are two types of exemption to the right of access, described in FOIA, ss.2(1) and (2). These are:

(a)   absolute exemptions; and
(b)   exemptions which might apply:

    (i)   if disclosure would prejudice certain interests (which are set out in the FOIA); and/or
    (ii)   for reasons of public interest.

The exemptions in (b), above, are known as qualified exemptions, because they can only apply where the public interest permits (see **Chapter 5** for an analysis of the public interest test) and, in some cases, where exemption is necessary to protect a specific interest (such as, for example, national security).

Of the 23 exemptions in the FOIA, only eight are absolute. These are listed in s.2(3). They are:

1.   information accessible to the applicant by other means (s.21);
2.   security matters (s.23);
3.   court records (s.32);

4. parliamentary privilege (s.34);
5. prejudice to the effective conduct of public affairs (s.36);
6. personal information (except to a limited extent, where the exemption is qualified (see further, **Chapter 5**)) (s.40);
7. confidential information (s.41); and
8. other legal prohibitions on disclosure (s.44).

The qualified exemptions are examined in **Chapter 5**.

4.4   APPLYING THE EXEMPTIONS

Whenever a public authority refuses to disclose information, it is required to explain why. This means citing the relevant exemptions and justifying their use in the particular context of the request.

In *Bowbrick* v. *Information Commissioner and Nottingham City Council* (case reference EA/2005/0006, 29 June 2006) the Information Tribunal examined the question of whether exemptions can be claimed for the first time at a late stage in the appeal process, i.e. at the Information Commissioner or Tribunal stage (having not previously been cited by an authority when responding to the request). The Tribunal held that it would be inequitable not to consider exemptions which were relevant, irrespective of when during the proceedings they were brought up. This approach was followed in *Mr Colin P England (1) and London Borough of Bexley (2)* v. *Information Commissioner* (case reference EA/2006/0060 & 0066, 10 May 2007) in which the Tribunal confirmed that there was nothing in the FOIA or in the Information Tribunal (Enforcement Appeal) Rules 2005, SI 2005/14 to prevent the Council amending its Notice of Appeal. Furthermore, 'it would be inconsistent with the Tribunal's own obligations to act in a manner that is compatible with individuals' human rights under the Human Rights Act 1998 for it to, on a technicality, require a disclosure that . . . would otherwise be protected by [a FOIA exemption]'.

In *Bowbrick* the Tribunal also explored whether the Information Commissioner has a positive duty to look for exemptions which might apply where not claimed by a public authority. It held that in general terms there is no such duty, but the Information Commissioner is not precluded from examining an exemption if it considers that another exemption has been misidentified.

4.5   ABSOLUTE EXEMPTIONS

The absolute exemptions apply to all information which falls within each of the categories listed above. In other words, the exemptions apply to whole *classes* of information. In assessing whether an absolute exemption applies, the only question is whether the information falls within one of the categories. If it does, then it is exempt. There is no test of public interest or prejudice.

If an absolute exemption applies, then the public authority does not have to disclose the information and may not even have to say whether it holds it, although it *is* required to tell the applicant which exemption it thinks applies, and why.

Each of the absolute exemptions is considered below.

4.5.1   Information accessible to the applicant by other means (s.21)

The purpose of this exemption is to ensure that public authorities do not become the natural first choice source for information which the applicant can get elsewhere. The FOIA does not cut across existing legal regimes which provide access to information, nor does it provide alternative means of access to information which is already freely available through commercial publishing operations or existing publicly funded provision. The FOIA is designed to supplement rather than duplicate the ordinary circulation of information to the public through the commercial electronic and print media and through existing library and archive services.

Provided the information requested is reasonably accessible by other means (FOIA, s.21(1)) then the exemption will apply. Information is reasonably accessible if (for example):

- it is made available in accordance with the authority's Publication Scheme (FOIA, s.21(3)) (in effect, an authority is not obliged to answer individual requests for information if it already makes that information generally available to everyone); or
- it is available by virtue of other legislation (FOIA, s.21(2)(b)), e.g., information which is accessible under the subject access rules in the Data Protection Act 1998 (DPA) or information about the environment which is available under the Environmental Information Regulations 1992 (EIR).

In *Mr Colin P England (1) and London Borough of Bexley (2)* v. *Information Commissioner* (case reference EA/2006/0060, 10 May 2007), the Information Tribunal considered the meaning of 'reasonably accessible'. Mr England had sought details of empty residential properties in the Bexley area, which the Council refused to disclose on the basis that the information was obtainable from the Land Registry website (**www.landreg.gov.uk**). The Tribunal considered whether the fact that only 70 per cent of land in Bexley was registered with the Land Registry was sufficient to engage the exemption in s.21. Bexley Council had argued that the requirement for reasonable accessibility will be satisfied where a requisite amount of information is available from another source. The Tribunal disagreed. The Tribunal held that the word 'reasonably' qualifies the word 'accessible'. Therefore 'reasonably accessible' applies to the mechanisms available to an applicant to obtain information. It does not mean that public authorities have no obligation to provide information where a 'reasonable amount' of information is available somewhere else.

In the *Transport for London* (TfL) Decision Notice (FS50075171, 5 May 2006), the Information Commissioner considered whether it was the accessibility of *individual* records that needed to be 'reasonable', or whether records as a whole should be considered. The applicant had sought files of prosecutions brought by London Bus Services Ltd (a subsidiary of TfL) since the start of 2003. TfL believed some of this information to be accessible in court records and therefore refused disclosure in reliance on s.21. The applicant argued that it would be unreasonable to expect him to retrieve court records from a large number of magistrates' courts where the individual records would be held. The Commissioner concluded that it was necessary to consider the accessibility of individual records rather than the effort required to assemble a collection of them all. In other words, reasonable accessibility is not a function of the volume of the information sought.

Note that information may still be 'reasonably' accessible (and therefore exempt under this section) even though it is only available on payment of a fee (FOIA, s.21(2)(b)), e.g. under the subject access regime in the DPA. Of course, where the cost of obtaining information by other means would be excessive, that might preclude use of the exemption.

Some factors to consider when assessing whether information is readily accessible are as follows.

- Is it is available to purchase through commercial outlets, or is it out of print?
- Is it mass produced in a large print run, or distributed only through scarce or specialist outlets?
- Is it available over the internet or through a public library?
- How easily can it be identified? Has it been catalogued or indexed?
- Is it ephemeral or has it been archived?
- Is it subject to onerous conditions of access or subsequent use?

Note, however, that there is a subjective element to the exemption, in the sense that the information must be reasonably accessible *to the applicant*. Consider the following points.

- Are any legal access rights available to the particular applicant (for example, Access to Health Records Act 1990, s.3, which provides that the holder of a health record shall allow access to the health record of a deceased person on application by that person's personal representative, by supplying them with a copy or an extract)?
- Does the applicant have access to otherwise closed or private sources of information, by virtue of some particular quality, entitlement or qualification?
- Does the applicant possess enhanced skills or resources which may bring otherwise inaccessible information within reach (e.g., research, technical or linguistic skills)?
- Is the applicant disadvantaged in some way (e.g., because of disability or educational or economic circumstances) which might render information inaccessible which would otherwise be readily accessible to the general public?

Information will not be exempt by virtue of its availability under other legislation if the relevant statutory obligation is only to make the information available for inspection.[1]

Importantly, this exemption does not apply to the requirement to confirm or deny, so even if the exemption means an authority does not have to make information available, the authority is still required to say whether or not it holds the information.

Where an authority does rely on this exemption, it should try as a matter of good practice to point the applicant to where, by other means, he or she can obtain the information requested.

Public archives and public records

Information held in public archive or by the Public Records Office may be FOIA exempt under s.21 if the information requested is catalogued and included in the relevant authority's Publication Scheme (or its parent authority's Publication Scheme).

The Public Services Quality Group of the National Council on Archives has produced a Standard for Access to Archives, providing guidance on what constitutes an acceptable level of service for archive repositories, including availability to the public. Where a personal visit to an archive is not practicable, some alternative should be made available, such as a paid research service or reference to a list of professional researchers.

Another point has been considered by the Information Tribunal in the context of s.21. In *Prior* v. *Information Commissioner* (case reference EA/2005/0017, 10 April 2007), the Tribunal noted that whether or not a complainant accepts the substance of the information provided is not a matter for consideration under the FOIA. The only obligation of a public authority is to provide the information it holds that fits the description specified in the request.

4.5.2 Security matters (s.23)

This exemption covers all information originating from or relating to one of the security services. Section 23 states that:

(1) Information held by a public authority is exempt information if it was directly or indirectly supplied to the public authority by, or relates to, any of the following bodies:

- the Security Service (i.e. MI5);
- the Secret Intelligence Service (i.e. MI6);
- the Government Communications Headquarters (i.e. GCHQ) (and this includes any unit or part of a unit of the armed forces which is required by the Secretary of State to assist GCHQ in carrying out its functions);
- the special forces;

- the Tribunal established under s.65 of the Regulation of Investigatory Powers Act 2000;
- the Tribunal established under s.7 of the Interception of Communications Act 1985;
- the Tribunal established under s.5 of the Security Service Act 1989;
- the Tribunal established under s.9 of the Intelligence Services Act 1994;
- the Security Vetting Appeals Panel;
- the Security Commission;
- the National Criminal Intelligence Service; and
- the Service Authority for the National Criminal Intelligence Service.

(2) A certificate signed by a Minister certifying that the information to which it applies was directly or indirectly supplied by, or relates to, any of the above bodies shall, subject to s.60 (which governs appeals against certificates), be conclusive evidence of that fact.

The exemption also applies to the duty to confirm or deny, to the extent that confirming or denying would involve disclosure of any exempt information (whether or not already recorded). It will therefore be appropriate in many cases for a department neither to confirm nor deny the existence of the information requested. It may equally be appropriate to rely on the exemption even where the department does not hold the information.

Application of the exemption in practice

The first part of the exemption refers to information directly or indirectly supplied by one of the security bodies, so the question of whether or not this applies will turn on the source rather than the content of the information requested. For this part of the exemption, the content of the information is irrelevant.

Insofar as the application of the exemption turns on the second part of it (i.e. whether information relates to any of the security bodies), it will be capable of covering a wide range of subject matter, whether of a policy, operational or administrative nature.

In relation to any particular item of information, it will be a question of fact whether it falls within s.23 or not. Where the origin of information is unclear, the exemption should be applied with care, and if possible after consultation with the author.

The FOIA does not specify how remote from the original source information needs to be before it ceases to be indirectly supplied by or related to one of the security bodies. As such, if it is possible to trace a discrete piece of information back through each transmission to its original source, then this would seem to be sufficient, however many hands it has passed through and even if the wording has changed along the way.

The s.23 exemption applies to all records, regardless of their age, including historical records, except that for historical records held by the National

95

Archives or the Public Record Office of Northern Ireland, s.23 ceases to be an absolute exemption after 30 years.

Ministerial certificates

Ministerial certificates require the signature of either a Cabinet Minister, the Attorney General or the Advocate General. It is not necessary to have a certificate to rely on s.23, but a certificate will normally reinforce a department's position in any legal proceedings, and determine the forum for hearing an appeal (the Information Tribunal rather than the Information Commissioner). As such, certificates are primarily relevant to enforcement proceedings and need not be served until such proceedings commence. Serving a certificate when answering a request will normally be premature and might involve unnecessary work, although departments should consider the need for a certificate at a reasonably early stage to take account of the time needed to prepare one.

Although s.23(2) provides that it is conclusive evidence that information falls within this exemption where it is certified as such by a Minister, this can still be challenged under s.60. Further, s.23 also only permits Ministers to certify specific information – which precludes the preparation of certificates in expectation of future requests. (Note, however, that certificates issued under s.24 (national security) *can* be general and prospective.)

Interaction with other exemptions

The security matters exemption may overlap with a number of other exemptions: namely, national security (s.24), defence (s.26), international relations (s.27) and the economy (s.29). There is nothing to prevent a department claiming exemption under several, or indeed all, these heads, if appropriate.

It is worth remembering, however, that except for national security, the other exemptions do not provide for ministerial certificates. Further, all of them are qualified exemptions and therefore subject to the public interest. This could give rise to procedural difficulties if an applicant challenges their efficacy. If, for example, a department claimed exemption under both the s.23 (security matters) and s.26 (defence) exemptions, then the route for appeal would be:

- an appeal to the Information Tribunal under s.60 against the s.23 certificate, by either the applicant or the Commissioner;
- a challenge by the applicant to the Commissioner on the balance of the public interest (although this may be adjourned pending the outcome of any s.60 appeal);
- a challenge by the applicant to the Commissioner on the s.26 exemption, although again, it may be appropriate for the Commissioner to adjourn this pending hearing of the s.60 appeal.

4.5.3 Court records (s.32)

Information contained in court records and other similar documents is absolutely exempt from FOIA disclosure. In essence, the exemption covers:

- any document served on or by a public authority; and
- documents held or created by a court, or a person conducting an inquiry or arbitration,

in each case, for the purposes of proceedings.

Documents served on or by a public authority

This covers documents created by the parties to litigation and will include information contained in:

- claim forms and statements of defence;
- committal documents in criminal proceedings;
- witness statements, medical and other experts' reports and exhibits;
- skeleton arguments;
- standard disclosure lists;
- public interest immunity applications and certificates;
- allocation questionnaires or pre-trial checklists (listing questionnaires);
- notices of a payment of money into court made pursuant to Part 36 of the Civil Procedure Rules;
- application notices;
- applications under Police and Criminal Evidence Act 1984, ss.76 and 78;
- trial bundles;
- response to a Request for Further and Better Particulars (Civil Procedure Rules 1998 (CPR) Part 18); and
- any other documents which are placed before a court for the purpose of a decision or ruling.

Where an authority is party to litigation, documents provided to it by the other parties under their disclosure obligations will normally be exempt. However, the exemption will not extend to information contained in exempt documents if the information is also held by the public authority in another form. So, for example, if an authority is litigating over a contract, the contract will not be exempt (assuming the authority holds a copy in its files) just because that contract is included in the authority's statement of case. This is because the opening line in s.32 reads 'Information held by a public authority is exempt information if it is held *only* by virtue of being held in [court documents etc.]' (FOIA, s.32(1)) (author's italics).

In practical terms, this means that information will usually only be susceptible to the s.32 exemption where it is known to the public authority solely because it is contained in documents served on the authority by another party in litigation, or where it is held by the authority solely because it was recorded in connection with litigation.

Documents held or created by a court

For the purposes of s.32, a 'court' includes a tribunal or other body exercising the judicial power of the State. As well as the civil and criminal courts (comprising magistrates' courts, county courts, the Crown Court, the High Court and the Court of Appeal), this includes the Judicial Committees of the House of Lords and the Privy Council, and the judicial functions of coroners. It would probably exclude the European Court of Justice and the European Court of Human Rights, which are not UK domestic courts. 'Proceedings' includes any inquest or post mortem.

This part of the exemption would cover information contained in documents such as:

- judgments and orders of the court which have not been published;
- notebooks of judges, tribunal members, coroners and other judicial officers;
- notices of hearings;
- summaries prepared by judicial assistants; and
- court or tribunal internal memoranda and correspondence which relate to particular proceedings.

The point about the s.32 exemption is that there are separate and specific regimes for access to information held by courts and tribunals, designed to give those bodies control over the information they hold. Special rules set out a comprehensive code governing the disclosure of court records and documents served in the course of proceedings. For example, rule 5.4 of the CPR deals with access to court documents in civil proceedings in county courts, the High Court and the Court of Appeal.[2] For certain types of proceedings (such as in the family court, where children need to be protected), only limited classes of persons may access court documents. The FOIA does not exist to provide indirect access to these records. The greater public interest is considered to lie in preserving the courts' own procedures for disclosure, and the s.32 exemption therefore functions to ensure that the courts can continue to control this.

There is a distinction, of course, between the courts themselves – which are not public authorities under the FOIA – and the government departments responsible for organising the court and tribunal systems (i.e. the Court Service and the Northern Ireland Court Service), which are. Information held by the latter is accessible under the FOIA in the normal way, as is information held by the police, the Legal Services Commission and the Legal Services Ombudsman.

The phrase 'created by ... a court' in s.32(1)(c) was considered by the Information Tribunal in *Alistair Mitchell* v. *The Information Commissioner* (case reference EA/2005/0002, 10 January 2005). The Tribunal concluded that in the context of sub-clause 32(1)(c) (as opposed to s.32(1)(a)), the phrase must be interpreted as referring to *judicially* created documents. On this basis it held that a court transcript was not an exempt document because it was not created by the judge.

It was the Information Commissioner's view in the *Doncaster Metropolitan Borough Council* decision (FS50080312, 7 August 2007) that s.32(2) should not be interpreted as requiring that the primary reason for holding information should be its status as a court record. The Commissioner did not accept the Council's argument that the FOIA requires him to consider what the primary purpose for holding the information is.

Documents held or created by a person conducting an inquiry

Inquiries will be subject to the FOIA unless they are legally independent of the sponsoring department. A public authority may therefore hold information which falls within s.32 either because it conducted an inquiry itself or because it was the inquiry's sponsoring department. However, there is a very important limitation on the application of the exemption to inquiries. The exemption can only apply where an inquiry has statutory constitution or is set up under Royal Prerogative (even if a judge heads the proceedings). This might include:

- inquiries which are required to be held by specific statutory provision;
- a discretionary inquiry or hearing designated by an order under s.16(2) of the Tribunals and Inquiries Act 1992 (the relevant order is the Tribunals and Inquiries (Discretionary Inquiries) Order 1975, as amended);
- an inquiry set up by the exercise of a statutory power (e.g. under Local Government Act 1972, s.250 or Children Act 1989, s.81);
- any inquiry to which the provisions of the Tribunals of Inquiry (Evidence) Act 1921 apply.

There are numerous examples of specific inquiries set up under an enactment.[3] Examples of inquiries which would normally fall outside the scope of s.32 are:

- departmental 'leak' inquiries;
- Lord Butler's review of the intelligence published prior to the invasion of Iraq on weapons of mass destruction;
- Sir Michael Bichard's inquiry arising from Ian Huntley's murder of Soham schoolgirls Holly Wells and Jessica Chapman;
- Lord Penrose's inquiry into the collapse of the mutual life assurer Equitable Life; and
- Lord Philip's inquiry into BSE.

Documents held or created by a person conducting arbitration

'Arbitration' is defined by reference to Part 1 of the Arbitration Act 1996, which applies only where there is a written arbitration agreement. Arbitration involves an impartial, independent third party hearing both sides (usually in private) and issuing a final and legally binding decision to resolve the dispute.

The exemption would normally apply to information contained in, for example:

- notes taken by an arbitrator;
- written decisions or reports of the arbitration;
- a written arbitration agreement that is created by a person conducting an arbitration;
- internal correspondence between persons involved in the conduct of an arbitration; and
- a letter from a person conducting an arbitration requesting further evidence.

4.5.4 Parliamentary privilege (s.34)

Information is exempt where necessary to prevent infringement of parliamentary privilege. Similarly, the duty to confirm or deny does not apply if or to the extent that exemption is required, for the same reason.

It is outside the scope of this book to discuss at length the nature of parliamentary privilege. It is sufficient for our purposes to note that while parliamentary privilege is not intrinsically regarded as a reason for secrecy, it is deemed a form of immunity applying to the House of Commons and House of Lords which is necessary for them to function independently, without external interference. The most significant privilege is the right of freedom of speech and proceedings in Parliament, which effectively means that MPs and peers cannot be sued or prosecuted for anything they say in debates or proceedings. As it applies to the FOIA, it means that no external authority can adjudicate on Parliament's right to withhold information where that right is exercised on grounds of parliamentary privilege.

Both the House of Commons and the House of Lords are public authorities for the purposes of the FOIA (individual MPs and peers are not) and both have Publication Schemes. Information included in these Publication Schemes will be exempt under s.21. For the most part, the exemption will apply to information generated and held by the Commons or Lords which are unpublished, such as:

- committee reports and report drafts;
- memoranda submitted to committees, and draft memoranda;
- internal papers prepared by the Officers of either House directly related to the proceedings of the House or committees (including advice of all kinds to the Speaker or Lord Chancellor or other occupants of the Chair in either House, briefs for the chairmen and other members of committees, and informal notes of deliberative meetings of committees);
- papers prepared by the Libraries of either House, or by other House agencies such as the Parliamentary Office of Science and Technology, either for

general dissemination to Members or to assist individual Members, which relate to, or anticipate, debates and other proceedings of the relevant House or its committees, and are intended to assist Members in preparation for such proceedings;

- correspondence between Members, Officers, Ministers and government officials directly related to House proceedings;
- papers relating to investigations by the Parliamentary Commissioner for Standards;
- papers relating to the Registers of Members' Interests; and
- Bills, amendments and motions, including those in draft, where they originate from Parliament or a Member rather than from Parliamentary Counsel or another government department.

As well as information generated and held by the Commons or Lords themselves, s.34 could extend to information held elsewhere (for example, by central government departments) if related to parliamentary proceedings. If so, then the department concerned must consult with the appropriate House authorities before disclosing. Importantly, although it is open to a department to refuse disclosure on s.34 grounds, only the House authorities can conclusively certify the exemption (as permitted by s.34(3)). Since any person breaching privilege may be punished by Parliament, failure to engage the exemption where it applies may result in serious sanctions. Departments should normally therefore seek advice from the relevant officials to ensure that privilege is asserted (and duly certified) where it is proper to do so. (For the House of Commons, the relevant official is the Speaker of the House, for the House of Lords, it is the Clerk of the Parliaments. Each House asserts privilege over its own material.) Particular care should be taken with requests for information contained in:

- any of the unpublished working papers of a select committee of either House, including factual briefs or briefs of suggested questions prepared by the committee staff for the use of committee chairmen and/or other members, and draft reports (most likely to be held by a department where a Minister is or has been a member of such a committee);
- any legal advice submitted in confidence by the Law Officers or by the legal branch of any other department, to the Speaker, a committee chairman or a committee, or any official of either House;
- drafts of motions, bills or amendments which have not otherwise been published or laid on the Table of either House;
- any unpublished correspondence between Ministers or department officials on the one hand, and any member or official of either House on the other, relating specifically to proceedings on any Question, draft bill, motion or amendment, either in the relevant House or in a committee; and
- any correspondence with or relating to the proceedings of the Parliamentary Commissioner for Standards or the Registrar of Members' Interests in the House of Commons.

Much information which is privileged is now routinely published by Parliament itself anyway, and this goes well beyond the record of proceedings. It includes internal administrative documents and even individual Members' expenditure against parliamentary allowances. Information published in this way does not cease to be privileged (it remains Parliament's decision whether or not to continue publication) but disclosure of published information cannot be taken as infringing parliamentary privilege in a way which would engage the s.34 exemption (although the information may be eligible for exemption under s.21, being reasonably accessible to the applicant other than under the FOIA).

Note that s.34 is not intended to enable the withholding of information which would be disclosable but for its being contained in parliamentary papers. So, while the draft of a memorandum responding to a select committee report may itself be privileged, factual information included in it may not be. The factual information would normally have to be disclosed unless it cannot be extracted without revealing what else is in the draft report.

There will also be a range of information which is not published by Parliament but which is also not related to parliamentary proceedings and therefore not protected by parliamentary privilege. The best examples of this are:

- papers prepared by the Libraries of either House or other House agencies, intended to provide general or specific background information on matters not currently under examination or expected or planned to be considered in formal proceedings of either House or their committees;
- Members' correspondence and other communications not specifically related to proceedings of either House or of one of its formally constituted committees (correspondence between a Member and a Minister about a constituency issue that is not the subject of proceedings is not privileged, but correspondence about a draft motion, amendment or Question is privileged);
- the deliberations of parliamentary bodies established by statute (although if they are discussing matters relating to the preparation of formal proceedings in Parliament, those deliberations may well be privileged);
- meetings of political parties and other committees.

4.5.5   Prejudice to the effective conduct of public affairs (s.36)

This is actually a qualified exemption (see **Chapter 5**), except in relation to information held by the House of Commons or House of Lords, where it is absolute, presumably for reasons of parliamentary privilege. A detailed analysis of s.36 is set out in **Chapter 5**.

4.5.6 Personal information (s.40)

The interface between freedom of information and data protection is extraordinarily complex. The key to understanding it is to recognise that neither regime is absolute. On the one hand, the FOIA promotes openness and transparency by requiring public authorities to disclose information proactively (through Publication Schemes) and on request. On the other, the DPA protects personal information by restricting the way our personal data can be used. Importantly, however, the basic principles in both cases are subject to exemptions. In the case of the FOIA, the exemptions permit public bodies to refuse to disclose information, and in the case of the DPA, they permit the use and disclosure of information with more freedom than would otherwise be allowed.

The exemption in s.40 relating to personal data acknowledges the tension between freedom of information and data protection and attempts to reconcile the two. It does so with some difficulty and a great deal of legislative contortion. As a result, s.40 is one of the most difficult exemptions to apply in practice.

The FOIA now extends the meaning of 'personal data' in the DPA to include all recorded information held by public authorities. Prior to the FOIA, the DPA covered all electronic records, but manual records were only caught if they were held in highly structured filing systems (such that personal data could be located easily, without having to flick through the pages (see *Durant* v. *Financial Services Authority* [2003] EWCA Civ 1746). The DPA still applies in this way to manual records held by organisations in the private sector.

The rules for dealing with requests for personal data depend on who is making the request – i.e. whether the requestor is the data subject himself, or a third party:

- *Subject access requests – i.e. requests made by the data subject himself or herself:* Subject access requests are absolutely exempt from the FOIA because they are covered by the regime in s.7 of the DPA. Any request for personal data made by the data subject can therefore be treated as a subject access request under s.7 of the DPA (although note that public authorities' obligations under s.7 of the DPA will now also apply to unstructured manual files). The purpose of s.40(1) of the FOIA is to ensure that the freedom of information regime does not duplicate or cut across the subject access regime under the DPA.
- *Requests for personal data by third parties:* These requests *do* fall within the FOIA regime, but the scope of the s.40 exemption and the way it applies varies. Section 40(2) provides that personal data requested by someone other than the data subject is exempt where either of two conditions apply, set out in s.40(3) and (4). The duty to confirm or deny is also excluded if either of these conditions apply. Within s.40(3) and (4) there are actually *three* exemptions:

- s.40(3)(a)(i) and (3)(b) provide an *absolute* exemption where disclosure of personal data to a third party would contravene any of the eight data protection principles (as set out in the DPA, governing the use of personal information);
- s.40(3)(a)(ii) provides a *qualified* exemption where disclosure of personal data to a third party would contravene s.10 of the DPA (that is, the right to prevent processing likely to cause damage or distress); and
- s.40(4) provides a *qualified* exemption where personal data is exempt from the data subject's own right of access by virtue of any of the provisions of Part IV of the DPA (that is, the exemptions in ss.27–39 which apply to things like national security, crime and taxation, and regulatory activity).

The cumulative effect of s.40(3) and (4) is that information which is protected from disclosure under the DPA cannot be obtained using the FOIA. This sounds straightforward enough, but it is far from easy to apply in practice. A detailed exposition of s.40(3) and (4), including the approach taken by the Information Commissioner and Information Tribunal, is set out in **Chapter 8**.

In the *Bristol North Primary Care Trust* decision (FS50066908, 10 April 2006), the Information Commissioner was asked to consider whether the s.40 exemption applied to footage from CCTV cameras, i.e. whether it constitutes personal data and, if so, whether its release would breach any of the data protection principles. Once the Commissioner had concluded that the footage did constitute personal data, he went on to consider whether disclosure would breach the data protection principles. In his view the capture of images of individuals on CCTV tapes could amount to an infringement of personal privacy. The public is generally expected to tolerate the use and disclosure of CCTV images for limited purposes, for example, use in a police investigation. However, allowing a general right of access would be to exceed the public's legitimate expectations. In addition, it was the Commissioner's view that if CCTV footage was available to the public on demand, this would not only adversely affect individuals' personal privacy, it would also undermine the intended use and purpose of the technology. Further, Art.8 of the European Convention on Human Rights (the right to respect for private and family life) was engaged and disclosure of footage would be an unnecessary and disproportionate interference by a public authority in an individual's private life. On the basis that disclosure of the information would put the Trust in breach of the data protection principles and Art.8 of the ECHR, the s.40 exemption has been correctly applied.

4.5.7   Confidential information (s.41)

Information which a public authority obtained from outside the organisation (including from another public authority) is exempt from disclosure if disclosure would be an actionable breach of confidence. Public authorities are also not obliged to confirm or deny possession of confidential information to the extent that this would in itself be an actionable breach of confidence.

Importantly, the exemption cannot apply to an authority's own confidential information (although it can still apply to information which is confidential to an authority's officers and staff) because s.41 refers to information 'obtained by the public authority *from another person*' (author's italics). Further, although government departments are treated as separate entities for FOIA purposes (FOIA, s.81(1)) a government department cannot claim s.41 exemption on the grounds that disclosure of information would be actionable by another government department (because the government cannot sue itself). The same applies between Northern Ireland departments, but not between a Northern Ireland department and a UK department.

What is confidential information?

The legal rules which define confidentiality are continually developing. It is outside the scope of this book to explore the law of confidence in detail.

The leading Information Tribunal case on s.41 is *Derry City Council* v. *Information Commissioner* (case reference EA/2006/0014, 17 October 2006). In that case, the Tribunal set out the common law test for confidentiality, as follows:

- does the information have the necessary quality of confidence to justify the imposition of a contractual or equitable obligation of confidence?
- was the information communicated in circumstances that created such an obligation?
- would disclosure be a breach of that obligation? and
- if this first part of the test is satisfied, would the public authority nevertheless have a defence to a claim for breach of confidence based on the public interest in disclosure of the information?

This test has been subsequently applied by the Tribunal in *McTeggart* v. *Information Commissioner and Department of Culture, Arts and Leisure* (case reference EA/2006/0084, 30 April/1 May 2007) and in *S* v. *Information Commissioner and General Registry Office* (case reference EA/2006/0030, 25 April 2005).

It is important for FOIA practitioners to note that even if the common law conditions for confidentiality are met, an action for breach of confidence will fail (and therefore the exemption will not apply) if disclosure is in the public interest. This is known as the public interest defence and derives from common law, not the FOIA. So, although the FOIA exemption for confidential information is absolute (i.e. not subject to a public interest test), if a public authority judges that a breach of confidence will not be actionable because the authority has a public interest defence to a claim, then the authority would normally have to disclose that information, notwithstanding its confidentiality.

In practice, information with some commercial value which is not easily available from other sources is likely to be confidential, as is information which an individual would consider confidential (e.g. a staff appraisal, salary details for junior employees, etc.). Three important factors must be assessed whenever a public authority is applying s.41:

- whether or not information is protected by confidentiality will depend largely on the circumstances in which it was obtained and whether, at the time, the authority expressly agreed to keep it confidential (there are guidelines in the Lord Chancellor's Section 45 Code of Practice (see below) on when an authority should agree to confidentiality restrictions);
- special considerations apply if the information in question is personal data; and
- if information is disclosed in breach of a duty of confidence, then the authority may be liable to a claim for damages; if, on the other hand, information is withheld when it should be disclosed, sanctions under the FOIA may apply. The application of s.41 must therefore be approached with care, and legal advice sought where appropriate.

The Tribunal examined the first limb of the common law test of confidence (whether information has the necessary 'quality of confidence' to make it worthy of protection) in *S* v. *Information Commissioner and General Registry Office* (case reference EA/2006/0030, 25 April 2005). The case arose from a request from an individual whose brother had died unexpectedly. The deceased's partner, who had been present at the death, had registered it with the General Registry Office (GRO) but the appellant had asked the GRO to amend the death certificate to reflect the fact that the deceased's mother had also been present. The GRO refused. The appellant subsequently asked for all documentation underlying the GRO's decision. The GRO did provide some information but refused to disclose a letter from the deceased's partner, on the basis that it was exempt under s.41. The letter had been sent in response to a request from the GRO, seeking clarification of her whereabouts at the time of her partner's death. She did not want the information in the letter disclosed to the applicant and further argued that there was nothing in the letter that the appellant was not already aware of. The Tribunal considered whether information loses its quality of confidence if it is already known to a FOIA applicant independently of a FOIA request. It held that it does not, on the basis that dissemination to a limited number of people (including the applicant) does not prevent information being considered confidential. Underlying the Tribunal's decision was the principle that every person will have a different perception of an event and each individual's recollection will vary, so that information known to an applicant may not in fact correspond exactly to information which an Authority holds. So while the facts underlying the content of the disputed letter may have been known to the applicant, the way in which those facts had been recalled by the letter's author imputed a personal

106

element to the information which meant that it should retain its confidentiality. Indeed, the Tribunal was satisfied that even where a synopsis of the information had been provided, the personal element would remain and with it the necessary quality of confidence.

The Tribunal was asked to consider some interesting questions regarding confidentiality and the application of s.41 in *Bluck* v. *Information Commissioner and Epsom & St Helier University NHS Trust* (case reference EA/2006/0090, 10 August 2007). The case arose from a request for the medical records of a deceased person. The deceased's mother sought hospital records for a period leading up to her daughter's death at Epsom & St Helier NHS Trust. The Trust refused disclosure on the basis that the information was confidential and could only be released with the consent of the deceased's next of kin (which had been refused). Citing the Court of Appeal decisions in *Coco* v. *Clark* [1968] FSR 415 (the leading authority on the law of confidence), *Ash* v. *McKennitt* [2006] EWCA Civ 1714 and the House of Lords decision in *AG* v. *Guardian Newspapers* [1990] 1 AC 109, Counsel for the appellant argued that:

1. there is a clear public interest in the disclosure of information in cases where a hospital has been negligent in the treatment of a patient, leading to that patient's death, the public interest lying in the fact that negligence is exposed and can be avoided in the future;
2. a claim of breach of confidence was not sustainable in the absence of any detriment likely to be suffered by either the deceased or her estate;
3. so much of the information contained in the deceased's medical records had already passed into the public domain that it no longer had the required quality of confidence; and
4. a claim of breach of confidence could not survive the death of the person whose private information was at issue and the personal representative of that person could not enforce, post mortem, any such claim which might have existed while they were alive.

Consequently, it was argued that any breach of confidence was not actionable as required by s.41(1)(b).

In relation to the appellant's first submission (public interest), the Tribunal held that the public interest in maintaining the s.41 exemption was not outweighed by the arguments for disclosure. If a patient was aware that his medical records may at some stage be disclosed to the public the patient may not give full disclosure to hospital staff, therefore risking an incorrect diagnosis and further harm. The Tribunal rejected the argument that the passage of time since death, the admission of negligence by the hospital and the extent to which information had already been released was sufficient to outweigh the public interest in maintaining confidence.

In response to the appellant's second submission (the requirement for detriment in order to sustain a claim of breach of confidence), the Tribunal interpreted the Court of Appeal's decision in *Ash* v. *McKennitt* to mean that, 'if disclosure would be contrary to an individual's reasonable expectation of maintaining confidentiality in respect of his or her private information, then the absence of detriment in the sense apparently contemplated . . . [by the appellant] is not a necessary ingredient of the cause of action'.

In relation to the appellant's third submission (public domain), the Tribunal decided that the information had not lost the necessary quality of confidence, because there was a significant amount of information contained in the medical records which had not been disclosed in earlier correspondence. This was obviously not known by the appellant (because she was not able to inspect the information) and therefore the challenge on this point failed.

In addressing the appellant's final point (claim for breach of confidence), the Tribunal took into account Counsel's contention that the absence of definitive authority on whether a duty of confidence survives death created a substantial doubt as to whether a claim for breach of confidence would succeed. In the absence of any compelling authority, all parties reverted to general principles. The appellant's case was that once a person has died, there is no one capable of enforcing a duty of confidence. The Information Commissioner and the hospital Trust argued that the basis of the equitable obligation of confidence stemmed from the purpose of a doctor's obligation of confidence and was therefore a legal, not just a moral and ethical, obligation (supported by the terms of the Hippocratic Oath). They argued that a doctor having accepted the obligation of confidence was an essential part of the doctor/patient relationship and it would be unconscionable for him to disclose information to the public either before death or afterwards. Consistent with the decision of Megarry J in *Coco* v. *Clark*, the Tribunal concluded that a duty of confidence is capable of surviving death. After a lengthy discussion of relevant case law and commentary, the Tribunal also decided that any breach of confidence would indeed be actionable by the deceased's personal representatives and therefore the requested information did constitute exempt information for the purposes of s.41.

Confidential information and the Lord Chancellor's Code of Practice

The overriding purpose of freedom of information is to ensure openness and transparency in the public sector. It will therefore be apparent to readers that sweeping confidentiality restrictions on information held by public authorities are necessarily incompatible with the FOIA. The Lord Chancellor's Code of Practice issued under FOIA, s.45 (referred to here as the 'Section 45 Code of Practice') sets out guidance on when public authorities should accept information in confidence, and also on when to consult third parties where an authority plans to disclose their confidential information.

In relation to information provided to a public authority by a third party:

- the public authority should only accept that information is in confidence where possession of the information is necessary in connection with the authority's functions and where it would not otherwise be provided;
- the public authority should not agree to hold information in confidence unless the information is genuinely confidential; and
- the public authority should only agree to express confidentiality provisions where these are capable of justification to the Information Commissioner.

Although the Section 45 Code of Practice does not have the legal force of the FOIA itself, it nevertheless has considerable clout. The Information Commissioner has a duty to promote its observance, and a legitimate expectation that authorities will comply with it. The courts will also normally refer to the Code when determining any question of compliance.

When considering whether to agree to hold information in confidence, here are some useful pointers:

- consider the nature of the interest to be protected and whether it is really necessary to hold information in confidence to protect that interest;
- consider whether it is possible to agree a limited duty of confidentiality, for example by clearly stating the circumstances in which the authority would disclose information;
- if the information will only be provided on condition that it is kept confidential, how important is the information in relation to the authority's functions?
- consider the nature of the person from whom the information is to be obtained and whether that person is also a public authority to whom the FOIA and the Section 45 Code of Practice applies (departments must be particularly cautious about agreeing to keep information confidential where the supplier of the information is also a public authority).

The Section 45 Code of Practice also deals with consultation with third parties where an authority cannot disclose third-party material without risking a breach of confidence. The Code says that:

- where disclosure cannot be made without consent (e.g. because this would in itself be a breach of confidence) the authority should consult the third party with a view to getting its consent to disclose, unless this is not practicable (for example because the third party cannot be located or because the costs of consulting would be disproportionate); and
- if the authority believes the cost of consulting to be disproportionate, then it should consider what is the reasonable course of action in the light of the requirements of the FOIA and the circumstances of the request.

In essence, if the authority has consent to disclose, then it will not be able to rely on s.41. If the authority notifies a third party of its intention to disclose and the third party objects, the authority may still disclose if it chooses, and the third party can only prevent disclosure by injunction (there is no mechanism under the FOIA for the third party to prevent disclosure). If the authority discloses without consulting at all, then the third party will have no redress under the FOIA. Its only remedy would be a claim against the authority for damages, perhaps with an injunction to prevent further disclosure.

The public interest defence to breach of confidence

As noted above, when considering the application of s.41, an authority must assess whether a public interest defence to a claim exists. If so, then the exemption cannot apply. The following principles should be applied when assessing the likelihood and force of a public interest defence:

- where a duty of confidence exists, there is a general public interest in favour of keeping that confidence;
- there is no general public interest in the disclosure of confidential information in breach of a duty of confidence – in other words, for a public interest defence to arise, there must be a specific factor in favour of disclosure;
- there is a public interest in ensuring public scrutiny of the activities of public authorities, so, if disclosure would enhance this scrutiny, this will weigh in favour of disclosure; examples might be:

    - information revealing misconduct or mismanagement of public funds;
    - information demonstrating that a public contract is not providing value for money;
    - information which would correct untrue statements or misleading acts by an authority;

- on the other hand, where the interests of a private person (whether an individual or an organisation) are protected by a duty of confidence, the public interest in scrutiny of public authority information is unlikely to override that duty (although this will be less compelling where a substantial period of time has passed since the information was obtained, as a result of which the harm which would have been caused has depleted);
- the FOIA itself has no influence on the nature of any public interest which attaches to the disclosure of information – so the fact that the FOIA might require disclosure were it not for s.41 is irrelevant;
- public authorities must have regard to the interests of the person to whom the duty of confidence is owed, but the authority's own interests are not relevant; and
- the identity of the person requesting the information and the reason for the request are both irrelevant – the question is not whether disclosure to the applicant would be a breach of confidence, but whether disclosure to

the public would be a breach (a request from a journalist or pressure group must be treated in the same way as a request from a person who is conducting historical research).

There is unlikely to be a public interest defence in cases where:

- the duty of confidence arises from a professional relationship;
- disclosure would affect the continued supply of important information (e.g. information from whistle-blowers); or
- disclosure would involve some risk to public administration or public or personal safety.

In the *Derry City Council* case (case reference EA/2006/0014, 17/18 October 2006), the Tribunal considered whether a concluded agreement between two parties (where one is a public authority) could constitute information provided by one of them to the other as required by s.41. In this case Ryanair sent a fax (marked 'private and confidential') to the Council (owner of Derry City Airport) setting out a number of terms for the operation of scheduled flights from London to Derry. No formal agreement was ever drawn up and so the parties were deemed to have conducted their business on the basis of the terms set out in the fax. Nearly six years after the fax was originally sent, the Belfast Telegraph wrote to the Council and made a FOIA request for information relating to its terms of business with Ryanair. The Council refused to disclose on the basis that the fax contained exempt information pursuant to s.41.

The Tribunal considered whether the information contained in the fax could constitute information provided by one party to the other, as required by the words 'from any other person' in s.41(1)(a). It reasoned that to characterise an agreement as a process by which a public authority obtained information from another party imposed too great a strain on the wording of s.41. On application to the facts, a formal agreement, irrespective of the form it took, could not be said to have been provided by one party to the other and the fax therefore fell outside the scope of the exemption.

In the context of the public interest defence in the context of a claim to confidentiality, the Tribunal was asked by counsel for the respondent to consider the Court of Appeal decision in *London Regional Transport* v. *Mayor of London* [2001] EWCA Civ 1491. The respondent argued that the public interest defence to a breach of confidence claim was applicable not just where there was some specific harm involved, but also where it was necessary to inform public debate. The Tribunal agreed with this submission to a certain extent but stressed that it is important to distinguish between (1) an issue on which the public is justifiably exercised at the time and (2) an issue of public interest which extends only as far as a half-hearted wish to be more fully informed on a matter of relatively low significance.

In addition, the Tribunal confirmed that in relation to the question of whether there is a public interest defence, there is no requirement to show exceptional circumstances and the defence is not confined to specific and confined categories of case (this approach was endorsed in *McTeggart* v. *Information Commissioner and Department of Culture, Arts and Leisure* (case reference EA/2006/0084, 30 April/1 May 2007)).

4.5.8 Other legal prohibitions (s.44)

Disclosures which are prohibited by other legal rules are also exempt from the FOIA. The FOIA does not cut across existing legal regimes which restrict access to information, nor does it provide alternative means of access to information which is expressly protected. At the time of writing, the DCA is engaged in a review of existing legislation to determine whether various statutory restrictions on disclosure of information are consistent with the FOIA. Where the DCA determines that restrictions are not consistent, the relevant statutes will be amended, using powers conferred by FOIA, s.75. Practitioners should therefore ensure they check up-to-date versions of any statutory provision where a restriction on disclosure may have existed in the past.

There are three types of existing legal provisions which will apply in this context:

* disclosures prohibited by statute;
* disclosures which would be incompatible with EU law; or
* disclosures which would be a contempt of court.

The requirement to confirm or deny also does not apply to the extent that doing so is restricted by other legal prohibition.

It will be immediately apparent that the exemption applies to any disclosure which is a criminal offence, or subject to regulatory, public or civil law restriction. It does not, however, extend to disclosures which are unlawful at common law (except by reason of contempt of court), so the FOIA is no basis for avoiding a disclosure which might be a tort or breach of contract. (Breaches of common law are dealt with, where appropriate, by specific exemptions, such as those covering breach of confidence (s.41) and defamation (s.79).)

There will be many bars to disclosure falling within this category, far too numerous to list here. The fundamental principle underlying the exemption is that the FOIA does not cut across other legal restrictions on disclosure. So, where disclosure is prohibited by the Official Secrets Act, the DPA or the Human Rights Act 1998, for example, the FOIA will not compel a public authority to make information available. There are similarly many restrictions relating to tax and social security, and various prohibitions on disclosure of information obtained in the course of investigations by bodies such as the Equal Opportunities Commission, the Commission for Racial Equality and the Parliamentary Commissioner for Administration. Certain information obtained by regulators such as the Financial Services Authority and utilities watchdogs like Ofgem, Ofwat and Ofcom will also be exempt, although the application of the exemption will depend on the circumstances in which the information was obtained by the watchdog and the precise scope of its statutory powers.

NOTES

1   For example, Commons Registration Act 1965, s.1 requires the keeping of registers of commons, and town or village greens. Section 3 provides that:

> any register maintained under this Act shall be open to inspection by the public at all reasonable times.

Although this does not preclude the provision of copies on request, the obligation does not go beyond allowing inspection and would therefore not engage the FOIA, s.21 exemption.

By contrast, the Trade Marks Act 1994, s.67(1), states that:

> after publication of an application for registration of a trade mark, the registrar shall on request provide a person with such information and permit him to inspect such documents relating to the application, or to any registered trade mark resulting from it, as may be specified in the request ... any request must be made in the prescribed manner and be accompanied by the appropriate fee (if any).

This meets all the requirements of FOIA, s.21(2)(b). The fact that payment of a fee may be required is irrelevant.

Similarly, the Births and Deaths Registration Act 1953, s.33(1), provides that:

> any person shall, on payment of a fee ... and on furnishing the prescribed particulars, be entitled to obtain from the Registrar General, a superintendent registrar or a registrar a short certificate of the birth of any person.

2   It allows anyone, on payment of a fee, to inspect and take a copy of a claim form which has been served, a judgment or order given or made in public, and, if the court gives permission, any other document. Where a person has the right to inspect a document without permission, a request can be made to the court staff. Where permission is required, application must be made to a judge.
3   Bloody Sunday Inquiry (Tribunals of Inquiry (Evidence) Act 1921), the Marchioness Inquiry (Merchant Shipping Act 1995) and the Victoria Climbie Inquiry (Children Act 1989, NHS Act 1971, Police Act 1996), to name but three.

CHAPTER 5

The qualified exemptions

Marcus Turle, Field Fisher Waterhouse LLP

5.1 INTRODUCTION

Chapter 4 looked at the absolute exemptions, which protect whole classes of information falling within the various categories set out in the Freedom of Information Act 2000 (FOIA). The qualified exemptions are very different. The qualified exemptions apply:

- only where the public interest permits – that is to say, only if the public interest in withholding information outweighs the public interest in disclosing it; and
- in some cases, only if disclosure would prejudice the interests described (such as, for example, the effective conduct of public affairs), and so for these exemptions the question arises not only of what interests they protect, but also the question of what prejudice means.

As noted, the public interest test applies to all the qualified exemptions. The prejudice test applies only to some. The prejudice-based exemptions relate to:

- national security (s.24);
- defence (s.26);
- international relations (s.27(1));
- relations within the UK (s.28);
- the economy (s.29);
- law enforcement (s.31);
- audit functions (s.33);
- the effective conduct of public affairs (s.36);
- health and safety (s.38); and
- commercial interests (s.43(2)).

The remaining qualified exemptions – for which only the public interest is relevant – relate to:

- information intended for future publication (s.22);
- international relations (s.27(2), which relates to information obtained from another state);

- investigations and proceedings conducted by public authorities (s.30);
- formulation of government policy (s.35);
- communications with Her Majesty, etc. (s.37);
- environmental information (s.39);
- personal information (s.40);
- legal professional privilege (s.42); and
- commercial interests (s.43(1), which applies only to trade secrets).

The exemptions to which the prejudice test does not apply are listed at **5.3**. The exemptions to which it does are listed at **5.4**.

Readers wishing to keep fully up to date with developments on the application of the exemptions are referred to the practical journal, *Freedom of Information* (**www.foij.com**).

5.2 APPLYING THE PUBLIC INTEREST TEST

There is no definition in the FOIA of 'public interest'. Indeed, the legislation says nothing at all on the subject, beyond the fact that in the case of two-thirds of the Act's exemptions, the public interest is a fundamental consideration. Section 2 says that if a public authority receives a request for information which may be subject to a qualified exemption, then the authority must apply the public interest test in considering whether or not to disclose that information. To be precise, the test is whether:

> in all the circumstances of the case, the public interest in maintaining the exemption outweighs the public interest in disclosing the information.

Given that 16 of the 23 FOIA exemptions are qualified, a good grasp of what we mean when we talk about the public interest is essential for the correct handling of FOIA requests.

There are other areas of English law to which public interest considerations apply, and all of them pre-date the FOIA. There is the public interest defence to claims for breach of confidence and for infringement of copyright. The Public Interest Disclosure Act 1998 protects whistle-blowers in the workplace on public interest grounds, intended to promote the detection and exposure of misconduct and malpractice likely to endanger employees. Even in these contexts, however, there is nothing which usefully serves as a working definition. As noted by Lord Hailsham, 'the categories of public interest are not closed' (*D* v. *National Society for the Prevention of Cruelty to Children* [1978] AC 171 at 230).

The lack of a definition emphatically does not make the law unclear, however. Nor is it the case that the absence of a definition makes assessing the public interest inherently difficult. On the contrary, the lacuna simply reflects the principle that the public interest in any given case will depend on the circumstances prevailing at the time. As the former Department for Constitutional Affairs (DCA) Guidance states, the public interest is 'an inherently dynamic concept' which will 'develop by decisions made within government and by the Information Commissioner and the Courts' (see DCA, 'Introduction to exemptions', Chapter 07: What is the public interest test? available online at **www.foi.gov.uk/guidance/exintro/chap07.htm**).

Already, a significant canon of material has developed in the form of Information Commissioner Decisions and, more importantly, judgments of the Information Tribunal. There is also official guidance from the Information Commissioner and from the Ministry of Justice (MoJ) (formerly the DCA).

5.2.1 The concept of the public interest

One very helpful judicial summary of the public interest comes from an Australian case, *Commonwealth of Australia* v. *John Fairfax Ltd* (1981) 32 ALR 485 (endorsed by the House of Lords in the *Spycatcher* case: *AG* v. *Guardian Newspapers (No.2)* [1990] AC 109) in which the court said:

> It is unacceptable in our democratic society that there should be a restraint on the publication of information relating to government when the only vice of that information is that it enables the public to discuss, review and criticise government action. Accordingly, the court will determine the Government's claim to confidentiality by reference to the public interest. Unless disclosure is likely to injure the public interest, it will not be protected. The court will not prevent the publication of information which merely throws light on the past workings of the government, even if it be not public property, so long as it does not prejudice the community in other respects. Then disclosure will itself serve the public interest in keeping the community informed and in promoting discussion of public affairs. If, however, it appears that disclosure will be inimical to the public interest because national security, relations with foreign countries or the ordinary business of government will be prejudiced, disclosure will be restrained.

In the early days of its passage through Parliament, the Freedom of Information Bill gave public authorities discretion to consider whether information should be disclosed on public interest grounds. This changed at the report stage, when consideration of the public interest was made a duty. Parliament recognised that for freedom of information to work there would have to be a fundamental shift from the historic Westminster culture of need-to-know to a new 'open' era of right-to-know. As a result, the legislation was redrafted to reflect the principle that 'information must be disclosed except where there is an overriding public interest in keeping specific information confidential'.[1]

5.2.2 The balancing exercise

The public interest test described in s.2 of the FOIA stipulates that a qualified exemption can only apply where the public interest in maintaining an exemption outweighs the public interest in disclosing information. The wording of s.2 has several significant implications. First, it requires public authorities to consider the public interest both for and against disclosure (or, more precisely, the public interest 'in maintaining the exemption' versus the public interest in disclosure). Only where the scales favour exemption can the duty to disclose be disapplied. Secondly, it sets the default at 'disclose'. That is to say, it imposes a general presumption in favour of disclosure unless and until this is outweighed by factors to the contrary. If the arguments are evenly balanced then the outcome must be to disclose. This presumption in favour of disclosure means that the burden of proof in justifying an exemption rests with the public authority. To do so, it must effectively be able to demonstrate two things: that there is a pressing need for non-disclosure, and that to override the right of access is a necessary and proportionate way of meeting that need.

The balancing exercise must therefore start from this general standpoint of competing interests determining an outcome. It does not, however, mean simply considering any public interest arguments which might be available. As the Information Tribunal has stated (*Bellamy* v. *The Information Commissioner*, case reference EA/2005/0023, 27 April 2006):

> not all public interest considerations which might otherwise appear to be relevant to the subject matter of the disclosure should be taken into account. What has to be concentrated upon is the particular public interest necessarily inherent in the exemption or exemptions relied upon.

The particular circumstances of each case are therefore absolutely vital in balancing public interest arguments. To underline this, the Information Tribunal has stated that public authorities must not maintain blanket policies for refusing information of a certain type:

> the public authority is not permitted to maintain a blanket refusal to disclose all information of a particular type or nature. The question to be asked is not: is the balance of public interest in favour of maintaining the exemption in relation to the type of information? The question to be asked is: is the balance of public interest in favour of maintaining the exemption in relation to this information, and in the circumstances of *this* case? The public authority may well have a general policy that the public interest is likely to be in favour of maintaining the exemption in respect of a specific type of information. However such a policy must not be inflexibly applied and the authority must always be willing to consider whether the circumstances of the case justify a departure from the policy.
> (*Hogan and Oxford City Council* v. *The Information Commissioner*, case references EA/2005/0026 and EA/2005/0030, 17 October 2006 (emphasis added))

From a purely operational perspective, given the nature of the public interest test and the fact that the burden of proof for justifying its application lies with the authority, whenever a decision maker comes to a view about where the balance lies, having assessed the relevant competing interests in the particular circumstances, he or she should clearly document:

- all the circumstances that have been considered;
- the specific public interests in favour of withholding information in the particular case, and the weight given to each;
- the specific public interests in favour of disclosure of information in the particular case, and the weight given to each;
- the considerations given to timescales; and
- the considerations given to partial disclosure (e.g. by redacting information which qualifies for exemption but disclosing everything else).

Aside from helping authorities to make assessments in the future, this will also provide the basis for a defence to any complaint or appeal.

5.2.3 Practical Guidance from the Information Commissioner

In his 'Freedom of Information Awareness Guidance No.3' the Information Commissioner has put forward some examples of factors which might apply in favour of disclosure when considering the public interest, and factors which are irrelevant.

Factors in favour of disclosure

1. *Furthering the understanding of issues of the day, and facilitating participation in public debate of those issues.*
2. *Promoting accountability for and transparency of decisions taken by public authorities.* This is because it will improve the quality of decisions and administration if authorities and officials have to provide reasoned explanations for their actions.
3. *Promoting accountability for and transparency of public expenditure.* For example, where public services are outsourced to the private sector there is a public interest in genuine competition and value for money – disclosure of information about gifts and expenses will also reassure the public of the probity of elected officials.
4. *Enabling individuals and companies to understand decisions made by public authorities affecting them, and where appropriate helping them to challenge those decisions.*
5. *Bringing to light information affecting public health and safety.* For example, the prompt disclosure of information by scientific and other experts may prevent accidents or outbreaks of disease and may also increase public confidence in official scientific advice.

Factors which are irrelevant

1. *A risk of information being misunderstood, either because it is technical or incomplete.* The Queensland Information Commissioner memorably

rejected the use of this factor on the ground that it is 'based on rather elitist and paternalistic assumptions that government officials and external review authorities can judge what information should be withheld from the public for fear of confusing it, and can judge what is necessary or unnecessary in democratic society': *Re Eccleston and Department of Family Services and Aboriginal and Islander Affairs* (1993) 1 QAR 60.

2. *A risk of embarrassment or loss of confidence.*
3. *The 'class' or 'type' of information is not of itself an argument against disclosure.* Although 'high level correspondence' may be more likely to have characteristics which make its disclosure contrary to the public interest.
4. *Public curiosity.* 'The public interest' is not the same as 'something which may be of interest to the public'.

In addition to these factors, Parliament has made it clear that the motives of the person making the request for information will not be relevant in application of the public interest test (Hansard, HL (series 5) vol 617, col 921 (17 October 2000), Lord Falconer):

> As far as public interest between disclosure on the one hand and the maintenance of exemption on the other is concerned, it has to be looked at objectively. One looks at the impact of disclosure, that is, making it public. What is the impact of the exemption being maintained? That should be looked at objectively rather than in terms of whatever the motive may be of the person applying. That does not mean that the motive of the person applying may not coincide with factors that could be relevant to what damage may be done and what assistance could be served by making the matter public. But individual motives will not be relevant to that.

5.2.4 Decisions of the Information Commissioner, and Information Tribunal judgments

Both the Information Commissioner and the Information Tribunal have considered the public interest when adjudicating on appeals brought before them, and there is now a considerable body of guidance to be obtained from an analysis of these cases. Those of most relevance are considered below in the context of the exemptions to which they relate.

5.3 CATEGORIES TO WHICH THE PUBLIC INTEREST TEST (BUT NOT THE PREJUDICE TEST) APPLIES

Information falling within these categories will be exempt only if the public interest in withholding information outweighs the public interest in disclosing it.

5.3.1 Information intended for future publication (s.22)

Most public authorities are now proactive about releasing information independently of their FOIA obligations. The s.22 exemption is intended to facilitate this process by ensuring that individual requests do not dictate publication timetables or force publication prematurely (unless, of course, the public interest requires this). In effect, the exemption allows authorities to manage proactive publication according to the particular exigencies of preparation, administration and other circumstances. So, for example, where an authority has commissioned a report for which a publication date has been set, s.22 may allow it to withhold the content of the report until the 'official' publication date, provided it is reasonable to do so.

To qualify for the exemption, information must meet three conditions:

- it must be held by the authority with a view to its publication by the authority or by someone else at some future date (although the precise date need not have been determined);
- the intention to publish must exist at the time the FOIA request is made; and
- it must be reasonable in all the circumstances for the authority to withhold the information until the future date of planned release.

'Publication' means any information which is addressed to the public at large or any section of it. For most public authorities this will therefore include the scheduled publication of announcements, press releases, speeches, interviews and articles, email bulletins, information available online and information retrievable electronically, including books, journals, periodicals and newspapers. For central government it will also include consultation papers, White Papers and Green Papers, reports and responses to select committee reports. Publication of research and statistics may also be covered.

What does 'with a view to publication' mean?

Section 22 can apply whether or not the actual date of publication has been determined, and whether or not publication will be by the authority itself or by someone else. The requirement that information must *already* have been held with a view to publication at the time the request is made means only that an authority cannot avoid disclosing something (for example, because it might be embarrassing) by deciding *when it receives a request* that the information will be published at some future date.

Information which an authority intends to pass on to another organisation for publication by it would normally also engage the exemption, as, perhaps, would information held by an authority which it has no intention of publishing itself, but which it knows will be published by someone else. Naturally, it is not enough in these circumstances that a decision whether or not to publish is pending.

A view to publication must be current and continuing, and in this sense will cover draft documents whilst a document is the current draft. Once a draft has been superseded, however, information which is removed from the subsequent draft will not normally be s.22 exempt unless there remains a justifiable ground on which it can still be said to be held with a view to publication (although, of course, other exemptions may apply instead).

Applying the public interest test

In relation to s.22, disclosure is planned at some future date anyway, therefore the public interest in this context turns not on whether to disclose, but on *when* – that is, on whether it is reasonable to withhold disclosure until the intended future date.

The public interest in allowing public authorities to release information in a manner and form, and at a time, of their own choosing is important. In the general run of public affairs, publication is planned and managed according to prevailing circumstances and authorities should rightfully be able to make their own arrangements. Considerations relevant to assessing the public interest might therefore include:

- the nature of the proposed publication timetable itself (the more distant, contingent or indeterminate the prospective publication date, the less heavily it might weigh in favour of exemption and the less reasonable delay might be);
- possible detrimental effects of early/delayed publication – for example, if disclosure might damage a third party's private interests or give rise unnecessarily to public concern, then this might favour withholding;
- whether simultaneous disclosure is a consideration in itself – advanced disclosure to a freedom of information applicant may be unfair to others;
- pre-publication procedures – whether immediate disclosure would undermine consultation with, or pre-publication disclosure to, a particular person (it is normally good practice, for example, to disclose information about a complaint to the complainant or the subject of the complaint before publication);
- publication procedures – for example, the reports of public inquiries are often published under the protection of the Parliamentary Papers Act to avoid defamation or other civil action;
- previous undertakings – for example, where ministers have promised to inform Parliament first about certain information, or where family members should be informed first about matters relating to a relative.

In the *Department of Education for Northern Ireland* decision (reference FS50123357), the Information Commissioner examined a request for disclosure of financial information relating to the South Eastern Education and Library Board (SEELB). The case focused on a report commissioned from KPMG following a statutory inquiry in 2004 and financial difficulties within SEELB resulting from overspending of £6 million in 2003/4 and 2004/5. The KPMG report was due for publication in October 2006, six months after the

FOIA request had been made, and the Department cited s.22, arguing that premature disclosure of the report would not be in the public interest because it would lead to considerable adverse press which would be highly damaging to the conduct of public affairs and the delivery of public services. The Commissioner noted that SEELB's financial difficulties had attracted considerable media coverage and that there is a public interest in transparency about issues of financial management and accountability in public authorities. At the same time, he acknowledged that what interests the public is not necessarily the same as what is in the public interest. In deciding that the public interest in disclosure was not outweighed by the public interest in maintaining the exemption, the Commissioner commented that the potential impact of media interest in an issue is not in itself a valid reason to withhold information which would inform the public about a matter of such importance as the financial health of an education board.

5.3.2   International relations[2]

Section 27 is a prejudice-based exemption except insofar as it relates to confidential information which is obtained from a foreign state or an international organisation or international court. Information from these bodies is exempt irrespective of any question of prejudice (but still subject to the public interest test).

An 'international court' is one established by a resolution of an international organisation of which the UK is a member, or by an international agreement to which the UK is a party. The International Court of Justice, European Court of Justice, International Criminal Court and European Court of Human Rights all qualify as international courts for FOIA purposes.

An 'international organisation' is one whose members include two or more states. For these purposes, a 'State' includes the government of any state, and any organ of government, such as a state's legislature and executive, and also territories outside the UK including Crown dependencies like Jersey and Guernsey, British Overseas Territories like Gibraltar, and territorial entities not necessarily recognised otherwise as states.

The UK itself need not be a member state for an organisation to qualify as an international organisation, so, as well as the United Nations and European Union, OPEC is covered, as is the Organisation of American States. The definition also extends to any organ of such an organisation, which would include, for example, the European Commission and European Parliament.

'Confidential information' is defined in s.27(3) as:

> information obtained ... at any time while the terms on which it was obtained require it to be held in confidence or while the circumstances in which it was obtained make it reasonable for the state, organisation or court to expect that it will be so held.

This allows for the possibility that a duty of confidence may arise by reasonable expectation or by express agreement. It is therefore wider than the s.41 exemption for confidential information generally, which reflects the common law position rather than the conventionally wider restrictions which parties agree by written contract. Also in contrast with s.41, s.27 is not conditional on a breach being actionable.

Applying the public interest test

Some examples of factors to consider when assessing the public interest as it relates to confidential information falling within s.27 are whether:

- disclosure would be contrary to international law (e.g. a breach of a treaty obligation);
- disclosure would undermine the UK's reputation for honouring its international commitments and obligations;
- disclosure is likely to undermine the willingness of the state, international organisation or court that supplied the information to supply other confidential information in future (or would be likely to have such an effect on the willingness of states, international organisations or courts in general);
- disclosure is likely to provoke a negative reaction from the state, international organisation or court that supplied the information, which would damage the UK's relations with them and/or its ability to protect and promote UK interests;
- disclosure is likely to result in another state, international organisation or court disclosing – contrary to the UK's interests – confidential information supplied to the UK; or
- the state, international organisation or court that supplied the confidential information has objected to its disclosure, and whether good relations with it are likely to suffer if the objection were ignored.

Authorities should also consider consulting the Foreign and Commonwealth Office when considering disclosing information which may affect the UK's international relations.

5.3.3 Investigations and proceedings (s.30)

In essence, s.30 serves to ensure that the FOIA cannot be used to circumvent the rules of disclosure governing criminal investigations and proceedings. There are two very separate exemptions within s.30 and each applies in distinct circumstances. The first, s.30(1), applies to information which has been held at any time for the relevant purposes – even if those purposes have since ceased to obtain. The second, s.30(2), focuses on the reasons for the acquisition of the information and applies only if it was obtained or recorded for purposes which are specified in s.30(3).

Section 30(1)

The s.30(1) exemption itself has three separate parts. The first (s.30(1)(a)) relates to information held relating to particular criminal investigations or proceedings[3] and applies to information which an authority has held at any time for an investigation which it has a duty to conduct in order to ascertain:

- whether a person should be charged with an offence; or
- whether a person charged with an offence is guilty of it.

The s.30(1)(a) exemption is primarily intended to cover information obtained by the police, National Criminal Intelligence Service or the Serious Fraud Office during the course of an investigation, and also information and evidence which leads to the bringing of charges, but it could also apply to criminal investigations conducted by organisations like:

- HM Revenue and Customs;
- the Department of Trade and Industry;
- the Department for Environment, Food and Rural Affairs;
- the Food Standards Agency;
- the Environment Agency;
- the Health and Safety Executive;
- the Financial Services Authority; and
- the Office of Fair Trading.

The s.30(1)(b) exemption applies to investigations which may lead to criminal proceedings which the authority has the power (but not necessarily the duty) to conduct. It is therefore relevant primarily to authorities with regulatory or investigatory functions who may conduct investigations with a view to deciding whether a person should be charged with a criminal offence.

Following on from s.30(1)(b), s.30(1)(c) applies to actual criminal proceedings which the authority has the power to conduct itself. The exemption will therefore apply to authorities such as the Crown Prosecution Service and any other public authority with prosecution functions.

Section 30(1) will not make exempt information which is unrelated to particular investigations or proceedings – such as statistics on conviction rates – but because it is not limited by time it will continue to apply to relevant information even after investigations and proceedings are finished (although, of course, the conclusion of proceedings may affect the application of the public interest test).

Section 30(2)

The s.30(2) exemption is not restricted to particular investigations or proceedings but is nevertheless quite narrow, being limited by two quite specific requirements.

First, it can only apply if the information in question was obtained or recorded for the purposes of the authority's functions in relation to one of four categories listed in s.30(2)(a)(i)–(iv). Secondly, the information must have come from confidential sources.

The authority's functions

Section 30(2) can only apply where information was acquired for the purposes of the authority's functions relating to:

(i)   investigations of the type referred to in s.30(1)(a); or
(ii) criminal proceedings which the authority has power to conduct; or
(iii) investigations conducted under the authority's statutory or prerogative powers[4] for any of the specified purposes (see below); or
(iv) civil proceedings[5] brought by an authority, or on its behalf.

In relation to part (iii), the specified purposes are:

(a)   for ascertaining whether any person has failed to comply with the law;
(b)   for ascertaining whether any person is responsible for any conduct which is improper;
(c)   for ascertaining whether circumstances exist or may arise which would justify regulatory action in pursuance of any enactment;
(d)   for ascertaining a person's fitness or competence in relation to the management of bodies corporate or in relation to any profession or other activity which he is, or seeks to become, authorised to carry on;
(e)   for ascertaining the cause of an accident;
(f)   for protecting charities against misconduct or mismanagement (whether by trustees or other persons) in their administration;
(g)   for protecting the property of charities from loss or misapplication;
(h)   for recovering the property of charities;
(i)   for securing the health, safety and welfare of persons at work; and
(j)   for protecting persons other than persons at work against risk to health or safety arising out of or in connection with the actions of persons at work (FOIA, s.31(3)).

One effect of the wording of s.30(2) appears to be that, if an authority sets up an inquiry which may reveal illegality, but which the authority does not have express statutory or prerogative power to conduct, then the information obtained or recorded for that inquiry will not be exempt, even if obtained from confidential sources.

Confidential sources

Confidential sources will usually be informants or whistle-blowers whose identity an authority would want to protect. It will not normally extend, however, to personnel working covertly to gather information, nor to information gathered using covert technology.

To engage s.30(2), the information itself need not be confidential, it is the relationship with the source which must be confidential. In practice, the personal information and confidential information exemptions may also apply to information obtained from confidential sources in which case ss.40 and 41 should be considered before looking at s.30(2). Examples of information likely to fall outside the ss.40 and 41 exemptions but within s.30(2) are:

- a diary with recorded appointments to meet an unnamed informer;
- details of surveillance and investigative techniques associated with the management of external confidential sources; and
- an indication that certain information has been obtained from an unnamed confidential source.

In *Alcock* v. *Information Commissioner and Chief Constable of Staffordshire Police* (case reference EA/2006/0022, 12 December 2006), the Tribunal confirmed that s.30(2) is a class-based exemption and therefore there is no need for prejudice to be shown for it to be engaged. In assessing the public interest in favour of disclosure it is relevant that the applicant already knows a substantial amount of the information sought.

Applying the public interest test

At the heart of s.30 lies the importance to law enforcement of public confidence in the investigations and proceedings to which the exemption refers. Public confidence can obviously be fostered by transparency, but it also requires the processes themselves to deliver justice effectively. As the White Paper on Open Government (Cm 2290, 1993) stated:

> There should be no commitment to disclose information which would help potential lawbreakers and criminals, put life, safety or the environment in danger ... Investigation of suspected crime must normally be kept secret from the suspect and others. Witness statements, names and addresses of witnesses and reports from the police and others to prosecutors could, if disclosed other than as required by the courts, jeopardise law enforcement or the prevention or prosecution of crime, or be extremely unfair to a temporary suspect against whom (in the event) no real evidence existed. It is in the interests of both the individuals concerned and the integrity of the prosecution process that material relating to both live and completed prosecutions and to prosecutions which do not go ahead can be kept confidential.

In balancing public interest considerations, public authorities will need to consider the potential effects of a disclosure and the nature and seriousness of the matter being pursued.

The ability of the police, HM Revenue and Customs and other public authorities to obtain information in pursuance of their investigative processes is critical to the prevention and detection of crime and to the integrity and effectiveness of the criminal justice system. Certain disclosures, particularly in relation to confidential sources, could have extremely serious consequences, lead to serious risk of injury or loss of life and be damaging to the willingness of other individuals to supply information.

When considering the balance of the public interest, a weighty consideration will be the extent to which disclosing or withholding information would:

- promote or diminish the chances of a successful prosecution, bringing future charges or making arrests;
- promote or diminish the chances of a fair trial;
- be fair to those who have not been prosecuted, in cases where a decision has been taken not to proceed;
- assist or hamper the gathering of intelligence information from confidential sources such as informants, whistle-blowers or calls to Crimestoppers;
- further the interests of justice through the participation of victims, witnesses, informants, suspects or offenders in investigations and proceedings – and either protect or endanger them as they do so;
- assist or impede other ongoing or future proceedings;
- prevent or facilitate the commission of crime.

In *Patrick Toms* v. *Information Commissioner* (case reference EA/2005/0027, 8 June 2006), the Information Tribunal considered the application of the public interest test in the context of s.30(1). It noted that the question of how competing public interests should be balanced does not constitute an exercise of discretion. The relevant question is whether the FOIA has been properly applied to the facts as found by the Information Commissioner. This is a mixed question of fact and law. In addition, the Tribunal noted that in assessing the balance of the public interest, 'regard should be had, inter alia, to such matters as the stage or stages reached in any particular investigation or criminal proceedings, whether and to what extent the information has already been released into the public domain and the significance or sensitivity of the information requested'.

5.3.4 Formulation of government policy (s.35)

The application of s.35 turns on the content of the information in question, and in particular whether it relates to the formulation or development of government policy.

The purpose of the exemption is to protect the internal deliberative process as it relates to policy making – in other words, to allow the government a 'safe space to protect information in the early stages of formulation' (*Office of Government Commerce* v. *Information Commissioner* (case reference EA/2006/0068 and 0080, 2 May 2007) where the threat of public exposure might otherwise compromise candid and robust discussions about policy. The exemption is intended to ensure

127

that the FOIA does not deter policy makers from full and proper deliberation, where, for example, the prospect of disclosure might discourage the exploration of extreme options, the keeping of detailed records and the taking of hard choices, or where disclosure might prejudice good working relationships, the neutrality of civil servants and ultimately the quality of government.

However, the Information Commissioner's view is that the exemption can only apply where there is clear, specific and credible evidence that the formulation or development of government policy would be materially undermined by the threat of disclosure under the FOIA.

In *Secretary of State for Work and Pensions (DWP)* v. *Information Commissioner* (case reference EA/2006/0040, 5 March 2007), the Information Tribunal examined s.35 and found that there should not be an automatic assumption that disclosure of the information will be harmful. Indeed, the Tribunal insisted that each case be considered in the light of its unique circumstances.

Government policy

'Policy' is not defined. According to the Information Commissioner, it will usually cover the development of options and priorities for Ministers who determine which options should be translated into political action, and when.

The Modernising Government White Paper refers to policy as the process by which governments translate their political vision into programmes and actions, to deliver outcomes or desired changes in the real world.

Policy can be sourced and generated in various ways. For example, it may come from Ministers' ideas and suggestions, manifesto commitments, significant incidents (such as a major outbreak of foot and mouth disease), EU policies or public concern expressed through letters, petitions and the like. Proposals and evidence for policies may come from external legal advisers, stakeholder consultation, or external researchers, as well as civil servants.

Importantly, policy is unlikely to include purely operational or administrative matters, or decisions about individuals. For instance, decisions about applications for licences or grants are not likely to involve the formulation of policy, but rather its application. Similarly, in most cases, information about an individual's freedom of information application will not fall into the category of information relating to the formulation or development of policy.

Government policy is seen as distinct from departmental or other types of policy. This implies policy which has had Cabinet input or represents the collective view of Ministers or which applies across government. It also implies some political process. Departmental policy will frequently be derived from and be identical to government policy, but where departmental policy applies only to the internal workings of the department it would not be caught (for example, departmental policy about working hours or estate management).

'Formulation' and 'development' of policy

These terms do not have precise meanings.

'Formulation' suggests the output from the early stages of the policy process, where options are generated and sorted, risks are identified, consultation occurs and recommendations and submissions are put to a Minister.

'Development' is sometimes used interchangeably with formulation, but also goes beyond it. It may refer to the processes involved in improving on or altering existing policy, for example through piloting, monitoring, reviewing, analysing or recording the effects of existing policy. At the very least, formulation and development suggests something dynamic – in the sense that something must be happening to the policy. The exemption cannot apply to a finished product, or a policy which has been agreed, is in operation or has already been implemented.

In *Secretary of State for Work and Pensions (DWP)* v. *Information Commissioner* (case reference EA/2006/0040, 5 March 2007) the Information Tribunal recognised that 'formulation' cannot and should not always be envisaged as a 'continuing process of evolution'. Where appropriate, the formulation process can be considered separately at each stage rather than as a continuum. The formulation in question in this appeal related to the national identity cards scheme and the Tribunal considered that it would be beneficial to treat the formulation as a two-stage process rather than an ongoing one. The first stage was made at a macro level: the decision to introduce a scheme. The second stage was planned on a micro level and related to the detailed implementation of the scheme at departmental level and secondary legislation. It therefore followed that information compiled for the purpose of formulating in the first 'macro' stage was not necessarily exempt simply because the micro stage was still ongoing at the time of the request.

The Tribunal re-affirmed this approach in *Office of Government Commerce (OGC)* v. *Information Commissioner* (EA/2006/0068 and 0080, 2 May 2007). This appeal also related to documentation generated in the course of the government's identity cards project. In this instance, the material requested was two Gateway Review reports. The Gateway process was introduced by the OGC in 2000 as the centrepiece of its initiative to promote best value for money in government procurements. Under the Gateway process a government programme or project should be examined at critical stages in its life cycle with the aim of ensuring that it can progress successfully from stage to stage.

In one of its longest reports to date, the Tribunal examined the definition of 'formulation'. Whilst accepting that the s.35 exemption was engaged, the Tribunal ultimately ordered disclosure. Its reasoning was that the requests were made 18 months after the reports had been produced, by which time the decision had already been taken to proceed with the introduction of ID cards and a Bill had been presented to Parliament for public debate. In other words, the 'formulation' value of the information was no longer current and could not compete with the considerable public interest in disclosing information about a controversial government project.

Factors to consider when applying the exemption

The following questions may be relevant to the application of the exemption:

- Would release of the information in this particular case make civil servants less likely to provide full and frank advice or opinions on policy proposals? (Would it, for example, prejudice working relationships by exposing dissenting views?)
- Would the prospect of future release inhibit consideration and debate of the full range of policy options (for example, if on reflection some of them seem extreme)?
- Would the prospect of release lead to civil servants defending everything that is or has been raised during deliberation (in anticipation, for example, of certain things later being discounted)?
- Would the possibility of future release deter the giving of advice which is ill-considered, vague, poorly prepared or written in unnecessarily brusque or defamatory language? Would the prospect of release in fact enhance the quality of future advice? (If so, then this would weigh in favour of release.)
- Is the main reason for applying the exemption to spare a civil servant or Minister embarrassment? (If so, then the exemption is not appropriate.)

Applying the public interest test

Arguments against disclosure might include:

- the need to maintain the quality of government policy making by facilitating free and frank exchanges between civil servants and the thorough consideration of all policy options, however extreme, without inducing the need to defend them;
- the need to maintain the quality of records, working relationships and a neutral civil service;
- the fact that the particular circumstances of the case indicate that public participation in the policy is inappropriate.

Arguments in favour of disclosure might include that:

- public participation in the policy is appropriate (in the sense of permitting people to contribute to policy prior to a final decision). Note:
  - participation cannot be meaningful without access to relevant recorded information about how policy decisions are reached, what

options are being considered and why some are excluded and others preferred;

- without public participation in key policy decisions, certain individuals or groups will enjoy undue influence in the policy-making process;
- a key driver for freedom of information is to provide access to information which will facilitate informed participation in the development of government proposals or decisions which are of concern to them;
- information disclosed prior to a decision being taken will facilitate more informed public debate;

- accountability for government decisions (i.e. the need for government to explain why something has happened, or to demonstrate sufficient rigour in taking account of all relevant considerations, including addressing legitimate objections, or that it is keeping its word and delivering what it has promised). Note:

  - disclosure of information is desirable where it may expose wrongdoing, the fact that wrongdoing has been dealt with or dispels suspicions of wrongdoing;
  - access to information under the FOIA may facilitate objective assessment, particularly where information obtained direct from the civil service (as opposed to government press offices) has not been spun;
  - there will usually be a strong public interest in favour of disclosure where a policy decision is going to lead to large scale public expenditure;
  - similarly, there will usually be a strong public interest in favour of disclosure where a policy decision involves departure from routine procedures or standard practice. (This was certainly the case with material relating to the identity cards scheme in the DWP case (see above), in which the public interest in disculsure outweighed the arguments for exemption. However, it is worth noting that in this case, the Tribunal ordered that the information be provided in redacted form in order to protect the identity of junior civil servants involved in the policy process.)

A good example of the application of the public interest test can be found in *Department for Education and Skills (DfES)* and *Information Commissioner* v. *Evening Standard* (case reference EA/2006/0006, 19 January 2007). A journalist asked the DfES to disclose the minutes of all senior management meetings at the department from June 2002 to June 2003 in relation to the setting of school budgets. The DfES initially refused the request, citing s.35(1)(a). The journalist's complaint to the Information Commissioner focused on the DfES's alleged failure to distinguish policy making (exempt under s.35) from operational decisions (not exempt under s.35). He also emphasised the considerable public interest in the information.

When weighing the arguments for and against disclosure, the Tribunal examined the following concerns in relation to the disclosure of minutes:

- loss of frankness and candour;
- danger of government by cabal;
- impact on record keeping; and
- potential damage to relations between civil servants and Ministers and to the accountability and role of civil servants in policy formulation.

The DfES's position, enunciated by several very senior officials (including Lord Turnbull, former Cabinet Secretary and head of the civil service, and Mr Paul Britton, Director General of the Domestic Policy Group in the Cabinet Office) hinged on 'grave adverse affects' which according to Mr Britton 'would inexorably result from the disclosure requested'. First, it was argued that the threat of future disclosure would discourage candour and boldness in the giving of advice, the consideration of options and the exchange of views. Secondly, Lord Turnbull referred to a series of 'secondary signals' which disclosure would send out. The loss of confidentiality in policy discussion, particularly in relation to the minutes of senior committees in close proximity to ministers, could threaten the role and integrity of the whole of the civil service. Such a relationship was an important constitutional safeguard which had served all governments well over the years. Public identification of a particular official with specific policy advice could also undermine the political neutrality of the civil service and exacerbate the suspicion sometimes exhibited by Ministers of an incoming administration towards an official apparently identified with a policy no longer in favour. The corollary to a politicised civil service was 'sofa government' or government by cabal, which is to say government influenced by special political advisers working independently of senior civil servants and therefore free of public scrutiny. There was also a concern that risk of disclosure would discourage the proper keeping of minutes.

The Tribunal was not convinced by these arguments and felt that the chilling effect outlined by the DfES was not sufficiently compelling to tip the public interest in favour of maintaining the exemption. On the risk to confidentiality it indicated that 'confidentiality is not always, we think, treated by ministers as sacrosanct'. On government by cabal, its view was that 'the use of political advisors rather than career civil servants goes back at least to Churchill and represents a growing trend, lamented by oppositions of whichever political complexion. Whether it is likely to accelerate if there is a greater risk of disclosure of the dealings of civil servants with each other and with ministers, we do not feel confident to predict. It will certainly not be curbed by any decision of ours'. On the likely negative effect on record keeping, it stated simply that 'Good practice should prevail over any traditional sensitivity as we move into an era of greater transparency'.

The Tribunal's analysis of the public interest provides useful guidance for decision makers. Broadly, the salient points are as follows:

- while the seniority of officials participating in recorded discussions may in some cases increase the sensitivity of the matters minuted, no information within s.35(1) is exempt simply on account of its status, its classification or of the seniority of those whose actions are recorded;
- the timing of the request is fundamental – disclosure of discussion of policy options while the policy is still in the process of formulation is highly unlikely to be in the public interest, unless for example it would expose wrongdoing within government; at the same time, factors of great relevance at the time of the recorded discussions or advice may carry little, if any, weight two years later – in this case a policy announcement had been made in July 2003 and implemented in July 2004; the request was made in January 2005; it was therefore clear that 'the time and space needed had been available and put to good effect';
- the words 'in all the circumstances of the case' indicate that, where appropriate, weighing the public interest may involve a consideration of any wider impact on the conduct of government (in this case, the 'secondary signals' enumerated by Lord Turnbull);
- that said, in judging the likely consequences of disclosure on officials' future conduct, we are entitled to expect of them 'the courage and independence' of highly educated and politically sophisticated public servants who understand the importance of their impartial role as counsellors to Ministers of conflicting convictions;
- there may be good reason in some cases for withholding the names of more junior civil servants who would never expect their roles to be exposed to the public gaze;
- we are entitled to expect of our politicians when they assume power in a department a substantial measure of political sophistication and fair-mindedness – to remove or reject a senior official because he or she is identified with a policy which has lost favour would betray a serious misunderstanding of the way the executive should work and would be unjust – it must be assumed that Ministers will behave reasonably and fairly towards officials who promoted policies which the new incumbent rejects; and
- the central question in every case is the content of the particular information in question – every decision must be specific to the particular facts and circumstances under consideration.

Accordingly, the Tribunal held that there was an overwhelming general public interest in transparent policy making on a funding matter of enormous public concern and so it ordered the information to be disclosed.

5.3.5 Communications with Her Majesty, etc. (s.37)

Section 37 relates to royal communications and honours. Information is exempt if it relates to:

133

- communications with Her Majesty, with other members of the Royal Family or with the Royal Household;[6] or
- the conferring by the Crown of any honour or dignity.

The duty to confirm or deny does not arise in relation to information which is exempt under s.37.

5.3.6 Environmental information (s.39)

Section 39 exempts information which an authority is obliged to make available in accordance with the Environmental Information Regulations 2004 (EIR), or would be obliged to make available but for an exemption in those Regulations.

The duty to confirm or deny does not apply to information which is exempt under s.39.

In essence, information which falls within the EIR must be processed in accordance with the EIR. The public interest test is applied by the EIR in the same way as it applies under the FOIA.

The EIR are dealt with in full in **Chapter 9**.

5.3.7 Personal information (s.40)

The s.40 exemption is for the most part an absolute exemption but there are limited circumstances in which it is only qualified. See **Chapter 8** for a full analysis of the interaction between the FOIA and the DPA.

5.3.8 Legal professional privilege (s.42)

Information which attracts legal privilege is FOIA exempt – subject to the public interest – from both the duty to disclose and the duty to confirm or deny (where this would in itself disclose information which is privileged).

Legal professional privilege (LPP) protects material from disclosure on the ground that a client must be sure that what he and his lawyer discuss in confidence will not be disclosed to third parties without his consent. Unfortunately, having been largely settled since the sixteenth century, the application of LPP has been significantly undermined following a Court of Appeal decision in *Three Rivers District Council* v. *The Governor and Company of the Bank of England* CA [2003] EWCA Civ 474 (*Three Rivers*). Widely criticised as artificial and impractical, it is fair to say the ramifications of the ruling have yet to be fully worked out. We are therefore in a state of considerable uncertainty. This is exacerbated by the FOIA's imposition of a public interest test in relation to LPP. This is another significant shift in the application of previously settled legal principles.

As a result of these changes to LPP, there are likely to be documents to which authorities would expect LPP to apply, but to which, in fact, LPP may not apply. Further, there may be documents to which LPP did apply at the time the document was produced, but to which privilege has later ceased to apply. In both cases, information which an authority would wish and expect to be FOIA exempt, will not be exempt (at least under s.42).

LPP is divided into two categories: legal advice privilege and litigation privilege.

Legal advice privilege

A communication is protected by legal advice privilege if it is made:

- confidentially; and
- between a client and his lawyer; and
- for the dominant purpose of seeking or giving legal advice or assistance.

Litigation privilege

A communication is protected by litigation privilege if it is made:

- confidentially; and
- for the dominant purpose of conducting or giving advice in relation to litigation, either pending or contemplated.

'Litigation' for this purpose covers adversarial proceedings. Adversarial proceedings are not defined, but include court proceedings and arbitration. Non-adversarial proceedings, such as inquiries or investigations, are excluded.

Unlike litigation privilege, legal advice privilege can only apply to communications passing directly between a lawyer and his client. Legal advice privilege cannot apply to correspondence between a lawyer and a third party, or between a client and a third party, even if the communication is for the purpose of obtaining information to be submitted to the client's lawyer.

The change to privilege introduced by the *Three Rivers* decision is that the Court of Appeal confined within narrow limits the persons who qualify as the client for the purpose of determining whether legal advice privilege applies. The *Three Rivers* case arose out of the collapse of BCCI following fraud on a vast scale perpetrated by its senior staff. The creditors and the liquidators of BCCI sued the Bank of England for misfeasance in public office in respect of its supervision of BCCI. The Bingham Inquiry was set up to consider whether the action taken by the UK authorities, including the Bank, had been appropriate and timely. Shortly after the inquiry was established, three Bank officials were appointed by the governor to deal with all communications between the Bank and the inquiry and with the Bank's solicitors in relation to the inquiry. They became known as the Bank's Inquiry Unit (BIU). The Bank received legal advice from its lawyers on every aspect of the presentation of its evidence and submissions to the inquiry. Preparatory work was carried out by the BIU including discussions with present and former Bank staff involved in the licensing or supervising of BCCI. The flow of factual information from the Bank to its lawyers was usually channelled through the BIU. Specific requests for factual matters to be investigated and reported to its lawyers were often made by its lawyers to the BIU who then delegated those fact finding tasks to others within the Bank. The Court of Appeal held that only the members of the BIU should be regarded as the client for the purpose of LPP.

The Bank submitted that communications from any employee should be treated as from the client because a company can only act through its employees. The Court of Appeal accepted that a company can only act through its employees but did not regard that as sufficient for determining whether privilege should apply. It said that 'information from an employee stands in the same position as information from an independent agent' and was thus not protected by legal advice privilege. Thus, not every employee of the client will be regarded as the client for the purpose of determining whether a document is protected by legal advice privilege.

The court held that confidential internal documents prepared for the purpose of instructing lawyers are not protected by legal advice privilege because such documents are not in themselves a communication between lawyer and client, or a document evidencing such communication. The court decided that legal advice privilege did not extend to documents prepared by the Bank's employees who were not part of the BIU:

- with the intention that they should be sent to and were in fact sent to the Bank's lawyers;
- which were said to have been prepared with the dominant purpose of the Bank obtaining legal advice but which were not in fact sent to the Bank's lawyers, whether or not prepared for submission to or at the direction of the Bank's lawyers, even if their effect was incorporated into documents which were sent to the lawyers;
- prepared otherwise than for the dominant purpose of obtaining legal advice but which were in fact sent to the lawyers.

The definition of 'client' has therefore become critical to determining whether a document is protected by legal advice privilege. Nevertheless, the Court of Appeal gave no guidance about how to determine who the client is. The client would seem to include in-house lawyers, senior officers whose duties include instructing the client's lawyers and those specifically appointed to communicate with the client's lawyers on particular matters.

Communications between an employer and his or her in-house lawyer where the lawyer is providing legal advice in his or her capacity as legal adviser will qualify for LPP, but where the lawyer acts in an administrative or executive capacity the communications will not be privileged.

Can privilege be lost?

Privilege can be lost where the underlying confidentiality in a document is lost or where the client waives the right to LPP in a document. Waiver of LPP for one document in a series of documents may, depending on the facts, also waive privilege in other related documents. The court will ensure fairness and prevent a party from cherry picking and waiving privilege only in those documents which assist it. Waiver of privilege in respect of part of a document will extend to the entire document, unless the subject matter of the remaining part is completely different.

Partial waiver should be distinguished from redaction of a document whereby privileged material is edited out: disclosure of the unprivileged part of the document will not waive privilege in the privileged part.

What is 'legal advice' for the purposes of LPP?

Most – but not all – communications between a lawyer and client will qualify as advice for the purpose of LPP. Legal advice is not confined to telling the client the law, provided that the advice is directly related to the performance by the solicitor of his or her professional duty as legal adviser of the client.

In *United States of America* v. *Philip Morris Inc & Ors and British American Tobacco (Investments) Ltd (Intervener)* [2004] EWCA CIV 330, the Court of Appeal said that the leading modern authority on the practical application of the principles governing privilege is still *Balabel* v. *Air India* [1988] Ch 317. In that case Taylor LJ said (at 330–1):

> The test is whether the communication or other document was made confidentially for the purposes of legal advice. Those purposes have to be construed broadly. Privilege obviously attaches to a document conveying legal advice from a solicitor to client and to a specific request from the client for such advice. But it does not follow that all other communications between them lack privilege. In most solicitor and client relationships, especially where a transaction involves protracted dealings, advice may be required or appropriate on matters great or small at various stages. There will be a continuum of communication and meetings between the solicitor and client. Where information is passed by the solicitor or client to the other as part of the continuum aimed at keeping both informed so that advice may be sought and given as required, privilege will attach. A letter from the client containing information may end with such words as 'please advise me what I should do'. But, even if it does not, there will usually be implied in the relationship an overall expectation that the solicitor will at each stage, whether asked specifically or not, tender appropriate advice. Moreover legal advice is not confined to telling the client the law; it must include advice as to what should prudently and sensibly be done in the relevant legal context.

A little later (at 331–2) Taylor LJ said that the scope of the privilege had to be kept within justifiable bounds. He stated in relation to documents recording information or transactions or recording meetings that:

> Whether such documents are privileged or not must depend on whether they are part of that necessary exchange of information of which the object is the giving of legal advice as and when appropriate.

The House of Lords in another *Three Rivers* decision unanimously endorsed the approach of the Court of Appeal in *Balabel* v. *Air India* [1988] Ch 317, and in particular Taylor LJ's comments.

There will always be borderline cases in which it is difficult to decide whether or not the advice is given in a legal context. Much will depend upon whether it is reasonable for the client to consult the special professional knowledge and skills of a lawyer. However, there will normally be a relevant legal context when a client seeks advice from a lawyer.

Litigation privilege

The test for determining whether litigation privilege can be invoked in relation to any communication where litigation has not commenced, is whether there was a real likelihood that litigation was reasonably in prospect at the time when the communication was made. There must be a real prospect of litigation as distinct from a mere possibility, but the prospect does not have to be more likely than not. The requirement that litigation be reasonably in prospect is satisfied if the party seeking to claim privilege can show that he or she was aware of circumstances which rendered litigation between himself or herself and a particular person a real likelihood.

Applying the public interest test

The public interest in maintaining the legal privilege exemption will normally be substantial because legal privilege itself derives from the public interest in maintaining confidentiality between lawyer and client. The guidance from the DCA on s.42 underlines this. It notes that where legal privilege applies, the balance of the public interest will usually weigh in favour of disclosure only in exceptional circumstances.

There are a number of factors which, as a matter of principle, will weigh in favour of maintaining LPP in the face of an FOIA request for privileged information:

- decisions by public authorities must be taken in a fully informed legal context;
- authorities require legal advice for the effective performance of their operations and that advice must be given by lawyers who are fully apprised of the factual background;
- legal advisers must be able to present the full picture, which will include arguments in support of their final conclusions and arguments that may be made against these (it is in the nature of legal advice that it will set out the arguments both for and against a particular view, weighing up their relative merits, and highlighting perceived weaknesses in any position);

- without such comprehensive advice, authority decision making may be compromised because it would not be fully informed;
- disclosure of legal advice could materially prejudice an authority's ability to protect and defend its legal interests;
- disclosure might unfairly expose a legal position to challenge and diminish the reliance which may be placed on the advice; and
- even where litigation is not in prospect, disclosure of legal advice may carry a risk of prejudicing an authority in future litigation, and legal advice connected with one department could have wider implications for other departments.

Public interest factors weighing in favour of disclosing privileged information might include that:

- circumstances are such that the government would waive privilege if litigation were afoot;
- departments should be accountable for the quality of their decision making and this may require transparency in the decision-making process and access to the information on which decisions were made; and
- in some cases there may be a public interest in knowing whether or not legal advice was followed.

In *Bellamy* v. *Information Commissioner and Secretary of State for Trade and Industry* (case reference EA/2005/0023, 27 March 2006), the Information Tribunal stressed the importance of legal professional privilege: 'under English law the privilege is equated with, if not elevated to, a fundamental right at least insofar as the administration of justice is concerned'. The Tribunal took the view that Mr Bellamy had failed to adduce sufficient considerations which would demonstrate that the public interest in justifying disclosure was outweighed by the public interest in maintaining the exemption. It commented that, 'there is a strong element of public interest inbuilt into the privilege itself. At least equally strongly countervailing considerations would need to be adduced to override that inbuilt public interest'.

There is a line of case law referred to in Bellamy which reinforces the intrinsic nature of LPP, culminating with *R. (Morgan Grenfell & Co Ltd)* v. *Special Commissioner or Income Tax* [2003] 1 AC 563. Here Lord Hoffmann remarked that: 'Legal profession privilege is a fundamental human right long established in the common law. It is a necessary corollary of the right of any person to obtain skilled advice about the law'. Several other cases echo this approach.

In *Kitchener* v. *Information Commissioner and Derby City Council* (case reference EA/2006/0044, 20 November 2006), when considering the public interest test, the Tribunal again reinforced the fundamental nature of legal professional privilege. It recognised that an inherent part of a fair trial is access to legal advice and representation. If either the lawyer or his client could be forced to disclose what either had said to the other, this would under-mine the very part of the process that our legal system seeks to protect. A client and his lawyer could not speak frankly if there was a possibility that disclosure might be ordered later.

The Tribunal in this case also commented on the fact that the exemption covered by s.42 is not absolute in nature. It noted that, since Parliament did not make it an absolute exemption, decision makers should take care not to make it one by default, by virtue of the force of the public interest in main-taining the exemption. This is not entirely consistent with the Tribunal's approach in *Bellamy* and it is not clear how decision makers should go about striking the right balance between, on the one hand, not treating s.42 as an absolute exemption, and on the other, giving it the appropriate weight given that legal professional privilege is considered such a cardinal principle.

A significant LPP case which did not reach the Information Tribunal but which resulted in the Information Commissioner issuing an Enforcement Notice concerned the Government's refusal to disclose advice from the Attorney General on the legality of military intervention in Iraq (Enforcement Notice of 22 May 2006). The Legal Secretariat to the Law Officers (LSLO) at the Attorney General's office had refused to disclose on the basis that the information at issue was covered by LPP and was therefore exempt under s.42. The Commissioner's decision is particularly interesting because he was obliged to weigh the fundamental nature of LPP against the need for the public to challenge and debate government decisions on a matter of such enormous importance and sensitivity.

During 2005 a multitude of requests were made seeking information relat-ing to the advice given by the Attorney General to the Prime Minister on the legality of military action in Iraq in 2003. In forming his opinion, the Commissioner considered two documents written by the Attorney General: one on 7 March and the other on 17 March 2003. A 17 March statement addressed to the House of Lords (in the form of a written answer) was already on the public record and therefore not part of the requested informa-tion. However, the Commissioner referred to it in his deliberations as to whether the public interest lay in favour of disclosing other contemporaneous information.

The 7 March advice was published by the government following a partial leak in April 2005. It was nevertheless part of the requested information at the time when the requests had been made and therefore the Commissioner deemed it necessary to consider whether or not it was exempt from disclosure under s.42.

In his Enforcement Notice the Commissioner's reasoning largely followed that of the Tribunal in Kitchener (above), namely that 'there must be a reason-able expectation that . . . [legal advice] . . . will remain confidential to ensure that the legal opinion is full and frank'. The Commissioner also acknowledged the long-standing convention that neither the advice of the Law Officers nor the fact that their advice has been sought is disclosed outside the government, a convention specifically recognised in para.24 of the Ministerial Code. The Commissioner also noted that the subject matter of the request required the reasons favouring non-disclosure to be applied with 'especial force in the context of a decision of such gravity, sensitivity and difficulty in policy terms, legal complexity and diplomatic sensitivity . . . and in the context of advice given personally by the Attorney General at the highest levels of government'.

The arguments in favour of disclosure centred around the ability of the public to 'understand, debate and challenge decisions taken by the government'. Here, 'there is a public interest in the government being able to demonstrate that the decision has been fully debated and that the appropriate advice has been sought from professional advisors'. There was also a public interest in understanding the legal basis for the decision to join the invasion of Iraq and to know that the government had acted in accordance with the rule of law. In particular, the Commissioner noted that it was important that the public understood the process which led from the 7 March advice to the 17 March statement since the latter came to an unequivocal conclusion and it was on this advice that the House of Commons relied when deciding to support military action by vote on 18 March 2003.

The Commissioner felt that there was a further public interest in disclosure arising from the uncertainty about the status and nature of the 17 March statement:

> It would have been reasonable for Parliament and the public to assume that the 17 March statement had been based on a thorough analysis of all relevant legal considerations and that its unequivocal conclusion reflected a similar conclusion . . . in an Opinion or Advice prepared by the Attorney General . . . it was a legitimate assumption that there was at least full consistency and continuity between the 7 March advice and the 17 March statement.

Following a series of government leaks which had preceded the Commissioner's consideration of the case, it had become public knowledge that the 7 March advice did not reach a firm conclusion. To this extent the 7 March advice and the 17 March statement were inconsistent and therefore the balance of public interest was tipped in favour of disclosure because the public might otherwise have been falsely led to believe that the decision to engage in military action was based on a 'firm and confident analysis'. In order to be satisfied that the decision in relation to Iraq was based as far as possible on a sound legal foundation, there was a public interest in understanding the chain of events between the 7 March advice and the 17 March statement.

In making his decision, the Commissioner was particularly conscious of the necessity of the government receiving legal advice in confidence. He acknowledged that LPP is a fundamental principle under English law but the fact that it had not been made an absolute exemption meant that there must be circumstances in which the public interest in disclosure was so strong that it could be overridden. The premise behind the implementation of the FOIA was that it enables the public to access information about the way the government has reached decisions and thereby seeks to improve trust and confidence.

The balance of the public interest did not require the disclosure of those parts of the requested information which were uncirculated drafts or documents of a preliminary, provisional or tentative nature or which might reveal legal risks, reservations or possible counter arguments as expressed by any of those involved in the provision of advice, or information informing that advice. However, the balance of the public interest did require the disclosure of those parts of the requested information which led to, or supported, the concluded views that were made public by the Attorney General in the 17 March statement.

By the Enforcement Notice dated 22 May 2006, the LSLO was required to publish a Disclosure Statement setting out the substance of all the recorded material within the requested information which led to or supported the views made public by the Attorney General in the 17 March statement.

5.3.9   Commercial interests (s.43(1))

There are two separate qualified exemptions under s.43 which serve to protect the legitimate interests of business. Section 43(1) applies to trade secrets, for which there is no requirement to assess the prejudice which disclosure might cause, because this is inherent in the meaning of a trade secret. If information is a trade secret, then it will be exempt, subject to the public interest. The duty to confirm or deny does not arise if compliance would defeat the purpose of the exemption.

There is no definition of a trade secret, either in the FOIA or in English law generally. However, the essence of a trade secret is generally taken to comprise three elements (*Lansing Linde Ltd* v. *Kerr* [1991] 1 WLR 251):

• it must be specific information used in a trade or business;
• it must not generally be known – which usually means that the owner must have limited, or at least not permitted, its widespread publication; and
• it must be information which, if disclosed to a competitor, would be liable to cause real or significant harm to the owner.

In 1997, the Law Commission, seeking views on the criminalisation of trade secrets as part of a Consultation Paper, identified four categories:

• formulae for highly specific products;
• technological secrets;
• strategic business information; and
• collations of publicly available information, such as databases.

These categories have not, however, been formally drafted into protected categories.

An analysis of s.43(2), and the application of the public interest test to s.43 generally, follows later in this chapter.

5.4   PREJUDICE-BASED EXEMPTIONS

The public interest test applies to each of the exemptions set out below in the usual way. However, unlike the exemptions referred to already, for the following group of exemptions to apply, disclosure of information must, or must be likely to, give rise to the prejudice referred to in each category. The prejudice itself need not be serious or substantial – any prejudice is sufficient – but it must at least be likely; a mere possibility of prejudice will not suffice.

It is conceivable of course that disclosure of information to one person might be prejudicial, whereas disclosure to someone else would not be. If so, then the correct approach is to consider whether widespread public disclosure of the relevant information would cause prejudice. For example, disclosing information about the specification of British army rifles might be judged harmless if the requestor is a retired colonel living in Dorset, but highly dangerous if the applicant is known to have sympathies with insurgent groups in Afghanistan. If it is likely that disclosure of information to the first applicant might find its way into the hands of the second (e.g. because our retired officer posts it on the internet), then this is clearly a factor to be built into the assessment of whether disclosure should be made.

An analysis of each of the prejudice-based exemptions follows.

5.4.1   National security (s.24)

Information which is not covered by the absolute exemption for security matters under s.23 will still be exempt if exemption is required to safeguard national security. The exemption applies also to the duty to confirm or deny.

Like s.23, s.24 also provides that certification by a Minister is conclusive evidence of exemption.

National security

The term 'national security' has never been defined in UK legislation, and both domestic and European courts have considered that the assessment of the threat to national security is essentially a matter for the executive. The courts here have accepted that it is proper to take a precautionary approach (see the House of Lords judgment in the appeal of Shafiq Ur Rehman against deportation, Secretary of State for the Home Department (11 October 2001 [2001] UKHL 47)) – that is, it is necessary not only to consider circumstances where actual harm has occurred or will occur to national security, but also to consider preventing harm, or the risk of harm, occurring.

Despite the absence of a definition, it is possible to infer certain statements about the meaning of national security from case law and statute.[7] For example:

- the security of the nation includes its well-being and the protection of its defence and foreign policy interests, as well as its survival;
- the nation does not refer only to the territory of the UK, but includes its citizens, wherever they may be, or its assets wherever they may be, as well as the UK's system of government; and
- there are a number of matters which UK law expressly recognises as constituting potential threats to, or otherwise being relevant to, the safety or well-being of the nation, including terrorism, espionage, subversion, the pursuit of the government's defence and foreign policies, and the economic well-being of the UK. However, these matters are not exhaustive. Government would regard a wide range of other matters as being capable of constituting a threat to the safety or well-being of the nation. Examples include the proliferation of weapons of mass destruction and the protection of the critical national infrastructure, such as the water supply or national grid, from actions intended to cause catastrophic damage.

As common sense would suggest, national security is not the same as the interests of the government of the day. Official information that would be embarrassing or inconvenient to the government if made public is not of itself a matter of national security.

As a qualified exemption, s.24 is contingent on two things. First, the test for reliance on the exemption is that non-disclosure should be required for the purpose of safeguarding national security. An authority must be prepared to demonstrate the need to withhold the information requested, and if steps could be taken to allow information to be disclosed while safeguarding national security in some other way, those steps will need to be considered. Secondly, even if exemption is required for this purpose, the exemption is also subject to the public interest.

Applying the public interest test

The public interest requires consideration of:

- whether, in all the circumstances of the case, the public interest in disclosing the information outweighs the public interest in withholding it; and
- if it is decided to withhold the information, whether the exemption from the duty to confirm whether or not the information is held is required for the purpose of safeguarding national security, and whether there is any overriding public interest in communicating the fact that a department holds the information, while not actually disclosing it.

In reality, of course, the public interest and the maintenance of national security are very closely allied. It is difficult in the abstract, therefore, to envisage circumstances where the former would override the latter. The circumstances would have to be fairly extraordinary, and presumably such that national security and the public interest were somehow in conflict.

5.4.2 Defence (s.26)

Section 26 makes information exempt if its disclosure would, or would be likely to, prejudice:

(a) the defence of the British Islands or any colony; or
(b) the capability, effectiveness or security of any relevant forces (meaning the armed forces and any forces cooperating with those forces).

This is a qualified exemption which turns not on the description of particular information but on the effects of disclosure. In every case, therefore, it is a question of assessing the risk of prejudice that disclosure may cause to the matters in (a) and (b), regardless of the content of the information, the kind of document in which the information is contained, or its source. In assessing prejudice, any prejudice is sufficient – it need not be significant, serious or substantial – but prejudice would normally have to be a likely consequence of disclosure, rather than a mere possibility.

Relevant examples falling within this exemption might be:

- defence policy and strategy, military planning and defence intelligence;
- the size, shape, organisation, logistics, order of battle, state of readiness and training of the armed forces;
- the actual or prospective deployment of those forces in the UK or overseas, including their operational orders, tactics and rules of engagement;
- the weapons, stores, transport or other equipment of those forces and the invention, development, production, technical specification and performance of such equipment and research relating to it;
- plans and measures for the maintenance of essential supplies and services that are or would be needed in time of conflict;
- plans for future military capabilities;
- plans or options for the defence or reinforcement of a colony or another country;
- analysis of the capability, state of readiness, performance of individual or combined units, their equipment or support structures; and
- arrangements for cooperation, collaboration, consultation or integration with the armed forces of other countries, whether on a bilateral basis or as part of a defence alliance or other international force.

Applying the public interest test

The public interest in avoiding prejudice to defence matters will be strong in most cases, so will outweigh the public interest in disclosure unless the harm or prejudice likely to result from disclosure would be trivial or minor.

There is at the same time widespread public interest in defence policy and the activities of the armed forces, so it is appropriate that the public should be able to understand how and why key decisions are taken. Where disclosure will inform debate, the public interest in disclosure will be weightier. Examples might include disclosure of information relating to:

- the safety of military personnel or loss of life;
- risks to the safety of civilians;
- the use of land or the environmental impact of military activity (for which s.39 may also be relevant);
- the factual and analytical bases used to develop defence policies; and
- the use of public funds.

Clearly the public interest will weigh against disclosure where this might undermine the conduct of a specific military operation or have an adverse impact on security or safety. Further, the disclosure of information in the face of an objection from an allied country, or in breach of a clear undertaking to preserve confidentiality, may well prejudice the UK's defence relations by restricting exchanges of information or by jeopardising military cooperation.

Related issues

Authorities which deal routinely with defence information will usually have their own specific clearance procedures for dealing with requests. Officials should always comply with such procedures because they will have been written to reflect the legal restrictions which apply to the organisation. The FOIA preserves all existing statutory prohibitions on disclosure, the breach of some of which is a criminal offence.

In many cases, it will also be appropriate for an authority to consult the Ministry of Defence before disclosing potentially exempt defence information.

5.4.3   International relations (s.27(1))[8]

Section 27 exempts from disclosure information which would, or would be likely to, prejudice:

- relations between the UK and any other state;
- relations between the UK and any international organisation or international court;
- the interests of the UK abroad; or
- the promotion or protection by the UK of its interests abroad.

Information, the disclosure of which is potentially covered by this exemption, spans a broad spectrum and could include, for example:

- reports on, or exchanges with, foreign governments or international organisations such as the EU, NATO, the UN, Commonwealth, World Bank or International Monetary Fund;
- information about the UK's activities relating to UK citizens or companies abroad, particularly their consular and commercial interests;
- information about other states' views or intentions provided in the course of diplomatic and political exchanges of views;
- details of inward and outward state visits and visits by Ministers and officials;
- information supplied by other states on diplomatic or other channels;
- discussion within the UK government on approaches to particular states or issues;
- information relevant to actual or potential cases before an international court; and
- details of the UK's position in multilateral or bilateral negotiations.

Applying the public interest test

The fundamental question when applying the public interest test under s.27 is whether the public interest in disclosure is outweighed by the damage or likely damage that would be caused to the UK's international relations, its interests abroad or its ability to protect and promote those interests.

For prejudice which is likely to be trivial – for example, where disclosure about the content of a discussion with a foreign official would be unlikely to provoke any significant negative reaction or have any significant detrimental effect on other states' willingness to have similar discussions with the UK in the future – then the public interest in disclosure is likely to prevail.

Correspondingly, for prejudice likely to be more serious – such as disclosure about the UK's attitude to an international issue of concern to a particular state which would provoke a strong negative reaction and could, for example, make it less likely that British companies would be awarded government contracts in future with that state – then the public interest in disclosing would have to be more specific and compelling to justify disclosure. The same would be true of a disclosure which would be likely to weaken significantly the UK's bargaining position in international negotiations, inhibit other governments' willingness to share sensitive information, or inhibit frankness and candour in diplomatic reporting.

5.4.4 Relations within the UK (s.28)

Section 28 will apply where disclosure would, or would be likely to, prejudice relations between any administration in the UK and any other such administration. The duty to confirm or deny does not apply to the extent that compliance would defeat the purpose of the exemption.

'Administration in the UK' means the UK government itself, and the various devolved administrations within the UK. These are:

- the Scottish administration;
- the Executive Committee of the Northern Ireland Assembly (which, at the time of writing, is suspended); and
- the National Assembly for Wales.

Local authorities and the Greater London Assembly are excluded, as are the Scotland, Northern Ireland and Wales Offices which are part of the UK government.

Section 28 applies – regardless of the nature or content of the information in question – where the effects of disclosure would, or would be likely to, prejudice relations between any of the administrations covered – that is, between the UK government and any of the devolved administrations, and also between any of the devolved administrations themselves.

In essence, there are now three devolved administrations within the UK, and the UK government represents UK interests in matters which are not devolved to Scotland, Wales or Northern Ireland. Policy responsibility for non-devolved matters is the responsibility of UK government Ministers and departments, and in these areas the Secretaries of State for Scotland, Wales and Northern Ireland are responsible for ensuring that the interests of those parts of the UK are properly represented and considered.[9]

Accordingly, there are two distinct circumstances in which s.28 might apply: where information requested under the FOIA has been obtained from or shared between administrations; and where information held by one administration could prejudice relations because that administration does not want other administrations to see it, or because other administrations would not want the information to be disclosed.

Information obtained from or shared between administrations

Under the terms of the Memorandum of Understanding between the UK administrations (MoU), all four are committed to the principle of good communication with one another, especially where one administration's work may have some bearing on the responsibilities of another. To enable each to operate effectively, they provide each other with policy information, including scientific and technical statistics, research results and, where appropriate, representations from third parties. Where necessary, they will in confidence:

- alert each other to relevant developments within their areas of responsibility, wherever possible prior to publication (although there are certain areas, notably national security and budget proposals, where prior notification is much less likely);

- give consideration to the views of the other administrations; and
- where appropriate, establish arrangements that allow for policies to be developed jointly between administrations.

The MoU also includes safeguards to ensure that information shared with other administrations is appropriately protected. In certain circumstances, this means that confidentiality is expected. In particular, the MoU provides that administrations will:

- state what restrictions there should be on information they share;
- treat information received in accordance with the restrictions they have agreed to respect;
- comply with the FOIA but in difficult cases refer back to the originator of the information; and
- accept that some information is subject to statutory or other restrictions and that there will be a common approach to the classification and handling of sensitive material.

An expectation of confidentiality will not be a conclusive demonstration of prejudice likely to result from disclosure, but it will be a relevant consideration.

Other information

There will be multifarious circumstances in which information shared between administrations might be prejudicial to relations if disclosed. Some examples might be:

- sensitive information about devolved matters which predate devolution, held by UK government departments but concerning devolved administrations;
- information held by devolved administrations relating to reserved or excepted matters;
- briefing or comments on another administration's plans or policies;
- an options analysis in an area of reserved policy which also includes an assessment of the operation of policy in a devolved area; and
- information about another administration which has come direct from a third party.

Note that, as with the other qualified exemptions, potential embarrassment is not enough to justify its use.

Applying the public interest test

The exigencies of open government have to be balanced with the political imperatives underlying the devolution settlement, namely trust, cooperation, information sharing and respect between the four administrations. The prospect of harming the effective functioning of the devolved relationships will be a significant factor in assessing whether to disclose information.

In weighing the public interest, it is important to consider the following:

- the wider public interest in freedom of information and any particular commitments given by administrations;
- the commitment to sharing information between the four administrations;
- the commitment to respecting confidential information shared between bodies;
- the nature and extent of prejudice to the relationships between administrations that might be caused by the disclosure of a particular piece of information;
- the importance of ensuring appropriate frankness and candour of discussion between administrations; and
- the extent to which other exemptions may be relevant.

The following are some examples where the public interest might favour withholding information:

- confidential briefings for UK Ministers provided for ministerial meetings;
- policy plans received from devolved administrations on a confidential basis which have not yet been announced;
- details of meetings between the four administrations the disclosure of which could impact on the effectiveness of such meetings;
- details of a sensitive UK negotiating position in the EU which, though reserved, impacts on devolved matters; and
- UK government assessments of politics and policies in the devolved administrations.

Examples where the public interest might favour disclosure are as follows:

- information which helps public understanding of the devolution settlement;
- information which would explain how decisions were taken (after an announcement has been made);
- details of negotiations which are no longer sensitive because of the passage of time; and
- cases where the administration which provided the information would have disclosed the information (even if a case can be made for non-disclosure).

5.4.5 The economy (s.29)

Information is exempt if disclosure would, or would be likely to, prejudice:

- the economic interests of the UK or any part of the UK;
- the financial interests of any administration in the UK.

The duty to confirm or deny does not arise to the extent that doing so would defeat the object of the exemption.

Economic interests

'Economic interests' include the central aim of government, to provide economic and financial management which supports the maintenance of a stable macroeconomic framework, maintains sound public finances and promotes UK economic prospects and productivity. Associated with these issues is the maintenance of a competitive financial services market, and efficient tax and benefits systems. The exemption exists in recognition of the instability and economic damage to the wider economy that could be caused by the disclosure of some information.

Financial interests

'Financial interests' means the efficient conduct of the financial aspects of government administration, to minimise the cost to the taxpayer. Public accountability necessitates that sufficient information is available to assess the probity and cost-effective nature of such dealings. This must be balanced against the damage to an administration's financial interests which might result if too much information is disclosed about its financial dealings, or if information is disclosed too soon after a particular event. This component of the exemption exists in recognition of the long-term cost to the taxpayer which could result from disclosure (premature or otherwise) of certain information.

The expression 'an administration in the UK' has the same meaning as in s.28.

The economic interests of the UK

This covers a considerable range of subject matter. It is likely that prejudice could result from disclosure of some of the following, where the information in question is sensitive:

- tax, national insurance and benefits policy;
- IMF loan programmes;
- financial stability discussions and support operations;
- firm-specific financial regulatory information;
- discussions with overseas financial authorities;
- analyses of macroeconomic policy;
- marketing trends, including interest rates and the framework of monetary policy and forecasts of government borrowing; and
- analyses of the effects of increases in public spending on wage and inflation pressures.

In most of these areas, the potential for prejudice is likely to turn on the timing of disclosure, particularly in cases where premature release could cause market instability.

The financial interests of an administration in the UK

Again, this covers a broad spectrum of subject matter. Examples of likely prejudicial disclosures include:

- allocation of gilts and Treasury bills at auctions/tenders to particular investors or market makers;
- government cash dealing and banking arrangements;
- UK reserves and foreign currency liabilities management and foreign exchange dealings;
- timing of large cash and stock transactions in the future;
- intended investment strategies;
- contracts details of PFI and PPP deals;
- auction bidding details (e.g. gilts, spectrum licences); and
- finances of public corporations.

Some examples of potentially prejudicial disclosures

These examples of potentially prejudicial disclosures are drawn from the DCA guidance on s.29. The list is only illustrative.

- information contained in Standing Committee and financial stability papers (of, for example, HM Treasury, the Bank of England, the Financial Services Authority);
- vulnerability assessments, for example of emerging market economies;
- gilt auctions – the size of offering at a gilt auction has a short-term but nevertheless significant sensitivity which could influence price and therefore the cost of borrowing for the government;
- budget information – release of budget information ahead of formal announcement, particularly in relation to tax and national insurance, might lead to pre-emptive action by companies and individuals, leading to a reduction in tax payable to the government;
- government cash flows and borrowing requirements – premature disclosure is likely to be market sensitive; and
- terrorism reinsurance – disclosure of information about claims could potentially prejudice the economic interests of a part of the UK.

Applying the public interest test

There is a legitimate public interest in the UK's economic policy, taxation and financial management, and release of some information will promote public understanding and informed debate (and, indeed, it has been government policy for some time to release information such as Monetary Policy Committee meeting minutes and the annual borrowing plans and gilt auctions calendar).

Some specific factors will weigh in favour of disclosure:

- the need to hold public authorities to account for their stewardship of public resources; and
- the objective of building public trust and establishing transparency in the operation of the economy so as to increase the credibility of economic policy decision makers and enhance the UK's reputation as a fair and honest business environment.

Factors weighing in favour of withholding information might include:

- where disclosure could result in financial instability within institutions or countries, either in the UK or abroad;
- where disclosure could pre-empt announcements on taxation, national insurance or benefits;
- where selective disclosure of the information could affect financial markets – financial regulation and government policy requires the transparent release of market sensitive data simultaneously to the whole market because this reinforces confidence in market integrity, thereby reducing the cost of capital in financial markets; selective or premature release of information undermines confidence in dealing in UK markets;
- where information has been obtained from confidential sources (e.g. overseas governments or regulators) and these would be damaged by disclosure and reduce the likelihood of information being made available in the future; and
- where the information consists of assessments of an institution's or economy's viability.

Authorities should consider consulting HM Treasury and/or other relevant government departments before releasing information which might fall within s.29.

In *Derry City Council* v. *Information Commissioner* (case reference EA/2006/0014, 17/18 October 2006), the Tribunal considered the relationship between economic interests and commercial interests. On the facts of the case, it concluded that the economic interests of the region depended on the commercial interests of the Council's airport. Consequently, if commercial interests were likely to be prejudiced then this would have a detrimental impact on the economic interests of the region and the exemption in s.29 would be engaged.

In the *HM Revenue and Customs* (HMRC) decision (FS50095271, 13 June 2007), the complainant had requested details of EC Treaty challenges to UK tax legislation. These contained details of estimates of the actual or potential cost to the exchequer of aspects of UK tax law being found to be in breach of the EC Treaty. HMRC withheld this information stating that it was exempt from disclosure under FOIA, s.29. They explained that the estimates were worst case scenarios which were extremely uncertain. Because of the level of uncertainty the Information Commissioner considered that the potential impact on investors from the release of the information gave rise to potential prejudice to UK economic interests. The Commissioner considered that the economy is sensitive to even small changes in investor confidence and disclosure of the information could lead to more than just a small change in investor confidence. Release of the EC Treaty challenges information could therefore pose a real or significant risk to the UK economy and s.29 was therefore engaged.

5.4.6 Law enforcement (s.31)

The application of s.31 turns on the likely *effects* of disclosure rather than the source of the information or the purpose for which it is held – which are covered under s.30. As such, s.31 will only be relevant in cases where s.30 is not. This therefore excludes from s.31 most substantive information relating to an authority's own law enforcement functions. However, s.31 is a considerably broader exemption than s.30, because it is relevant to information which authorities hold for the law enforcement purposes of other bodies.

The exemption operates by reference to a list of law enforcement interests which might be prejudiced by disclosure of information. Some are very wide, others very specific. Information is exempt if its disclosure would, or would be likely to, prejudice:

(a) the prevention or detection of crime;
(b) the apprehension or prosecution of offenders;
(c) the administration of justice;
(d) the assessment or collection of any tax or duty or of any imposition of a similar nature;
(e) the operation of immigration controls;
(f) the maintenance of security and good order in prisons or in other institutions where persons are lawfully detained;
(g) the exercise by any public authority of its functions for any of certain specified purposes (see below);
(h) any civil proceedings which are brought by or on behalf of a public authority and arise out of an investigation conducted for any of the certain specified purposes by or on behalf of the authority exercising either prerogative powers or powers conferred by or under any enactment; or
(i) any inquiry held under the Fatal Accidents and Sudden Deaths Inquiries (Scotland) Act 1976 to the extent that the inquiry arises out of an investigation of the type referred to in paragraph (h) above.

The duty to confirm or deny does not arise to the extent that compliance would prejudice any of these matters.

As will be clear, paragraphs (a)–(f) stand by themselves and refer to a series of law enforcement interests which could be prejudiced by disclosure.

Paragraphs (g)–(i) can only apply in relation to the specified purposes set out below (FOIA, s.31(2)):

(a) to ascertain whether any person has failed to comply with the law;
(b) to ascertain whether any person is responsible for any conduct which is improper;
(c) to ascertain whether circumstances exist or may arise which would justify regulatory action in pursuance of any enactment;
(d) to ascertain a person's fitness or competence in relation to the management of bodies corporate or in relation to any profession or other activity which he is, or seeks to become, authorised to carry on;
(e) to ascertain the cause of an accident;
(f) to protect charities against misconduct or mismanagement in their administration (whether by trustees or other persons);
(g) to protect the property of charities from loss or misapplication;
(h) to recover the property of charities;
(i) to secure the health, safety and welfare of persons at work; and
(j) to protect persons other than persons at work against risk to health or safety arising out of or in connection with the actions of persons at work.

The prevention or detection of crime and the apprehension or prosecution of offenders

The above terms appear throughout English law and have no special meaning within the context of the FOIA. They may apply specifically or in general terms. Examples of circumstances in which potential prejudice (i.e. resulting from disclosure) may make the exemption bite are:

- intelligence about anticipated criminal activities (disclosure here has a high potential to prejudice the prevention or detection of the crime in question, and the apprehension of the alleged offenders);
- information relating to planned police operations, including specific planned operations, and policies and procedures relating to operational activity;
- information relating to the identity and role of police informers (to which a number of other exemptions are also likely to be relevant, including those under ss.30, 38, 40 and 41);
- information relating to police strategies and tactics in seeking to prevent crime (the disclosure of such information has a high potential to undermine legitimate police objectives carried out in the public interest);
- information disclosure of which would facilitate the commission of any offence; and

- information disclosure of which would prejudice the fair trial of any person against whom proceedings have been or may be instituted (to which, again, a number of other exemptions may also be relevant, particularly, with reference to s.44, in relation to disclosures which would breach Art.6 of the European Convention on Human Rights).

APPLYING THE PUBLIC INTEREST TEST

Maintaining confidence in law enforcement and the criminal justice system is obviously crucial to the public interest, but it is a consideration which can weigh both for and against disclosure. Much is done through police and community consultation (and the media) to keep citizens informed about the ways in which the police carry out their responsibilities. On occasions, however, there will be some tension between this emphasis on openness and the need to maintain the confidentiality of specific operations or policies. Similar considerations will apply to other law enforcement bodies.

It is also important to be aware that prejudice may arise incrementally, as well as from a single disclosure. Clearly, disclosure of information on a single specific police operation designed to apprehend alleged offenders could be prejudicial. What, though, about disclosures of more general information relating to police strategies and tactics? Such disclosure may undermine legitimate police objectives and hamper future operational activity by limiting the value of those strategies and tactics once disclosed (or by providing valuable intelligence to perpetrators of crime).

Examples of specific considerations which might be relevant to this section include:

- the effects of crime on individuals – for example, it would not be in the public interest to disclose details of a surveillance operation and thus potentially compromise that operation, where the target was a person suspected of a series of violent assaults;
- the effects of crime on society – for example, it may not serve the public interest to disclose in advance the arrangements for an operation to combat graffiti and other criminal damage in a specific area; and
- the effects of crime on the economy – for example, it may be against the public interest to disclose specific police strategies for action against those failing to pay fines or other penalties.

The administration of justice

There is no definition of the administration of justice, but it should be interpreted broadly. In particular:

- the exemption does not only concern the operation of the courts – justice is administered through courts and tribunals, through arbitrators, and through alternatives to litigation;

156

- all categories of justice are included (criminal, civil, family or administrative), as are matters which may not fit into that classification or which are general in nature;
- justice may be administered by professional judges and adjudicators, or by lay magistrates or panel members, or by jurors;
- administration of justice need not imply an adversarial context – it includes non-contentious or uncontested business, and inquisitorial processes (such as inquiries and coroners' courts);
- ensuring public access to justice is part of the administration of justice; and
- the administration of justice may be prejudiced in an individual case, or by something happening to the general process by which justice is delivered.

In the normal course, the administration of justice could be prejudiced by disclosures relating to:

- the operation of the judicial appointments system;
- the ability of a judge to deliver justice effectively, fairly and fearlessly in a particular case;
- the ability of a judge, or of the judiciary, to deliver justice effectively in more general terms;
- the business of the running of the courts and tribunals (though other exemptions might also be relevant);
- the enforcement of sentences and the execution of judgments;
- the ability of litigants to bring their cases, or a particular case, to court;
- the prospects of a fair trial taking place;
- the effectiveness of relationships between different agencies involved in the administration of justice (for example, premature disclosure of plans to redistribute functions between different agencies could lead to a breakdown of cooperation);
- a range of other matters and systems that support the administration of justice (e.g. the operation of the legal aid system, or IT systems – disclosure of the security measures on computer systems would facilitate unauthorised access and thereby make them vulnerable to interference); and
- the maintenance of an independent and effective legal profession.

APPLYING THE PUBLIC INTEREST TEST

Clearly, the public interest in the administration of justice is very high. However, in addition to this, there is a public interest in the separation of powers between courts and the executive. This effectively means that there is a public interest in the government acknowledging that the administration of justice is within the courts' particular domain, and in recognising that the courts are, constitutionally, the ultimate arbiters of the law.

As such, although the nature, degree and likelihood of prejudice to the administration of justice will be an essential part of weighing the balance of public interest, government recognition of the courts' position means that authorities should take particular care whenever concluding that the public interest in avoiding prejudice is outweighed. Circumstances where prejudice in a particular case is outweighed by the prevention of prejudice more generally might be one example of where the balance may lie in favour of disclosure. There may be other circumstances, particularly at the administrative margins of the administration of justice (as opposed to the judicial centre of the system), where the operational impact of a prejudicial disclosure is more diffuse, and considerations of administrative transparency weigh more strongly. Precisely because prejudice to the administration of justice encompasses such a wide range of circumstances, the specific factors relevant to individual cases may be particularly important to the operation of this exemption.

In *Mr Colin P England and London Borough of Bexley* v. *Information Commissioner* (case reference EA/2006/0060&66, 1/2/5 May 2007) counsel for the respondent argued that the exemption in s.31(1)(a) did not apply to information relating to empty properties in Bexley, as it was not specifically collated for crime prevention purposes. The Tribunal rejected this submission on the basis that the exemption does not contain any express link to the purpose for which information has been obtained, or the function of the public authority. Previous decisions (e.g. *Hogan* v. *Oxford County Council* EA/2005/0026&30) had all concerned information collected for specific crime prevention purposes. However, the Tribunal felt that this was only coincidental and there is no explicit reference to support the proposition that s.31(1)(a) does not apply to information obtained otherwise than for specific crime prevention purposes.

Tax

Taxes, duties and impositions of a similar nature includes:

- income tax;
- corporation tax;
- VAT;
- insurance premium tax;
- petroleum revenue tax;
- national insurance contributions;
- climate change levy;
- excise duties (for example, on tobacco, oil, beer, spirits and wine);
- motor vehicle duties;
- air passenger duty; and
- stamp duty.

Disclosures likely to be prejudicial to the assessment or collection of these levies include:

- details of plans to close tax loopholes;
- information held in relation to the tax affairs of companies or individuals;
- information which informs plans for future investigations;
- third-party information which aids the collection of tax or duties; and
- details of strategies, investigative practices or even negotiating tactics used to assist in the collection of taxes or duties.

APPLYING THE PUBLIC INTEREST TEST

There is a strong public interest in having stable and secure public finances. These are crucial to the stability and sustainable growth of the UK economy and to the delivery of resources to fund public services. An efficient and well administered tax system also improves the competitiveness of business and supports the government's social and welfare objectives. A central requirement of a modern and fair tax system is that everyone pays the proper amount of tax and receives the benefits to which they are entitled. Tax avoidance and evasion reduce the revenue available for delivering public services, and distort the incentives that the tax system aims to offer, unfairly shifting a greater tax burden on to honest and compliant taxpayers.

Of course, disclosure of information promotes public awareness of how taxes work, which helps make it simpler for individuals and business to pay taxes. Authorities should take into account the public interest in the proper administration of taxation both in general and in particular cases, and in the avoidance of disruption or distortion of markets, or of the successful delivery of tax policy objectives.

Operation of immigration controls

'Immigration controls' is not defined in the FOIA but it will obviously cover the physical immigration controls at points of entry into the UK, as well as the arrangements made (whether in or under legislation, or as a matter of policy or procedure) in connection with entry into, and stay in, the UK, including the investigation of offences relating to immigration.

Clearly, the disclosure of information would be prejudicial under this head if its release into the public domain would help people to evade immigration controls (although, as long as that is likely to be the consequence of release, the information itself need not be about immigration controls).

Examples of circumstances where disclosure might prejudice the operation of immigration controls include disclosure of:

- information about the extensive counterfeiting of travel documents of a particular country, on the basis of which travel documents issued by that country should be subjected to particular scrutiny. In this case, the disclosure of the information or the identity of the targeted country might be prejudicial because it could alert counterfeiters (and persons making use of their services) to use another country's travel documentation;

- information which would reveal an incidence of suspected illegal working which is to be investigated by the immigration service. In this case, the disclosure of the information about the proposed investigation might be prejudicial because it could alert employers of the illegal workers in advance and allow them to escape investigation; and

- information on proposed changes to visa regimes. The imposition or amendment of visa regimes usually takes place with little or no notice to the public. This is because visa regimes are generally introduced to prevent evasion or abuse of immigration controls by nationalities who, over time, have been shown to pose a higher risk of evasion or abuse than other nationalities when seeking to enter the UK. Therefore, the disclosure of information relating to visa regimes could, in some cases, prejudice the operation of immigration controls because it would encourage persons from the countries which are due to be affected to seek to enter the UK before the changes are introduced, thus avoiding the more stringent regime which has necessarily been developed.

APPLYING THE PUBLIC INTEREST TEST

Immigration controls are important in order to regulate entry to and settlement in the United Kingdom, in which there is a clear public interest.

In the immigration context, there are a number of public interest considerations which may favour disclosure in the context of a particular request. There is a public interest in ensuring that there is public confidence in the operation of our immigration controls, and one way to ensure this is to keep the public informed of policies, developments and proposals for the future, and the reasons underlying them. Linked with this is the public interest in ensuring that the public have access to correct information. Immigration is an emotive issue and inaccurate information should not be allowed to circulate uncorrected in the public domain.

It is in the public interest to provide information which confirms the performance of immigration control – for example, by providing statistics on the number of passengers and applications that are handled by the Immigration and Nationality Directorate. There is also a public interest in establishing that the implementation of immigration control is carried out in accordance with the published statements and policies by providing, wherever possible, details of implementation of immigration control.

There is also a public interest in ensuring that those who are subject to immigration controls are aware of those controls and how they operate, as this may discourage such persons from seeking to enter the UK illegally.

Equally there are a number of public interest considerations which may, in the context of a particular request, favour non-disclosure. For example, there is a public interest in ensuring that:

- people are not able to evade or abuse our immigration controls in order to enter the UK illegally;
- the efficiency and integrity of our immigration controls are not undermined; and
- investigations into suspected immigration offences can be conducted effectively.

Maintenance of security and good order in prisons

'Security' and 'good order' are not defined in the FOIA but common sense suggests that 'security' will include everything related to the secure custody of detainees, the safety of the prison population, and the detection and prevention of activity (criminal or otherwise) prohibited under prison rules. It is likely that good order refers to measures intended to counter individuals' disobedience or concerted indiscipline, and which promote a safe and orderly prison regime. Note, however, that this exemption is intended to preserve not only security and good order in prisons but also in 'other institutions where persons are lawfully detained'. This includes young offenders' institutions, secure hospitals, secure training centres, local authority secure accommodation and immigration detention and removal centres.

Since the exemption focuses on the effects of disclosure, information would presumably cause harm if its release would compromise security, lead to the breakdown of good order or impair an institution's ability to restore either.

A key aspect of this, therefore, is the need to ensure that changes to prison routine are introduced in a carefully managed way, with prisoner reaction being assessed and expectations managed so that when the change is introduced there is not an immediate adverse reaction that may put staff and prisoners at risk. Premature release of information about a potentially unpopular policy change could therefore be prejudicial. Hypothetical examples of information relevant to good order might be information about proposed changes in the home detention curfew (or tagging) policy, or incentives and earned privileges scheme, or information about changes in meal times or arrangements for visits.

An example of security-related information might be information detailing the times and routes of prisoner escorts, and information relating to good order may include, for example, the strategy for dealing with concerted prisoner indiscipline or the contingency plans for responding to other types of incident.

Conversely, information on physical security at a prison which is assessed as having little or no impact on the risk of prisoner escape if disclosed, might not be considered to prejudice security and should therefore be disclosed.

There is a public interest in ensuring public confidence in the operation of the prison system, which may be achieved by informing the public of policies, developments and proposals for the future. The public interest is clearly not served, however, by releasing information which may aid prisoners to escape, may cause unrest, or may put anybody within an institution at risk.

Sections 31(1)(g), (h) and (i)

As noted above, these exemptions operate only where:

- disclosure would prejudice one of the processes in s.31(1)(g), (h) or (i); and
- that process is for one of the purposes listed in s.31(2); and
- the public interest allows.

The following paragraphs assess the application of each paragraph of s.31(1) in turn.

SECTION 31(1)(G) – FUNCTIONS OF A PUBLIC AUTHORITY

'Functions' refers to an authority's powers and duties. These derive either from statute or from the royal prerogative, and the connected purposes in s.31(2) indicate that the provision is chiefly concerned with those systems operated by authorities to ensure that proper standards of conduct and safety are met. Notwithstanding this, though, s.31 does not limit the application of the exemption to particular central functions, since in reality very many authorities and departments exercise functions for the purpose of ascertaining whether any person has complied with the law (s.31(2)(a)), ascertaining whether any person is responsible for any conduct which is improper (s.31(2)(b)), ascertaining the cause of an accident (s.31(2)(e)), or securing the health, safety and welfare of persons at work (s.31(2)(i)).

SECTION 31(1)(H) – CIVIL PROCEEDINGS ARISING OUT OF STATUTORY OR PREROGATIVE INVESTIGATIONS

'Civil proceedings' certainly comprises non-criminal legal action before a court or tribunal, but it could stretch to include other proceedings such as, for example, some forms of regulatory enforcement proceedings. Much will depend on the terms of any regulatory regime, and on the particular circumstances involved.

The prejudice in question must be to the civil proceedings themselves, but there is no need to give that an artificially narrow interpretation. It is capable, for example, of applying to prejudice to the authority's position in such proceedings.

The proceedings must arise, directly or indirectly, out of an investigation. The investigation, in turn, must have been conducted for one of the specified purposes in s.31(2), though the same is not true for the proceedings themselves (even if, in practice, this will be likely). For example, having ascertained that someone has improperly disclosed sensitive information to journalists, a public authority may attempt to prevent publication of that material by a breach of confidence action.

The investigation must have been conducted either:

- by virtue of the royal prerogative (many investigations undertaken by government departments are undertaken under prerogative powers, because the residual source of their legal powers – where not expressly conferred by statute, for example – resides in the Crown; this is particularly the case regarding investigations in the context of the internal management of government departments); or
- by or under an enactment – that is to say, by virtue of provisions in an Act of Parliament or in an instrument made under powers contained in an Act (this will include, in particular, statutory regulations).

Both the civil proceedings and the investigation may be undertaken either by the authority itself, or by another body on the authority's behalf.

This provision has potential to overlap with s.31(1)(c) (the administration of justice) and with ss.32 (court records) and 42 (legal professional privilege). The general public interest considerations likely to be engaged are therefore those relating to the administration of justice and the proper conduct of legal proceedings.

SECTION 31(1)(I) – INQUIRIES UNDER THE FATAL ACCIDENTS AND SUDDEN DEATHS INQUIRY (SCOTLAND) ACT 1976

The 1976 Act provides for public inquiries to be held in respect of fatal accidents, deaths of persons in legal custody, sudden, suspicious or unexplained deaths, or deaths which occur in circumstances giving rise to serious public concern. As the Lord Advocate's powers to investigate deaths in Scotland under this legislation are wide-ranging, this provision will have relevance to UK government departments operating in Scotland in a wide variety of circumstances where a death occurs, even where the death does not occur in legal custody. For Whitehall departments, these will of course be in areas of reserved policy/operations, such as, for example, defence (deaths of MoD service personnel based in Scotland) or immigration (deaths of asylum seekers in Home Office detention in Scotland), and in such cases the relevant exemptions (s.26, s.31, etc.) may also apply.

Like s.31(1)(h), this provision is limited by the following factors:

- the prejudice must be to the inquiry;
- the exemption applies only to the extent that the inquiry arises out of an investigation;

- the investigation must have been conducted for one of the purposes specified in s.31(2); and
- the investigation must have been conducted under statutory or prerogative powers (although not necessarily under the 1976 Act itself).

Some statutes, which have their own provisions about inquiries into deaths, expressly allow for the disapplication of the 1976 Act, to prevent a death triggering two parallel statutory inquiries. Examples include s.14(7) of the Health and Safety at Work etc. Act 1974, and s.271(6) of the Merchant Shipping Act 1995. Such provisions will limit the application of this exemption.

The s.31(2) purposes most likely to be relevant to the investigations referred to in connection with the 1976 Act are:

- ascertaining whether any person has failed to comply with the law;
- ascertaining whether any person is responsible for any conduct which is improper;
- ascertaining whether circumstances which would justify statutory regulatory action exist; and
- ascertaining the cause of an accident.

APPLYING THE PREJUDICE TEST

In *Hogan and Oxford City Council* v. *Information Commissioner* (case reference EA/2005/0026,30, 5 October 2006), the Tribunal provided guidance on the application of the prejudice test in the context of s.31. Mr Hogan sought to obtain specific details of motor vehicles licensed with the DVLA where the Registered Keeper of the vehicle was the local authority. This information was eventually provided by the Council with the exception of the Vehicle Identification Numbers (VINs) which were withheld in reliance on s.31(1)(a). The Tribunal considered in some detail the application of the prejudice test. When considering the existence of prejudice, public authorities should consider that disclosure is effectively being made to the general public as a whole, since any disclosure may not be subject to conditions governing subsequent use. It suggested that the test involves three steps:

1. identifying the applicable interests within the relevant exemption;
2. considering the nature of the prejudice being claimed; and
3. considering the likelihood of the occurrence of prejudice.

(This approach was subsequently applied in *Reith v. Information Commissioner and London Borough of Hammersmith & Fulham* (case reference EA/2006/0058, 13 April 2007).)

In elaborating on the third point the Tribunal expressed the view that the chance of prejudice being suffered should be more than a hypothetical or remote possibility, there must be a real and significant risk.

On this basis there are two possible limbs on which a prejudice-based exemption may be engaged. First, where the occurrence of prejudice to the specified interest is more probable than not. Secondly, where there is a real and significant risk of prejudice, even if it cannot be said that the occurrence of prejudice is more probable than not. In general terms, the greater the likelihood of prejudice, the more likely that the balance of public interest will favour maintaining the qualified exemption in question. In this particular case, the Tribunal found that there was evidence in favour of disclosing the VINs to Mr Hogan and indeed the applicant himself presented persuasive evidence. However, the Tribunal ultimately decided that disclosure of the VINs would be likely to prejudice the prevention or detection of crime and therefore they were exempt from disclosure under s.31(1)(a).

The Tribunal in *Hogan* also briefly considered the application of the public interest test. Ultimately, they said, it is incorrect to consider whether the balance of the public interest lies in favour of maintaining the exemption in relation to a specific type of information. The correct consideration is rather: does the balance of public interest lie in favour of maintaining the exemption in relation to *this specific type of information and in the circumstances of this case*? If a public authority has a general policy in favour of maintaining the exemption in respect of a specific type of information, then the policy should not be inflexibly applied and the authority must always be willing to consider whether the circumstances justify a departure from policy.

5.4.7   Audit functions (s.33)

This exemption is intended to protect the effectiveness of the audit functions of certain public authorities. It applies where the disclosure of information would, or would be likely to, *prejudice* an authority's functions relating to (a) the audit of the accounts of other public authorities; or (b) the examination of the economy, efficiency and effectiveness with which other public authorities use their resources in discharging their functions (FOIA, s.33(1)). The duty to confirm or deny does not apply to the extent that doing so would defeat the purpose of the exemption.

While much of the information that an auditor holds could be disclosed and may indeed be prepared with a view to publication, there may be cases where disclosure would prejudice the audit function.

Disclosure might prejudice audit functions in the following ways:

- Relations with audited bodies and audit third parties may be compromised – there may be information that originates from an audited body which, if disclosed, could harm relations between the auditors and that body, and so affect the ability of the auditors to carry out their functions effectively.
- Disclosure may interfere with audit methods – in the interests of an audit's effectiveness, it may be important that details of the audit method, including,

for example, the specific files that the auditor intends to examine, are kept from the audited body before the audit takes place. Disclosure of audit methods after an audit may also prejudice subsequent audits where, for example, an auditor intends to use the same method. Similarly, releasing information about how the auditing body derives its conclusions could also prejudice the audit function.

- Public reporting and scrutiny – before publication, many public sector auditors discuss their emerging findings and draft report with the audited bodies and other affected parties to ensure accuracy and completeness of the evidence on which they base their conclusions and recommendations. In the case of the National Audit Office (NAO), it may also be under a duty to inform Parliament first of the findings of its reports. If information from an audit were disclosed before official publication, this may pre-empt the proper reporting process and could lead to preliminary findings – which had not been fully tested – being given the same currency as fully tested conclusions. This may undermine the fairness of the audit process and create a misleading impression of both the auditor and the body being audited, possibly causing unwarranted damage to either reputation. In these circumstances the audit function would clearly be prejudiced.

In *Office of Government Commerce and Information Commissioner* (EA/2006/0068 and 0080), the Tribunal re-affirmed previous Tribunal decisions which established that the phrase 'would prejudice' means that a prejudicial effect is 'more probable than not'. Further, 'would be likely to prejudice' should be read as 'there is a real or significant risk of prejudice'.

Applying the public interest test

There is a strong public interest in ensuring that auditors can effectively carry out audits of public authorities. Much of the information that auditors produce is made available for the same general public interest reasons that support the principles of the FOIA. These include:

- making the reasons for a public body's decisions evident;
- enhancing the scrutiny and improving the accountability of public bodies;
- contributing to public debate; and
- increasing public participation in decision making.

The audit process facilitates the accountability and transparency of public authorities for decisions taken by them, which in turn facilitates accountability and transparency in the spending of public money. In general, most value for money audits lead to a public report with these express aims. There is therefore a clear public interest in protecting the effectiveness of the audit process. However, there is also a counterbalancing public interest in making available information which would lead to greater public confidence in the integrity of the audit process by allowing scrutiny, not only of the audited body, but also of the auditor's performance. In many cases the balance of the public interest will change over time, with the key issue likely to be whether the final report has been published.

Auditing departments and agencies must be aware of the confidentiality requirements of legislation that governs the particular bodies they audit. For example the external auditor of HM Revenue and Customs, the NAO, is bound by the Finance Act 1989, which makes it a criminal offence to disclose taxpayers' information.

5.4.8 The effective conduct of public affairs (s.36)

The s.36 exemption recognises the critical role in effective government of free and frank discussion. However, s.36 can only apply in cases where the information in question is not exempt under s.35 (although the two may be claimed in the alternative). It is therefore likely that s.36 will tend to apply to areas which do not relate to policy – such as management, delivery and operational functions. Further, s.36 exempt information need not relate to government Ministers. It can include any advice and discussion taking place at official level.

The fundamental difference between ss.35 and 36 is that the latter turns on the effects of disclosure rather than the nature of the information itself. In other words, s.36 can apply irrespective of what the information is, if disclosure:

> would, or would be likely to . . . *inhibit* the free and frank provision of advice . . . or the free and frank exchange of views for the purposes of deliberation . . . or would otherwise *prejudice*, or would be likely to prejudice, the effective conduct of public affairs (author's italics).

Importantly, s.36 is contingent on the reasonable opinion of a qualified person, which means that it can only apply with the authority of one of the officials listed in s.36(5). This indicates that s.36 must be used with great deliberation.

What do 'advice' and 'exchange of views' cover?

There is very little guidance on what is meant by these terms. 'Advice' can be internal (e.g. from officials to Ministers) or external (e.g. from third parties). It includes any advice whether made by an authority, or to it. Any 'exchange of views' is limited only by having to be for the purposes of deliberation. This will include processes of decision making, opinion forming or evaluation, but is likely to exclude casual or trivial exchanges.

The term 'inhibit' does not feature elsewhere in the FOIA. It suggests a suppressive effect, in other words a situation where communications would be less likely to be made, or would be made in a more reticent or circumscribed fashion, or would be less inclusive.

In considering its effects, it may be relevant to consider whether disclosure may:

- make it more likely that the person offering advice will be unwilling to do so in future;
- inhibit that person from offering unwelcome advice;
- make it more likely that the person being advised will not ask for advice in future;
- have a similar inhibiting effect on other people in future;
- make it more likely that advice will be given that is materially different because of the possibility of disclosure;
- make people less likely to engage in discussion (whether oral or written) as part of the deliberative process;
- distort or restrain that discussion; or
- result in pressure being brought to bear on officials to provide particular advice.

What does the 'effective conduct of public affairs' cover?

This provision deals with situations which fall outside the other specific circumstances covered by s.36. Little guidance is available so far, but during debates on the Bill, Lord Falconer explained that it is intended to cover residual cases which cannot be foreseen, but where it is necessary to withhold information in the interests of good government. It is a broadly expressed residual exemption, therefore a clear justification would have to be provided when seeking to rely on it (and it is also subject to ministerial authorisation).

In relation to statistical information only, information which an authority holds is exempt if disclosure would:

- prejudice the free and frank provision of advice; or
- prejudice the free and frank exchange of views for the purposes of deliberation; or
- otherwise prejudice the effective conduct of public affairs.

This exemption can only be applied to non-statistical information if the authority is authorised by government to exercise discretion.

In *Guardian Newspapers (1) and Heather Brooke (2)* v. *Information Commissioner and BBC* (case reference EA/2006/0011&13, 8 January 2007), the Tribunal discussed two questions of law which are relevant to decision makers seeking to rely on s.36. First, the Tribunal considered the application of s.36(2)(b), and specifically the question of whether disclosure of information might be 'inhibiting', the meaning of 'would be likely to' and the meaning of 'reasonable opinion', in the context of the requirement for the exemption to apply 'in the reasonable opinion of a qualified person'. Secondly, it examined the application of the public interest to the information in the minutes themselves. The case concerned the disclosure of the minutes of the BBC Governors' meeting which took place on the day the Hutton Report was released: 28 January 2004. The BBC had refused to disclose, claiming exemption under s.36 on the grounds that publication would inhibit the free and frank exchange of views for the purposes of deliberation in governors' meetings.

The application of s.36(2)(b)

In interpreting the phrase 'would or would be likely to', the Tribunal followed the decision of Munby J in *R* v. *Secretary of State for the Home Office* [2003] EWHC 2073. This requires that the mischief in question (the 'inhibition' of free and frank deliberations) would 'probably' occur (i.e. with a greater than 50 per cent chance, on the balance of probabilities), or that there would be a 'very significant and weighty chance' that it would occur, even if the risk fell short of being more probable than not.

In consideration of the interpretation and application of 'reasonable opinion', the Tribunal concluded that 'the substance of the opinion must be objectively reasonable'. This statement is in conflict with the Commissioner's guidance on the same point, which states that he considers the phrase to mean an opinion 'which lies within the bounds of reasonableness or range of reasonable opinions'. In the Tribunal's view, the substance of the opinion must merely be 'objectively' reasonable in order to satisfy the wording of the Act.

The Tribunal also considered whether the process by which the opinion was arrived at was relevant. It concluded that in order to satisfy the statutory wording 'the opinion must be both reasonable in substance and reasonably arrived at'. It would certainly undermine the purpose of the FOIA (to provide a general right of access to information) if the qualified person were not required to give proper consideration to all relevant matters.

In the event, the Tribunal somewhat fudged its judgment by declaring itself unable to decide whether or not the decision of the BBC Board of Governors (to withhold the minutes) was a reasonable one, and so accepting the Commissioner's conclusion that it had indeed been reasonable. However, it goes on to say that should a higher court also recognise that the process by which the opinion is arrived at is relevant in assessing its reasonableness, and also that the proper consideration of specific relevant evidence is an essential feature of the process, then the Tribunal would regard the opinion to be unreasonable. This is a somewhat bizarre conclusion.

To summarise, the Tribunal determined that both the reasonableness of the opinion and the reasonableness of the process by which the opinion is reached are relevant considerations. Public authorities should therefore expect to have to adduce specific relevant evidence in support of reliance on s.36(2)(b). At the same time, the Tribunal's approach in the case suggests that unless and until we have judicial authority on the point, it will be difficult to challenge the application of s.36(2)(b) other than on public interest grounds.

THE PUBLIC INTEREST TEST

The Tribunal made several observations when considering the application of this test:

- In assessing the balance of public interest, the passage of time will have an important bearing – in general, the public interest in maintaining an exemption will diminish over time.
- It is not the Commissioner's role to decide whether or not the qualified person's opinion is correct, he must only give weight to the opinion and use it as an important factor in his assessment of the balance of public interest.
- The qualified person's opinion only gives an indication of the likelihood that disclosure would inhibit the free and frank exchange of views – it does not necessarily imply any particular view as to the severity or extent of such inhibition or to the frequency with which it may occur – it is for the Commissioner to form a view on these.
- The importance and sensitivity of the subject matter of deliberations are not the same thing. The subject matter of the minutes considered in this case were of very high importance but their contents could hardly be considered sensitive when they were in the public domain a matter of hours following the meeting.
- Deliberations on many other topics would have a greater requirement for a period of secrecy, such as details of commercial plans or negotiations, proposals for cuts in services or staff numbers etc.
- A public authority has an obligation to make sure meetings/deliberations are recorded in the form of proper minutes, regardless of whether or not disclosure to the public is anticipated at a later date.

In addition, the Tribunal commented on the meaning of 'qualified person' in s.36(5)(o)(ii). It was surprised by the BBC's view that authorisation entitled them to delegate the decision to any individual governor. If an authorisation given to a public authority itself under s.36(5)(o)(ii) entitled it to delegate the task of the qualified person to an individual of their choice, then the subsection would be unnecessary. It was the Tribunal's view that the opinion must be the opinion of the authority's primary decision-making organ, in this case the Board of Governors.

The Tribunal concluded by allowing the appeal because in its opinion, at the time the information request was made, the public interest in maintaining the s.36 exemption did not outweigh the public interest in disclosing the information contained in the minutes of the BBC Governor's meeting on 28 January 2004.

5.4.9   Health and safety (s.38)

Section 38 exempts information if its disclosure would, or would be likely to, (a) endanger the physical or mental health of any individual; or (b) endanger the safety of any individual (FOIA, s.38(1)). 'Endanger' connotes risk of harm rather than harm itself.

The following are some examples of disclosures with an evident potential for the kind of endangerment to which this exemption applies:

- those which would allow individuals, groups or firms to be identified or located and consequently targeted and attacked for their beliefs or practices, including work in controversial scientific areas;
- disclosure of plans and policies relating to the accommodation of individuals, or groups of individuals, where disclosure could lead to their being threatened or harassed (e.g. asylum seekers);
- disclosure of information about negotiations with kidnappers, where disclosure could endanger the safety of hostages; and
- disclosure of sensitive or graphic information about deceased individuals which could cause serious distress to particular individuals such as family members, particularly if they were not previously aware of the details.

Of course, information relating to health and safety may often be environmental information within the meaning of the EIR. If such information is environmental information, exemption from the FOIA under s.39 must be claimed and the disclosure of that information should be considered under the EIR.

Applying the public interest test

It is never in the public interest to endanger the health and safety of any individual. However, more generally, details to be considered will include:

- the size of the risk involved, the likelihood of the outcome in question, and the extent to which steps might be taken to reduce or manage that risk;
- the nature and seriousness of the resulting outcome were that risk to materialise;
- the possibility that disclosure would help to protect the health or safety of other individuals; and
- the possibility that the anticipated danger could be prevented or managed by other, reasonable, precautions.

There is a public interest in disclosing information in order to reduce the potential danger to people and to increase their personal freedom by making them aware of various risks and enabling them to take appropriate action. A certain level of trust is necessary if the recommendations and information supplied by departments with specific responsibilities to inform the public of health and safety issues are to be acted upon. This trust may be enhanced by a high level of disclosure.

The *NHS Direct* decision (reference FS500108885, 30 July 2007) gives an indication of when the Information Commissioner will consider that the public interest in disclosing information is outweighed by the public interest in maintaining the s.38 exemption.

NHS Direct provides health advice and information via a confidential telephone service. In this case the Commissioner was asked to consider whether disclosure of the equivalent geographic numbers of NHS Direct's 0845 numbers would, or would be likely to, endanger the health and safety of individuals. As the service's geographic numbers were not networked through a central computerised system and were not always located within a call centre, a member of the public ringing such a number would likely experience a delay in answer, routing to an inappropriate adviser, or no answer at all. Furthermore, a proportion of NHS Direct's calls are immediately referred to 999 emergency services, Accident and Emergency wards, or for the urgent attention of GPs. NHS Direct deemed that a delay in response to such a call, or no answer at all, could endanger the health and welfare of individuals. NHS Direct also argued that releasing geographic numbers would inevitably require staff to be allocated to these numbers resulting in prioritisation of these calls over those coming through on 0845 numbers. This might also have the effect of relatively minor issues being dealt with first. As a consequence, there would be longer waiting times on 0845 calls and further risks to the health and safety of callers on this number also. NHS Direct therefore refused to disclose, citing s.38.

In assessing the balance of public interest in his decision, the Commissioner recognised that there is a public interest in the public being able to access information about the cost effectiveness of public services. However, there is also a competing public interest in maintaining confidence in the effective operation of the NHS Direct service and the health and safety of the public should not be put at risk by disclosing geographic numbers unless it is safe to do so. An increased likelihood of risk to the health and safety of individuals using the NHS Direct service was in itself a powerful public interest argument against disclosure. In considering the systems operating at the time that the request for information was made, the Commissioner was satisfied that there was a real risk that disclosure of geographic numbers could damage the efficient and effective service that NHS Direct was already providing and therefore could endanger the health and safety of individuals using the service. In this case, because the endangering of public health and safety was such a strong argument, the public interest in maintaining the exemption outweighed the public interest in disclosure and therefore NHS Direct was not required to disclose its geographic numbers to the applicant.

Other statutes and policies

There may be legal prohibitions on disclosing information which would endanger an individual's health or safety. The most relevant examples include the Rehabilitation of Offenders Act 1974 and s.28 of the Health and Safety at Work etc. Act 1974. It is important to be alert to the possibility of such information being environmental information within the meaning of the EIR, in which case, exemption from the FOIA under s.39 is the necessary route.

5.4.10　Commercial interests (s.43(2))

The s.43 exemption has already been addressed as it applies to trade secrets (FOIA, s.43(1)). As a separate point, s.43(2) provides a more general category of exemption for commercially sensitive information if the disclosure of information would, or would be likely to, prejudice someone's commercial interests (including the authority's own). The duty to confirm or deny does not arise if compliance would defeat the purpose of the exemption.

Commercial interests are wider than trade secrets and apply – theoretically, at least – to any activity related to the business, trade or profession of any person or organisation. An organisation's commercial interests might, for example, be prejudiced where a disclosure would be likely to:

- damage its business reputation or the confidence that customers, suppliers or investors may have in it;
- have a detrimental impact on its commercial revenue or threaten its ability to obtain supplies or secure finance; or
- weaken its position in a competitive environment by revealing market sensitive information or information of potential usefulness to its competitors.

Examples of information the disclosure of which may have particular potential to damage commercial interests include:

- research and plans relating to a potential new product;
- product manufacturing cost information;
- product sales forecast information;
- strategic business plans, including, for example, plans to enter, develop or withdraw from a product or geographical market sector;
- marketing plans, to promote a new or existing product;
- information relating to the preparation of a competitive bid;
- information about the financial and business viability of a company; and
- information provided to a public authority in respect of an application for a licence or as a requirement of a licence condition or under a regulatory regime.

Importantly, s.43(2) can apply to an authority's own commercially sensitive information as well as to such information held by the authority relating to outside organisations.

In January 2006, the Information Tribunal explored the following question in *John Connor Press Associates Limited* v. *The Information Commissioner* (Appeal Number EA/2005/0005): should an authority be required to disclose financial information which might prejudice its own bargaining position during contemporaneous contractual negotiations and a third party's bargaining power for future commercial transactions?

In the winter of 2004–2005, the National Maritime Museum (NMM) held an exhibition of artwork by Conrad Shawcross. This exhibition was one of a series of contemporary art events staged under the NMM's 'New Visions' programme. In January 2005, John Connor Press Associates Limited (JCPA) asked the NMM to disclose all documentation and correspondence relating to any payments made to the artist for the exhibition. The NMM duly disclosed the contract together with three invoices and some miscellaneous correspondence which revealed substantial details about the transaction. Crucially though, all financial information had been redacted. The NMM relied upon s.43(2), stating that disclosure would be likely to prejudice the commercial interests of both NMM and Conrad Shawcross.

The Information Commissioner held that, in the light of the 'active and contemporaneous negotiations for a project of a similar nature', the public interest in maintaining the s.43(2) exemption outweighed the public interest in disclosure. The Information Tribunal overruled this decision. The key element to note was the Tribunal's interpretation of the phrase 'likely to prejudice' in s.43(2). The Tribunal insisted that this expression must mean that 'the chance of prejudice being suffered should be more than a hypothetical or remote possibility; *there must be a real and significant risk*' (emphasis added).

The following reasons were given: (1) the information already disclosed would have provided any prospective exhibitor with a significant amount of valuable information; (2) it had already been disclosed that the NMM had, very unusually, agreed to contribute to the cost of the artist's materials (a piece of information which significantly decreased the bargaining value of the financial information withheld); and (3) the nature of the works made by Conrad Shawcross and the subsequent artist with whom NMM was negotiating were sufficiently different that they could not be valuably compared.

The Information Commissioner was asked to consider a similar situation in the *BBC* decision (FS50133791, 30 July 2007). Here the applicant sought financial information in relation to an animated television series obtained by the BBC from an independent production company (such companies being referred to as 'IPCs'). The BBC refused disclosure of this information in reliance on s.43(2), indicating that its release would have an adverse effect on its commercial interests. The BBC put forward three prejudice arguments:

1. disclosure would provide the BBC's competitors with valuable pricing information which could have the effect of distorting the market for IPCs, increasing the likelihood of competitors coordinating their bids against the BBC;
2. disclosure would have a prejudicial effect on the BBC relative to its commercial rivals and its relationship with IPCs would be compromised; and
3. if the information was disclosed, the BBC would be in breach of its obligation of confidentiality to this particular IPC and this may have an adverse effect on further dealings.

In summary, the Commissioner agreed with all three of these arguments and was satisfied that the s.43(2) exemption was engaged in this instance.

Prejudice to a third party's commercial interests

Public authorities will hold a great deal of information which falls within s.43(2) because disclosure would cause commercial damage to third parties.

Third party commercially sensitive information will come into the possession of public authorities in a number of ways, for example:

- as a result of legal, regulatory or licensing requirements;
- in the course of policy development – for example, information obtained, usually voluntarily, to inform and influence the development of policy, or changes to law or regulation;
- through providing support for business – for example, information provided by a company or trade association to a public authority to obtain advice, help with a specific project, and/or financial assistance; and
- through contracts, for example for products, services or research.

Authorities may also procure commercial information as a product of their own research, for example when conducting assessments of product performance and financial viability. They will hold commercial information on various products and services in their role as purchasers.

Areas of particular sensitivity

Certain areas of activity in which all authorities are involved are likely to carry particular risks in relation to commercially sensitive information.

One such area is procurement. All public authorities buy goods and services, and a great deal of information which changes hands during the procurement process will be commercially sensitive. Some examples of information to which s.43 is most likely to apply include:

- *information relating to general/preliminary procurement activities:* for example, market sounding information; information relating to programme, project and procurement strategies; and contextual information about the authority, its business objectives and plans;

- *information relating to supplier selection:* e.g. qualification information for potential bidders; information about requirements including specifications; details of the qualification process; and details of qualified bidders;
- *information relating to contract negotiation and award:* e.g. bids; papers about capabilities of bidders, evaluations of bids, negotiating briefs and recommendations; the contract; information about successful bid and bidder; and information about other bids and bidders; and
- *information relating to contract performance and post-contract activities:* e.g. information about implementation; information about performance; information about contract amendments with supporting papers; and information which may be provided and reviewed by third parties (e.g. consultants/auditors).

The requirements of the public procurement regime should also be taken into account in relation to the possible disclosure of information. The EC Public Procurement Directives, implemented in the Public Works Contracts Regulations 1991, the Public Services Contracts Regulations 1993 and the Public Supply Contracts Regulations 1995, recognise that the interest of suppliers in sensitive information supplied by them in a procurement must be respected and that both the interest of suppliers and the public interest may mean that certain information relating to a contract award is withheld from publication.

The new Consolidated Public Procurement Directive (2004/18/EC), yet to be implemented in the UK, continues to recognise these interests and prohibits the disclosure of information which suppliers have designated as confidential in a procurement, except as provided by the Directive and by national law.

When considering likely public interest considerations; there are lessons to be learned from overseas.

Experience of the enforcement of access to information legislation in Ireland is instructive in this area, although care should be taken not simply to read across from the Irish experience, as the freedom of information regime is similar but not identical. The picture in Ireland tends to support the view that the public interest in the disclosure of procurement-related information is not sufficiently strong to override the harm that may be done to commercial interests before the award of the contract. However, the public interest in making information available after the award of the contract – such as the total tender price and evaluation details of the successful tenderer, along with information about the fee rates and other details necessary to understand the nature of the services contracted – was found to be much stronger.

A second area is public authorities' commercial interests in the disclosure or publication of information. FOIA obligations to disclose information apply to copyright information as well as to other information. However, the commercial effects of disclosure on the copyright holder (including the authority itself if it is the copyright owner) should be considered, where relevant, in relation to s.43. Of course, copyright protection in a work will continue to subsist even if information is disclosed under FOIA. A copyright holder may therefore enforce its copyright against any successful FOIA applicant who then sought to exploit that information in breach of the copyright.

Applying the public interest test

There is a public interest in protecting the commercial interests of both the private sector (which plays an important role in the general health of the economy) and the public sector (whose commercially related functions need in any event to be exercised in the wider context of the public interest).

Conversely, there is a general public interest in the disclosure of commercial information in order to ensure that:

- there is transparency in the accountability of public funds;
- there is proper scrutiny of government actions in carrying out licensing functions in accordance with published policy;
- public money is being used effectively, and that departments are getting value for money when purchasing goods and services;
- departments' commercial activities, including the procurement process are conducted in an open and honest way; and
- business can respond better to government opportunities.

Factors that might weigh in favour of the public interest in withholding information in this area include:

- where disclosure would make it less likely that companies or individuals would provide the department with commercially sensitive information in the future and consequently undermine the ability of the department/ agency to fulfil its role;
- where disclosure would be likely to prejudice the commercial interests of the department by affecting adversely its bargaining position during contractual negotiations which would result in the less effective use of public money;
- where disclosure would, as a consequence, make it more difficult for individuals to be able to conduct commercial transactions or have other dealings with public bodies which are not typical commercial transactions – for example, where an organisation obtains a grant or financial assistance from a public authority – without fear of suffering commercially as a result. It would not, for example, be in the public interest to disclose information about a particular commercial body if that information was not common knowledge and would be likely to be used by competitors in a particular market to gain a competitive advantage.

177

NOTES

1 Hansard, HL (series 5) vol 619, col 143 (14 November 2000), Lord Falconer.
2 See also **5.4**.
3 Criminal proceedings include proceedings before a court martial or a standing civilian court.
4 There are very many investigations carried out under either statutory or preroga-tive powers, too numerous to cover in full here. Some examples are inquiries under the Health and Safety at Work etc. Act 1974, s.14 and investigations under the Financial Services and Markets Act 2000, s.169. As a rule, most investigations carried out by statutory bodies will be statutory investigations, and investigations carried out by central government departments will be either statutory investiga-tions or carried out under prerogative powers.
5 'Civil proceedings' is not defined but will certainly include legal proceedings which are not criminal proceedings, before a court or tribunal. It is possible that in some cases the phrase might have a wider meaning, perhaps including certain forms of statutory regulatory enforcement action.
6 The 'Royal Household' is not defined but can be taken to mean those individuals who are authorised to act on behalf of a member of the Royal Family (such as their employees, agents and servants, and including members of the Private Offices of each of the Royal Family) in the carrying out of public, official and constitu-tional affairs. Contractors who supply to the Royal Household (e.g. holders of Royal Warrants) do not form part of it. Certain members of the government Whips' offices in both Houses of Parliament are formally members of the Royal Household (senior government Whips in the Commons are designated the Treasurer and Comptroller of the Household; the Vice Chamberlain also serves as a senior government Whip; junior government Whips in the Lords are Lords and Baronesses in Waiting). The activities of these individuals as government Whips are not covered by s.37.
7 E.g. Security Service Act 1989, Intelligence Services Act 1994, Radioactive Substances Act 1993, Water Industry Act 1991, Control of Pollution Act 1974, Offshore Safety Act 1992, Town and Country Planning Act 1990.
8 See also **5.3**.
9 Details of the relationships between the administrations, and their respective responsibilities, is set out in Cm 5240, an inter-administration Memorandum of Understanding. A summary of the terms of the MoU is available online at **www.foi.gov.uk/guidance/exguide/sec28/annex_a.htm**.

CHAPTER 6

Implications for the private sector

Hugh Tomlinson QC, Matrix Chambers

6.1   INTRODUCTION

It has been widely recognised that freedom of information legislation can have a substantial impact on the private sector. Although the Freedom of Information Act 2000 (FOIA) only places duties of disclosure on public authorities, it potentially allows any applicant to have access to any information held by the public sector. Any information which has been provided[1] to public authorities[2] by businesses is potentially disclosable to *any* applicant.[3] This includes a huge range of information about the activities of the private sector. The information will have come into the hands of public authorities for a wide variety of reasons, such as through the process of taxation, or as a result of regulation or direct commercial relationships between public and private sectors.

As many commentators have pointed out, the FOIA represents both a threat and an opportunity for the private sector. The threat is that commercially sensitive material will be made available to competitors or the media with potentially adverse consequences. The opportunity is for the private sector to obtain a huge range of commercially valuable information at extremely modest cost.[4]

The threat of public disclosure of private sector confidential commercial material is the most immediate issue. Private bodies provide a wide range of sensitive information to public authorities. The threats of disclosure include matters such as the following:

- when a business wins a government contract, that competitors will learn the price and contractual levels of performance and might be able to find the results of performance reviews;
- when a business loses a bid, that competitors may be able to discover details of the bid;
- when a private body has been the subject of a regulatory investigation or inquiry, that competitors or the media might be able to discover details.

If private bodies wish to protect confidential commercial information from disclosure they must take steps do so. It is clear that marking a document confidential will no longer be a guarantee that the public (including business competitors and the media) will be prevented from gaining access to it. It is necessary to consider a wide range of carefully targeted measures to provide as much protection as possible for information which has been or will be given to public authorities.

The opportunities arising from the FOIA are less immediate but potentially of even greater importance. Material held by public authorities provides the private sector with a huge information resource – available at modest cost. Using this resource involves detailed analysis of the kinds of commercially useful information which might be held by public authorities and the making of focused requests aimed at obtaining disclosure of information which can be put to commercial use.

A number of commentators have pointed out that, in the first two years of the operation of the FOIA, the private sector has been slow to make use of the opportunities on offer. It has been estimated that only 20 per cent of requests to local authorities came from business,[5] in contrast to the position in, say, Canada, where 40 per cent of requests have come from business. It may be that attention has been concentrated on 'defensive' measures, to ensure that competitors do not obtain access to information which is given to public authorities. It seems likely that as the operation of the FOIA becomes more familiar, the private sector will make more use of the opportunities on offer.

The impact of the FOIA on the private sector is likely to increase. In October 2007 the Ministry of Justice (MoJ) announced a three-month public consultation on extending the coverage of freedom of information to additional bodies, including contractors who provide services to public authorities.[6]

In an examination of the impact of the FOIA on the private sector, this chapter will address the four main areas detailed below:

- *FOIA exemptions and the private sector:* This section deals with the operation of the exemptions in the FOIA which are likely to be relevant when commercially important information is held by public authorities, focusing, in particular, on the confidentiality and commercial interests exemptions in ss.41 and 43 of the FOIA.
- *FOIA requests and the supplier of information:* The position of private bodies in relation to FOIA requests for information which they have supplied to public authorities is considered, in relation to both consultation and express contractual provision.
- *Practical steps for protecting information:* The risks faced by private bodies are examined together with practical steps which might be taken to protect information from disclosure under the FOIA.
- *Making use of the FOIA:* This section covers the opportunities available for private bodies to obtain information under the FOIA.

In order to keep up to date with developments, readers are referred to the practical periodical, *Freedom of Information* (**www.foij.com**).

6.2   FOIA EXEMPTIONS AND THE PRIVATE SECTOR

6.2.1   Introduction

Section 1 of the FOIA creates a general right of access to information held by public authorities. This means 'information recorded in any form' (FOIA, s.84) and includes information held by another person on behalf of the authority (FOIA, s.3(2)(b)). It does not, however, include information held by a public authority on behalf of another person (s.3(2)(a)). By virtue of s.1(1), any person who requests information (s.84) from a public authority is entitled (a) to be informed in writing by the public authority whether it holds information of the description specified in the request; and (b) if it does, to have that information communicated to him.

This general right of access is, of course, subject to a series of exemptions. Some of these are absolute: if information falls into one of the categories of information which is absolutely exempt from disclosure, then the public authority has no duty to disclose under the FOIA. (It may, however, be entitled to disclose the information voluntarily.) There are seven absolute exemptions:

- s.21: information accessible by other means;
- s.23: information supplied by or relating to bodies dealing with security matters;
- s.32: information contained in court records;
- s.34: where exemption from the duty of disclosure is required to avoid an infringement of parliamentary privilege;
- s.40: where the information constitutes personal data of which the applicant is the data subject;[7]
- s.41: where disclosure of the information would constitute an actionable breach of confidence;
- s.44: where disclosure is prohibited by statute.

Other exemptions are qualified – they are subject to a test of prejudice and/or public interest. If the information falls into any of these categories, a balancing exercise must be undertaken to determine whether, in all the circumstances of the case, the public interest in excluding the duty to confirm or deny, or in maintaining the exemption, outweighs the public interest in disclosing whether or not the public authority holds the information or in communicating the information. There are 16 qualified exemptions:

- s.22: information intended for future publication;
- s.24: information required for the purpose of safeguarding national security;
- s.26: information the disclosure of which would be likely to prejudice defence;
- s.27: information the disclosure of which would be likely to prejudice international relations;

- s.28: information the disclosure of which would be likely to prejudice relations between administrations within the UK;
- s.29: information the disclosure of which would be likely to prejudice the economic interests of the UK or the financial interests of any administration within the UK;
- s.30: information held for the purpose of criminal investigations and proceedings and investigations conducted by public authorities;
- s.31: information the disclosure of which would be likely to prejudice law enforcement;
- s.33: information the disclosure of which would be likely to prejudice the exercise of audit functions;
- s.35: information relating to the formulation of government policy;
- s.36: information the disclosure of which would be likely to prejudice the effective conduct of public affairs (this is sometimes described as hybrid exemption);
- s.37: information relating to communications with Her Majesty and in relation to honours;
- s.38: information the disclosure of which would be likely to prejudice health and safety;
- s.39: information which is subject to disclosure under the EIR;
- s.42: information in relation to which a claim to legal professional privilege could be maintained;
- s.43: information which constitutes a trade secret or the disclosure of which would be likely to prejudice commercial interests.

It should be noted that a request is for information and not documents. This means that one document may contain some pieces of information which are non-exempt, some which are subject to an absolute exemption and some which require the application of a public interest test.

All these exemptions are potentially relevant to the private sector. Commercially sensitive information may be covered by a whole range of possible exemptions. In most cases, however, the interest being protected by the exemption is of the nature of a *public* one which the public authority is likely to be careful to protect. For example, it seems likely that a public authority holding sensitive information about defence systems would rely on the exemption in s.26. However, in the case of two exemptions, what is being protected is a *private* interest. In such a case, private bodies will wish to take steps to ensure that such interests are being properly protected by public authorities. The exemptions in question are those concerning confidential information (s.41) and information which constitutes a trade secret or whose disclosure is likely to prejudice commercial interests (s.43). The operation of these two exemptions is of considerable importance to the private sector. They will be considered in the next three sections.

6.2.2   The confidential information exemption[8]

Introduction

The FOIA is designed to protect confidential information which private bodies have supplied to public authorities from disclosure to applicants. Section 41 provides:

(1)   Information is exempt information if –

   (a)   it was obtained by the public authority from any other person (including another public authority), and
   (b)   the disclosure of the information to the public (otherwise than under this Act) by the public authority holding it would constitute a breach of confidence actionable by that or any other person.

(2)   The duty to confirm or deny does not arise if, or to the extent that, the confirmation or denial that would have to be given to comply with section 1(1)(a) would (apart from this Act) constitute an actionable breach of confidence.

The term 'actionable breach of confidence' is not defined but it appears to mean a claim which would be upheld by the courts (not merely a claim that is arguable).[9] In other words, the absolute exemption applies only if it can be shown that a disclosure of the information by the public authority would, in the circumstances – and putting the FOIA to one side – be an actionable breach of confidence. The public authority and, if there are appeals, the Information Commissioner, the Information Tribunal and the High Court will have to decide whether or not an action for breach of confidence by the supplier of the information would have succeeded.

The information covered

In order to be exempt information under s.41, the information must be 'obtained from any other person' – in other words, the exemption does not cover the public authority's own information. The Information Tribunal has held that a concluded contract between a public authority and a third party does not fall within s.41(1)(a) (*Derry City Council* v. *Information Commissioner* 11 December 2006, para.32(c)). Whether information regarding the pre-contractual negotiating position of the parties falls within s.41 will depend on the circumstances (*ibid.*, para.32(d)). This means that the whole of any contract with a public authority is potentially disclosable, 'no matter how confidential the content or how clearly expressed the confidentiality provisions' (*ibid.*, para.32(e)). However, s.41 may still apply to confidential technical information set out in a contract (*ibid.*). Furthermore, contracts potentially fall under the exemption in s.43 of FOIA, which is discussed below.

Requirements for breach of confidence

The importing of the common law concept of breach of confidence into the FOIA makes the assessment of the applicability of the s.41 exemption an extremely difficult exercise. (The Office of Government Commerce suggests that if an exemption under s.41 is likely, a public authority should seek legal advice, see *FOI (Civil Procurement) Policy and Guidance*, p.6; the guidance is available at **www.ogc.gov.uk/documents/FOI.pdf**.) The precise limits of breach of confidence are still being explored in case law and public authorities will, inevitably, approach the issue in different ways. As a result, it will be very difficult to predict whether, in a given case, the exemption will protect a particular piece of information. An essential first step is the analysis of the requirements for establishing an actionable breach of confidence[10] as explained in the case law.

In *Derry City Council* v. *Information Commissioner* (11 December 2006, para.30) the Information Tribunal approached the issue of breach of confidence by considering four[11] questions:

1. Did the information have the necessary quality of confidence to justify the imposition of a contractual or equitable obligation of confidence?
2. Was the information communicated in circumstances that created such an obligation?
3. Would disclosure be a breach of that obligation?
4. Would there nevertheless be a defence to a claim for breach of confidence based on the public interest in disclosure of the information?

In relation to the first question, the basic attribute of confidentiality is inaccessibility – the information must not be common knowledge (*Saltman Engineering* v. *Campbell Engineering* (1948) 65 RPC 203, 215). Information which is in the public domain cannot be confidential. In a well-known passage in the *Spycatcher* case in the House of Lords, Lord Goff said:

> . . . the principle of confidentiality only applies to information to the extent that it is confidential. In particular, once it has entered what is usually called the public domain (which means no more than that the information in question is so generally accessible that, in all the circumstances, it cannot be regarded as confidential) then, as a general rule, the principle of confidentiality can have no application to it.
>
> (*Attorney General* v. *Guardian Newspapers (No.2)* [1990] 1 AC 109 at 282)

The Court of Appeal has recently offered the following definition of 'confidential information':

> information will be confidential if it is available to one person (or a group of people) and not generally available to others, provided that the person (or group) who possesses the information does not intend that it should become available to others.
>
> (*Douglas* v. *Hello! (No.3)* [2006] QB 125)

Confidentiality does not depend on the establishment of absolute secrecy. This is another way of saying that the question as to whether a particular item of information is in the public domain is not an all or nothing one. As was said in *Franchi* v. *Franchi* [1967] RPC 149, 153: 'It must be a question of degree depending on the particular case, but if relative secrecy remains, the plaintiff can still succeed'.

The concept of relative secrecy has not been fully analysed in the authorities but a number of points are clear, as follows:

- The fact that information is known to a small number of people does not mean that it is no longer confidential (see, e.g. *Franchi* v. *Franchi* [1967] RPC 149, 152).
- Information which is only accessible by carrying out specialist research which requires background knowledge and the expenditure of time may still be confidential.[12] So, in *Attorney General* v. *Greater Manchester Newspapers*, (2001) *The Times*, 7 December it was held that information which was accessible in a specialist part of a public library to a person with specialist knowledge was not in the public domain. (See also *R.* v. *Solicitors Complaints Bureau, ex p. Wylde* (6 October 1996), 'information available to the public can nonetheless remain confidential where in practice it is difficult or impractical to obtain information from the public source'.)
- The fact that the public can only obtain a particular item of information on the payment of a fee or subject to some other restriction does not mean that the information is confidential. (See, e.g. *Melton Medes Ltd* v. *Securities and Investments Board* [1995] Ch 137 (information not confidential if disclosed in court because the transcript can be obtained for a fee).)
- Information is not confidential if it is generally available to the public, for example, in the press or from public records.

In relation to the second question, the law imposes a duty of confidence whenever a person receives information he knows or ought to know is fairly and reasonably to be regarded as confidential.[13] Although in the vast majority of cases, this duty will arise out of some transaction or relationship between the parties, this is not necessary to establish the duty. It is now recognised that this second requirement need not be met if it is plain that the information is confidential (*Douglas* v. *Hello! (No.3)* [2006] QB 125).

In relation to the third question, there must be an actual or threatened use of the information for a purpose other than that for which it was imparted to the confidant (see generally *Coco* v. *AN Clark (Engineers) Ltd* [1969] RPC 41). There is no need for the claimant to show detriment where personal information is involved (see *Bluck* v. *Information Commissioner*, Information Tribunal, 17 September 2007, paras.14–15). However, where the 'confider's' interest is purely a commercial one, it may be necessary to show that disclosure will cause damage.

The issues arising under the fourth question have been expressed in a number of ways in case law. Whilst considering the *Spycatcher* case Lord Goff said:

> although the basis of the law's protection of confidence is that there is a public interest that confidences should be preserved and protected by the law, nevertheless that public interest may be outweighed by some other countervailing public interest which favours disclosure. This limitation may apply, as the learned judge pointed out, to all types of confidential information. It is this limiting principle which may require a court to carry out a balancing operation, weighing the public interest in maintaining confidence against a countervailing public interest favouring disclosure
>
> (*Attorney General* v. *Guardian Newspapers (No.2)* [1990] 1 AC 109, 282)

This is sometimes referred to as a public interest defence, or could also be seen as an element of the tort.

The weighing or balancing exercise referred to by Lord Goff takes on different forms in different kinds of cases, considered below:

- In some cases the public interest in disclosure will simply outweigh the public interest in preserving confidentiality. This was once known as the iniquity defence but is now recognised as being more general.
- This principle has been held to justify disclosure of suspected criminal conduct (*Malone* v. *Metropolitan Police Commissioner* [1979] Ch 344), disclosure of fraudulent business practices (*Gartside* v. *Outram* (1857) 26 Ch 113), alleged corruption by a local authority (*Preston Borough Council* v. *McGrath* (2000) *The Times*, 19 May), dangerous medical practices which endanger the public (*Schering Chemicals Ltd* v. *Falkman Ltd* [1982] 1 QB 1), dangerous medical hazards (*W* v. *Egdell* [1990] 1 Ch 359), information about cults (*Hubbard* v. *Vosper* [1972] 2 QB 84 (in relation to a book about Scientology)) and information concerning the functioning of the Intoximeter device (*Lion Laboratories* v. *Evans* [1985] QB 526 (this case established that the justification of the disclosure of confidential information did not depend on establishing an iniquity)).
- In the rare case where commercial confidential information is also private, then, if there is a disclosure to the media, it is necessary to carry out a balancing exercise between privacy and freedom of expression (*Campbell* v. *MGN* [2004] AC 457).
- In the case of the disclosure of information concerning the expenditure of public money, there are strong freedom of expression arguments in favour of disclosure, although the public interest must be assessed on the basis of proportionality considerations arising under Art.10(2) of the European Convention on Human Rights. (See the discussion in *London Regional Transport* v. *Mayor of London* [2003] EMLR 4, especially 57–8 (Sedley LJ).)
- In the case of commercial information, it appears that the public interest in the free flow of commercial information (i.e. the same public interest

which renders contracts in restraint of trade void) means that commercial and industrial confidentiality only attaches to:

> specific information which an enterprise needs to keep confidential in order to protect its competitive position, not general knowledge of business organisation or methods.
> (*R.* v. *Secretary of State for Transport, ex p. Alliance against the Birmingham Northern Relief Road* [1999] Env LR 447, 475)

The fourth question means that although s.41 contains an absolute exemption, there is substantial opportunity for the person making the request to raise, and the public authority to consider, public interest arguments in favour of disclosure, particularly where there is any suggestion that the information relates to actual or potential wrongdoing. However, in contrast to the approach to 'qualified exemptions' under FOIA, the presumption is that confidentiality should be preserved unless outweighed by countervailing factors (see *Derry City Council* v. *Information Commissioner, Information Tribunal*, 16 December 2006, para.34(m)). (Under FOIA there is an 'assumption' rather than a 'presumption' in favour of disclosure, see *Department of Trade and Industry* v. *Commissioner, Information Tribunal*, 10 November 2006 (paras.42–3).) See also *Hertfordshire County Council* (FS50086121, 1 February 2007, para.62) in which the Information Commissioner said that, in confidentiality case 'the test applicable is . . . a balancing of the public interest in putting the information in the public domain and the public interest in maintaining the confidence; if the factors balance equally then the confidence should be maintained'.

The person making the request for disclosure can raise public interest arguments based on government openness, but these can only be general arguments and cannot be based on the FOIA itself. This is because the test as to whether information falls within the s.41 exemption is whether a disclosure otherwise than under the FOIA would constitute an actionable breach of confidence. In other words, what must be considered is whether, but for the FOIA, the disclosure of the information would have been a breach of confidence. This appears to have the result that the public interest in open access to information underlying the FOIA is not a relevant consideration and the definition of confidentiality cannot be influenced by the terms of the FOIA itself. (Contrast the position in Canada, *Air Atonabee* v. *Canada (Minister of Transport)* (1989) 27 CPR (3d) 180, 198, and the United States, *Critical Mass Energy Project* v. *Nuclear Regulatory Commission* (1991) 942 F.2d 799, D.C. Cir, CA, where the definition of 'confidentiality' under freedom of information statutes is less restrictive than at common law.)

The s.41 exemption in practice

The s.41 exemption has been relied on in a number of cases considered by the Commissioner and the Information Tribunal. It has been emphasised that a public authority which relies on this exemption needs to provide a explanation as to the basis on which it is said to be applicable. The Scottish Information Commissioner has provided a helpful checklist as what an authority is expected to provide:

- Precise details of the specific information believed to fall within the scope of the exemption;
- Details of why that specific information should be considered to have been obtained from another person;
- Details of why the information should be considered to have the necessary quality of confidence;
- Evidence that the information was received in circumstances which imposed an obligation to maintain confidentiality;
- Details of why the disclosure would cause damage to the person who communicated the information.

(*Docherty* v. *Lothian NHS Board*, Decision 190/2007, 22 October 2006, para.35)

A number of types of commercial information passing between public authorities and third parties have been found not to be exempt under this section:

- Information supplied in support of a tender did not have a 'sufficient quality of confidence' (*Pembrokeshire County Council*, FS50067633, 6 June 2006).
- Agreements between Ryanair and Derry City Council concerning the use of Derry City Airport (*Derry City Council* v. *Information Commissioner, Information Tribunal*, 11 December 2006).
- Information relating to private equity investments made by a local authority was not within the exemption because the public interest in disclosure overrode the public interest in maintaining confidentiality (*Hertfordshire County Council*, FS50086121, 1 February 2007).
- Contracts for the sale of land were not confidential, and valuations and other related material which were more than six years old no longer had the necessary quality of confidence (*Oxford City Council*, FS500090744, 1 February 2007).
- Information as to the identity of grant assessors engaged by the Department for Trade and Industry (DTI) in relation to a wave energy conversion system. The fact that the DTI had promised that the advices given by the assessors would be 'confidential' was not sufficient to imbue information as to the names of the assessors and those present at the assessment meetings with the quality of confidence for s.41 purposes (*Department for Trade and Industry*, FS50069394, 13 February 2007).

The s.41 exemption has only been successfully relied on by public authorities to resist the disclosure of information concerning private sector third parties in a small number of cases:

- A report provided to a local authority by a charitable company relating to its management of a sports arena. The Commissioner accepted that the contents of the report were confidential and that the public interest did not override the duty of confidentiality (*Boston Borough Council* FS50064581, 6 April 2006).
- A report and supporting information concerning Equitable Life was confidential and covered by express confidentiality provisions in the terms of engagement with the actuarial consultants (*Financial Services Authority*, FS50094583, 5 July 2007).
- An executable version of the economic model used by the National Institute for Clinical Excellence in its assessment of various Alzheimer's drugs. The model was confidential and, after detailed consideration of the 'public interest' considerations, the Commissioner decided its disclosure would constitute an actionable breach of confidence (*National Institute for Clinical Excellence*, FS50082569, 27 September 2007).

6.2.3   The trade secrets exemption

Trade secrets are protected by a qualified exemption. By s.43(1), information is exempt information if it constitutes a trade secret. The FOIA does not define 'trade secret' and the English courts have not sought to provide any comprehensive definition of the term (see the discussion of the English law in *Ansell Rubber Co Pty Ltd* v. *Allied Rubber Industries Pty Ltd* [1972] RPC 811) nor to define the precise difference between this and confidential business information. The definition usually cited is that set out in *Lansing Linde Ltd* v. *Kerr* [1991] 1 WLR 251:

> information which, if disclosed to a competitor, would be liable to cause real (or significant) harm to the owner of the secret. I would add first, that it must be information used in a trade or business, and secondly that the owner must limit the dissemination of it or at least not encourage or permit widespread publication.

The Information Commissioner has suggested that, when attempting to decide whether information is in fact a trade secret it is helpful to ask:

- Is the information used for the purpose of a trade?
- Is it obvious from the nature of the information or, if not, has the owner made it clear that he or she considers releasing the information would cause them harm or be advantageous to their rivals?
- Is the information already known?
- How easy would it be for competitors to discover or reproduce the information for themselves?[14]

This appears to be wide enough to cover anything which a private body does which is unique to it, which gives it a competitive edge and which is not generally known. It potentially covers not just product-related information but also working practices and approaches (Office of Government Commerce, *FOI (Civil Procurement) Policy and Guidance*, p.9; the guidance is available at **www.ogc.gov.uk/documents/FOI.pdf**).

It is plain that the notion of trade secret includes not only secret formulae for the manufacture of products but also innumerable other pieces of information, such as technical knowledge and experience associated with manufacture of particular goods, and information relating to sales, prices and customers which would be of advantage to competitors.

If a public authority is of the view that information does constitute a trade secret, then the duty to disclose and the duty to confirm or deny do not apply if public interest in maintaining the exemption outweighs public interest in disclosing the information (FOIA, s.2(2)(b)). The public interest in maintaining this exemption involves consideration of matters such as the maintenance of intellectual property rights and the need to protect the flow of commercial secrets to public authorities.

It is of the essence of a trade secret that it is confidential: if it is in the public domain it loses its quality of secrecy. It is difficult to see how the conditional exemption in s.43(1) adds anything to the absolute exemption in s.41.

6.2.4 The prejudice to commercial interests exemption[15]

If the disclosure of information is prejudicial to commercial interests then it is covered by a qualified exemption. By s.43(2), information is exempt information if its disclosure 'would, or would be likely to, prejudice the commercial interests of any person (including the public authority holding it)'.

When considering whether disclosure 'would, or would be likely to, prejudice' commercial interests, the Information Tribunal has held (*Hogan* v. *Information Commissioner* 17 October 2006, paras.30–34; see also *Derry City Council* v. *Information Commissioner* 11 December 2006, paras.17–28) that the proper approach is as follows:

- The nature of the 'prejudice' being claimed must be considered. The decision maker must show that there is some causal relationship between the potential disclosure and the prejudice and that the prejudice is 'real, actual or of substance'.
- The likelihood of the occurrence of the prejudice must be considered. 'Likely to prejudice' has been interpreted as meaning that the chance of prejudice being suffered should be more than a hypothetical or remote possibility: there must be a real or significant risk (*John Connor Press Associates* v. *Information Commissioner* 25 January 2006, para.15). The alternative limb of disclosure 'would prejudice' places a stronger evidential burden on the public authority than showing that disclosure is 'likely to prejudice'.

If a public authority is of the view that disclosure of the information would be likely to prejudice commercial interests, then the duty to disclose and the duty to confirm or deny do not apply if the public interest in maintaining the exemption outweighs the public interest in disclosing the information (FOIA, s.2(2)(b)).

The s.43 exemption in practice

The s.43 exemption has been considered by the Commissioner and the Information Tribunal in a number of cases. In some cases the public authority has failed to demonstrate that disclosure 'would or would be likely to prejudice' commercial interests. For example:

- Information concerning the payments made to an artist by the National Maritime Museum (*John Connor Press Associates* v. *Information Commissioner*, Information Tribunal, 25 January 2006).
- Information regarding the cost and sale price of shares involving Invest NI and private companies – although it was accepted that the position would have been different in relation to continuing negotiations (*Invest (Northern Ireland)* FS500739979, 24 July 2006).
- A report concerning the hull of a ship in the process of construction. The Commissioner took into account the fact that considerable information concerning a dispute between the shipbuilder and client was already in the public domain (*Maritime and Coastguard Agency*, FS50105734, 25 September 2006).
- Information about alleged malpractice by a third party some years earlier which had been found to be unproven. This did not give rise to a significant risk of reputational damage sufficient to prejudice commercial interests (*Medicines and Healthcare Products Regulatory Agency*, FS50076806, 22 January 2007).
- Information about the amounts paid to an artist commissioned to make a video portrait of David Beckham (*National Portrait Gallery*, FS50082255, 30 January 2007).
- Information as to the identity of grant assessors engaged by the DTI in relation to a wave energy conversion system (*Department for Trade and Industry*, FS50069394, 13 February 2007).
- Information as to the amounts paid by the BBC to six insurers. Although this information could enable other insurers to gain an insight into the requirements of the tender for insurance business, they would still have to go through the tender process. The insurers would not suffer real commercial prejudice as a result of other clients knowing what they charged the BBC (*BBC*, FS50105262, 27 March 2007).
- Information as to the names of companies identified as using inappropriate charges in setting premiums when selling endowment mortgages. Although s.43 was engaged, the public interest in disclosure outweighed the public interest in maintaining the exemption (*Financial Services Authority*, FS50075781, 7 August 2007).

The exemption has been successfully relied on by public authorities to resist the disclosure of a variety of information concerning private sector third parties:

- Information concerning rent, repairing terms and costs in relation to a proposed development of a surgery using a private developer (*Farndon Green Medical Centre*, FS50065663, 3 April 2006).
- Information in relation to development of land, including tender documentation supplied by developers (*Guildford Borough Council* FS50070214, 18 July 2006).
- Information concerning the operation of the Royal Mail's 'Smart Stamp' service. Disclosure was likely to allow competitors to use the technology, harm the Royal Mail's relationship with suppliers and undermine the integrity of the system (*Royal Mail*, FS50126145, 28 March 2007).
- Correspondence between the owner of an 'old master' and the National Gallery. The disclosure was likely to damage the commercial interests of the Gallery and the owner and the public interest in maintaining the exemption outweighed the public interest in disclosure (*National Gallery*, FS50107548, 21 May 2007).
- A report and supporting information concerning Equitable Life. The disclosure would damage the commercial interests of Equitable Life Assurance Services and the public interest in maintaining the exemption prevailed (*Financial Services Authority*, FS50094583, 5 July 2007).

6.2.5 Summary

In summary, the effect of these exemptions is that a public authority should not disclose information which has been supplied to it by a private body if:

- such disclosure would constitute a breach of confidence (s.41);
- the information is a trade secret (s.43(1)); or
- disclosure of the information would be likely to prejudice the private body's commercial interests (s.43(2)).

In practice, there is a high degree of overlap between the three exemptions. (Although, because the first is an absolute exemption it is likely to be the most important in practice.) For example, any detailed financial information supplied by a private body in a procurement context is likely to fall within both s.41 and s.43(2). However, information contained in contracts will usually only be protected under s.43.

Whether or not a particular piece of information falls within one of these exemptions is a fact-sensitive question which will depend on matters such as:

- the precise nature of the information: to what extent is it in the public domain, and how commercially sensitive is it?

- the circumstances in which the information was supplied to the public authority: whether, for example, it was made clear at the time that the private body regarded the information as confidential;
- when the information was supplied: other things being equal it is likely that commercial sensitivity will diminish over time and information supplied, say, five or 10 years ago is much less likely to be exempt than information supplied in relation to a current contract;[16]
- whether there are any public interest considerations: for example, in general there is a public interest in knowing how public money is spent – this may mean that public authorities will disclose global figures for sums paid under supply contracts, but not the detailed breakdown of these figures.

6.3 FOIA REQUESTS AND THE SUPPLIER OF INFORMATION

6.3.1 Introduction

The private body which has supplied confidential information or trade secrets to a public authority has no statutory right to be consulted when an applicant asks for disclosure of this information. In other words, in contrast to some other jurisdictions, there are no formal reverse freedom of information procedures: the supplier of information has no formal status under the FOIA. Under the statute, it is the public authority alone which must deal with the complex analysis required to determine whether the s.41 or s.43 exemptions apply.

There are, however, two potential ways in which a private body can protect its position in relation to FOIA requests for information which it has supplied to a public authority. These are:

- by making representations to the public authority in a process of consultation with the public authority;
- by reliance on express provision in its contracts with the public authority.

6.3.2 Consultation

Although there is no statutory right for the supplier of information to be consulted before information is disclosed, the Section 45 Code of Practice makes it clear that consultation should take place where the views of the third party may assist the public authority to determine whether an exemption applies or where the public interest lies (para.35).

Paragraph 27 of the Section 45 Code provides that:

In some cases it will be necessary to consult, directly and individually, with [those who supply public authorities with information] in order to determine whether or not an exemption applies to the information requested, or in order to reach a view on whether the obligations in section 1 of the Act arise in relation to that information. But in a range of other circumstances it will be good practice to do so; for example where a public authority proposes to disclose information relating to third parties, or information which is likely to affect their interests, reasonable steps should, where appropriate, be taken to give them advance notice, or failing that, to draw it to their attention afterwards.

This provision places public authorities under a public law obligation to consult with the suppliers of information. This obligation is enforceable in judicial review proceedings in the Administrative Court.

Where information appears to be confidential, public authorities will consult the suppliers of information. If a request for information is refused by the public authority the applicant has four levels of appeal: internal, Information Commissioner, Information Tribunal and High Court. The supplier of information needs to be kept aware of the progress of any appeal against a decision to refuse information with a view to intervening if its interests are adversely affected. (Although there is nothing in the FOIA or the Codes requiring the public authority to keep a consulted information supplier informed of the result of an appeal, it is suggested that there would be a public law duty to do so, in order to make consultation rights effective.)

If the request for information is accepted by the public authority, then the third party whose information is released has no right of appeal under the FOIA. It would, however, have two possible remedies:

- an application for judicial review of the public authority's decision to release the information;
- a High Court action for breach of confidence against the public authority.

There are no reported cases in which such applications have been made and it appears that disclosure disputes which have arisen have, to date, been dealt with by agreement.

6.3.3 Contractual provisions

Introduction

Public authorities cannot contract out of the FOIA. They may be obliged to disclose information in response to requests even if they have agreed not to do so (see later in this section). Nevertheless, the terms of contracts with private bodies may be highly relevant to the disclosure decisions which public authorities will have to make.

Many private bodies seek to impose contractual confidentiality obligations on public authorities. The Section 45 Code makes it clear that public authorities must consider these clauses with care before agreeing to them. Paragraph 32 states that:

When entering into contracts with non-public authority contractors, public authorities may be asked to accept confidentiality clauses, for example to the effect that information relating to the terms of the contract, its value and performance will not be disclosed. Public authorities should carefully consider the compatibility of such terms with their obligations under the Act. It is important that both the public authority and the contractor are aware of the limits placed by the Act on the enforceability of such confidentiality clauses.

The Commissioner draws attention to this clause in his Awareness Guidance No.2 (see p.5). However, it should be noted that the Section 45 Code makes it clear that there are circumstances in which the preservation of confidentiality between public authority and contractor is appropriate, and must be maintained, in the public interest (para.33). It suggests that where there is good reason to include non-disclosure provisions in a contract, public authorities should consider the desirability, where possible, of making express provision in the contract identifying the information which should not be disclosed and the reasons for confidentiality. The Scottish Information Commissioner has summarised the position in this way:[17]

> information should only be accepted in confidence if it is necessary for the authority to obtain that information in order to carry out its functions and it would not otherwise be provided or could not otherwise be obtained. Authorities should not agree to hold information in confidence if it is clearly not confidential in nature
> (*Foote* v. *Aberdeenshire Council*, Decision 27/2007, 12 February 2007, para.27)

Confidentiality clauses

Confidentiality clauses obviously have an important role to play in the FOI context. They are particularly helpful if they clearly identify the information that may be exempt. It should, however, be borne in mind that the terms of the contract itself cannot constitute 'information' for the purposes of s.41: in order to provide protection the clause should relate to information supplied whether as part of the tender process or in accordance with the terms of the contract itself (see **6.2.2**).

Although information covered by a confidentiality clause will not automatically attract the protection of s.41, a well-drawn confidentiality clause will be of considerable assistance to the public authority when it is considering an FOIA request.[18]

Clearly, a confidentiality clause will not be compatible with the FOIA if it relates to information which is not, in fact, confidential. In such circumstances, the public authority will be obliged to disclose the information to an applicant (unless, of course, some other exemption applies).

Public authorities will take particular exception to confidentiality clauses which purport to give private bodies a veto over the disclosure of any information, whatever its precise status.

In order to provide maximum protection in the context of FOIA applications, a confidentiality clause should:

- carefully identify (if necessary by reference to a schedule) the information which is said to be confidential. It is important that the clause is not too widely drawn. The more widely drawn the clause the greater the risk that the public authority will disclose in any event;
- give the reasons why the information is confidential (again, this could be in a schedule) (Section 45 Code, para.34). A provision to this effect is likely to be useful both to the public authority when responding to an FOIA request and to the private body when it is being consulted by the public authority.

It should be noted that the FOIA does not affect the contractual position as between the public authority and a private body. If a public authority agrees that it will not disclose information in a particular category, then a disclosure of such information will constitute a breach of contract even if the public authority had an obligation to disclose. In other words, because no FOIA exemption applied, e.g. even if information is not, in fact, confidential within the meaning of s.41 this will not prevent its disclosure from being a breach of a provision which deems it to be confidential. The Information Commissioner has pointed out that public authorities risk putting themselves in a dilemma: where they cannot avoid breaching either their statutory or their contractual obligations (see Information Commissioner *Annexe to Awareness Guidance No.5: Public Sector Contracts* (updated January 2006), p.3). This point may be of particular importance in relation to pre-FOIA contracts with very widely drawn confidentiality clauses.

Consultation provisions

The Section 45 Code suggests that express consultation provisions might be included in public authority contracts (Section 45 Code, para.34). Although there is no English case law on the topic, such a clause would plainly be enforceable. (This was accepted by the New Zealand Court of Appeal in *Astra Pharmaceuticals* v. *Pharmaceutical Management Agency Limited* [2000] NZCA 345, para.37.) The point could be dealt with simply by making it a contractual requirement that the public authority consults with the private body according to an agreed timescale. Bearing in mind the fact that a public authority, in general, has only 20 days to respond to a FOIA request (FOIA, s.10(1)), the timescale must necessarily be a tight one. The following is suggested:

- notification by the public authority of requests within five working days;
- a response by private body within five days;
- notification by the public authority of its disclosure decision within three days.

It may also be useful to include a contractual mechanism for resolving disputes. This could involve, for example, the appointment of an agreed person as adjudicator to decide whether or not a particular exemption applied. However, it is again important to bear in mind the tight timescales laid down by the FOIA, and any adjudication mechanism must be capable of dealing with disputes within a matter of a few days.

If a dispute cannot be resolved by consultation or a dispute resolution mechanism then, in the last resort, it will be necessary to seek an interim injunction to restrain disclosure. This could be sought in the Administrative Court (in the course of an action to challenge the decision to disclose). However, in a s.41 case the most straightforward course will be to seek an injunction in the Chancery Division to restrain a breach of confidence. It should, however, be noted that if the FOIA applicant is a media organisation (or is a person intending to publish the information sought) the test for granting an injunction will not be the balance of convenience but the higher test of whether the applicant would be likely to succeed at trial.[19] As at the time of writing, there are no reported cases in which such an application has been made.

6.4 PRACTICAL STEPS FOR PROTECTING INFORMATION

6.4.1 Introduction

Against this statutory and contractual background, it is now possible to consider the practical steps which private bodies can take to protect their information from disclosure. It has been suggested that:

> The logical framework for the steps which need to be taken to protect confidential information is based on answers to the following questions:
>
> - who in the company provides what information to which public authorities?
> - is it clearly recognised which parts of this information are confidential, why and for how long?
> - is confidentiality claimed effectively when or before the information is submitted?
> - has the system been tested to give assurance that the company's information is being treated appropriately by the public authority, and does the public authority have up to date details of who to contact if requests are made for access to it?
> (Amos and Innes, *A Guide for Business to the Freedom of Information Act 2000* (Constitution Unit), 2001)

These questions can usefully be addressed under two general headings:

- *information audit and other steps:* covering the identification of the commercially sensitive information which has been and is being provided to public authorities, and review of the effectiveness of confidentiality arrangements;

- *cooperation with public authorities:* ranging from informal approaches to ascertain the approach being taken to disclosure, to agreed contractual mechanisms for dealing with FOIA issues.

These measures are considered further below.

It should be borne in mind that an essential first step for any private body is to raise awareness amongst its own staff. Staff involved in the provision of information to public authorities, in particular those in sales, marketing and management positions, should be familiar with the way in which the FOIA operates and of the detail of the exemptions. They should also be apprised of the way in which information is likely to be handled by public authorities.

6.4.2   Information audit and other steps

Introduction

There are a number of possible steps to be taken in order to protect commercially valuable information from disclosure under the FOIA:

- a review should be conducted of the information given to public authorities in the past;
- clear policies and procedures should be established for the management of information and for claiming confidentiality;
- care should be taken, in particular, to segregate information into that which is confidential and that which is non-confidential, and the basis on which confidentiality is being claimed should be clearly set out.

Past information

Private bodies should begin by reviewing the commercially sensitive material which has been submitted to public authorities in the past. Particular areas of concern include:

- tender documentation;
- supply contracts;
- service performance reports;
- collaborative private/public research results;
- information supplied to regulators – for example, in the context of an investigation or inquiry.

Different public authorities are likely to take different approaches to the disclosure of these types of information. It should, however, be noted that the Office of Government Commerce has produced an *Information Disclosure Policy* which deals in detail with information obtained at each stage of the contract process, setting out working assumptions about disclosure (see Office of Government Commerce, *FOI (Civil Procurement) Policy and Guidance*, Annex A, pp.31–35; the guidance is available at **www.ogc. gov.uk/documents/FOI.pdf**).

When material has been identified, an assessment of its continuing sensitivity should be carried out. As a general rule, the older the material the less sensitive it is likely to be. When the sensitive material has been identified then one or more of the following steps can be taken:

- Some material may no longer be needed by the public authority – for example, detailed tender documentation where the bid was not successful. In these circumstances, the public authority could be asked to return the material and to confirm that it no longer holds copies.
- Where it is clear that the public authority continues to require the material, it could be asked to provide express confirmation that it recognises that it is confidential (or is a trade secret) and that it would apply the s.41 or s.43(1) exemptions if an FOIA request is made for this information.
- If the material is such that disclosure would cause prejudice to the private body, then a written explanation of the prejudice could be given to the public authority and its confirmation could be sought that it would apply the s.43(2) exemption if an FOIA request is made for this information.

In relation to material which is already held, the public authority could be asked to agree a consultation procedure of the type which private sector bodies would wish to include in future contracts (see **6.3.3**). Such a procedure would, potentially, be of advantage to both the public authority and the supplier of the information as it would provide informed input into the disclosure decision, and a degree of protection for the public authority against breach of confidence claims.

Future disclosure

In relation to future contracts, an audit can be conducted at the pre-tender stage in order to ascertain what information is likely to be sensitive in the future and how long it is likely to remain sensitive. When this has been done the information could be listed in an appendix to the contract (this approach is suggested by the Information Commissioner; see *Annexe to Awareness Guidance No.5: Public Sector Contracts*, p.2). The Office of Government Commerce has suggested that this approach should be taken and that discussions on this point should be included within general contract negotiations (see Office of Government Commerce, *FOI (Civil Procurement) Policy and Guidance*, p.6).

A number of practical measures might be taken when preparing and submitting documents to public authorities.

- Sensitive material could be clearly marked and segregated to avoid the risk of inadvertent disclosure. Confidential documents could be watermarked or supplied in a different form or on paper of a different colour from non-confidential ones.

- In some circumstances, documents could be submitted in two versions: one disclosable and one confidential.
- Consideration should be given to whether it is necessary to hand over information to public authorities. In some circumstances, documents could be made available for inspection only.
- Private bodies should avoid providing additional voluntary information to public authorities.
- A record should be kept of all sensitive information supplied, the claims for confidentiality which have been made and the grounds for such claims given to the public authority.

Monitoring

If a private sector body has concerns that a public authority is likely to make inappropriate disclosures of its information, then a simple cross-check can be carried out using a third party or surrogate data agency[20] – what has been called the 'mystery shopper' procedure. An FOIA request can be made for the information from the public authority to see whether it will, in fact, be disclosed.

6.4.3   Cooperation with public authorities

It is obviously of central importance for private bodies to establish effective communication with public authorities in relation to FOIA disclosure issues. The aim of such communication is to:

- identify the kinds of information which should be kept from disclosure;
- establish a mechanism for consultation in relation to FOIA requests;
- agree confidentiality provisions and procedures for identifying sensitive material;
- agree policies for document retention and return.

As already discussed, private bodies should take the provisions of the FOIA into account when entering into new contracts with public authorities (see **6.3.3**). This should be discussed at the tendering stage and properly drawn contracts should contain clear express provision in relation to confidentiality and consultation. Useful general guidance on both is provided by the Office of Government Commerce (*FOI (Civil Procurement) Policy and Guidance*), which has also prepared model confidentiality clauses (see Office of Government Commerce, 'Model Confidentiality Clauses', available at **www.ogc.gov.uk/ documents/Model_FOIA_confidentiality_clauses.doc**).

6.5 MAKING USE OF THE FOIA

The FOIA can be an important business tool. A substantial proportion of freedom of information requests in the United States are made by businesses seeking information concerning their competitors and the activities of government. There have been a number of requests by UK businesses aimed at obtaining such information under the FOIA. For example, in one case the Information Commissioner ordered disclosure of information about private equity investments made by a local authority requested by an employee of a company which collated and sold statistical reports on investment funds and investment opportunities (*Hertfordshire County Council*, FS50086121, 1 February 2007).

A private sector body which believes that public authorities might hold information which is of commercial value to it should carefully target its requests, perhaps engaging the services of a surrogate data agency with experience of making requests. A useful technique is the so-called 'jigsaw' request – seeking by means of a number of coordinated requests to identify the missing pieces of the information jigsaw.

The useful information available under the FOIA could include:

- details of previous bids by competitors, including matters such as pricing, personnel levels and competency;
- contract compliance and performance data, which reveal how competitors' contracts have been performed;
- background information relating to procurement decisions and the regulatory climate, for example, working party and consultants' reports;
- clients' evaluation criteria, which show exactly how previous bids have been evaluated and contract decisions reached;
- the health and safety records of competitors or reports of health inspectors.

It should be remembered that not all transactions between the public and private sectors are subject to contracts. Information relating to some of these more informal dealings will generally be less restricted. FOIA requests could be made in relation to subjects such as lobbying of government departments, or hospitality provided by competitors to public authorities.

6.6 CONCLUSION

Although the FOIA has no direct application to the private sector, it is likely to have a significant impact on the activities of any private body which has substantial dealings with the public sector. Suppliers of goods and services to the public sector must carefully consider the information which they have provided, and will in the future provide, in the course of contractual relationships or other dealings. In the absence of careful protective measures there is a serious risk that sensitive material may become available to competitors and the media. The provisions of the FOIA are complex and, in relation to commercially sensitive material, import complex private law concepts. Public authorities require careful guidance as to the types of information which they can properly disclose to applicants under the FOIA. Contracts should be drafted to identify the material which is sensitive and the general reasons why it is sensitive. The consultation provisions of the Section 45 Code should be strengthened by express contractual mechanisms.

The FOIA also presents an important opportunity for the private sector to obtain commercially useful information from the public sector. A vast range of material is available in relation to both the activities and approach of government and the activities of commercial rivals.

NOTES

1   The duty to disclose applies to information held at the time when the request was received – it does not matter when the information was provided. In that sense, the FOIA has retrospective effect, covering information supplied to or obtained by public authorities at any time in the past.
2   That is, bodies listed in Sched.1 to the FOIA (to which the Financial Services Authority and a number of others have been added since enactment) and 'publicly owned companies' as defined by s.6. Lord Falconer stated that over 100,000 public authorities are subject to the FOIA.
3   Applications can be made by any person and the reason for the application is, in general, irrelevant. Applications can be made anonymously through surrogate data agencies – i.e. agencies which make requests in their own names so that the public authority does not know the identity of the ultimate client.
4   Public authorities can charge for photocopying and postage but will not charge for the costs of locating the information if this is less than £450 (on the basis of £25 per person-hour), or £600 in the case of central government.
5   See Frontier Economics, *Independent Review of the Impact of the Human Rights Act*, October 2006, p.35: 60 per cent of requests were from private individuals and 10 per cent from journalists.
6   See *Freedom of Information Act 2000: Designation of additional public authorities*, Consultation Paper CP 27/07, 25 October 2007. The options being considered include building information obligations into contracts and making an order under s.5 of FOIA to designate private contractors as public authorities in respect of certain functions or services.
7   This is a complex exemption which has some qualified elements and is therefore sometimes described as a hybrid exemption, see **Chapter 8** for a full discussion.
8   See generally, Information Commissioner, *Freedom of Information Act Awareness Guidance No.2: Information provided in confidence* (updated January 2006).
9   See Lord Falconer, Hansard HL, Vol.617, 17 October 2000, col.2; see the discussion in P. Coppel, *Information Law* (2007), §25–007; and see Department for Trade and Industry, FS50069394, 13 February 2007, para.42.6: 'A mere chance of success is not sufficient to satisfy s.41'.
10 It should be noted that the position is now slightly different in relation to private information – misuse of private information is developing as a separate tort (see

Campbell v. *MGN* [2004] 2 AC 457 and *Douglas* v. *Hello! (No.3)* [2006] QB 125). In the present context we are concerned with commercially confidential information and breach of confidence is the relevant form of the tort.

11 For the first three, see *Coco* v. *A N Clark (Engineers) Ltd* [1969] RPC 41, 47; *Murray* v. *Yorkshire Fund Managers* [1998] 1 WLR 951; as to the fourth see *Lion Laboratories* v. *Evans* [1985] QB 526 and *Attorney General* v. *Guardian Newspapers (No.2)* [1990] 1 AC 109, 214 and (in relation to private information), *Campbell* v. *MGN* [2004] 2 AC 457.

12 See the discussion in F. Gurry, *Breach of Confidence* (1984), pp.70–1.

13 Per Lord Nicholls, *Campbell* v. *MGN* [2004] 2 AC 457, §14: in relation to information about an individual's private life the tort is now better described as 'misuse of private information', see note 10.

14 Freedom of Information Act, Awareness Guidance No.5, p.3; see also *Smith* v. *Dundee City Council*, Scottish Information Commissioner Decision 216/2006, 28 February 2006, paras.30–8 and see *Searle Australia* v. *Public Interest Advocacy Centre* (1992) 108 ALR 163.

15 See generally, Information Commissioner, *Freedom of Information Act Awareness Guidance No.5: Commercial Interests*.

16 In *Cartlidge* v. *Scottish Executive* (Decision 28/2005, 3 October 2005) the Scottish Information Commissioner noted that 'Information contained in concluded and terminated contracts decreases in sensitivity with the passage of time' but concluded that, in relation to a contract which terminated some eight months before the request, 'not enough time has passed . . . to sufficiently degrade the commercial sensitivity of the information'.

17 See also his pre-FOIA decision in *Sturgeon* v. *Scottish Prison Service* (Case 02/04, 24 November 2004) in which he said 'companies must be made aware that if they expect to be successful in bidding for contracts paid for from the public purse, then they will operate under reasonable terms of scrutiny and openness provided for by the freedom of information legislation' (para.60).

18 See generally, Information Commissioner *Annexe to Awareness Guidance No.5: Public Sector Contracts* (updated, January 2006), p.3.

19 As laid down by s.12(3) of the Human Rights Act 1998, see *Cream Holdings* v. *Banerjee* [2005] 1 AC 253.

20 For this term see note 2 above.

CHAPTER 7

Freedom of information and the media

Keith Mathieson, Reynolds Porter Chamberlain

7.1 INTRODUCTION

The word 'media' does not appear anywhere in the Freedom of Information Act 2000 (FOIA). The FOIA does not give the media any kind of preferential treatment. Newspapers, broadcasters and journalists have the same rights of access as everyone else.

Nonetheless, there are at least two good reasons for considering the application of the FOIA to the media.

First, the media collectively are among the most frequent users of the FOIA. Lord Falconer, the Secretary of State for Constitutional Affairs at the time the Act came into force, said that in the first month of the FOIA's operation about half of the requests made of central government came from people identifying themselves as reporters.[1] More recently, Lord Falconer claimed that government-commissioned research showed that journalists accounted for about 16 per cent of the costs of FOI requests of central government.[2]

Secondly, the law recognises that the media occupy a unique position in society and enjoy certain special privileges. The courts have recognised the media's function as the eyes and ears of the public and have confirmed the importance of the role discharged by the media, including investigative journalists, in the expression and communication of information. Most people only hear of information obtained through the FOIA via the media.

It would not be going too far to say that if the FOIA fails the media, then it fails the public.

7.2 EXPERIENCE SO FAR

In the period of almost three years since the FOIA came into force, it has undergone a fairly thorough road test by journalists. Authoritative data concerning the success rates of FOI requests by the media is not available. Published material suggests, however, that the experience has been mixed (information in this section, where not otherwise attributed, is derived from *Media Lawyer*, March 2005).

7.3   MEDIA SUCCESSES – INFORMATION OBTAINED

There are numerous instances of the successful exercise by the media of rights of access to information under the FOIA. Some of these successes have been a straightforward outcome of the FOIA process; others have been obtained only after lengthy appeals to the Information Commissioner and the Information Tribunal.

The *Financial Times* (FT) obtained some 300 pages of documents in response to a request of the Treasury for 'details of government studies on the aftermath and lessons to be learnt from Black Wednesday [i.e. 16 September 1992, the day the UK withdrew sterling from the European Exchange Rate Mechanism]'. The manner in which the FT's request was handled sheds interesting light on central government's approach to freedom of information requests and will be explored further later in this chapter.

The *Guardian* has published a number of important stories based upon information released pursuant to freedom of information requests. On 23 March 2005 it published for the first time details of EU subsidies received by British farmers and agricultural companies. On 16 March 2005, following 36 simultaneous FOI applications, it published national data about the individual mortality rates of cardiac surgeons practising in the NHS.

On 8 January 2007 the *Guardian*, together with Heather Brooke, the FOI campaigner, won a victory at the Information Tribunal for disclosure of the minutes of a BBC Governors' meeting in the wake of the Hutton Report on the circumstances surrounding the death of Dr David Kelly and the subsequent resignation of the BBC's Chairman and Director General.

The BBC has a dedicated web page (**http://news.bbc.co.uk/1/hi/in_depth/ uk/2006/foi**) headed 'How the BBC has used the Freedom of Information Act'. This details numerous stories, among the more recent of which concern the number of foreigners stopped for drink driving, the contents of documents generated by Gordon Brown while Rector of Edinburgh University and the cost of police investigations into the Channel 4 show 'Big Brother'.

In February 2007, following a ruling by the Information Tribunal, the Department for Education and Skills was required to comply with a request by the *Evening Standard* for disclosure of the minutes of high-level meetings within the department about the 2003 schools funding crisis.

Regional newspapers and broadcasters have taken advantage of the FOIA to obtain from local government and other decentralised bodies all kinds of information such as details of private finance schemes to build local hospitals and pay hikes for chief fire officers.

7.4   MEDIA FAILURES – INFORMATION REFUSED

By no means all applications by the media for disclosure of information have been successful. One newspaper group has said it is the information that has been refused, rather than that provided, which has characterised its experience of the FOIA so far.

In a front page article on 2 February 2005 headed 'Is this freedom of information?', *The Independent* listed 10 freedom of information requests it had made together with the answers received:

- *Iraq war: legal advice*

  Q: Please disclose the legal advice given by the Attorney General on the legality of the war with Iraq.

  A: No. It is exempt as legally privileged information. (Attorney General)

- *Iraq war: legal discussions*

  Q: Please disclose all ministerial and senior military officer correspondence on the subject of the legality of the war/conflict with Iraq.

  A: No. There is no obligation under the Act to disclose this information. (Ministry of Defence)

- *Railways*

  Q: Please disclose material concerning Stephen Byers' decision to declare Railtrack insolvent in autumn 2001.

  A: It would not be possible to respond to this request within the appropriate cost limit. (Department for Transport)

- *Olympic bid*

  Q. Please disclose the assessment of the original candidates to head the Olympic bid following interviews that led to the appointment of Barbara Cassani.

  A. No. Interview notes have probably been disposed of. (Greater London Authority)

- *Belmarsh*

  Q: Please disclose all the open evidence against the Belmarsh detainees.

  A: No, this would be too costly. Some of the information might also be exempt. (Home Office)

- *Primary schools*

  Q: How many primary schools in England still have outside lavatories?

  A: The department does not hold this information. (Department for Education and Skills)

- *Lord Irvine's flat*

  Q: Please disclose documents relating to the redecoration of the Lord Chancellor's residence, including costings, since 1997.

  A: No. The question is almost certain to exceed the appropriate cost limit. (Department for Constitutional Affairs)

- *Smoking*

  Q: Please let us see papers relating to the DTI investigation into BAT.

  A: The department holds such information, [but] the information itself is being withheld as it falls under the exemption in section 44 of the Act. (DTI)

- *Casinos*

  Q: Please provide minutes of meetings held between officials at the Department of Culture, Media and Sport and executives of US gaming companies.

  A: We need extra time to determine if this is in the public interest. (DCMS)

The Independent claimed to have made 70 FOI inquiries of which only 10 had been successful. In the newspaper's view, the government's new era of openness more closely resembled a catalogue of obfuscation and evasion. Other newspapers have reported similar experiences. Indeed, the FOIA has generated a new kind of news story in which the refusal of government to provide information in response to a FOIA request becomes the story itself.

A paper by the Constitution Unit of University College, London published on 24 April 2007 sought to explore how journalists had used the FOIA during its first 21 months of implementation. The authors' findings were based primarily on interviews with journalists but drew also on an analysis of national newspaper articles in which information obtained through the FOIA appeared. The paper found that there was significant disappointment with the operation of the FOIA, in particular with the slow response time and the ineffectiveness of the system of appeals against refusals.

The in-house lawyer for one national newspaper group has spoken publicly about her group's experience of central government's approach to freedom of information requests.[3] She highlighted the following tendencies:

- unacceptably undifferentiated reasons for refusal, e.g. saying 'all the information falls within one or more of the following exemptions';
- lack of particularity when explaining the basis for reliance on exemptions;
- failure to provide advice and assistance (as required by FOIA, s.15) by, for example, referring the journalist to another government department;
- unexplained redaction of documents;
- identical refusals from different departments in response to slightly different requests, suggesting pre-prepared and/or centralised responses.

7.5   HOW EFFECTIVE IS THE FOIA FOR THE MEDIA?

It is impossible to obtain reliable and systematic data on the use of FOIA by the media. Journalists are not required to identify themselves when making FOIA requests and while published articles often reveal the source of stories to be information obtained pursuant to FOIA requests, those articles by their nature concern only successful requests and not those requests in which public authorities have refused to give the information requested. Nonetheless, as studies such as those of the Constitution Unit cited above demonstrate, it is still possible to reach some conclusions concerning the effectiveness of FOIA for the media. Such conclusions are based not just on practical experience but also on certain inherent features of the FOIA. So far as the media are concerned, the most serious drawbacks of the FOIA are as follows:

1. the width and variety of the applicable exemptions;
2. the public interest test;
3. the fee regime;
4. the time for compliance;
5. the cumbersome appeals procedure; and
6. the lack of any specific protection from civil action arising from publication of information released under the FOIA.

This chapter deals with each of these issues in turn and there will also be consideration of the way in which public authorities may seek to limit the impact of freedom of information. Additionally, some practical ways in which the media can make the most of the FOIA are suggested.

7.5.1 The exemptions

The exemptions are explored in detail in **Chapters 4** and **5**. The purpose of mentioning them here is because collectively they constitute the greatest impediment to the flow of information to the media.

It is hard to exaggerate the sheer breadth of the exemptions contained in the FOIA. The scope and complexity of the exemptions are graphically illustrated by the amount of space they take up in the FOIA itself. While the general right of access to information held by public authorities occupies a few lines of one section of the FOIA, the exemptions occupy no fewer than 24 lengthy sections plus an additional section outlining their general effect. The Department for Constitutional Affair's (DCA) guidance notes on the exemptions are voluminous. The guidance notes to s.26 (Defence), for example, which are not untypical, cover 13 printed pages (*FOI full exemptions guidance*, available at **www.foi.gov.uk/guidance/exguide/sec26/chap01.htm**). The *General Guidance on Use of Exemptions in the FOI Act* covers 21 printed pages (available at **www.foi.gov.uk/guidance/exguide/intro/index.htm**).

The number and scale of the exemptions offer public authorities immense scope for withholding information in response to media, or indeed other, requests. Moreover, the exemptions cover the very areas – crime, immigration, national security, law enforcement, government policy, etc. – in which the media are most interested.

The following categories of exemption are those most commonly encountered by the media, particularly when dealing with central government:

Information supplied by, or relating to, bodies dealing with security matters (s.23)

This provision, which confers an absolute exemption, potentially covers a very wide category of information. In the words of the DCA's procedural guidance:

> In so far as the exemption relates to the source, rather than the content of the information it is not possible to give an indicative list of the types of information that may be covered by section 23. In so far as the application of the exemption turns on whether information 'relates' to the security bodies, it will be capable of covering a range of subject matter of a policy, operational or administrative nature. In relation to any particular item of information, it will be a matter of fact as to whether it falls under section 23 or not. However this may sometimes be a question of degree, or indeed be difficult to ascertain if evidence relating to the origin of the information is not available or is inconclusive. Each request that potentially involves sensitive information, has a national security element or relates, even indirectly, to the Security Bodies, will need to be considered on a case by case basis to ensure that a correct response is made. Where there is any doubt, the originator of the document containing the information should be consulted. Particular consideration needs to be given to cases where no specific information from or relating to a security body is held, but that absence could in itself amount to information falling within this exemption – for example by confirming an absence of security involvement in circumstances where that absence was a significant fact.
>
> (DCA, *FOI full exemptions guidance* 'Section 23 – Information Supplied by, or Related to, Bodies Dealing with Security Matters', ch.2, available at **www.foi.gov.uk/guidance/exguide/sec23/chap02.htm**)

A further twist is that, if a public authority reveals that it has no information supplied by or relating to a security body, that fact may itself amount to information about the security body:

> Officials should bear in mind that acknowledging that no information supplied by or relating to any of the Security Bodies is held may in itself constitute information about one of the Security Bodies, and that in some circumstances it may be appropriate to apply the 'neither confirm nor deny' provision under section 23(5) *even when no information is held* [emphasis added].
>
> (DCA, *FOI full exemptions guidance* 'Section 23 – Information Supplied by, or Related to, Bodies Dealing with Security Matters', ch.3, available at **www.foi.gov.uk/guidance/exguide/sec23/chap03.htm**)

Two decisions by the Information Commissioner serve to demonstrate the use of the exemption in practice. In both cases the public authority's reliance on the exemption was upheld.

In the first case[4] the complainant asked North Yorkshire Police (NYP) for information about the cost to the force of policing protests at RAF Menwith Hill. NYP refused to provide the information, citing (albeit at a late stage) the exemption contained in s.23. The Commissioner decided that s.23 was engaged and being an absolute exemption, was not subject to the public interest test. NYP was therefore entitled to withhold the information.

In the second case[5] the complainant asked the Cabinet Office whether the Wilson Doctrine remained in force and on how many occasions MPs' phones had been tapped. The Doctrine states that if the telephone calls of Members of Parliament are tapped, the Prime Minister will make an announcement to that effect at a time he judges to be consistent with the requirements of national security; equally, any alteration to the Doctrine would be similarly announced when the Prime Minister considered it safe to do so. The Cabinet Office refused the request, relying on s.23 (and also s.24), and declined to confirm or deny whether it held the requested information. The Commissioner upheld the refusal of the request.

Investigations and proceedings conducted by public authorities (s.30); law enforcement (s.31)

These closely connected categories of exemption are qualified exemptions and are therefore subject to the application of the public interest test.

In outline, s.30 covers (a) information held for the purposes of any investigation conducted by the public authority with a view to criminal proceedings; or (b) information obtained or recorded by the authority for the purposes of various kinds of investigation, including those of a criminal nature, and which relates to the obtaining of information from confidential sources.

As the DCA guidance notes point out, s.30 is plainly directed towards police investigations and also to criminal investigations conducted by a wide variety of other bodies such as HM Revenue and Customs and the Health and Safety Executive (DCA, *FOI full exemptions guidance* 'Section 30 – Investigations and Proceedings Conducted by Public Authorities', ch.2, available at **www.foi.gov.uk/guidance/exguide/sec30/chap02.htm**). The wording of the section is sufficiently wide to put most information held by police forces and other bodies exercising powers of criminal investigation well beyond reach of the media.

To the extent that s.30 does not apply, s.31 may nevertheless justify the withholding of information.

Section 31 makes exempt information the disclosure of which could prejudice a wide variety of law enforcement interests, including the prevention or detection of crime, the administration of justice, the collection of taxes and the operation of immigration controls. However, the section extends well beyond what most of us would recognise as law enforcement. It makes exempt, for example, information the disclosure of which could prejudice a public authority's investigation into the cause of an accident.

As the guidance note to s.31 makes clear: 'This exemption covers a very large number of aspects of what may generally be termed "law enforcement" ' (DCA, *FOI full exemptions guidance* 'Section 31 – Law Enforcement', available at **www.foi.gov.uk/guidance/exguide/sec31/chap01.htm**).

Between them ss.30 and 31 draw something of a veil over the work of law enforcement agencies generally. In one case concerning the application of s.30[6] the complainant requested from Surrey Police CCTV footage relating to the highly publicised murder of schoolgirl Milly Dowler in 2002. The footage was understood to show the last public sighting of Milly. The police refused to provide this information, citing s.30. The Information Commissioner upheld the refusal, being satisfied that the public interest in maintaining the exemption outweighed the public interest in disclosure.

In other cases, however, the Commissioner has declined to uphold the public authority's reliance on ss.30 and 31. One such case[7] concerned a request for information on a number of thefts from Royal Mail delivery vans. Other cases concerned the release of a 'private' letter to Tony Blair from the Financial Services Authority[8] and the publication of information on the number and rank of judges and magistrates who had been disciplined for misuse of departmental computer systems, including for the use of viewing pornography.[9]

Court records, etc. (s.32)

Information held by the courts is fully outside the scope of the FOIA because courts are not public authorities for the purposes of the FOIA.

One might nonetheless think that information in court records held by other public authorities might be accessible. Unfortunately this is not the case. Section 32 provides an additional obstacle to media organisations wishing to obtain information deriving from court documents as it provides an absolute exemption for such information if it is held by public authorities only by virtue of being contained in a document filed with a court, served on or by a public authority, or created by a court for the purposes of proceedings in a particular matter. Those proceedings may include inquests and arbitrations.

This wide category of information would cover information contained in all kinds of court documents, including statements of case and witness statements. It is important to note that the exemption applies only where the information is held by the public only by virtue of being contained in a document of the description set out in s.32. If the information is held by virtue of some other reason, the exemption does not apply.

One case considered by the Information Commissioner[10] concerned a request by an applicant for all information in files relating to his complaint to the Patent Office. The Patent Office disclosed all the information it held apart from one statement. Release of the statement was refused as it was created solely for the purpose of an inquiry under the Register of Patent Agent Rules 1978 and therefore exempt under s.32(2)(a). The Commissioner upheld the Patent Office's reliance on the exemption.

Parliamentary privilege (s.34)

Section 34, which is an absolute exemption, covers an extensive range of parliamentary material.

The DCA's guidance confirms the wide scope of the exemption (DCA, *FOI full exemptions guidance* 'Section 34 – Parliamentary Privilege', available at **www.foi.gov.uk/guidance/exguide/sec34/chap02.htm**). It says that the exemption is most likely to be relevant to information contained in documents in the following categories:

- committee reports, and drafts thereof;
- memoranda submitted to committees, and drafts thereof;
- internal papers prepared by the Officers of either House directly related to the proceedings of the House or committees (including advice of all kinds to the Speaker or Lord Chancellor or other occupants of the Chair in either House, briefs for the chairmen and other members of committees, and informal notes of deliberative meetings of committees);
- papers prepared by the Libraries of either House, or by other House agencies such as the Parliamentary Office of Science and Technology, either for general dissemination to Members or to assist individual Members, which relate to, or anticipate, debates and other proceedings of the relevant House or its committees, and are intended to assist Members in preparation for such proceedings;
- correspondence between Members, Officers, Ministers and government officials directly related to House proceedings;
- papers relating to investigations by the Parliamentary Commissioner for Standards;
- papers relating to the Registers of Members' Interests;
- Bills, amendments and motions, including those in draft, where they originate from Parliament or a Member rather than from Parliamentary Counsel or another government department.

Additionally, the DCA advises public authorities that particular care should be taken in relation to requests for information about or contained in:

- any of the unpublished working papers of a select committee of either House, including factual briefs or briefs of suggested questions prepared by the committee staff for the use of committee chairmen and/or other members, and draft reports: these are most likely to be in the possession of a department as a result of a Minister being, or having been, a member of such a committee;
- any legal advice submitted in confidence by the Law Officers or by the legal branch of any other department to the Speaker, a committee chairman or a committee, or any official of either House (even if s.42 (legal professional privilege) would in any case be likely to apply);
- drafts of motions, bills or amendments, which have not otherwise been published or laid on the Table of either House;
- any unpublished correspondence between Ministers (or departmental officials) on the one hand, and, on the other hand, any member or official of

either House, relating specifically to proceedings on any Question, draft bill, motion or amendment, either in the relevant House, or in a committee;
• any correspondence with or relating to the proceedings of the Parliamentary Commissioner for Standards or the Registrar of Members' Interests in the House of Commons.

The Information Commissioner has upheld a claim by the Treasury Committee of the House of Commons for a s.34 exemption in respect of a request for three files. The files contained correspondence, briefs and a draft report from the Treasury Committee's 1995–1996 inquiry into 'Financial services regulation: self-regulation at Lloyd's of London'.

Formulation of government policy (s.35); prejudice to effective conduct of public affairs (s.36)

The scope of the exemption for information relating to the formulation and development of policy has been something of a battleground between the media and government. The exemption has been the subject of three important rulings by the Information Tribunal: *DfES* v. *Information Commissioner* (EA/2006/0006); *Secretary of State for Work and Pensions* v. *Information Commissioner* (EA/2006/0040); and *HM Treasury* v. *Information Commissioner* (EA/2006/0041). In all three cases the Tribunal upheld, or largely upheld, the Commissioner's decisions that the exemption did not apply to the information in question.

It is apparent from these rulings that central government departments have been insufficiently rigorous in their determination of the considerations which properly govern application of the exemption. In the Work and Pensions case the Tribunal observed that the department:

> made no real attempt in the Refusal Notice to consider factors in favour of disclosure in order to undertake the balancing exercise required under section 2(2)(b). Even in the evidence before this Tribunal the [department] appears to have made no serious attempt to rectify this position and . . . only seemed to recognise one public interest in favour of disclosure, namely informed public debate. Instead the [department] has concentrated on putting forward factors in favour of maintaining the exemption. These factors have been largely put forward at a general level as they might apply to any claim for a section 35(1)(a) exemption, and have not necessarily been applied to all the circumstances of this case.

At para.75 of its judgment in the DfES case the Tribunal set out the correct principles to be applied in relation to s.35. These principles have been adopted in subsequent cases and it is to be hoped that central government will take careful note of the relevant principles before placing future reliance on the exemption. The Tribunal has made it very clear that government has been wrong to treat what is plainly a qualified exemption as tantamount to an absolute exemption. It has stressed the importance of considering the specific information in question in each case rather than relying on general objections of principle to the release of policy-related information. It has set out the correct basis on which the public interest balancing exercise should be undertaken. And while accepting that disclosure of discussions of policy options, whilst policy is in the process of formulation, is highly unlikely to be in the public interest, the Tribunal has urged a rigorous approach to the analysis of the information in question, including issues of timing, in determining whether the information should be released. The Tribunal has rejected the notion that the process of a policy development and formulation is a 'seamless web': there may be distinct stages of policy formulation, each of which may require separate consideration. Finally, the Tribunal has emphasised in the context of s.35 the assumption underlying the FOIA that the disclosure of information held by public authorities is in itself of value and in the public interest.

There has been a tendency on the part of government to rely in support of the s.36 exemption on blanket assertions similar to those advanced in support of the s.35 exemption. The Tribunal has made it equally clear in relation to s.36 that mere assertion of harm is not enough to ground a valid claim for exemption and that there must be proper evidence in support of such a conclusion: see, for example, *Guardian Newspapers and Heather Brooke* v. *Information Commissioner* (EA/2006/0011 and EA/2006/0013).

Personal information (s.40)

Section 40 contains a mixture of absolute and qualified exemptions concerning personal data, the effect of which will be to make exempt a great deal of information of a personal nature.

The relationship between freedom of information and data protection legislation is fully dealt with in **Chapter 8**. In short, s.40 places serious limitations on the media's ability to obtain personal data about individuals. The general scheme is that personal data about third parties will not be disclosed if disclosure would breach the data protection principles contained in the Data Protection Act 1998 (DPA). Even if the data protection principles would not be breached, unless the public interest justifies disclosure, an exemption will still apply if the data subject could not himself access the data under the DPA, or has objected to disclosure under s.10 of the DPA.

It seems likely that the effect of s.40 will be to protect personal privacy at the expense of freedom of information. A recent decision by the Information Commissioner[11] concerned the identities of those to whom the Prime Minister had sent Christmas cards. The Cabinet Office refused the request for a list of Christmas card recipients on various grounds including the exemption under s.40(2). The Commissioner decided that the exemption did apply to those persons on the list who had no public profile since such persons had a reasonable expectation that their identities would be kept private and the publication of such information would be unfair. In another case[12] the Commissioner upheld reliance on the s.40 exemption by Gloucestershire County Council in relation to a request for the names and addresses of those who had signed a petition concerning the review of a farm tenancy.

Confidential information (s.41)

Section 41 contains an absolute exemption for information the disclosure of which would be an actionable breach of confidence by a third party. A breach of confidence will be actionable not only where a public authority has expressly agreed to keep certain information confidential but also where it has received information in circumstances in which the law has imposed an obligation of confidence even though no specific confidentiality undertaking has been given.

Public authorities receive all kinds of information in confidence and frequently enter into confidentiality agreements, for example in relation to commercial contracts. The scope of the s.41 exemption is accordingly very wide indeed.

As the DCA guidance points out, the application of this exemption is essentially a legal question which calls for the careful interpretation and application of the law of breach of confidence (DCA, *FOI full exemptions guidance* 'Section 41 – Information Provided in Confidence', available at **www.foi.gov.uk/guidance/exguide/sec41/chap02.htm**). Public authorities are reminded that if the exemption is wrongly applied and information is wrongly disclosed, a public authority may in some circumstances be exposed to legal action for breach of confidence. Public authorities are encouraged to take legal advice on the applicability of this exemption.

In view of the complexity of the law and public authorities' understandable reluctance to expose themselves to the risk of legal action by third parties, it seems highly likely that public authorities will take a cautious view of this exemption, tending to favour non-disclosure. It is likely, therefore, to be difficult for journalists to gain access to information which might reasonably be considered to be commercially sensitive.

The National Institute for Health and Clinical Excellence (NICE) was found by the Information Commissioner to have properly relied upon s.41 in declining a request for sight of the economic model used for the assessment of drugs for the treatment of Alzheimer's disease.[13] The Commissioner adopted the approach taken to the application of s.41 by the Information Tribunal in *Derry City Council* v. *The Information Commissioner* (EA/2006/0014), finding that the disclosure of the model would breach the duty of confidence NICE owed to the academic institution which had developed it.

7.5.2   The public interest test

In relation to information subject to a qualified exemption, the public authority is, of course, required to consider whether the public interest in maintaining the exemption outweighs the public interest in disclosure. As discussed in **Chapter 5**, this is not a straightforward analysis. Freedom of information law in certain other jurisdictions requires the decision maker to be satisfied, before withholding information, that the disclosure of the information would be contrary to the public interest. Such a test is likely to involve a general assessment of the public interest, enabling a broad range of matters to be considered as part of the balancing exercise. By contrast, the public interest imposed by the FOIA in relation to qualified exemptions is a more focused test. It does not involve consideration of all aspects of the public interest that weigh against disclosure, but instead involves specific consideration of the public interest in maintaining the particular exemption under consideration. In other words, the public interest test will vary according to the nature of the exemption: public interest factors favouring disclosure of defence information, for example, will not necessarily be the same factors as those favouring disclosure of economic information.

Helpfully for the media and applicants generally, the DCA's guidance on the public interest test begins as follows:

> The starting point whenever considering the balance of the public interest is that there is a general public interest in disclosure. In contrast, there is no general public interest in public authorities withholding information.
>
> (DCA, *Exemptions guidance*, 'Introduction to exemptions', available at **www.dca.gov.uk/foi/guidance/exintro/chap07.htm**)

The guidance invokes Lord Falconer's words during the passage of the legislation: 'information must be disclosed except where there is an overriding public interest in keeping specific information confidential' (*Hansard* HL, 14 November 2000, col.143).

As the guidance says, however:

> the assessment of the public interest is a judgment in which policy and legal interpretations are both involved to some degree: it is an inherently dynamic concept. The law and practice of the public interest test will develop by decisions made within Government and by the Information Commissioner and the courts.
>
> (DCA, *Exemptions guidance*, 'Introduction to exemptions', available at **www.dca.gov.uk/foi/guidance/exintro/chap07.htm**)

There will inevitably be concern among media groups that, despite the pro-disclosure rhetoric, public authorities will nonetheless apply the public interest test in a manner that is too restrictive. The DCA's guidance on application of the public interest test to certain of the exemptions suggests that disclosure will be in the public interest only in exceptional circumstances. For example, in relation to s.24 (national security), the guidance says:

> There is obviously a very strong public interest in safeguarding national security. If non-disclosure is required to safeguard national security, *it is likely to be only in*

exceptional circumstances that consideration of other public interest factors will result in disclosure.

(DCA, *FOI full exemptions guidance*, 'Section 24 – National Security', available at **www.foi.gov.uk/guidance/exguide/sec24/chap03.htm**; emphasis added)

In relation to s.37 (communications with Her Majesty), the guidance says:

It is a fundamental constitutional principle that communications between the Queen and her Ministers and other public bodies are essentially confidential in nature and there is therefore a fundamental public interest in withholding information relating to such communications . . .

Openness in government can increase public trust and engagement. The FOI Act requires the public interest to be balanced before a final decision can be taken about whether or not to disclose. But for the reasons indicated above, *it is likely to be in exceptional circumstances* only that the public interest will come down in favour of disclosure of this information to the extent that it is to any degree confidential or private.

(DCA, *FOI full exemptions guidance*, 'Section 37 – Communications with Her Majesty, with other Members of the Royal Household, and the Conferring by the Crown of any Honour or Dignity', available at **www.foi.gov.uk/guidance/exguide/sec37/chap103.htm**; emphasis added)

In relation to other qualified exemptions, the advice is less categorical but it still provides much scope for public authorities to resist disclosure. See, for example, the guidance on s.30 (investigations and proceedings conducted by public authorities):

The factors to be taken into account in considering the balance of the public interest will depend upon the circumstances of the particular case. In determining whether the public interest in withholding the information outweighs the public interest in disclosing the information, one or more of the following factors may be of assistance, namely, the extent to which either disclosing or withholding information would:

- promote or diminish the chances of a successful prosecution, bringing future charges, or making arrests;
- promote or diminish the chances of a fair trial taking place;
- be fair, in cases where decisions have been taken not to proceed, to those who have not been prosecuted;
- assist or hamper the gathering of intelligence information from confidential sources (e.g. informants/whistleblowers/calls to Crimestoppers);
- further the interests of justice in the participation of victims, witnesses, informants, suspects or offenders in investigations and proceedings – and either protect or endanger them as they do so;
- assist or impede other on-going or future proceedings;
- prevent or facilitate the commission of crime.

(DCA, *FOI full exemptions guidance*, 'Section 30 – Investigations and Proceedings Conducted by Public Authorities', available at **www.foi.gov.uk/guidance/exguide/sec30/chap03.htm**)

If the public interest test is applied too narrowly, access to information will be unnecessarily and unjustifiably impeded. The responsibility for applying the test properly rests with public authorities in the first instance, but it is up to the media, as collectively one of the most prominent user groups, to satisfy themselves that the test is being applied consistently and conscientiously and to raise with the Information Commissioner all cases in which it appears that public authorities are failing to do so. The decisions of the Commissioner and the Tribunal regarding the public interest test should be regarded thus far as encouraging for the media and requesters generally: see, for example, the careful analysis of where the public interest lay in *DfES* v. *Information Commissioner* (EA/2006/0006).

7.5.3 The fee regime

Any discussion of the FOIA fee regime requires some understanding of the relevant terminology, for which readers are referred to earlier chapters of this book.

The appropriate limit of the cost of disclosing information is the limit beyond which a public authority is entitled to refuse a request. Under current regulations, the appropriate limit is £600 for Parliament and central government (equivalent to 24 working hours) and £450 for other public authorities (equivalent to 18 working hours): Freedom of Information and Data Protection (Appropriate Limit and Fees) Regulations 2004, SI 2004/3244. In determining the appropriate limit, the only costs to be considered are those of locating, editing and putting the information into a suitable format for disclosure.

If a request would cost less than the appropriate limit, and there is no other basis for refusing the request, the public authority must comply with the request. It is entitled to make a charge but the charge may only relate to the costs of:

- putting the information in the applicant's preferred format, so far as this is reasonably practicable;
- reproducing any document containing the information, e.g. photocopying or printing; and
- postage and other forms of communicating the information.

No staff costs are chargeable, only tangible costs such as copying, postage and fax.

If a request would cost more than the appropriate limit, a public authority is quite simply entitled to refuse to deal with it. This has the ironic consequence that the media may be deprived of access to information on costs grounds in cases of particular size, complexity and importance while getting free access to trivial information on the ground that it is cheap and easy to retrieve.

A public authority is not obliged to comply with a request in a case where the maximum limit is exceeded even if a media organisation is prepared to pay the authority's costs of retrieving the information. Some public authorities may of course choose to comply in these circumstances, in which case they may charge fees representing the total time spent in responding to the request. While it is up to particular public authorities to decide if they wish voluntarily to provide information where the appropriate cost limit is exceeded, they should remember their obligations to provide advice and assistance. In its fees guidance, the DCA advises public authorities planning to turn down a request for reasons of cost or to charge a high fee that they should contact the applicant in advance to discuss whether the scope of the request might be modified so as to bring the costs of responding within the appropriate limit.

There is not much indication so far that public authorities will be willing to provide information in cases where the appropriate cost limit is exceeded. Indeed, the cost limit may well be regarded by some public authorities as a useful means of avoiding disclosure. Some public authorities have already announced that, where requests exceed the appropriate limit, it will be their policy to exercise their legal right not to respond.

Towards the end of 2006 the Government proposed two major changes to the FOI Fees Regulations (Freedom of Information and Data Protection (Appropriate Limit and Fees) Regulations 2004, SI 2004/3244). First, authorities would have been able to include the time they spend thinking about a request, consulting others about it and deciding whether the information should be released as well as the costs of searching for and extracting the requested information. A second proposal would have allowed the costs of unrelated requests made by the same individual or organisation to be aggregated and refused if their combined cost exceeded the limit. Those changes would, in the words of the Campaign for Freedom of Information 'have made it easier for public authorities to refuse requests on costs grounds and severely restricted the amount of information that could be obtained under the Act'. Following a consultation exercise and robust representations by the media and other organisations, the Government announced on 25 October 2007 that it no longer intended to proceed with its proposed changes.

7.5.4   The time for compliance

Most journalists do not operate according to the kind of timetable envisaged by the FOIA for compliance with requests for information – a limit of 20 working days (see FOIA, s.10). In the world of news media, 20 working days is a very long time.

A journalist working on a story is simply not going to be able to wait for a public authority to answer his or her request. Even if the authority deals with the request promptly, the information is likely to come back weeks after the journalist's copy deadline has passed, particularly if the authority takes advantage of the extension of time permitted by s.10(3) of the FOIA for qualified exemption cases where the public interest needs to be considered. Public authorities have frequently said they require further time for this purpose.

In many cases, public authorities appear to have forgotten that their obligation is to respond 'promptly' and the 20-day limit is just that: a limit rather than a recommended response time. Many public authorities ignore their statutory obligations altogether. The 20-day time limit is widely seen as a 'soft' deadline with no effective sanction for its breach.

If a request is refused, and a review and/or appeal becomes necessary, the problem is compounded by the additional time taken by that process, explained further below.

It follows that the FOIA may be of limited use to news journalists working against daily or weekly news pressures. Its effectiveness may be restricted to specialist or investigative reporters working to much longer timescales or on specific projects or investigations. In its paper cited above, the Constitution Unit of University College, London concluded that the time taken by public authorities to respond to requests, coupled with the lengthy appeals process, seriously limited the practical effectiveness of the FOIA for journalists other than those engaged on investigative or historical stories.

7.5.5 The appeals procedure

If the media are dissatisfied with the manner in which a freedom of information request has been dealt with by a public authority, they can seek to have the matter reviewed. In practice, how effective is the review process likely to be?

In the first instance, a media applicant will normally have to pursue the public authority's own complaints procedures. These will vary between one authority and another. Some public authorities, for example the Foreign Office, have opted for a no-frills review: dissatisfied applicants are invited simply to apply for an internal review. Other authorities, for example the Department of Health, have opted for a more formal style of investigation.

It is possible that these complaints procedures may result in the release of information previously withheld. There is, however, a perception by some sections of the media that in most cases this will not happen and that in the majority of cases the need to comply with the public authority's own complaints procedure will simply constitute an unwelcome delay in the prosecution of its appeal to the Information Commissioner.

As fully discussed elsewhere in this book, a person dissatisfied with a public authority's decision has the right, once he or she has exhausted any relevant complaints procedure, to take the matter to the Information Commissioner. From there he or she has the right to appeal to the Information Tribunal and then, on a point of law, to the High Court.

The FOIA does not prescribe time limits for these review steps. In its booklet *Your right to know – how to complain* (obtainable through **www.information commissioner.gov.uk**) the Information Commissioner says that an initial response to a complaint, which will 'outline the steps we will take', will be sent to the complainant within 28 days. It appears that in all cases the Information Commissioner will initially attempt to resolve the matter informally and only if that proves to be impossible will he issue a Decision Notice under s.51. At the same time as issuing a Decision Notice, the Information Commissioner will provide details of the right to appeal to the Information Tribunal.

Further insights into the procedures likely to be employed by the Information Commissioner are to be found in the Memorandum of Understanding (MoU) between the Information Commissioner and government departments (available at **www.foi.gov.uk/memorandum.pdf**). This provides that where the Information Commissioner receives a complaint, he will send details of the complaint to the relevant department within 10 working days of receipt. The department will then be required to provide all relevant information as quickly as possible and in any event within 20 working days.

The MoU further provides that the Information Commissioner 'will contact both the Department and the Complainant, whenever appropriate, throughout his consideration of a complaint and, in any event, will normally provide progress reports every 28 days'.

In relation to Decision Notices, the MoU says that before issuing a Decision Notice, the Information Commissioner will consider issuing a non-statutory Preliminary Decision Notice and invite the department to comment on it within 28 working days. The Information Commissioner undertakes to consider any such comments before deciding to serve a Decision Notice under s.50.

If the Information Commissioner does decide to issue a Decision Notice, the MoU provides that the Information Commissioner will, following service of the notice on the department and the complainant, give both parties a reasonable period of time to digest the notice before making it publicly available.

Appeals to the Information Commissioner have been taking between six and 18 months to complete. Appeals to the Information Tribunal take several more months. In some case it has taken over two years following the refusal of a request for the media to get a final ruling from the Tribunal.

It is apparent from the above that any media organisation dissatisfied with a public authority's decision will have to exercise considerable patience in its dealings with both the Information Commissioner and, in all probability, the Information Tribunal. In many cases, it may be imagined that the media will take the view that by the time any appeal is resolved, the story may no longer be worth publishing and for that reason an appeal is simply not worthwhile.

7.5.6 Civil liability arising from publication of information released under the FOIA

Journalists are, to state the obvious, in the business of publishing information. Under UK law, publication can be a hazardous occupation. The publication of false, defamatory or private information may give rise to various kinds of

221

liability, including defamation, malicious falsehood, misuse of private information, breach of confidence and breach of the Data Protection Act. The publication of someone else's original material may give rise to an action for copyright infringement.

If published material consists of, or is based on, information released under the FOIA, does this afford the media any protection against liability?

The short answer to this question is no: the law does not give any special protection to the publication of information provided under the FOIA.

Section 79 of the FOIA does provide protection to public authorities where information communicated by a public authority contains defamatory matter. In such a case, the publication to the applicant is privileged unless the publication is shown to have been made with malice.

Section 79 plainly does not confer privilege upon the subsequent publication of defamatory matter by the media. The extent, if any, to which privilege will apply to such a publication will depend on an analysis of the nature and occasion of the media publication and the application of the law of defamation to that publication. It appears unlikely that the courts will place much emphasis on the fact that published information was derived from an FOIA request. In assessing the applicability of privilege, the courts will be more concerned with (a) the nature of the information itself; and (b) the circumstances of publication. In relation to Reynolds privilege, however, which requires a consideration of the status of the published material, it may sometimes be relevant that the material was considered appropriate for disclosure to the media under FOIA (*Albert Reynolds* v. *Times Newspapers Limited* [2001] 2 AC 127; see also *Jameel and others* v. *The Wall Street Journal Europe Sprl* [2006] All ER (D) 132 (Oct)).

In relation to copyright, s.50 of the Copyright, Designs and Patents Act 1988 provides that 'where the doing of a particular act is specifically authorised by an Act of Parliament, whenever passed, then, unless the Act provides otherwise, the doing of that act does not infringe copyright'. While this provision may provide some protection for public authorities who provide copyright material to the media, it offers no protection to any media organisation that may subsequently publish copyright material (though some other defence to copyright infringement may of course apply).

It follows that the media publish information at their own risk. The FOI regime confers no protection on them and, while in a great many cases publication will pose little or no risk, that will not be so in all cases. It is important, therefore, that the media understand that the FOIA provides access to information: it does not provide a licence to publish.

7.5.7 Control of communications versus freedom of information

Most governments recognise the importance of controlling the flow of information and, where possible, the message being communicated. How is the desire to control official communications to be reconciled with the liberalisation of access to information inherent in FOI legislation?

There is an obvious risk that central government in particular will try to subvert the use of the FOIA by journalists in such a way as to embarrass it. Some indication of the sensitivity of government to the FOIA's potential to generate scoops was evident in an announcement by Lord Falconer, made just before FOIA came into force, in which he made it clear that journalists cannot expect to keep for themselves information generated in response to an FOIA request.

On 29 December 2004 Lord Falconer announced that 'when government departments receive requests under the FOI legislation which are of general public interest, government departments will publish the responses'. On the face of things this is tough to argue against. As Lord Falconer put it:

> It is a fundamental principle of the UK legislation that authorities should treat FOI requests in exactly the same way, regardless of who asks for the information . . .
> Some members of the media seem to be taking what might be seen as a more partisan view, arguing that responses to their inquiries made under FOI should be kept secret for them . . .
> I find this response hard to fathom. Surely media organisations, for so long campaigners for open government and for freedom of information, cannot be suggesting that their own commercial interests are of greater importance to them than the public's right to know.
>
> (*Guardian*, 29 December 2004)

Suggesting that the media are more interested in preserving their own scoops than the public's right to know may be clever politics, but it appears to have little to do with furthering the media's role in promoting the FOIA. If the FOIA is to work effectively, it is important that journalists have an interest in using it. If they are to be deprived of stories by the government information machine, there will be little incentive to use the FOIA. As the *Guardian* itself said in response to Lord Falconer's announcement:

> The courts have long recognised that most media companies are commercial organisations as well as providers of news . . . Ferreting information out of Whitehall will often be time-consuming and expensive. Editors will be reluctant to assign reporters to long and labour-intensive investigations if the fruits of their inquiries will be released to every other journalist before they even have a chance to publish it themselves. This is not a wish to keep information 'secret for journalists'. No editor would object to all the documents being placed in the public domain immediately after publication. It is a simple question of timing. This sly little announcement reeks of Lord Falconer having been nobbled by a Sir Humphrey. He should think again.
>
> (*Guardian*, 30 December 2004)

There are other ways governments can – and do – deal with unwelcome FOI requests by journalists. An academic study of the use by journalists of

FOI legislation in Canada has shown that requests by journalists (and members of opposition parties) are routinely subjected to special vetting procedures.[14] While there is little evidence to suggest that valid requests by journalists are improperly rejected, there is evidence showing that this so-called 'amber lighting' procedure delays the response to the request, sometimes in such a way as to frustrate the story altogether since by the time the information is released, the matter is no longer newsworthy. Alternatively, the government has in the meantime 'spiked' the story by making a pre-emptive statement of its own or even by taking pre-emptive action such as, in the case of allegations of financial malpractice, organising an independent audit to investigate the matter.

As it happens, there is already some insight into how central government approaches FOI requests because the Treasury mistakenly sent to the BBC copies of internal Treasury documents which describe the Treasury's deliberations on a request by the *Financial Times* for information about 'Black Wednesday', the day in 1992 when Sterling withdrew from the European exchange rate mechanism. The BBC duly published the documents on its website (see **http://news.bbc.co.uk/1/hi/uk_politics/4250399.stm**).

The documents show that a standard template exists for answering FOI requests. The template is divided into three sections as follows:

- Part 1: Detail of question;
- Part 2: Draft reply to questioner;
- Part 3: Background note.

Part 3 is further divided as follows:

- *Section A: Summary of information being recommended for disclosure*. The template explains that this section should include:

  whether or not any exemptions were considered and a brief description as to how the public interest test was applied in the case of qualified exemptions. This is subject to Part C on section 36 exemptions below.

- *Section B: Summary of information not being recommended for disclosure because an exemption applies*. The template says:

  Please include an account of what exemption is being applied, and, in the case of qualified exemptions, how the public interest test was applied. This is subject to Part C on section 36 exemptions below.

- *Section C: Section 36 exemptions*. The template says:

  Please highlight whether or not a case for an exemption under section 36 arises. This relates to the effective conduct of public business and needs to be signed off by a Minister. To do this, you should:

  - Attach the paper or specific sections to be considered under Section 36;
  - Attach an analysis of the relevance of the exemption.

- *Section D: Process by which decisions have been reached*. The template says: To complete this section you should:
  - Give the name of the *Director* who has signed off the draft reply;
  - State that the Information Rights Unit and Treasury Legal Advisers have been consulted;
  - State whether there are any related requests within the Treasury or outside that you know of (for example if it is a round robin);
  - State whether the request has gone to the DCA clearing house.

The relevant civil servant marked the relevant documents in three colours: *pink* for those parts he thought should be exempted; *yellow* for those parts where exemptions were considered but ruled out; and *green* for those parts which were outside FOI exemptions but 'raised potential presentational issues'.

An important reason for disapplying exemptions that might otherwise have applied was the fact that the former Prime Minister, John Major, had discussed aspects of the information sought in his published autobiography. The civil servant noted that certain information – criticism of the French – was potentially embarrassing but there was 'little case' for exempting.

The application of the exemptions in Part 3 Section B of the document was, broadly, reflected in the draft letter to the *Financial Times* journalist who had requested the information. The exemptions relied on were s.27 (international relations), s.29 (the economy) and s.35 (formulation of government policy). The public interest relied on was partly that disclosure of the information, which included details of conversations with foreign officials, could inhibit the free and frank exchange of information. Further public interest justifications arose from the following considerations:

- references to losses incurred by other central banks as a result of UK borrowings should be excluded as 'it could be more difficult to enter into future financial transactions with these banks and others if they could not be sure if details of their transactions would be made public or not';
- a part of the document which referred to the Bank of England's operational tactics as 'sub-optimal' was redacted on the ground that questioning the way the Bank handled the Black Wednesday episode 'would potentially damage our credibility and effectiveness in future intervention episodes';
- final, but unpublished, economic forecasts were withheld even though they were 13 years old. According to the memo:

Clearly, economic forecasts constitute advice and opinion that are highly important in the setting of economic policy. We recommend that you decide that their disclosure would inhibit the free and frank exchange of views and that disclosure would lower the quality of economic policy advice.

In relation to these forecasts, the memorandum noted that Treasury lawyers had advised that in view of the age of the forecasts:

it could be difficult to sustain the argument that they should not be disclosed if [the journalist] complains about their non-disclosure. They consider that the Information Commissioner may well take a different view of the application of the public interest test in this case.

It is revealing that Treasury officials, despite legal advice to the contrary, preferred to recommend non-disclosure. This may suggest that not all civil servants had – at least at that time – switched their default setting from 'this should be kept quiet unless' to 'this should be published unless'. (For further guidance issued by the government on the release of information, see the 'working assumptions' for requests for information posted under 'Handling specific types of request' at **www.foi.gov.uk/practitioner/handlingrequests.htm**.)

It will be noted that the template mentioned provides for special consideration to be given in all cases to the possible applicability of the s.36 exemption (prejudice to effective conduct of public affairs). In the case of the Black Wednesday documents, the civil servant concluded that s.36 was inapplicable because s.35 applied and s.36 can apply only where information is not exempt by virtue of s.35. However, the memorandum still drew attention to a number of comments which were 'potentially excludable' under s.36, though the case was 'not compelling' in view of the passage of time. These comments included such remarks as 'Mrs Thatcher's removal of her veto on ERM membership was determined by her own increasing weakness'. It would surely be hard for even the most FOI-resistant of civil servants to argue persuasively that such a comment might have a prejudicial effect on the conduct of public affairs over a decade later.

What is perhaps most striking about the Treasury's approach to the *Financial Times* request is the care it took over how to respond. This may to some extent reflect the fact that at the time the FOIA was still in its infancy, and it no doubt also reflects the Treasury's conscientiousness. It would seem also to reflect, though, a certain discomfort with the FOI regime and even a degree of fear about what may be let out of the bag and what the media might do with it. Presentational issues are raised more than once and it is interesting that before any documents were released, the former Prime Minister and Chancellor were both supplied with copies of the documents by the Treasury. The purpose of doing so appears to have been to give the former Prime Minister and Chancellor the opportunity to prepare in advance their responses to the inevitable press enquiries. It is difficult to see any objection to that. What would be objectionable would be to provide such documents in order to provide third parties with the opportunity to object to the documents' release. The FOIA contains no provision for third parties to veto the release of information.

The Black Wednesday request was not sent to the DCA clearing house referred to in Part 3 of the template. The clearing house is described in the DCA guidance as 'the central point of expertise, guidance and advice for all FOI requests which raise sensitive issues and have Whitehall-wide implications'. It is envisaged that the clearing house will deal with requests of the following types:

- requests which obviously involve cross-Whitehall issues;
- round robin requests, such as those relating to departmental financial information;
- requests raising difficult issues about the application of sensitive exemptions, for example those relating to the policy-making process (advice to Ministers, ministerial letters), cabinet correspondence or papers, national security or international relations, commercial confidentiality or legal advice;
- requests for which ministerial certificates may have to be considered; and
- particularly difficult mixed requests.

The clearing house is a ready mechanism whereby FOIA requests could be vetted by central government – compare the amber-lighting process in Canada referred to above. It is earnestly to be hoped that the clearing house will be used for the purposes envisaged by the guidance and not to subvert the legitimate use of the FOIA by the media.[15] It is, however, worth recording that a number of national newspaper journalists already believe that the process of releasing information under the FOIA has become politicised and that the first instinct of some government departments is to refuse information which might lead to a negative story. Journalists have also observed the differing approaches of government departments, some departments being conspicuously more forthcoming with information than others. They have also noted that while some public authorities have helpfully published logs of information disclosed, enabling the media and others to see at a glance what information is available, others have either failed to do so or have failed to update their logs.

7.6   THE MEDIA AS PUBLIC AUTHORITIES

Four media organisations are classed as 'public authorities' under the FOIA, but only in respect of 'information held for purposes other than those of journalism, art or literature'. They are the BBC, Channel 4, S4C and the Gaelic Media Service.

These organisations have had to implement the FOIA themselves, at the same time as making use of it to obtain information for their own programmes. In practice, this dual role has not caused any significant problems for the broadcasters. When the BBC responded to the Government's consultation on changes to the fees regulations (see above), it made clear that its primary interest was as a user of the FOIA, rather than as a public authority.

One big issue for the broadcaster public authorities has been the extent to which the FOIA applies to them, both in terms of (a) what procedure should be applied and (b) what is meant by 'purposes other than those of journalism art or literature'? These issues have been explored in *Sugar* v. *The Information Commissioner and the British Broadcasting Corporation* (EA/2005/0032), which at the time of writing is pending before the Court of Appeal.

In January 2005, Mr Sugar made a request to the BBC for disclosure of a confidential, internal review of news coverage about the Middle East, which had been prepared by a senior BBC journalist. The BBC maintained that as at the date of Mr Sugar's request, the review was held for the purposes of journalism and so was exempt from the FOIA. The Information Commissioner agreed and Mr Sugar appealed to the Information Tribunal.

The Information Tribunal considered two main issues. Firstly, did it have jurisdiction to hear the appeal at all, given that the FOIA only applies to the BBC in relation to material held for purposes other than, inter alia, journalism? Secondly, was the material held for such purposes? The Tribunal decided that it had jurisdiction, and went on to find that whilst the review had been held initially for the purposes of journalism, such purposes had changed when the document was later considered by a high-level, internal BBC management board.

The BBC appealed both decisions, in the first High Court action brought under the FOIA. It explained that it was doing so not because of the content of the review itself, but because the underlying principles had important resource implications.

Mr Justice Davis decided that the Tribunal did not have jurisdiction. He held that:

> it is only in respect of information held by the BBC otherwise than for the purposes of journalism, art or literature that the BBC is a public authority subject to the requirements of Part 1 to Part V of the FOIA. In respect of information not so held the BBC is not a public authority subject to Parts 1 to V of the FOIA.

He went on to find that since the Information Commissioner had agreed with the BBC that the information was held for the purposes of journalism, no decision notice had been issued, meaning that the Tribunal did not have jurisdiction. Accordingly, both earlier decisions of the Information Tribunal were overturned.

The decision is significant for the BBC, and those interested in its affairs. It means that where a request is outside the scope of the FOIA, the BBC is not a 'public authority' and so does not have to comply with duties such as that under s.16 to provide advice and assistance. Where the Information Commissioner agrees that the FOIA does not apply, a requestor's only route of challenge is to bring judicial review proceedings: they cannot appeal to the Tribunal.

Mr Justice Davis also had to consider a related judicial review claim brought by Mr Sugar against the Information Commissioner, challenging his decision that the review was held for the purposes of journalism. In rejecting the claim, the judge made clear that he thought that to seek judicially to define the phrase 'held for the purposes other than journalism, art or literature' would be 'both an impossible and futile exercise'. He continued:

The context and circumstances in which the issue arises need to be considered; and by reference to the factual situation in each case, the matter becomes one of assessment and judgement, albeit an assessment or judgment potentially capable of being challenged on public law grounds.

What is clear from the decisions of Mr Justice Davis, the Information Tribunal and the Information Commissioner is that the phrase 'journalism' is not going to be interpreted too narrowly. It will extend beyond reporters' notebooks and production paperwork and will likely include materials held for the purposes of improving future journalism, such as the review in the *Sugar* case. Where material is held for more than one purpose, the decisions so far accept the need for the dominant purpose to be identified.

There are likely to be a number of further cases on the extent to which FOIA applies to the four broadcasters and what is meant by 'journalism, art or literature'. Clarification will also be needed at some stage on whether 'journalism, art or literature' in fact covers all output or just certain types of programmes, and what happens when there is a change in the purpose for which a document is held, for example due to the passage of time.

7.7   PRACTICAL CONSIDERATIONS FOR MEDIA APPLICANTS

- Consider whether the information might be available from other sources before making a FOI request: those sources may produce the information more quickly and cheaply.
- Make the request for information as specific as possible.
- If the request is refused as being unclear, or because the public authority claims not to hold the information in question, remind the authority of its duty to provide advice and assistance.
- Anticipate possible objections to the request on grounds of cost. Try to confine the request within reasonable bounds.
- Consider making the request in some other (consenting) person's name if it appears the public authority may treat a request from a media representative differently.
- If the request is refused, consider whether the terms of the refusal satisfy FOI requirements. Is it clear why the request has been refused? If not, insist that the authority gives a proper reason for its refusal.
- Be prepared to challenge refusals. Remind public authorities that they have a discretion to provide information despite (a) the availability of exemptions; and (b) the fact that to comply with the request may exceed the appropriate cost limit.
- Where a refusal is based on a qualified exemption, take a critical look at the public interest justification for the refusal. The decision to withhold must be based on sound and specific reasoning.

NOTES

1   Inaugural DCA/Constitution Unit lecture on freedom of information, 25 January 2005: **www.dca.gouk/speeches/2005/lc250105.htm**.
2   Source: Robert Verkaik, 'Freedom of Information Act misused, says Falconer' *The Independent* 22 March 2007 (available at **http://news.independent.co.uk/uk/legal/article2381051.ece**).
3   Louise Hayman, address to IBC Media Law Conference, London, 17 March 2005.
4   Case Ref: FS50074342, Date: 21/12/2006, Public Authority: North Yorkshire Police (available at **www.ico.gov.uk/upload/documents/decisionnotices/2006/fs50074342.pdf**).
5   Case Ref: FS50086063, Date: 11/07/2006, Public Authority: Cabinet Office (available at **www.ico.gov.uk/upload/documents/decisionnotices/2006/decision_notice_fs50086063.pdf**).
6   Case Ref: FS50086301, Date: 30/07/2007, Public Authority: Surrey Police (available at **www.ico.gov.uk/upload/documents/decisionnotices/2007/fs_50086301.pdf**).
7   Case Ref: FS50118873, Date: 09/08/2007, Public Authority: Royal Mail (available at **www.ico.gov.uk/upload/documents/decisionnotices/2007/fs_50118873.pdf**).
8   Case Ref: FS50133972, Date: 20/09/2007, Public Authority: Financial Services Authority (available at **www.ico.gov.uk/upload/documents/decisionnotices/2007/fs_50133972.pdf**).
9   Case Ref: FS50074348, Date: 27/03/2007, Public Authority: Department for Constitutional Affairs (available at **www.ico.gov.uk/upload/documents/decisionnotices/2007/decision_notice_fs50074348.pdf**).
10 Case Ref: FS50099396, Date: 03/07/2007, Public Authority: UK Intellectual Property Office (available at **www.ico.gov.uk/upload/documents/decisionnotices/2007/fs_50099396.pdf**).
11 Case Ref: FS50080115, Date: 26/03/2007, Public Authority: Cabinet Office (available at **www.ico.gov.uk/upload/documents/decisionnotices/2007/fs_50080115.pdf**).
12 Case Ref: FS50086626, Date: 13/03/2007, Public Authority: Gloucestershire County Council (available at **www.ico.gov.uk/upload/documents/decisionnotices/2007/fs_50086626.pdf**).
13 Case Ref: FS50082569, Date: 27/09/2007, Public Authority: National Institute for Health and Clinical Excellence (available at **www.ico.gov.uk/upload/documents/decisionnotices/2007/fs_50082569.pdf**).
14 Alasdair S. Roberts, 'Spin Control and Freedom of Information: Lessons for the United Kingdom from Canada', *Public Administration*, Vol.83 No.1, 2005 (pp.1–23), Blackwell Publishing Ltd (available online from **www.blackwell-synergy.com** using the 'Quick Link' search box).
15 Jack Straw, Home Secretary, HC 7 Dec 1999 340 HC Official Report (6th series) col.174.

The author gratefully acknowledges the assistance of Jaron Lewis and Catrin Llewellyn of Reynolds Porter Chamberlain in the preparation of this chapter.

CHAPTER 8

Relationship between freedom of information and data protection

Antony White QC, Matrix Chambers

8.1 INTRODUCTION

At first blush, legislation concerned with data protection and legislation concerned with freedom of information would seem to pull in opposite directions. The Data Protection Act 1998 (DPA) is a measure designed to safeguard individual privacy, whereas the Freedom of Information Act 2000 (FOIA) is a measure designed to secure open access to information. They have very different origins and objectives, yet they share a common regulator (the Information Commissioner) and have in many respects a similar enforcement regime (through decisions of the Information Commissioner and the Information Tribunal). They deal with overlapping subject matter so there must of necessity be an interface between the two Acts. This chapter explores the differences between the two pieces of legislation and their interaction.

In this chapter, section **8.2** explains the different origins of the two Acts and the main ways in which they differ. Section **8.3** provides a brief overview of the DPA, drawing attention to the amendments introduced into that Act by the FOIA. Section **8.4** explores the manner in which the two Acts interact through the medium of s.40 of the FOIA. Section **8.5** discusses relevant decisions of the Information Commissioner and Information Tribunal.

8.2 LEGISLATIVE HISTORY OF THE TWO ACTS AND THE PRINCIPAL DIFFERENCES

8.2.1 History of the DPA

The political climate of the late 1960s and early 1970s which fostered the introduction of race and sex discrimination legislation also resulted in increasing concern about personal privacy. No fewer than eight Bills concerned with different aspects of privacy were introduced into Parliament during this period, but none received government support.[1] In 1972, the government-appointed Committee on Privacy, chaired by Kenneth Younger, produced its report (Cmnd 5012, 1972). The Younger Report set out a series of proposed guiding principles for the use of computers which manipulated personal data. In 1978, the government-appointed Data Protection Committee chaired by Sir Norman Lindop produced a further report recommending data protection legislation (Cmnd 7341, 1978). A government White Paper with proposals for legislation followed in April 1982 (Cmnd 8539, 1982). This led to the enactment of the Data Protection Act 1984. The 1984 Act was novel and complex legislation which had only limited impact.

On 24 October 1995 the European Parliament and the Council of the European Union adopted Directive 95/46/EC on the Protection of Individuals with Regard to the Processing of Personal Data and on the Free Movement of Such Data. As Brooke LJ observed in *Douglas* v. *Hello! Ltd* [2001] QB 967 at para.56, this Directive 'was self-avowedly concerned with the protection of an individual's Convention rights to privacy'.[2] This view of the Directive was echoed by Lord Phillips MR giving the judgment of the Court of Appeal in *Campbell* v. *MGN Ltd* [2003] QB 633 where he stated at para.73:[3]

> The Directive was a response to the greater ease with which data can be processed and exchanged as a result of advances in information technology. Foremost among its aims is the protection of individuals against prejudice as a consequence of the processing of their personal data, including invasion of their privacy.

The DPA was passed to implement Directive 95/46/EC in domestic law (*Douglas* v. *Hello! Ltd* [2001] QB 967, para.56; *Campbell* v. *MGN Ltd* [2003] QB 633, para.72). The DPA largely follows the form of the Directive (*Campbell* v. *MGN Ltd*, para.72). It follows that in interpreting the DPA it is appropriate to look to the Directive for assistance. Lord Phillips MR explained in *Campbell* v. *MGN Ltd* at para.96:

> The Act should, if possible, be interpreted in a manner that is consistent with the Directive. Furthermore, because the Act has, in large measure, adopted the wording of the Directive, it is not appropriate to look for the precision in the use of language that is usually to be expected from the Parliamentary draftsman. A purposive approach to making sense of the provisions is called for.

In addition to informing its interpretation, the European origin of the DPA means that in applying the DPA the Information Commissioner, the Information Tribunal and the ordinary courts must all be guided by the principle of proportionality. In particular, the principle of proportionality must govern any sanctions applied in the operation of the domestic legislation which implements the Directive (see *Criminal Proceedings Against Lindqvist* [2004] QB 1014, ECJ). This principle of proportionality is likely to be of particular importance in any situation where competing rights or societal values, enshrined in or recognised by the European Convention on Human Rights (ECHR), are in play – for example competing rights of privacy and freedom of expression (as in *Campbell* v. *MGN Ltd* [2003] QB 633), or the competing privacy rights of two different individuals (as in *W* v. *Westminster City Council* [2005] EWHC 102 (QB), Tugendhat J).

8.2.2   History of the FOIA

In contrast to the DPA, the FOIA has no European origin. The European Court of Human Rights has consistently declined to interpret Art.10 of the ECHR as providing a right of access to officially held information (see *Leander* v. *Sweden* (1987) 9 EHRR 433, and *Guerra* v. *Italy* (1998) 26 EHRR 357). The same approach is evident in domestic cases in which reliance has been placed on Art.10 in an attempt to obtain open access to government inquiries into foot and mouth disease and medical misconduct (*R. (Persey)* v. *Secretary of State for Environment etc.* [2003] QB 794, *R. (Howard)* v. *Secretary of State for Health* [2003] QB 830), or access to royal wills (*Brown* v. *Executors of the Estate of HM Queen Elizabeth the Queen Mother* [2007] EWHC 1607 (Fam) at [68] (reversed on other grounds by the Court of Appeal: [2008] EWCA Civ 56)).

A Freedom of Information Act was a 1997 manifesto commitment of the incoming Labour Government. A White Paper (Cm 3818, 1997) proposed radical changes with a view to promoting open government and transparent decision making. Freedom of information legislation had been introduced elsewhere in the common law world at a much earlier stage (in the United States there has been a Freedom of Information Act since 1966, and in Australia, Canada and New Zealand FOI legislation was enacted in 1982). The Freedom of Information Bill introduced by the government drew upon experience in other common law jurisdictions, as well as on the values protected by the rights introduced into domestic law by the Human Rights Act 1998. The government recognised that legislation required a delicate balance of the right to know against the right to privacy and confidentiality.[4]

The FOIA was passed on 30 November 2000 but most of its provisions were not brought into force until 1 January 2005. On the day it was brought into force, then Secretary of State for Constitutional Affairs, Lord Falconer, stated:

> We have caught up with other countries, and, in many cases, we have overtaken them. We have studied the experience of other countries to enable us to introduce one of the most generous freedom of information regimes in the world. The need to know culture has been replaced by a statutory right to know.

8.2.3   Similarities and differences between the two Acts

The fact that the DPA was passed to implement an EU Directive, whereas the FOIA has no European origin, might be thought to indicate a significant difference of approach in the two pieces of legislation. However, their difference in origin may not be particularly significant when it comes to their operation and application. Of course the DPA will be interpreted and applied in a manner consistent with the Directive which it implemented, whilst no such interpretative tool is available for the FOIA. However, the European principle of proportionality is rapidly becoming established in the field of English public law,[5] where the FOIA is located, and in the private law of confidentiality (see *Campbell* v. *MGN Ltd* [2004] 2 AC 457), with which the FOIA is necessarily concerned. In these circumstances the general approach to the interpretation and application of the two Acts is likely to be consistent. A consistent approach to their interpretation and operation is also called for by the fact that the FOIA introduces significant amendments into the DPA, and by the fact that s.40 of the FOIA expressly refers to and incorporates substantial parts of the DPA when dealing with personal information, as explained further below.

Two further important links between the two statutes should be emphasised. First, both Acts have at their core a right of access to information. This is self-evident in the case of the FOIA. In the case of the DPA, the primary right provided to data subjects is the right of access under s.7 of the DPA to personal data of which they are the subject. As Laddie J emphasised in *Johnson* v. *Medical Defence Union Ltd* [2005] WLR 750, para.19, the other rights provided to data subjects under ss.10–14 of the DPA are all dependent upon the data subject being able to discover, through the exercise of the right of access provided by s.7, whether and in what fashion personal data is being processed by a data controller. The right of access under s.7 of the DPA is given special status by s.27(5) of the DPA which provides that it shall have effect 'notwithstanding any enactment or rule of law prohibiting or restricting the disclosure, or authorising the withholding, of information'.[6] Thus both Acts are fundamentally concerned with access to information. Secondly, as already noted, the two Acts share a common enforcement regime, with the Information Commissioner and Information Tribunal established under s.6 of the DPA for the purposes of both Acts (see DPA, s.6(1) and (3), as amended by the FOIA).

There are, of course, also significant differences between the two Acts. The most significant of these are as follows:

- The DPA, in general terms, provides for rights against any data controller. A data controller may be a private individual, a small private company, a charitable organisation, a partnership, a large quoted company, or a public authority. By contrast, the FOIA provides rights only against public authorities.
- Under the DPA rights are, in general, provided only to data subjects, which are defined as living individuals. By contrast, the rights under the FOIA are conferred upon any person, which will include natural persons, companies, statutory or other bodies, and unincorporated associations.
- The information with which the DPA is concerned is confined, in general, to data relating to a living individual who can be identified from the data. The FOIA is concerned with all kinds of information.
- The DPA is, in general, concerned with information processed on computer equipment or contained in structured filing systems. The FOIA extends to information recorded in any form. (In certain specific situations the FOIA provides that information includes unrecorded information – see e.g. s.51(8).)

Further, it is apparent that a statute which entitles any person to request from a public authority any information recorded in any form has the potential to interfere with a measure designed to promote informational self-determination[7] for individuals. The manner in which these competing objectives are reconciled through s.40 of the FOIA is considered in **8.4** below. It is first necessary to have a basic understanding of the operation of the DPA.

8.3 OVERVIEW OF THE DPA

8.3.1 Key concepts

Sections 1–5 of the DPA define a number of key expressions and set the territorial limits of the Act.

'Data'

'Data' is defined by s.1(1), as amended by the FOIA 2000, to mean information which:

(a) is being processed by means of equipment operating automatically in response to instructions given for that purpose;
(b) is recorded with the intention that it should be processed by means of such equipment;
(c) is recorded as part of a relevant filing system or with the intention that it should form part of a relevant filing system;
(d) does not fall within paragraph (a), (b) or (c) but forms part of an accessible record as defined by Section 68; or
(e) is recorded information held by a public authority and does not fall within any of paragraphs (a) to (d).

In broad terms, paragraphs (a) and (b) of this definition of data refer to information which is or is intended to be processed on computer equipment. Paragraph (c) of the definition extends to information recorded as part of, or intended to form part of, a relevant filing system. A 'relevant filing system' means any set of information relating to individuals which, although not computerised, is structured either by reference to individuals or by reference to criteria relating to individuals in such a way that specific information relating to a particular individual is readily accessible (s.1(1)). In *Durant* v. *Financial Services Authority* [2003] EWCA Civ 1746; [2004] FSR 28 the Court of Appeal gave a narrow interpretation to the expression 'relevant filing system', concluding at para.48 that 'Parliament intended to apply the Act to manual records only if they are of sufficient sophistication to provide the same or similar ready accessibility as a computerised filing system' (per Auld LJ, with whom Mummery and Buxton LJJ agreed). Paragraph (d) of the definition makes specific provision for health records, educational records and the accessibility of public records (see s.68 and Scheds.11 and 12).

Paragraph (e) of the definition of data was inserted by the FOIA. It extends the reach of the DPA to cover unstructured manual records held by public authorities (*Smith* v. *Lloyds TSB Bank plc* [2005] EWHC 246 (Ch), Laddie J at para.27), but not other data controllers.

'Data subject', 'personal data' and 'sensitive personal data'

Section 1(1) of the DPA also defines a 'data subject' as an individual who is the subject of personal data. 'Personal data' is defined as data which relate to a living individual who can be identified from such data or from such data and other information which is in the possession of, or is likely to come into the possession of, the data controller. It includes any expression of opinion about the individual and any indication of the intentions of the data controller or any other person in respect of the individual.

In *Durant* v. *Financial Services Authority* [2003] EWCA Civ 1746; [2004] FSR 28 the Court of Appeal also gave a narrow interpretation to the expression 'personal data'. It held that the question of whether data referring to an individual amounts to an individual's personal data:

> depends on where it falls in a continuum of relevance or proximity to the data subject as distinct, say, from transactions or matters in which he may have been involved to a greater or lesser degree . . . there are two notions that may be of assistance. The first is whether the information is biographical in a significant sense, that is, going beyond the recording of the putative data subject's involvement in a matter or an event that has no personal connotations, a life event in respect of which his privacy could not be said to be compromised. The second is one of focus. The information should have the putative data subject as its focus rather than some other person with whom he may have been involved or some transaction or event in which he may have figured or have had an interest, for example, as in this case, an investigation into some other person's, or body's, conduct that he may have instigated. In short, it is information that affects his privacy, whether in his personal or family life, business or professional capacity (per Auld LJ in para.28. Mummery and Buxton LJJ agreed).

This guidance was followed by the Court of Session, Inner House, in *The Common Services Agency* v. *The Scottish Information Commissioner* [2006] CSIH 58 in ruling that statistical information, although based on the medical histories of children with leukaemia, was no longer biographical in a significant sense and was accordingly not personal data for the purposes of the Freedom of Information (Scotland) Act 2002 and the DPA.

Some types of personal data are identified as 'sensitive personal data' in relation to which particularly stringent requirements are applied. Section 2 of the DPA identifies sensitive personal data as personal data in relation to the data subject consisting of information as to:

(a) his racial or ethnic origin;
(b) his political opinions;

(c) his religious beliefs or other beliefs of a similar nature;
(d) whether he is a member of a trade union;
(e) his physical or mental health or condition;
(f)   his sexual life;
(g) the commission or alleged commission by him of any offence; or
(h) any proceedings for any offence committed or alleged to have been com-
      mitted by him, the disposal of such proceedings or the sentence of any
      court in such proceedings.

A noteworthy omission from this list is any reference to finance, taxation
or similar matters.

'Data controller' and 'data processor'

In general the rights provided by the DPA are rights against a 'data controller', meaning a person who (either alone or jointly or in common with
other persons) determines the purposes for which and the manner in which
any personal data are, or are to be, processed. A 'data processor' is any person
other than an employee of a data controller who processes data on behalf of
the data controller.

'Processing'

The expression 'processing', in relation to information or data, is defined
extremely widely. It embraces the obtaining, recording or holding of information or data or the carrying out of any operation or set of operations on the
information or data including:

- organisation, adaptation or alteration of the information or data;
- retrieval, consultation or use of the information or data;
- disclosure[8] of the information or data by transmission, dissemination or
  otherwise making it available; or
- alignment, combination, blocking, erasure or destruction of the information
  or data.

The width of the definition of processing was emphasised by the Court of
Appeal in the *Naomi Campbell* v. *MGN Ltd* case. However, the apparent
width of the definition of processing must now be read in the light of the later
decision of the Court of Appeal in *Johnson* v. *Medical Defence Union Ltd*
(2007) 96 BMLR 99. In that case the Court of Appeal held by a majority that
the carrying out of a 'risk assessment review' by the MDU, following which
the claimant's membership was terminated, had not involved the 'processing'
of his personal data within the terms of the DPA. The majority judgments
take a much narrower view of the concept of 'processing' under the DPA
from that taken by the Court of Appeal in the *Naomi Campbell* case. The

majority in *Johnson* divided the series of operations involved into three phases. The first and third phases (retrieval of information from a computer and recording of the review outcome on a computer) amounted to processing, although this was not complained of or unfair. The second phase (the exercise of individual judgment in relation to information retrieved from the computer) did not amount to processing even where the result of the review was subsequently recorded electronically. Arden LJ dissented, holding that the operation as a whole amounted to processing. The majority view is (as Arden LJ points out) difficult to reconcile with the *Naomi Campbell* case.

The 'special purposes'

The special purposes, which are relevant to certain exemptions and remedies, are defined in s.3 of the DPA as any one or more of the following:

(a) the purpose of journalism;
(b) artistic purposes; and
(c) literary purposes.

The 'data protection principles'

Section 4(4) of the DPA sets out the basic statutory duty of all data controllers, which is to comply with the data protection principles in relation to all personal data. The data protection principles are set out in Part I of Sched.1 to the Act (s.4(1)). Part II of Sched.1 provides guidance on the interpretation of the data protection principles (s.4(2)). Schedule 2 (which applies to all personal data) and Sched.3 (which applies only to sensitive personal data) set out conditions applying for the purposes of the first data protection principle (s.4(3)).

The eight data protection principles set out in Part I of Sched.1 are as follows:

1. Personal data shall be processed fairly and lawfully and, in particular, shall not be processed unless:

    (a) at least one of the conditions in Sched.2 is met; and
    (b) in the case of sensitive personal data, at least one of the conditions in Sched.3 is also met.

2. Personal data shall be obtained only for one or more specified and lawful purposes, and shall not be further processed in any matter incompatible with that purpose or those purposes.
3. Personal data shall be adequate, relevant and not excessive in relation to the purpose or purposes for which they are processed.
4. Personal data shall be accurate and, where necessary, kept up to date.
5. Personal data processed for any purpose or purposes shall not be kept for longer than is necessary for that purpose or those purposes.

6. Personal data shall be processed in accordance with the rights of data subjects under the DPA.
7. Appropriate technical and organisational measures shall be taken against unauthorised or unlawful processing of personal data and against accidental loss or destruction of, or damage to, personal data.
8. Personal data shall not be transferred to a country or territory outside the European Economic Area (EEA) unless that country or territory ensures an adequate level of protection for the rights and freedoms of data subjects in relation to the processing of personal data.

Part II of Sched.1 to the DPA contains important guidance on the interpretation of the first, second, fourth, sixth, seventh and eighth principles. Paragraphs 1 and 2 of Part II of Sched.1 are of particular significance in that they impose requirements of fairness in relation to the obtaining of data.[9] It is also important to understand how the sixth principle operates. Paragraph 8 of Part II of Sched.1 provides that a person is to be regarded as contravening the sixth principle only if he contravenes one or more of ss.7, 10, 11, 12 or 12A of the DPA. Such contraventions can only occur if a data subject has invoked the rights provided by those sections.

Schedules 2 and 3 each contain a list of conditions. At least one of the Sched.2 conditions must be met before the first data protection principle can be satisfied in relation to any processing of personal data. If the personal data in question is sensitive personal data, the first data protection principle will not be satisfied unless, in addition, at least one of the conditions in Sched.3 is also met.[10]

8.3.2 Territorial limits

Section 5 sets out the territorial limits of the application of the DPA. In general it applies to a data controller in respect of any data only if:

*   the data controller is established in the UK[11] and the data are processed in the context of that establishment;[12] or
*   the data controller is established neither in the UK nor in any other EEA state but uses equipment in the UK for processing the data otherwise than for the purposes of transit through the UK.

Export of data to a country or territory outside the EEA may contravene the eighth data protection principle. Note, however, that a person does not transfer data to a country or territory outside the EEA simply by loading the data on to an internet page which may be accessed from other countries (see *Criminal Proceedings Against Lindqvist* [2004] QB 1014, ECJ at p.1038, paras.69–71).

8.3.3 Part II of the DPA: data subject rights

Part II of the DPA provides for the rights of data subjects and others. These are:

- the right of access to personal data (ss.7–9A);
- the right to prevent processing likely to cause damage or distress (s.10);
- the right to prevent processing for purposes of direct marketing (s.11);
- rights in relation to automated decision taking (s.12);
- rights of data subjects in relation to exempt manual data (s.12A);
- entitlement to compensation for failure to comply with certain requirements (s.13);
- rectification, blocking, erasure and destruction (s.14).

It is a noteworthy feature of the rights provided by ss.7–12A (although not ss.13 or 14) that the first step in enforcing the rights is the service of a written notice by the data subject. In the case of such rights the court can only have a role if such self-help proves ineffective.

Right of access to personal data

As already noted, the right of access to personal data may be seen as the primary right conferred on data subjects by the DPA. The nature of the right was described in the following terms by Laddie J in *Johnson* v. *Medical Defence Union Ltd* [2005] 1 WLR 750, paras.20–1:

> Section 7(1)(a) allows the individual to find out whether personal data about him are being processed and Section 7(1)(b) allows him to find out how they are being processed if Section 7(1)(a) is answered in the affirmative. There is no pre-condition that the individual believes or can demonstrate a prima facie case that the data controller has any of his personal data nor is there a pre-condition that, if any such personal data are held, the individual believes or can demonstrate a prima facie case that they are being processed improperly. Section 7 is not concerned with whether the data controller is acting improperly. Therefore the purpose of these provisions is to make the processing of personal data transparent. Because there is nothing in this to limit applications to cases where the data controller has acted in some way improperly, he may charge a fee for complying with a data request under this section (Section 7(2)(b)). The section also contains provisions which allow the data controller to refuse requests for information, at least in part, where compliance might disclose the identity of third parties.

The right of access to personal data is exercised, in the first instance, by a data subject serving on a data controller a request in writing and, if required, paying a fee up to a prescribed amount (s.7(2)). Unless the data controller reasonably requires further information in order to satisfy himself of the identity of the data subject or in order to locate the information which the data subject seeks, and has informed the data subject of that requirement, the data controller must comply with the request within 40 days (s.7(3), (8) and (10)).

Where the data controller cannot comply with the request without disclosing information relating to another individual who can be identified from that information he may be able to refuse to comply with the request, either wholly or in part, if that other person does not consent to the disclosure (ss.7(4)–(6) and 8(7)). A data controller who has previously complied with a request by an individual is not obliged to comply with a subsequent identical or similar request by that individual unless a reasonable interval has elapsed since compliance with the previous request (s.8(3)).

Subject to the matters referred to in the preceding paragraph, a data subject is entitled in response to a request made under s.7(1):

(a) to be informed by any data controller whether personal data of which that individual is the data subject are being processed by or on behalf of that data controller;

(b) if that is the case, to be given by the data controller a description of:

  (i)   the personal data of which that individual is the data subject;
  (ii) the purposes for which they are being or are to be processed; and
  (iii) the recipients or classes of recipients to whom they are or may be disclosed;

(c) to have communicated to him in an intelligible form:

  (i)   the information constituting any personal data of which that individual is the data subject; and
  (ii) any information available to the data controller as to the source of those data; and

(d) where the processing by automatic means of personal data of which that individual is the data subject for the purpose of evaluating matters relating to him such as, for example, his performance at work, his creditworthiness, his reliability or his conduct, has constituted or is likely to constitute the sole basis for any decision significantly affecting him, to be informed by the data controller of the logic involved in that decision-taking.

Under s.7(9) if a court is satisfied that a data controller has failed to comply with a request in contravention of the provisions of s.7, the court may order him to comply with the request. Under s.15(2) the court may inspect the information which the data subject has requested in order to see whether s.7 has been complied with, but it shall not, unless it determines that question in the data subject's favour, require the information to be disclosed to him. In *Johnson* v. *Medical Defence Union Ltd* [2005] 1 WLR 750 Laddie J held that s.15(2) did not prevent a data subject whose application to the court under s.7(9) had failed from obtaining disclosure of documents relating to the processing of his or her personal data in subsequent substantive proceedings for breach of the data protection principles. Section 8 contains supplementary provisions relating to the operation of s.7, and s.9 modifies the operation of s.7 where the data controller is a credit reference agency.

Section 9A, which was introduced by the FOIA, provides an important modification to the operation of s.7 where the information requested by a data subject is unstructured personal data held by a public authority. In such

241

a case the public authority is not obliged to comply with s.7(1) in relation to any unstructured personal data unless the request contains a description of the data (s.9A(2)). Even if the data are described by the data subject in his request, the public authority is not obliged to comply with s.7(1) if it estimates that the cost of complying with the request in relation to those data would exceed the appropriate limit.[13] The effect of s.9A is to increase significantly the right of access to personal data held by public authorities. Whereas other data controllers will only have to search structured manual filing systems which meet the narrow definition of a relevant filing system laid down by the Court of Appeal in *Durant*, public authorities will have to conduct much more extensive searches. The burden imposed upon public authorities in relation to unstructured personal data held by them is limited, outside the operation of s.7, by s.33A of the DPA.

Right to prevent processing likely to cause damage or distress

By s.10(1) an individual is entitled by notice in writing to a data controller to require the data controller at the end of a reasonable period to cease, or not to begin, processing any personal data in respect of which he is the data subject, on the ground that, for specified reasons:

(a) the processing of those data or their processing for a particular purpose or in a particular manner is causing or is likely to cause substantial damage or substantial distress to the data subject or another; and

(b) that damage or distress is or would be unwarranted.

The right to serve a notice under s.10(1) does not apply if the data subject has given consent to the processing, or if the processing is necessary for the performance of a contract with the data subject or for the taking of steps at the request of the data subject with a view to entering into a contract, or if the processing is necessary for compliance with any legal obligation of the data controller (other than an obligation imposed by contract), or if the processing is necessary in order to protect the vital interests of the data subject (see s.10(2) and Sched.2, paras.1–4).

The data controller must respond within 21 days of receiving a notice under s.10(1) stating whether he has complied or intends to comply with the request, and if not, why not (s.10(3)). If the data controller fails to comply with the notice, a court may order him to take such steps for complying with it as the court thinks fit (s.10(4)).

Right to prevent processing for purposes of direct marketing

Section 11(1) entitles a data subject to serve a notice in writing on a data controller requiring the latter at the end of a reasonable period to cease, or not to begin, processing personal data for the purposes of direct marketing. If the data controller fails to comply with the notice the court may order him to do so (s.11(2)).

Rights in relation to automated decision taking

Section 12(1) entitles a data subject to serve a notice in writing on a data controller requiring the data controller to ensure that no decision taken by or on behalf of the data controller which significantly affects the data subject is based solely on the processing by automatic means of personal data for the purpose of evaluating matters such as, for example, performance at work, creditworthiness, reliability or conduct. The data controller must respond within 21 days stating whether he intends to comply with the notice (s.12(3)). Certain types of automated decision making are exempt (s.12(4)–(7)). A court may order a data controller who has failed to comply with a notice under s.12(1) to reconsider his decision or take a new decision which is not based solely on automatic processing of personal data (s.12(8)).

Rights of data subjects in relation to exempt manual data

Under s.12A, which applies only until 24 October 2007,[14] a data subject is entitled to serve a notice in writing requiring a data controller to rectify, block, erase or destroy exempt manual data which are inaccurate or incomplete. The expression 'exempt manual data' means manual data held immediately before 24 October 1998 or accessible records within s.68 (s.12A(4)(b) and Sched.8, para.14). If the data controller fails to comply with the notice the court may order him to do so (s.12A(3)). The expressions 'inaccurate' and 'incomplete' are both defined: 'inaccurate' is defined in s.70(2); 'incomplete' is defined in s.12A(5).

Compensation for failure to comply with certain requirements

Section 13 provides that an individual who suffers damage by reason of any contravention by a data controller of any of the requirements within the DPA is entitled to compensation (s.13(1)). An individual who suffers distress as well as damage is entitled to compensation from the data controller for that distress (s.13(2)(a)). Even if the individual does not suffer damage, he is entitled to compensation for distress if the contravention of which he complains relates to the processing of personal data for the special purposes (s.13(2)(b)). It was under this provision that Morland J awarded damages for distress to Naomi Campbell ([2002] EMLR 617).

Rectification, blocking, erasure and destruction

A data subject may apply to the court where personal data of which he or she is the subject is inaccurate, and the court may order the data controller to rectify, block, erase or destroy such data and any expression of opinion which appears to the court to be based on the inaccurate data (s.14(1)). Specific provision is made for situations in which the data controller has obtained the inaccurate data from the data subject or a third party (s.14(2)), and for informing third parties of the court's decision (s.14(3)). The court also has a power, which is not limited to inaccurate data, to require the rectification, blocking, erasure or destruction of data in relation to which there has been a contravention by a data controller of any of the requirements of the DPA which has caused damage to the data subject entitling him to compensation where there is a substantial risk of further contravention (s.14(4)).

8.3.4 Part III – notification and registration requirements

Sections 16–26 of the DPA make provision for the registration of data controllers. Under s.17, processing without prior registration is prohibited. Breach of that prohibition is a criminal offence (see s.21), but it has been held that failure to register does not, of itself, give rise to a private law cause of action: *Murray* v. *Express Newspapers plc and anor* [2007] EWHC 1908 (Ch). Supplementary provision is made in relation to fees and other matters.

8.3.5 Part IV – exemptions

The provisions of Part IV of the DPA, read together with Regulations made thereunder and with Sched.7 to the DPA, provide a number of important exemptions from the requirements of the Act. These provisions are extremely complex and in a work of this nature it is impossible to provide more than a bare summary.

The first point to note is that s.27(1), which introduces the exemptions which follow, explains that the exemptions may relate either to data or to processing. The distinction between exempting data, and exempting the processing of it, was significant in relation to the interpretation of the media exemption in s.32 by the Court of Appeal in *Campbell* v. *MGN Ltd* [2003] QB 633.

The various exemptions make either data or processing of different sorts exempt from different provisions or sets of provisions. Throughout Part IV two expressions are used as shorthand formulae for different sets of provisions. These two expressions are:

- 'the subject information provisions', which means (a) the first data protection principle to the extent to which it requires compliance with Sched.1, Part II, para.2 (one of the requirements relating to fairness in the obtaining of data from the data subject or other sources); and (b) s.7 (the right of access to personal data);
- 'the non-disclosure provisions', which means (a) the fair and lawful requirement of the first data protection principle; (b) the second, third, fourth and fifth data protection principles; and (c) ss.10 and 14(1)–(3).

Notwithstanding the introduction of these two shorthand formulae, some of the exemptions make data or processing exempt from a wider set of provisions – see for example the exemption in relation to national security under s.28. Other exemptions apply only in relation to s.7 – see for example the exemption in relation to personal data processed for research purposes provided by s.33(4). Other exemptions refer to Part II of the DPA (which includes s.7) without referring specifically to s.7 – see, for example, s.33A.

The types of data and/or processing of data exempt from some or all of the provisions of the DPA are as follows:

- s.28 – national security;[15]
- s.29 – crime, taxation and unlawful benefit claims;
- s.30 – health, education and social work;[16]
- s.31 – regulatory activity (the definition of 'relevant regulatory functions' in s.31(2) is extremely wide) (s.31 is amended and the exemption extended by s.200 of the Local Government and Public Involvement in Health Act 2007);
- s.32 – journalism, literature and art;[17]
- s.33 – research history and statistics;
- s.33A – manual data held by public authorities;[18]
- s.34 – information available to the public by or under any enactment (such enactments do not include the FOIA; this exclusion is necessary in order to avoid circularity);
- s.35 – disclosure required by law or made in connection with legal proceedings;
- s.35A – parliamentary privilege;
- s.36 – domestic purposes;
- s.37 – miscellaneous exemptions. These are:

  - Sched.7, para.1 – confidential references given by the data controller;
  - Sched.7, para.2 – prejudice to combat effectiveness of the armed forces;
  - Sched.7, para.3 – data processed for the purposes of judicial appointments, the appointment of Queen's Counsel or the conferring of any honour or dignity;
  - Sched.7, para.4 – Crown employment and Crown or ministerial appointments (see the Data Protection (Crown Appointments) Order 2000, SI 2000/416);
  - Sched.7, para.5 – management forecasts and management planning;
  - Sched.7, para.6 – corporate finance information to the extent that information might emerge which would be price sensitive or might damage the economic or financial interests of the United Kingdom (see the Data Protection (Corporate Finance Exemption) Order 2000, SI 2000/184);
  - Sched.7, para.7 – negotiations with the data subject;
  - Sched.7, para.8 – examination marks;
  - Sched.7, para.9 – examination scripts;

- Sched.7, para.10 – legal professional privilege;
- Sched.7, para.11 – privilege against self-incrimination;
- s.38 – further exemptions made by Order of the Secretary of State. These are (see the Data Protection (Miscellaneous Subject Access Exemptions) Order 2000, SI 2000/419):

  - human fertilisation and embryology;
  - adoption records and reports;
  - statement of child's special educational needs;
  - parental orders, records and reports.

8.3.6 Part V – enforcement

Sections 40–50 of the DPA contain provisions relating to enforcement by the Information Commissioner and appeals to the Information Tribunal.

Section 40 empowers the Information Commissioner to serve an Enforcement Notice if satisfied that a data controller has contravened or is contravening any of the data protection principles. An Enforcement Notice may require the data controller to take specified steps or to refrain from any processing of personal data or specified personal data, and may require the data controller to rectify, block, erase or destroy inaccurate data and to notify third parties.

Section 42 provides that any person who believes himself to be directly affected by any processing of personal data may request the Information Commissioner to assess whether it is likely or unlikely that the processing has been or is being carried out in compliance with the DPA. On receiving such a request the Information Commissioner shall decide how to proceed, taking into account, in particular, whether or not the person making the request is entitled to make an application for access to the personal data under s.7. This tends to emphasise again that the right of access under s.7 is the primary right afforded by the DPA.

Section 43 empowers the Information Commissioner to serve an Information Notice on a data controller in order to pursue a request under s.42 or in order to obtain information for the purpose of determining whether the data controller has complied or is complying with the data protection principles. Such an Information Notice will require the data controller to furnish the Information Commissioner with information in such form as may be specified.

Sections 44–6 make specific provision relating to enforcement where the personal data are, or are claimed to be, being processed for the purposes of journalism, art or literature, including provision for service of a Special Information Notice which may be served with a view to ascertaining whether data are being processed only for such purposes.

Section 47 makes a failure to comply with an Enforcement Notice, Information Notice or Special Information Notice a criminal offence.

Sections 48–9 provide that a person served with an Enforcement Notice, an Information Notice or a Special Information Notice may appeal to the Information Tribunal against the Notice. The appeal is a full appeal on facts and law and may involve the fresh exercise of discretion. A further appeal on a point of law lies to the High Court.

Section 50 and Sched.9 provide the Information Commissioner with powers of entry and inspection, subject to the issue of a warrant by a circuit judge.

8.3.7 Part VI – miscellaneous and general provisions

Sections 51–4 and 58–9 make further provision relating to the functions of the Information Commissioner and the Information Tribunal. Section 51 imposes general duties on the Information Commissioner to promote good practice, disseminate information, give advice and issue Codes of Practice. By s.52 the Information Commissioner's reports and Codes of Practice must be laid before Parliament. Section 53 gives the Information Commissioner power to grant legal assistance in cases of substantial public importance. Section 54 sets out the Information Commissioner's role in relation to international cooperation and obligations in the area of data protection. Section 58 prevents any enactment or rule of law from prohibiting the provision of information to the Information Commissioner. Section 59 imposes obligations of confidentiality on the Information Commissioner and his staff in relation to information obtained under the DPA or under the FOIA.

Section 55 creates the criminal offence of unlawfully obtaining personal data. It is subject to a public interest defence. However, the defence depends upon it being established that the processing actually is in the public interest, which is surprising given that the exemption for the media from most types of civil liability under s.32 only requires a reasonable belief that the processing is in the public interest. The Government has indicated that it will consider this anomaly when legislating to increase the maximum sentence for an offence under s.55.

Sections 56–7 render ineffective contractual terms requiring the production by a data subject of certain data which he or she could obtain from a data controller. In essence these provisions are designed to prevent an employer from obliging an employee to disclose criminal records, health records or other details. There is a public interest exemption.

8.4 INTERFACE BETWEEN THE DPA AND THE FOIA: S.40 AND EXEMPTION BY INCORPORATION

8.4.1 The purpose and structure of s.40

Section 40 of the FOIA contains strikingly complex provisions which govern the interaction between that Act and the DPA. The complexity arises as a result of the legislative technique used in s.40 to establish sets of potential exemptions from the duties imposed on a public authority under s.1 of the FOIA by incorporating substantial parts of the DPA.

The key to understanding the provisions of s.40 is to bear in mind three points:

1. Where a living individual makes a request to a public authority for personal data (within the meaning of s.1(1) of the DPA) of which he or she is the data subject (again within the meaning of s.1(1) of the DPA), that request cannot be dealt with by the public authority under the FOIA, but must be dealt with by the public authority under the DPA.

2. Where, however, (a) a living individual requests personal data of which he is not the data subject (i.e. information relating to another living individual); or (b) a request for personal data is made by a person who is not a living individual (e.g. a company, partnership or unincorporated association), the request must be dealt with by the public authority under the FOIA but will be subject to potential exemptions (absolute and/or qualified) arising from the provisions of the DPA which are incorporated by reference into s.40(3) and (4).

3. A separate provision (s.40(5)) provides for exemptions in relation to the public authority's duty to confirm or deny under s.1 of the FOIA. There is an absolute exemption from this duty where a request for personal data is made by a living individual who is the data subject. In other cases the exemption from the duty to confirm or deny is qualified, even if there is an absolute exemption from the duty to communicate the information requested.

Bearing these three points in mind, the provisions of s.40 may be broken down into four component parts as outlined below.

1. Section 40(1) provides:

> Any information to which a request for information relates is exempt information if it constitutes personal data [as defined in DPA, s.1(1) – see s.40(7)] of which the Applicant is the data subject [as defined in DPA, s.1(1) – see s.40(7)].

This is the provision which prevents a living individual using the FOIA to request personal data of which he is the data subject from a public authority. It provides for an absolute exemption: s.2(3)(f)(i). The policy of the legislation is that such requests are outside the scope of the FOIA and must be pursued under s.7 of the DPA. In furtherance of this policy the definition of data (and hence of personal data) in s.1(1) of the DPA was amended by the FOIA to extend to any recorded information held by a public authority. In practice, in accordance with the requirements of good public administration, any request under the FOIA falling within s.40(1) will be dealt with by the public authority as a data subject access request under s.7 of the DPA. The public authority will be under no duty even to confirm or deny under the FOIA (s.2(1)(a) and s.40(5)(a)), but will be obliged to respond to the request in accordance with s.7 of the DPA.

2. Section 40(2)–(4) provides as follows:

    (2)   Any information to which a request for information relates is also exempt information if:

        (a) it constitutes personal data which do not fall within sub-section (1); and

        (b) either the first or the second condition below is satisfied.

    (3)   The first condition is:

        (a) in a case where the information falls within any of the paragraphs (a) to (d) of the definition of 'data' in Section 1(1) of the Data Protection Act 1998, that the disclosure of the information to a member of the public otherwise than under this Act would contravene:

            (i) any of the data protection principles; or

            (ii) section 10 of that Act (right to prevent processing likely to cause damage or distress); and

        (b) in any other case, that the disclosure of the information to a member of the public otherwise than under this Act would contravene any of the data protection principles if the exemptions in section 33A(1) of the Data Protection Act 1998 (which relate to manual data held by public authorities) were disregarded.

    (4)   The second condition is that by virtue of any provision of Part IV of the Data Protection Act 1998 the information is exempt from section 7(1) of that Act (data subject's right of access to personal data).

These subsections contain the absolute and qualified exemptions which may apply where information which constitutes personal data (as defined in DPA, s.1(1) – see s.40(7)) is requested from a public authority by a living individual who is not the data subject (i.e. the person to whom the personal data relates), or by a legal person such as a company, firm or unincorporated association. The operation of these potential exemptions is considered further below. It is, however, worth noting at the outset that where s.40(3)(a)(i) or (b) applies an absolute exemption is conferred (see s.2(3)(f)(ii)), whereas if s.40(3)(a)(ii) or s.40(4) applies, a qualified exemption is conferred.

3. Section 40(5) provides:

    (5)   The duty to confirm or deny:

        (a) does not arise in relation to information which is (or if it were held by the public authority would be) exempt information by virtue of sub-section (1); and

        (b) does not arise in relation to other information if or to the extent that either:

(i) the giving to a member of the public of the confirmation or denial that would have to be given to comply with section 1(1)(a) would (apart from this Act) contravene any of the data protection principles or section 10 of the Data Protection Act 1998 or would do so if the exemptions in section 33A(1) of that Act were disregarded; or

(ii) by virtue of any provision of Part IV of the Data Protection Act 1998 the information is exempt from section 7(1)(a) of that Act (data subject's right to be informed whether personal data being processed).

This part of s.40 confers a qualified exemption in relation to the duty to confirm or deny. It confers a qualified exemption because s.40(5) is not one of the provisions listed in s.2(3). However, although in general the effect of s.40(5) is to confer qualified exemptions, the combined effect of s.40(5)(a) and s.2(3)(f)(i) is to confer an absolute exemption from the duty to confirm or deny where a request for information falls within s.40(1).

4. Section 40(6) provides:

(6) In determining for the purposes of this section whether anything done before 24 October 2007 would contravene any of the data protection principles, the exemptions in Part III of Schedule 8 to the Data Protection Act 1998 shall be disregarded.

As noted above, Part III of Sched.8 to the DPA relates to the processing during the second transitional period (24 October 2001 to 23 October 2007 – see DPA, Sched.8, Part 1, para.1(2)) of manual data which was held prior to 24 October 1998. The effect of s.40(6) is to reimpose, for the purposes of s.40, restrictions on the processing of such data during the second transitional period which are disapplied by para.14(2) or para.14A of Part III of Sched.8 to the DPA. This will not impact on the rights of data subjects under the DPA, but will impact upon the rights of living individuals who are not the data subject or other persons to obtain personal data relating to others under the FOIA.

8.4.2 The operation of subsections 40(2)–(4)

The threshold requirement

The potential exemptions provided by subsections 40(2)–(4) of the DPA are only engaged where a public authority receives a request for information which constitutes personal data from a living individual who is not the data subject or from a legal person such as a company, firm or unincorporated association. This threshold requirement is set out in s.40(2)(a). In simple terms it requires a request for personal data relating to a living individual who is not the person making the request. As was pointed out earlier in this chapter when explaining the operation of the DPA, the expression 'personal data' has been given a narrow interpretation by the Court of Appeal in *Durant* v.

Financial Services Authority [2004] FSR 28 (see also *Smith* v. *Lloyds TSB Bank plc* [2005] EWHC 246 (Ch) at paras.30–1). Information is not personal data simply because it makes reference to a living individual. It must be information which is biographical in a significant sense, which has the data subject as its focus rather than some other person with whom he may have been involved or some transaction or event in which he may have figured or have had an interest (*Durant* v. *Financial Services Authority* [2004] FSR 28, para.28). If the information to which a request relates crosses this threshold, it will be exempt information if either the first condition (set out in s.40(3)), or the second condition (set out in s.40(4)) is satisfied.

The first condition

The first condition, set out in s.40(3), has two limbs, (a) and (b). Limb (a) is itself subdivided into two parts, (i) and (ii). As already noted, part of the first limb (s.40(3)(a)(i)) and the second limb (s.40(3)(b)) of the first condition confer absolute exemptions; the second part of the first limb (s.40(3)(a)(ii)) confers a qualified exemption.

The difference between the two limbs of the first condition is that the first limb (s.40(3)(a)) applies where the information requested falls within any of paras.(a)–(d) of the definition of data in s.1(1) of the DPA. This is a reference to the definition of data prior to its amendment by the FOIA. As explained in **8.3.1**, paras.(a) and (b) of the definition of 'data' refer to information which is or is intended to be processed by means of computerised equipment, para.(c) refers to information recorded or to be recorded as part of a relevant filing system,[19] and para.(d) is limited to accessible records defined by s.68 of the DPA.

The second limb of the first condition, contained in s.40(3)(b), relates only to information falling within para.(e) of the definition of data in s.1(1) of the DPA. It will be recalled from **8.3.1** that para.(e) of the definition of data was inserted by the FOIA and extended the definition of data to include all recorded information held by a public authority not falling within paras.(a)–(d) of the definition. In essence, para.(e) covers unstructured manual records held by public authorities.

The first part of the first limb of the first condition (s.40(3)(a)(i)), and the second limb of the first condition (s.40(3)(b)) confer an absolute exemption (s.2(3)(f)(ii)). That absolute exemption applies where the disclosure of the information in question to a member of the public[20] otherwise than under the FOIA would contravene any of the data protection principles. For the purposes of the second limb of condition 1, when assessing whether such disclosure would contravene any of the data protection principles the exemptions contained in s.33A(1) of the DPA are disregarded (s.40(3)(b)). For the purposes of the first part of the first limb there is no comparable disapplication of any of the exemptions from the data protection principles contained in the DPA, from which it would appear that the assessment required under that part of the first limb is whether the disclosure to a member of the public would contravene any of the data protection principles insofar as they are applied by the DPA to the kind of data in question.[21]

The data protection principles are contained in Part I of Sched.1 to the DPA and are set out in **8.3.1**. Guidance on the interpretation of the data protection principles is provided in Part II of Sched.1 to the DPA. Since the data protection principles cover all aspects of processing of data, and processing is widely defined to include obtaining, recording, holding, organising, adapting, altering, retrieving, consulting or using the data as well as disclosing it, only certain parts of certain of the data protection principles would appear to have an impact on an assessment of whether there should be disclosure of the information in question to a member of the public.

The data protection principles most likely to apply to the first part of the first limb, and to the second limb, of the first condition are those following below. In the decisions to date of the Information Commissioner and Information Tribunal relating to s.40 of the FOIA it has been the first data protection principle which has been of primary importance, although the second data protection principle has also been relevant in certain cases.

- *The first data protection principle* – Personal data shall be processed fairly and lawfully and, in particular, shall not be processed unless:

  (a) at least one of the conditions in Sched.2 is met; and
  (b) in the case of sensitive personal data, at least one of the conditions in Sched.3 is also met.

As explained above, the first data protection principle imposes three cumulative requirements: the data must be processed fairly and lawfully; at least one of the conditions in Sched.2 must be met; and, in the case of sensitive personal data, at least one of the conditions in Sched.3 must also be met. As to the first of these requirements, although the provisions of s.40 will be capable of rendering disclosure of the information to a member of the public lawful, such disclosure will not be treated as fair unless the data controller complies with para.2 of Part II of Sched.1 to the DPA. In essence this paragraph requires certain information to be provided to the data subject where the data has been obtained from that data subject, and, with limited exceptions, requires the same information to be provided to the data subject where the information has been obtained from another source. The practical consequence of these requirements is that the disclosure of personal data by a public authority is unlikely to be fair unless the public authority has taken all reasonably practicable steps to contact the data subject and provide him with the requisite information. So far as the second and third requirements of the first data protection principle are concerned, the focus in the cases to date has tended to be on para.6 of

Sched.2 to the DPA. In cases involving sensitive personal data it is possible that condition 7(1)(b) of Sched.3 to the DPA will be met.[22]

- *The second data protection principle* – Personal data shall be obtained only for one or more specified and lawful purposes, and shall not be further processed in any manner incompatible with that purpose or those purposes.

  It is likely that this data protection principle may be contravened by disclosure of information to a member of the public, on the basis that information obtained for one purpose (e.g. medical treatment, social service functions, education or rating) will be disclosed to a stranger in a manner incompatible with that purpose.[23] Paragraph 6 of Part II of Sched.1 to the DPA suggests that there may be a contravention of the second data protection principle where it is disclosed to a person who intends to use it for a purpose other than that for which the public authority obtained it.

- *The third data protection principle* – personal data shall be adequate, relevant and not excessive in relation to the purpose or purposes for which they are processed.

  The disclosure of irrelevant or excessive personal data would contravene this principle. However, provided a public authority limits the disclosure to that which is relevant and necessary it will not contravene this principle.

- *The sixth data protection principle* – personal data shall be processed in accordance with the rights of data subjects under the DPA.

  This principle might be contravened if the data subject had served a notice on the public authority under s.10 of the DPA requiring it not to disclose personal data relating to him on the ground that such disclosure would be likely to cause the data subject or another person substantial damage or substantial distress which would be unwarranted.

- *The eighth data protection principle* – personal data shall not be transferred to a country or territory outside the EEA unless that country or territory ensures an adequate level of protection for the rights and freedoms of data subjects in relation to the processing of personal data.

  Although it has been suggested[24] that this principle is unlikely to have particular relevance to disclosure of information under the FOIA, it is not safe to assume this will be the case. In a press release issued on 1 January 2005 to coincide with the coming into force of the FOIA, then Secretary of State for Constitutional Affairs, Lord Falconer, pointed out that 'anyone, of any nationality, and living anywhere in the world, will be able to make a written request for information'.[25] If a public authority receives a request for personal data from a country outside the EEA, there is no reason why a transfer of the data in question to that person will not be covered by this principle. The public authority must consider the matters listed in para.13 of Part II of Sched.1 to the DPA when deciding whether an adequate level of protection for the rights and freedoms of data subjects in relation to the processing of personal data exists in the country or territory from which the request was received and to which the data are to be transferred.

The second part of the first limb of the first condition (set out in s.40(3)(a)(ii)) confers a qualified exemption where the information falls within para.(a)–(d) of the definition of 'data' in s.1(1) of the DPA and the disclosure of the information to a member of the public would contravene s.10 of the DPA. Such a contravention could only occur where the data subject had served a notice in writing under s.10(1) of the DPA requiring the data controller to cease, or not to begin, processing of personal data in respect of which he or she is the data subject on the ground that the processing was causing or was likely to cause substantial damage or distress to the data subject or to another which was or would be unwarranted. It should be a simple matter for the public authority to check whether such a written notice has been received from the data subject.

The second condition

The second condition, set out in s.40(4), is that by virtue of any provision of Part IV of the DPA the information is exempt from s.7(1) of that Act. This confers a qualified exemption. When considering the provisions of Part IV of the DPA (which are summarised in **8.3.5**) it is important to bear in mind that information is exempt from s.7(1) where the relevant exemption refers either:

(a) to Part II of the DPA (where s.7 appears); or
(b) to the subject information provisions (defined in s.27(2) of the DPA) (which includes s.7); or
(c) specifically to s.7.

The relevant exemptions are:

- s.28 – national security;
- s.29 – crime, taxation and unlawful claims for benefit;
- s.30 – health, education and social work;
- s.31 – regulatory activity;
- s.32 – journalism, literature and art;
- s.33 – personal data processed for research purposes;
- s.35A – parliamentary privilege;
- s.36 – domestic purposes; and
- s.37 – the following paragraphs of Sched.7:
  - (1) confidential references given by the data controller;
  - (2) information prejudicial to the combat effectiveness of the armed forces;
  - (3) judicial appointments/appointments of Queen's Counsel/honours and dignities;

(4)   Crown employment and Crown or ministerial appointments;
(5)   management forecasts and management planning;
(6)   corporate finance;
(7)   negotiations with the data subject;
(8)   examination marks;
(9)   examination scripts;
(10)   legal professional privilege;
(11)   privilege against self-incrimination.

- s.38 – miscellaneous exemptions made by Order of the Secretary of State:

  – human fertilisation and embryology;
  – adoption records and reports;
  – statement of child's special educational needs;
  – parental orders, records and reports.

A public authority, even if it acts in perfectly good faith in performing what it understands to be its obligations under the FOIA, may if it errs in its approach to the law, be held liable for infringing the Art.8 (ECHR) rights of affected individuals (compare *R. (Robertson)* v. *City of Wakefield Metropolitan Council* [2002] QB 1052 and *W* v. *Westminster City Council* [2005] EWHC 102 (QB)). It is therefore important for public authorities to adopt a methodical, structured approach to the operation of s.40.

Persons requesting information under the FOIA, and public authorities responding to such requests, may find it helpful to adopt the following step-by-step approach to the operation of s.40.

1. Consider first whether the information to which the request relates constitutes personal data as defined by s.1(1) of the DPA, in the light of the interpretation given to that definition by the Court of Appeal in *Durant* v. *Financial Services Authority* [2004] FSR 28. If the information requested does not constitute personal data s.40 will not apply.

2. If the information to which the request relates constitutes personal data, consider whether the applicant is the data subject of the data for the purposes of s.1(1) of the DPA. If so, s.40(1) confers an absolute exemption, and there is no obligation on the public authority to confirm or deny or to communicate information. However, the public authority should, consistently with the principles of good public administration, process the request as a subject access request under s.7 of the DPA.

3. If the information to which the request relates constitutes personal data, but the applicant is not the data subject of the data, consider whether either the first part of the first limb of the first condition (set out in s.40(3)(a)(i)), or the second limb of the first condition (set out in s.40(3)(b)) applies to make the information exempt on the grounds that disclosure of the information to a member of the public otherwise than under the FOIA would contravene any of the data protection principles.

4. If that is not the case, consider whether the second part of the first limb of the first condition (set out in s.40(3)(a)(ii)) applies on the grounds that disclosure of the information to a member of the public otherwise than under the FOIA would contravene s.10 of the DPA. If so, consider the usual public interest test required in the case of a qualified exemption.

5. If neither of the limbs of the first condition is satisfied, move on to consider whether the second condition (set out in s.40(4)) is satisfied on the grounds that the information in question is exempt from s.7(1) of the DPA by any provision of Part IV of that Act. If so, a qualified exemption is conferred and again the usual public interest balancing exercise must be conducted.

8.5 DECISIONS OF THE INFORMATION COMMISSIONER AND INFORMATION TRIBUNAL

There have been more than 100 decisions by the Information Commissioner relating to s.40 of the FOIA, and about a dozen appeals to the Information Tribunal in which s.40 has been considered. In a work of this nature it is not possible to provide a detailed digest of the decisions of the Commissioner and Tribunal, but certain themes emerging from the cases can be identified.

Decisions of the Information Commissioner

A substantial number of the cases before the Information Commissioner have concerned requests for information relating to employees of public authorities. These cases have established that, in general, the names, positions and salaries of public employees, particularly senior employees, should be disclosed. The basis for this is that such public employees must reasonably expect that accountability and transparency in relation to the use of public resources and the performance of public functions requires the disclosure to the public of who is paid what to do what job.[26] Expenses claims by public employees, councillors and MPs have been disclosed for similar reasons.[27] However, names of public employees will not be released where there is evidence of a risk to personal safety,[28] nor will the private addresses[29] or private telephone numbers[30] of public employees be released. The qualifications of particular public employees will not be released where this would enable their religious beliefs to be ascertained.[31] In appropriate cases redacted copies of contracts of employment may be released to show employment practices without disclosing personal data relating to individual employees.[32] Information relating to disciplinary investigations in respect of individual employees will not usually be released,[33] but in exceptional circumstances (for example, where the investigation revealed a culture of bullying at the highest level[34]) it may be. Details of compromise agreements relating to the termination of employment will not usually be released,[35] although a summary which respects the privacy of the employee may be.[36] Details of the background and qualifications of unsuccessful applicants for public office will not be disclosed.[37]

A similar approach can be seen in decisions by the Information Commissioner relating to information about the holders of licences or authorisations. Details were not released of the identities of individuals licensed to carry out experiments on animals because of the risk to their personal safety.[38] Details of individual egg producers were not released for the same reason.[39]

A number of cases have considered the release of information relating to informants or complainants. Information relating to the identity of complainants to the Standards Board for England,[40] the Civil Aviation Authority,[41] the Charity Commission[42] and local authorities[43] has not been disclosed. The Information Commissioner reasons that such complainants would reasonably expect their identities to be kept confidential and therefore the release of such details to the public would be unfair and contrary to the first data protection principle.

Unsurprisingly, requests for information about, or capable of identifying, individual hospital patients have not been upheld.[44]

In almost all of these cases the exemption under consideration has been the absolute exemption provided by s.40(2) and (3)(a)(i), and the focus has been on whether disclosure of the information to the public would breach the data protection principles. The Information Commissioner's approach is to consider first whether the disclosure would be unfair. If it would not be unfair, the next issue is whether one of the conditions in Sched.2 to the DPA is satisfied. The condition which usually falls for consideration is that set out in para.6 of Sched.2. This requires a balance to be struck between the legitimate interest of the public in disclosure of the information and the prejudicial impact which disclosure will or may have on the privacy of the person to whom the information relates. In this way although the exemption is an absolute one, its application in practice involves something closely akin to the public interest balancing exercise required in the case of qualified exemptions.

In a more limited category of cases the exemption under consideration has been the qualified exemption provided by s.40(2) and (3)(a)(ii). As explained above, this can only apply where the person to whom the information relates has served a notice on the public authority under s.10 of the DPA. The Information Commissioner has been alive to the possibility that a person who fears that his or her conduct may be criticised might serve a s.10 DPA notice with a view to discouraging the public authority from disclosing information under the FOIA. In such circumstances the qualified exemption requires an intense scrutiny of the factors relevant to the public interests in favour of and against disclosure. In one case the Information Commissioner found that the more subjective and non-factual the information is, the stronger will be the public interest in its non-release.[45]

Decisions of the Information Tribunal

In *Corporate Officer of the House of Commons* v. *Information Commissioner* EA/2006/0074–76, 9/8/07 the Chairman of the Tribunal, John Angel, provided in para.22 a clear explanation of how the absolute exemption provided by s.40(2) and (3)(a)(i) or (3)(b) works in practice:

> if A makes a request under FOIA for personal data about B, and the disclosure of that personal data would breach any of the data protection principles, then the information is exempt from disclosure under the Act . . . This is an absolute exemption . . . Hence the Tribunal is not required to consider whether the public interest in maintaining the exemption outweighs the public interest in disclosure . . . However . . . the application of the data protection principles does involve striking a balance between competing interests, similar to (though not identical with) the balancing exercise that must be carried out in applying the public interest test.[46]

Like the Information Commissioner, the Tribunal in its approach to s.40 of FOIA has drawn a clear distinction between public life and public activities of persons to whom information relates on the one hand, and their private lives and activities on the other. This emerges clearly from the decisions of the Tribunal relating to MPs' expenses[47] and to the disclosure of names and official telephone numbers and email addresses of public employees.[48]

The Tribunal has also adopted the same approach as the Information Commissioner to the release of the identity of a complainant or informant, holding that such a person is entitled reasonably to expect that their identity will be kept confidential so that its release to the public will be unfair and accordingly a breach of the first data protection principle.[49]

One decision of the Tribunal shows the impact of the second data protection principle (personal data shall be obtained only for one or more specific and lawful purpose, and shall not be further processed in any manner incompatible with that purpose) in this area. The Tribunal refused to allow the release to the public of addresses of unoccupied properties which had been obtained by the public authority for council tax purposes.[50] This decision is consistent with earlier decisions of the Information Commissioner refusing to order the release of data obtained for a specific purpose.[51]

Finally, a decision of the Tribunal which is of considerable practical significance emphasises that information can be released consistently with s.40 in redacted form. In the case in question, details of prosecutions for selling alcohol to underage persons were released with names and other information which might enable individuals to be identified redacted.[52]

Readers wishing to keep fully up to date with decisions of the Information Commissioner are referred to the regular periodical, *Freedom of Information* (**www.foij.com**).

8.6 CONCLUSION

Both the DPA and the FOIA have at their core a right of access to information. In the case of personal biographical information liable to impact on an individual's right of privacy, the individual to whom the information relates has a right of access under the DPA but not under the FOIA. If other individuals or legal persons seek access to information relating to another living individual they must do so under the FOIA, and their right of access to such information is subject to a large number of exceptions which s.40 of the FOIA incorporates by reference from the DPA. In this way, the two Acts seek to balance respect for a living individual's autonomy and dignity by giving access to and control over personal data, against the public interest in the free flow of information held by public authorities with a view to promoting greater participation in the democratic process and transparency of public decision making. The balancing mechanism is complex and a methodical, step-by-step approach to s.40 will be required in practice if the mechanism is to operate in the manner intended by Parliament. The decisions of the Information Commissioner and Information Tribunal discussed above provide practical guidance on the application of the s.40 exemption.

NOTES

1   Zinser, *The United Kingdom Data Protection Act 1998: International Data Transfer and its Legal Implications* [2005] ICCLR 80, note 2.
2   For an analysis of the decision in the *Douglas* case, see *Privacy & Data Protection* (**www.pdpjournal.com**), Vol.5, Issue 6, pp.9–12.
3   In a passage unaffected by the subsequent appeal in that case to the House of Lords: [2004] 2 AC 457.
4   *Hansard*, HL (Series 5) Vol.612, cols.823–30 (20 April 2000).
5   See e.g. Fordham, *Judicial Review Handbook*, 4th edn. (2004) section P58 and cases there discussed; *De Smith's Judicial Review*, 6th edn (2007), paras. 11-073 to 11-085.
6   Carey in *Data Protection: A Practical Guide to UK and EU Law*, 2nd edn. (2004) observes at p.153 that this gives the subject access right special status.
7   See Professor Ian Lloyd's *Guide to the Data Protection Act 1998*, para.4.6 (1998).
8   In *Campbell* v. *MGN Ltd* the Court of Appeal held that publication of data in a newspaper amounted to processing where the information in question had previously been processed on computer equipment: [2003] QB 633, para.106.
9   In *Campbell* v. *MGN Ltd* at first instance ([2002] EMLR 30) and again in *Douglas* v. *Hello! Ltd (No.3)* [2003] 3 All ER 996 it was held that data obtained by means of surreptitious photography had not been fairly obtained. In each case the Court placed reliance on *R.* v. *Broadcasting Standards Commission ex p. BBC* [2001] QB 885 where the Court of Appeal recognised that surreptitious photography is regarded as objectionable. See also *R.* v. *Loveridge* [2001] EWCA Crim 973. Contrast *Murray* v. *Express Newspapers plc and anor* [2007] EWHC 1908 (Ch) at [73] where Patten J appears to have held that surreptitious photography in the street was not of itself an unfair obtaining of data.

10 These requirements, together with the requirement of the first data protection principle that personal data shall be processed fairly and lawfully are cumulative: *Campbell* v. *MGN Ltd* [2002] EMLR 30, paras.102, 119. The Court of Appeal did not disagree with this part of the trial judge's analysis – see [2003] QB 633, para.88.

11 See s.5(3). An individual is established in the UK if ordinarily resident here. A company is established in the UK if incorporated under the law of any part of the UK. A partnership or unincorporated association is established in the UK if formed under the law of any part of the UK. Any other person who maintains in the UK an office, branch or agency through which he carries on any activity, or a regular practice, is also established here.

12 This requirement may give rise to difficult questions where data is processed by the UK office of a multinational concern.

13 See the Freedom of Information and Data Protection (Appropriate Limit and Fees) Regulations 2004, SI 2004/3244, reg.3. The appropriate limit is £600 in the case of a government department, the House of Commons or House of Lords, the Northern Ireland Assembly or the National Assembly for Wales, or the armed forces of the Crown. In the case of any other public authority the appropriate limit is £450.

14 See Sched.13 – the period between 24 October 2001 and 23 October 2007 is referred to in the DPA as the second transitional period. There were a number of provisions relating to the first transitional period which ended on 23 October 2001. These are no longer of relevance.

15 Provision is made for a conclusive ministerial certificate subject to review on administrative law principles by the Information Tribunal. See s.28(2)–(7) and *Baker* v. *Secretary of State for the Home Department* [2001] UKHRR 1275.

16 See the Data Protection (Subject Access Modification) (Health) Order 2000, SI 2000/413; the Data Protection (Subject Access Modification) (Education) Order 2000, SI 2000/414; the Data Protection (Subject Access Modification) (Social Work) Order 2000, SI 2000/415.

17 Under s.32(4)–(5) there is a complete bar on pre-publication injunctive relief. Under s.32(1)–(3) there is a public interest exemption which applies both to pre-publication processing and to publication itself: *Campbell* v. *MGN Ltd* [2003] QB 633.

18 In the case of personal data relating to appointments or removals, pay, discipline, superannuation or other personnel matters this exemption extends to all of the provisions in Part II: s.33A(2). In relation to other personal data held in manual form by public authorities the exemption is more limited, and in particular the fourth data protection principle (which requires data to be accurate and up to date) and the sixth data protection principle so far as it relates to the rights conferred by ss.7 and 14, remain in effect: s.33A(1).

19 See **8.3.1** – in *Durant* v. *Financial Services Authority* [2004] FSR 28 the Court of Appeal gave a narrow interpretation to the expression 'relevant filing system', limiting it to structured filing systems with their own internal indexation or search facility, i.e. manual records only if they are of sufficient sophistication to provide the same or similar ready accessibility as a computerised filing system (para.48).

20 The focus in s.40(3)(b) on disclosure to a *member of the public* can be significant. In FS50069257 York Hospitals NHS Trust, 7/11/05, disclosure of information provided by third parties in relation to the investigation of a grievance was refused even though certain of the third parties had consented to the disclosure of the information to the applicant. The question was not whether disclosure to the applicant would involve a breach of the data protection principles but whether disclosure to a member of the public would do so. See also FS50066908 Bristol North Primary Care Trust, 10/4/06 – where disclosure *to the public* of CCTV footage would be an

unwarranted interference with privacy rights disclosure of that footage would not be ordered.

21 Coppel, *Information Rights* (2004) at p.627 points out that this has the odd consequence that the applicability of one of the exemptions under the DPA makes it easier to obtain disclosure under the FOIA. This is indeed surprising – the exemptions under the DPA are largely designed to hold the balance between the rights of the data subject and the rights of and burden upon data controllers. It is not self-evident that the same exemptions are apt where access to personal data held by a public authority is claimed by someone who is not the data subject.

22 For a contrary view see Coppel, *Information Rights*, pp.631–2.

23 This appears to be the view of Wadham and Griffiths in *Blackstone's Guide to the Freedom of Information Act 2000*, 2nd edn. (2005) para.10.4.3. A contrary view is adopted by Coppel, *Information Rights*, p.629 where it is suggested that the prohibition on further processing contained in the second half of the second data protection principle is directed to voluntary disclosure rather than disclosure in accordance with a statutory obligation. No authority is cited for this assertion which receives no support from Art.6(1)(b) of the Directive upon which the second data protection principle is based.

24 Coppel, *Information Rights*, p.630.

25 Department for Constitutional Affairs Press Release, 1 January 2005.

26 An early and much followed decision on senior public employees' salaries was FS50062124, Corby Borough Council, 25/8/05. See for further examples FS50068973, Calderdale Borough Council, 24/11/05 (names of employees who had traveled to Australia at the Council's expense), FS50093734, Newry and Mourne Health and Social Services Trust, 5/6/06 (salary and pension details), and FS501102474, BBC, 11/12/06 (fees paid to presenters for charity programme). A similar approach has been taken under the Canadian Freedom of Information legislation – see *Canada (Information Commissioner)* v. *Canada (Commissioner of the RCMP)* [2003] 1 SCR 66.

27 See in relation to MPs' expenses FS50071194, House of Commons, 22/2/06. There have been three appeals to the Information Tribunal on MPs' expenses – see note 47 below.

28 See e.g. FS50083545, Home Office, 8/6/06 (probation officers). In several cases the Commissioner has noted that the names of individuals working in laboratories where experiments are conducted on animals, or in prisons, would not be released for the same reason.

29 See e.g. FS50103031, Waveney District Council, 5/6/06.

30 See e.g. FS50073576, Richmond Upon Thames LBC, 29/6/06.

31 See FS50063659, DFPNI, 12/7/05.

32 See FAC0064579, Southend on Sea NHS Primary Care Trust, 15/3/06.

33 See e.g. FS50068026, BBC, 27/7/06, FS50086131, Newcastle upon Tyne Hospitals NHS Trust, 9/8/06, FS50068004, Governing Body of Boston Grammar School, 26/9/06.

34 FS50081576, Department of Culture, Leisure and Arts, 5/10/06. An appeal to the Information Tribunal was allowed in part: *McTeggart* v. *Information Commissioner and Department of Culture Arts and Leisure* EA/2006/0084, 4/6/07, and further disclosure ordered.

35 FS50071454, City and County of Swansea, 2/10/06, FS50075602, Architects' Registration Board, 12/2/07.

36 FS50068239, Denbighshire County Council, 27/7/06.

37 See FS50086317, HM Treasury, 3/10/06.

38 FS50082472, Home Office, 19/4/06.

39 FS50089403, DEFRA, 20/12/06.
40 FS50064699, Standards Board for England, 1/8/05.
41 FS50065361, Civil Aviation Authority, 18/10/05.
42 FS50093053, Charity Commission, 4/7/06.
43 FS50093233, New Forest DC, 30/1/07.
44 See e.g. FS50080302, East Sussex Hospitals NHS Trust, 7/6/06.
45 FS50080302, East Sussex Hospitals NHS Trust, 7/6/06.
46 In *Corporate Officer of the House of Commons* v. *Information Commissioner* EA/2007/0060-63; 0122-3; 0131, 26/2/08, the Information Tribunal recognised (at paras.53–5) that recital 72 to the Data Protection Directive requires account to be taken of the principle of public access to official information.
47 See *Corporate Officer of the House of Commons* v. *Information Commissioner* EA/2005/0015–16, 16/1/07, *Corporate Officer of the House of Commons* v. *Information Commissioner* EA/2006/0074–76, 9/8/07 and *Corporate Officer of the House of Commons* v. *Information Commissioner* EA/2007/0061-3; 0122-3; 0131, 26/2/08.
48 See *DFES* v. *Information Commissioner and Evening Standard* EA/2006/006, 19/2/07 (names of officials) and *MOD* v. *Information Commissioner* EA/2006/0027, 20/7/07 (names and official telephone numbers and email addresses of MOD employees).
49 See *Alcock* v. *Information Commissioner and Chief Constable of Staffordshire Police* EA/2006/0022, 3/1/07.
50 See *England* v. *London Borough of Bexley and Information Commissioner* EA/2006/0060, 10/5/07. The Information Commissioner has held on two occasions that 'low sensitivity' information consisting of the addresses of council-owned properties can be released so long as there is no evidence that this might impact on vulnerable individuals housed in such properties – see e.g. FS50082890, Mid Devon DC, 4/5/06.
51 See FS50075171, Transport for London, 5/5/06 (information obtained for the purposes of revenue protection and prosecution not released), FS50070184, London Borough of Sutton, 24/5/06 (information obtained for trading standards purposes not released) and FS50084360, Plymouth City Council, 23/8/06 (information obtained for care agency purposes not released).
52 *Lancashire County Council* v. *Education Commissioner* EA/2006/0047, 27/3/07.

CHAPTER 9

The Environmental Information Regulations 2004

Professor Brian Jones and Christopher Rees,
Herbert Smith LLP

9.1   INTRODUCTION

Although the main focus of this book is the rights of access to information provided by the Freedom of Information Act 2000 (FOIA), it is important for readers to note that where the information requested by an applicant is 'environmental information' the provisions of the FOIA do not apply.

Instead there exists a parallel legal regime of access to information under the Environmental Information Regulations 2004 (EIR), SI 2004/3391. As will become apparent in this chapter, the access regime under the EIR differs in significant ways from that contained in the FOIA.

The EIR came into operation on 1 January 2005, implementing EU Council Directive 2003/4 on public access to environmental information. They supersede earlier Regulations dating from 1992 (SI 1992/3240, subsequently amended by SI 1998/1447) themselves implementing an earlier EU measure: Directive 90/313 on freedom of access to information on the environment.

In the context of environmental information, rights of access to information are therefore not entirely new (in contrast to rights of access to non-environmental information under the FOIA) and some UK and European Court of Justice (ECJ) case law under the earlier Regulations and Directive remains relevant to the interpretation of the recently revised rules.

The purpose of this chapter is to describe the main features of the EIR, and to draw attention to the more important differences between rights of access to environmental information and the rights of access under the FOIA to other kinds of information.

9.2   WHY A SEPARATE AND DIFFERENT REGIME?

In relation to rights of access to environmental information, the UK is subject to particular obligations under international law – namely the 1998 Aarhus Convention on Access to Information, Public Participation and

Access to Justice in Environmental Matters;[1] and also under EU law – Council Directive 2003/4 on public access to environmental information.

Rather than draft the FOIA so that access to all information would be governed by rules equivalent to the Aarhus/EU rules which only apply to environmental information, the approach adopted by the Government was to create the two separate legal regimes indicated above.

9.2.1   Mutual exclusivity of the two regimes

In any case where a request for information involves or includes a request for information which is environmental information, the rules set out in the EIR will apply to the application. Insofar as the requested information may also include information which is not environmental information, the rules within the FOIA will apply to that other information (this is the practical effect of s.39 of the FOIA, as modified by reg.20 of the EIR).

9.2.2   How do the two regimes compare?

As the discussion which follows will demonstrate, there are many differences between the two regimes. Some provisions within the respective regimes which may seem broadly similar differ quite significantly in terms of detail; and on certain matters the rules differ starkly in content.[2]

The aim of this chapter is to give a clear message that will resonate, bell like, in the minds of our readers long after they have turned this page. The cautionary message is: 'never assume that the answer to any particular question will be the same under each of the two regimes'.[3]

Although this basic message will become more apparent as this chapter progresses it may be useful here to flag two of the key differences between the two regimes:

- The bodies subject to obligations to disclose information differ significantly as between the two regimes. In particular there are entities not subject to FOIA obligations which do have duties of disclosure of information under the EIR.[4]
- The exceptions to the duty to disclose are broadly similar within the two regimes but are by no means identical.[5] It is essential to look closely at the detailed formulation of each exemption within each regime. In general, however, it may be said that exemptions from the duty to disclose information are more narrowly drawn under the EIR than under the FOIA (but not always: see e.g. reg.12(4)(e) protecting internal communications where the exemption under the EIR appears on its face to be broader than any equivalent under the FOIA).

At the same time as stressing significant differences between the FOIA and the EIR it should be noted that some attempt has been made to 'marry up' the procedural and enforcement aspects of the two regimes. So, for example, time periods for disclosure are broadly the same, and jurisdiction in relation to disputes has been conferred in relation to both regimes upon the Information Commissioner and the Information Tribunal.

9.2.3 Breadth of the definition of 'environmental information'

The key concept of environmental information is a broad one. It extends well beyond what might in common parlance be thought to fall within that phrase: as has been evident in the number of cases to date in which a public authority has mistakenly dealt with a request for such information under the wrong legal regime.

The breadth of the concept was stressed in *Ofcom* v. *Information Commissioner and T-Mobile (UK) Ltd* (September 2007), where the Information Tribunal referred to recital 10 of the EU Directive:

> The definition of environmental information should be clarified so as to encompass information in any form on the state of the environment, on factors, measures or activities affecting or likely to affect the environment or designed to protect it, on the cost-benefit and economic analyses used within the framework of such measures or activities and also information on the state of human health and safety, including contamination of the food chain, conditions of human life, cultural sites and built structures in as much as they are, or may be, affected by any of these matters.

The breadth of the concept of environmental information can best be demonstrated by setting out the definition within the EIR. This provides that 'environmental information' means:

> any information in written, visual, aural, electronic or any other material form on –
>
> (a) the state of the elements of the environment, such as air and atmosphere, water, soil, land,[6] landscape and natural sites including wetlands, coastal and marine areas, biological diversity and its components, including genetically modified organisms, and the interaction among these elements;
> (b) factors, such as substances, energy, noise, radiation or waste, including radioactive waste, emissions, discharges and other releases into the environment, affecting or likely to affect the elements of the environment referred to in (a);[7]
> (c) measures (including administrative measures), such as policies, legislation, plans, programmes, environmental agreements, and activities affecting or likely to affect the elements and factors referred to in (a) and (b) as well as measures or activities designed to protect those elements;
> (d) reports on the implementation of environmental legislation;
> (e) cost-benefit and other economic analyses and assumptions used within the framework of the measures and activities referred to in (c);
> (f) the state of human health and safety, including the contamination of the food chain, where relevant, conditions of human life, cultural sites and built structures inasmuch as they are or may be affected by the state of the elements of

265

the environment referred to in (a) or, through those elements, by any of the matters referred to in (b) and (c).

This definition of environmental information is identical to that contained in Art.2(1) of Directive 2003/4; which itself draws closely from that within the Aarhus Convention (see Art.2(3)).

The ambit of this definition is significant. As indicated above, if information is environmental information it may be requested of a broader range of bodies than if not environmental information; and if information is environmental information it may be that exemptions which would apply to other kinds of information (so as to protect from disclosure) will not apply.

Some idea of the breadth of the concept of 'environmental information' may be gained from decisions of the Information Tribunal holding the following to be environmental information:

- Various items of information, believed to be held by a local council, relating to two highway schemes which eventually did not materialise, but believed to evidence a council decision to reduce the contribution to be sought in relation to the schemes from Tesco in connection with the development of its store in Beverley: *Robinson* v. *Information Commissioner and East Yorkshire Council* (October 2007).

- Copies of statements obtained from individuals concerning an application to modify the definitive rights of way map maintained by the local authority. The information sought concerned the route of a path and information concerning its use, and therefore fell within the reference to 'landscape' in reg.2(1)(a): *Dainton* v. *Information Commissioner and Lincolnshire County Council* (September 2007).

- Information held by Ofcom on the location, ownership and technical attributes of mobile phone cellular base stations. It was argued, variously, that the information sought fell within reg.2(1) as being (a) information on energy, radiation or emissions affecting or likely to affect the air or atmosphere; (b) information on the state of human health in as much as such health might be affected by such energy, radiation or emissions operating through the air or atmosphere; and/or (c) information on built structures. The Information Tribunal ruled that radio wave radiation from a base station fell within the concept of an 'emission'; that radio wave emissions were, in any event, 'energy' and 'radiation', and that whether or not (as a matter of science) the waves affect the air or atmosphere which they travel through, they do affect the solid components of the natural world referred to in reg.2(1)(a); that even were evidence available to show the deleterious affect on human health of radio waves, information on base station emissions would not qualify as information *on* the state of human health – rather, it would be information on factors suspected of affecting human health; and that although base stations were 'built structures', information about such structures is not per se 'environmental information' – it would only be such if the information was concerned with how the structure was itself affected by a factor such as radiation or energy: *Office of Communications* v. *Information Commissioner and T-Mobile (UK) Ltd* (September 2007) at paras.21–9. Further, the Tribunal held that the names of base station operators should be regarded as 'environmental information', as it would be artificial to hold that whereas information about, for example, radiation was environmental information the identity of its producer was not (see para.31).

- Information relating to legal advice obtained by a local planning authority in relation to the need for planning permission for a fence at a residential property, and the legality of certain local authority decisions and actions: the barrister's advice was held to relate to 'landscape': *Burgess* v. *Information Commissioner and Stafford Borough Council* (June 2007) at para.29.
- In Decision FER0069117 (12 February 2007) the Information Commissioner held that legal advice about a subject which fell within the concept of 'environmental information' should equally be regarded as 'environmental information' (see paras.15 and 16).
- A local authority report containing information about possible prosecution or enforcement action for breaches of planning controls. This was 'environmental information' as being information on measures affecting land and landscape: *Benjamin Archer* v. *Information Commissioner and Salisbury District Council* (May 2007).

Further, in Information Tribunal cases the following have been *assumed* to be environmental information:

- Information dating back some forty years relating to flood risk and flood protection and believed now to be in the possession of the Environment Agency: *Bromley and others* v. *Information Commissioner and the Environment Agency* (August 2007).
- Information in the possession of the Export Credits Guarantee Department evidencing inter-government-department communications relating to an export credit application in relation to the Sakhalin II oil and gas project: *Friends of the Earth* v. *Information Commissioner and Export Credits Guarantee Department* (August 2007) at para.12.
- Licences, agreements, drawings held by the Port of London Authority in relation to the construction and extension of Temple Pier: *Port of London Authority* v. *Information Commissioner and John Hibbert* (May 2007).
- Information held by Network Rail in relation to flooding near a railway line and in relation to work carried out on, and the future use of, a particular branch line: *Network Rail Limited* v. *Information Commissioner* (July 2007).
- Advice provided to the Deputy Prime Minister prior to that Minister taking his decision to reject a planning inspector's recommendation, and to grant planning permission for the construction of a controversial

50-storey residential tower near Vauxhall Bridge: *Rt Hon Lord Baker of Dorking* v. *Information Commissioner and the Department for Communities and Local Government* (June 2007).

- Legal advice relating to the enforceability of a s.106 planning agreement and other planning matters, in the context of proposed night-time flights at Kent International Airport: *Kircaldie* v. *Information Commissioner and Thanet District Council* (July 2006).

In Decision FER0072936 (28 March 2007) the Information Commissioner analysed two reports ('Milne' and 'Qatargas II') comprising risk assessments in relation to proposed liquid natural gas terminals at Milford Haven, and drew the following conclusions as regards whether they comprised 'environmental information':

> The Commissioner has examined the Milne report in the light of the definition at regulation 2(1). The report was commissioned by the Authority to assess the risk of explosion and gas release from LNG carriers. It presents scenarios based on available evidence and testing and is not specific to Milford Haven. The Port Authority has argued that, while the report does contain information on the characteristics of LNG, it does not relate specifically to its impact upon the state of the elements of the environment. Whilst he acknowledges that the arguments in this case are finely balanced, the Commissioner believes that the report does fall within the definition of environmental information contained in regulation 2(1)(b). This is because the report deals with potential scenarios that involve 'releases into the environment', that are 'likely to affect' the elements of the environment referred to in regulation 2(1)(a), principally the air and atmosphere. The Commissioner has further looked at whether the Milne report in its entirety consists of environmental information, or whether it would be possible for the Port Authority to extract only those elements of the report that fall within the definition of environmental information. However, it is the Commissioner's view that, as the vast majority of the report consists of environmental information, it would be impossible to redact any non-environmental information without diluting the meaning of the information. Accordingly, the Commissioner believes that the Port Authority should treat the whole report as falling within the jurisdiction of the regulations. The Qatargas II report is a risk assessment identifying hazards, consequences and possible mitigating measures relating to the use of Milford Haven for importing LNG. Such hazards include environmental, financial and other problems. The Port Authority has accepted that some information within the report falls within the definition at regulation 2(1)(f). This is because some information relates to the state of human health and safety, as it is affected by the state of the elements of the environment referred to in (a), particularly the air and atmosphere. The Commissioner also considers the report to fall within the definition of environmental information at regulation 2(1)(c).

Similarly, in *Decisions FER0099394 and FER0099394* (14 November 2007) the Information Commissioner took a quite robust approach, holding that pricing and financial information within a waste management PFI contract was so inextricably linked to the fundamentally 'environmental' nature of the contract that it would be a 'false distinction to consider such information as not being environmental'.

9.2.4 Bodies subject to obligations under the EIR: the EU legislative background

The definition of 'public authority' under the EIR is based closely on the wording of the EU Directive (see Art.2(2)), which in turn reflects the definition contained in the Aarhus Convention (see Art.2(2)).

Whereas the FOIA has adopted an approach of listing by name the bodies to which the Act's obligations apply, the approach as regards environmental information has been to describe entities not by name but by reference to certain characteristics.

Although the concept of public authority is significantly broader in relation to environmental information than under the FOIA, there has been, and remains, some uncertainty as regards just how broadly the definition within the EIR should be interpreted.

Early differences of view as to the breadth of the concept of public authority under the EIR can be explained, at least in part, by examination of the legislative history of the EU Directive which those Regulations purport to implement.

In summary, the legislative history shows that within the European Commission's initial Proposal for the Directive the definition of 'public authority' was substantially broader in scope than that which emerged in the final text of the adopted Directive.

In the initial Proposal the definition suggested was:

Public authority shall mean:

(a) government or other public administration at national, regional or local level;
(b) any legal or natural person having public responsibilities or functions, or providing public services, relating directly or indirectly to the environment under the control of a body or person falling within (a);
(c) any legal person entrusted by law, or under arrangements with a body or person falling within (a) or (b), with the operation of services of general economic interest which affect or are likely to affect the state of elements of the environment.

This Proposal was acknowledged by the Commission to go further than was necessary in order to meet Aarhus Convention requirements. In particular, the Proposal's reference to bodies entrusted 'with the operation of services of general economic interest which affect or are likely to affect the state of elements of the environment' would have produced a Directive which would have been clearly applicable to public utility services generally, across the fields of water, waste, electricity, nuclear power and so on.

When the matter came before the European Parliament's lead Committee on this Directive (its Environment Committee) an amendment to the definition of public authority was immediately proposed with a view to aligning the wording of the Directive more closely with that of the Aarhus Convention. At first reading, the European Parliament adopted this proposed amendment.

At this point the Commission produced an amended Proposal (June 2001) in which it accepted the Parliament's approach that the Directive should adopt the same definition of public authority as contained in the Aarhus Convention. In particular the definition in the amended Proposal no longer referred to bodies whose functions were likely to 'affect' the environment. Rather, the definition was now couched in significantly narrower terms: in terms, that is, of bodies having public responsibilities or functions 'in relation to the environment'.

The definition contained in that amended Commission Proposal was to all intents and purposes the same as that which was adopted in the final Directive.

Given the significant changes which occurred to the definition of public authority during this EU legislative process it is important to be wary of early statements about what the Directive was intended to achieve, since these may better reflect the Commission's original intentions than its intentions when putting forward the amended Proposal.

With these remarks in mind we can turn to the definition of public authority within the EIR.

9.2.5 Meaning of 'public authority' within the EIR

The EIR define 'public authority' (reg.2(2)) as comprising:

(a) government departments;
(b) certain other public authorities as defined in FOIA, s.3(1) (with some exceptions);
(c) any other bodies or other persons which carry out functions of public administration; and
(d) any other bodies or other persons which are under the control of a person falling within (a), (b) or (c) above and:

  (i)   have public responsibilities relating to the environment;
  (ii)   exercise functions of a public nature relating to the environment; or
  (iii) provide public services relating to the environment.

Public authorities within categories (a) and (b)

Categories (a) and (b) seem reasonably self-explanatory.

Public authorities within category (c)

Category (c) serves to bring squarely within the scope of the EIR a variety of entities which perform what may legitimately be regarded as functions of public administration notwithstanding that they may be organisationally independent of governmental entities falling within (a) or (b). This would seem to cover those branches of government which have over past decades been hived off to executive agencies. Note, moreover, that the functions of public administration performed by these bodies need not be functions which are in any respect environmental.

That a body can only fall within category (b) if it performs administrative functions was emphasised by the Information Tribunal in *Network Rail Limited* v. *Information Commissioner* (July 2007). It was not sufficient for a body to be a 'public body'[8] or to 'perform functions of a public nature', or to 'perform public functions' (formulae relevant in other contexts, such as having obligations under the Human Rights Act 1998 or being amenable to judicial review under Civil Procedure Rules 1998 (CPR) rule 54.1). In the words of the Tribunal: 'Public functions plainly extend beyond administration.'

The Tribunal looked closely at the functions of Network Rail and concluded that:

> even if Network Rail Ltd is a body which carries out public functions, it is not a body which carries out public administrative functions.

In so concluding, the Tribunal was influenced by statement made by Blackburne J in *Griffin* v. *South West Water Services Ltd* [1995] IRLR 15:

> South West Water is no more an 'administrative body' because it 'administers' a service (the supply of water and sewerage services) than is a company carrying on a business, manufacturing and distributing sweets, because such as company 'administers' that enterprise.

And also:

> SWW's primary function as a supplier of water and provider of sewerage services, is to be contrasted with administrative functions such as town planning, court administration, and any of the myriad functions of the civil service.

Referring to Network Rail Limited, the Tribunal commented:

> NRL . . . runs a rail system, just as SWW ran a water supply and sewerage service. It does not administer anything, save in the sense that it runs its own business. It is not a regulator; that is the role of the Office of Rail Regulation. Unlike its predecessor it does not set rail safety standards.

Similar issues arose in *Port of London Authority* v. *Information Commissioner and John Hibbert* (May 2007). The Information Tribunal here, however, concluded that the Port of London Authority (PLA) was, in contrast to Network Rail, a body performing functions of 'public administration'. In forming that view the Tribunal focused, amongst other things, on the nature of the statutory duties imposed on the PLA, and the powers conferred on the PLA to regulate others. Having so decided, the Tribunal addressed an argument that even if the PLA was a body carrying out public administration, it was not exclusively such – it also performed functions which were akin to those of a commercial organisation. PLA argued that the information sought related to such commercial activities and that in relation to those activities it was not a 'public authority' for the purposes of the EIR. The Tribunal acknowledged that in principle an organisation may be a public authority in respect of some information it holds and not a public authority in respect of other information (see also on this point the Decision of the Information Commissioner in *Decision FER0090259* involving Environmental Resources Management Ltd). On the facts, however, the Tribunal did not consider this to be a case in which the commercial activities cited by PLA could properly be regarded as separable from the PLA's public functions. A significant factor behind this conclusion was that the PLA was a non-profit-making organisation and any income from 'commercial' activities was used to defray costs of its public administrative responsibilities.

Public authorities within categories category (d)

Category (d) is more controversial. It brings within the scope of the EIR a variety of entities which are not government bodies and which do not perform functions of public administration.

The aim of category (d) appears to be to ensure that private law entities which perform certain functions that at one time may have been regarded as functions of the state shall not, simply as a consequence of the privatisation of that function, fall outside the scope of the EIR.

It is important to note, however, that category (d) does not purport to bring all privatised industries within the scope of the EIR. For an entity to fall within category (d) it must satisfy both of the following conditions:

- it must be under the control of a body which is a public authority within one of categories (a), (b) or (c); and
- it must have public responsibilities relating to the environment, or exercise functions of a public nature relating to the environment, or provide services relating to the environment.

Unfortunately none of the above phrases is defined either in the EIR or in the Aarhus or EU texts. It would appear to be the intention of the Convention, the Directive and the Regulations that companies exercising what are essentially environmental functions shall be subject to the duties of disclosure of environmental information in cases where those companies have been afforded only a very limited degree of operational freedom from governmental control.

In contrast, companies which do not perform environmental functions, or which do perform such functions but do so with some substantial operational freedom from governmental prescription would seem not to fall within the EIR.

In interpreting the key phrases it would seem probable that the mere fact that a company's activities have significant *impacts* on the environment

272

should not be regarded as the same as the company *having responsibilities in relation to the environment, providing services in relation to the environment or having public functions in relation to the environment*.[9]

Further, the concept of 'under the control of' a governmental body would seem to suggest something rather more than merely that a company operates in a field of activity which is, in the general public interest, closely regulated by government. It would seem to import the notion of government having some rather substantial degree of managerial control over the running of the company.[10]

It will clearly be necessary for companies to consider, limb by limb, whether they fall within the scope of the definition of public authority within the EIR. Where there is room for argument a company may well opt to withhold information requested, putting the onus on the applicant to refer the matter to the Information Commissioner for resolution, with further recourse later perhaps to the Information Tribunal and the courts.

For the moment the message should be that:

- the notion of public authority under the EIR is clearly broader than the equivalent concept under the FOIA;
- the concept certainly extends to a range of companies which might be surprised to find themselves so described;
- the concept does not extend as broadly as intended initially by the European Commission;
- each case should be taken on its merits, looking to see how far the characteristics of the company in question match the key statutory tests described above.

The leading decision on this matter to date is that of the Information Commissioner in Decision FER0090259 (7 June 2006). This concerned the status of a commercial entity (Environmental Resources Management Ltd) which was under contract with the Regional Assembly of the North East of England (RANE) to produce a report which was by statute required to be prepared by or on behalf of that Assembly. The Information Commissioner concluded that ERM Ltd was a 'public authority' in this situation and so was a proper subject of an information access request for information on this matter which it held. The Information Commissioner's reasoning was as follows:

> The Commissioner's view is that ERM are, for the purposes of the information request set out in this notice, subject to the EIR. The Commissioner's general approach is to adopt a broad interpretation of the definition of 'public authority' in the EIR to bring it in line with the directive. This avoids the problem of public sector bodies contracting out public services in order that legal obligations, such as the obligation to disclose environmental information, may be avoided. It is therefore wholly possible that there may be cases where external service providers to public authorities are subject to the provisions of the EIR. It is also possible that organisations may be public authorities in respect of some of the information they hold and not others. [The Regional Assembly – RANE] is a public authority because it, 'carries out functions of public administration.' The Strategic

Environmental Assessment Regulations require public authorities to carry out or secure the carrying out of environmental assessments. By contracting out the carrying out of the environmental assessment the public authority is fulfilling its own statutory obligation. Through this contract, RANE has delegated a public function to ERM, and ERM, for the purposes of this case are therefore subject to the provisions of the EIR because in carrying out an environmental assessment it is under the control of a public body and is exercising functions of a public nature relating to the environment.

If this Decision is correct its implications may be quite far-reaching – given the very broad scope afforded the concept of environmental information, and given the fact that local authorities and other governmental bodies contract out much of the research and other work involved in the exercise of their various statutory functions. Commercial concerns undertaking such tasks appear to be regarded, in law, as themselves exercising the function of the body for whom the task is being performed. This is, perhaps, to have extended the scope of the concept of 'public authority' a step too far. It is unclear, for example, how the more general obligations imposed on 'public authorities' apply to bodies such as ERM Ltd – e.g. the general duty to disseminate information under Regulation 4. It may be that a more limited interpretation of reg.2(2)(d)(ii) would be preferable. It might be better for information requests to be focused on the body which is clearly a 'public authority' (here, RANE) and for that body to be required to disclose all information which is held on its behalf by contractors (e.g. information provided to ERM Ltd by RANE on a returnable basis) and all information which has been provided to that public authority in the performance of contractual obligations (e.g. the contracting party's report and supporting data). Information created by the contracting party and not passed over to the public authority as an aspect of its performance of the contract would not, under this analysis, be regarded as accessible information in the hands of a 'public authority'.

Less controversially, the Information Commissioner has held that Sutton and East Surrey Water plc is a 'public authority' for the purposes of the EIR. The company is a water undertaker under the Water Industry Act 1991. It was appointed and is regulated by a government department (and so is 'controlled' by a public authority), and has 'public responsibilities relating to the environment'. The Commissioner also regarded the company as falling within limb (c) above – as a body 'carrying out functions of public administration' in that it administers the public water supply on behalf of the government (*Decision FER0162211* – 12 November 2007).

9.2.6 Regulations not applicable to public authorities exercising certain functions

The rights of access and the public authority obligations summarised below are expressly stated not to apply in relation to any public authority to the extent that that authority is acting in a judicial or a legislative capacity (reg.3(3)).

9.2.7 The Houses of Parliament

The Regulations do not apply to either House of Parliament to the extent that this is required to avoid an infringement of the privileges of either House (reg.3(4)).

9.2.8 General duty to disseminate information

In addition to duties to respond to particular requests for environmental information, public authorities to which the EIR apply are under a general duty progressively to make the environmental information which they hold available to the public by electronic means which are easily accessible. Further, each public authority must take steps to organise the environmental information relevant to its functions with a view to active and systematic dissemination to the public of that information (reg.4(1)(a) and (b)). (By virtue of reg.4(2) the use of electronic means to make information available or to organise information is not required in relation to information collected before 1 January 2005 in non-electronic form.) This obligation does not, however, extend to any information covered by the exemptions to the duty to disclose information, as set out in reg.12 (reg.4(3)).

For the purposes of this and other provisions of the EIR environmental information is held by a public authority if the information:

(a) is in the authority's possession and has been produced or received by the authority; or

(b) is held by another person on behalf of the authority (reg.3(2)).

DEFRA Guidance suggests that:

> Any information in the possession of the public authority or which is stored elsewhere and is held by a natural or legal person on behalf of, or solely in connection with, services provided to a public authority is 'held' by it.

In Information Commissioner *Decision FER50102786* (21 November 2007) it was held that information about aircraft noise at Robin Hood Airport which was available to a local authority as a matter of contractual right from a third party computer and was accessible via a telephone line was information 'in the authority's possession' within reg.3(2)(a) above.

The information which is required by the EIR to be disseminated must include at least:

(i) texts of international treaties, conventions or agreements, and of Community, national, regional or local legislation on the environment or relating to it;

275

(ii) policies, plans and programmes relating to the environment;

(iii) progress reports on the implementation of the items referred to in (i) and (ii) above when prepared in electronic form by public authorities;

(iv) national (and where appropriate, regional and local) reports on the state of the environment published at regular intervals not exceeding four years – such reports to include information on the quality of, and pressures on, the environment;

(v) data or summaries of data derived from the monitoring of activities affecting, or likely to affect, the environment;

(vi) authorisations with a significant impact on the environment and environmental agreements (or a reference to the places where such information can be requested or found);

(vii) environmental impact studies and risk assessments concerning the environmental elements referred to within the definition of 'environmental information' (reg.4(4)(a)).[11]

There must also be disseminated facts, and analyses of facts, which the public authority considers relevant and important in framing major environmental proposals (reg.4(4)(b)).

9.2.9 The general duty to make environmental information available on request

Regulation 5 imposes a general duty that public authorities should upon request make available to an applicant environmental information which it holds (or which is held by another on its behalf) (reg.5(1)). The duty does not apply where the environmental information is 'personal data of which the applicant is the data subject' (reg.5(3)). There is no requirement that the request should be in writing, and certainly the request does not need to be a request explicitly for access under one or other of the statutory access regimes. No obligations apply in relation to information no longer held by the public authority or by any person on its behalf; save in the case where the public authority has passed the information over to a different public authority (see **9.2.12**). Where information was not held by the public authority at the time of the request but is acquired by the authority prior to its decision regarding disclosure, the Information Commissioner will regard it as good practice for the public authority to regard that information as disclosable (subject to the operation of an exemption).

Under the EIR the general duty to make environmental information available on request applies notwithstanding any enactment or rule of law that would prevent the disclosure of information in accordance with the EIR (reg.5(6)). This rule, it should be noted, is directly the opposite of the principle found in the FOIA. FOIA, s.44 provides an absolute exemption from disclosure for information that is prohibited from being disclosed by another Act or Community obligation.

Requests for environmental information may be made by any person (the applicant is not required to demonstrate any particular interest in the matter), and unless one of the exceptions described below applies, public authorities are required to make requested information available as soon as possible, and no later than 20 working days after receipt of a request. This 20-day period may, however, be extended by the public authority to 40 working days in cases where this is reasonably believed by the public authority to be necessary in the light of the complexity and[12] volume of the information requested. The necessity in question may here relate either to the business of actually providing the information requested within the 20-day period, or the difficulty within that period of making a decision that the information should not be disclosed (reg.7(1)). Any decision to extend the 20-day period must be taken by the public authority and notified to the applicant within that 20-day period (reg.7(3)).

Prima facie the public authority must make the information available in such form or format as the applicant requests. However, this presumption is displaced where it is reasonable for the public authority to make the information available in some other form or format or the information is already publicly available and accessible to the applicant in another format (reg.6(1)).

There is also a potentially far-reaching obligation under the EIR that the information 'shall be up to date, accurate and comparable, so far as the authority reasonably believes' (reg.5(4)). It is presently unclear how proactive public bodies must be to ensure on an ongoing basis that information in their possession meets these requirements.

For example, the scope of obligations imposed on a public authority where the authority is aware that its latest information is out of date or inaccurate is not clear. Is it sufficient merely to make these shortcomings clear, or is there an obligation to correct the shortcoming by updating or securing more accurate information? If the information is not made available in the form or format requested, the public authority must explain (in writing if requested) the reason for this as soon as possible and no later than 20 days from the receipt of the request for the information, and inform the applicant of his or her rights to make representations under reg.11 and to take advantage of applicable appeal and enforcement mechanisms. See reg.6(2).

9.2.10 Charging

In relation to charging for the provision of information, a distinction is drawn in the EIR between recoupment by a public authority of the costs it incurs in providing the information requested by an applicant, and recoupment of costs incurred merely in affording on-site access to that information.

A public authority may not make any charge for allowing an applicant access to any public registers of environmental information which it holds; nor may it make any charge in relation to the examination of requested information at the place which the public authority makes available for that examination (reg.8(2)).

However, outside these two situations a public authority may charge the applicant for making the requested information available to the applicant (reg.8(1)). (It seems clear that no charge may be made in relation to refusals of information.) It was not initially clear whether the expression 'making the requested information available' related only to the cost of copying and trans- mitting retrieved information to the applicant, or whether it also embraces the cost of retrieving that information internally. The matter seemed finely bal- anced as a matter of interpretation. However, in *Markinson* v. *Information Commissioner* (March 2006) the Information Tribunal made clear that the costs of locating and retrieving information were not relevant to a public authority's assessment of its charge for making that information available once located and retrieved: see para.33(c). This view of the law seems confirmed also by Information Commissioner *Decision FS50079628* (29 November, 2007) – see paras.20–5: time taken manually to sort and separate documents, and time taken to redact documents not time taken in 'making the documents available'.

The charge imposed by a public authority may must not exceed an amount which the public authority is satisfied is a reasonable amount (reg.8(3)).[13] The concept of reasonableness of charge is not further defined. In a case in 1999 (*Commission* v. *Federal Republic of Germany*, Case C–217/97 (1999)) the European Court of Justice took the view, in relation to the reasonable charge for supplying information criterion of the earlier EU Directive, that charges set at a level which would serve to deter persons from seeking access to information would frustrate the main aims of the Directive, and so would not qualify as rea- sonable. This is of particular significance in the light of the fact that, unlike under the FOIA, there is no provision under the EIR permitting a public authority to refuse to disclose information because of the disproportionate expense likely to be involved. (Under the FOIA an exception exists where the cost of complying with a request will exceed the 'appropriate limit' (currently £600 for central government and £450 for local government) within the mean- ing of Fees Regulations made under ss.9, 12 and 13.) In certain circumstances a request involving a public authority in very substantial expense may fall within the manifestly unreasonable exemption (see further **9.2.13**). However, there may be circumstances where the public interest in the matter being disclosed is suffi- ciently great to render the request not manifestly unreasonable, despite the fact that disclosure may be at substantial public expense.

In *Markinson* v. *Information Commissioner* (March 2006) the Information Tribunal considered an appeal on the part of an individual who had been charged £6 for a copy of each planning or building control decision he requested, and 50p for each sheet within the planning file which he wanted photocopied. In his decision the Information Commissioner had noted the subjective wording of reg.8(3) – 'an amount which the public authority is satisfied is reasonable' – and felt therefore unable to substitute his own judgment as to reasonableness for that of the local authority. On appeal the Tribunal drew attention to the wording of Art.5(2) to the EU Directive:

> Public authorities may make a charge for supplying environmental information but such charge shall not exceed a reasonable sum.

The Tribunal declined to accede to an argument that reg.8(3) should be interpreted in any way other than it's ordinary meaning in order that it should be rendered consistent with the EU Directive. Instead the Tribunal concluded that the 'subjective' wording of the Regulation was consistent with the EU Directive:

> It seems to us that the UK Government was not obliged to re-state the precise language of Article 5(2) in the Regulations. It was left with some discretion, or margin of appreciation . . .

On that basis the role of the Commissioner and the Tribunal was not to ask whether the sums charged in any particular case were or were not reasonable sums; rather it was to ask whether any reasonable public authority could have regarded such sums as reasonable: applying the principles for review of subjectively worded conferments of power laid down by the House of Lords in *Secretary of State for Education and Science* v. *Tameside Metropolitan Borough Council* [1977] AC 1014.

The Tribunal therefore asked two questions: (i) did the local authority honestly believe its charges to be reasonable, and if so (ii) whether that belief was a belief that a reasonable local authority, properly directing itself to the relevant law and facts, could have held.

On close examination of the reasoning processes which had, it seemed, led the council to the level of charges which it had set, the Tribunal found that all relevant considerations had not been taken into account by the local authority: for example, there was Guidance on such charges issues by the Office of the Deputy Prime Minister, and this appeared to have been ignored by the local authority. The Tribunal indicated in its final Decision that the ODPM's indicative figure of 10p per page for photocopying charges should apply unless an authority could show good reason why this sum should be exceeded.

Public authorities are required to publish and make available to applicants a schedule of their charges, and also information on the circumstances in which a charge may be made or may be waived (reg.8(8)). Non-binding DEFRA Guidance recommends that central departments and local authorities should waive charges where costs incurred are less than the prescribed sums relevant as regards waiver of charges for requests made under the FOIA.

A public authority may require payment of its proposed charge in advance of making the environmental information available to the applicant. Where the public authority opts to do so it must inform the applicant of this fact, and also of the amount of the charge, within 20 working days of receipt of the request for the information (reg.8(4)). (In calculating the 20 working days within which the public authority must disclose the information the period from the date of such notification and the payment of the advance charge is ignored: see reg.8(6).) In such circumstances the applicant has 60 working days from the date of such notification within which to pay the charge, and trigger the duty to disclose the information (reg.6(5)). Although the duty to disclose will lapse if the charge is not paid within this 60-day period there is no reason why a further, albeit identical, request could not be made by the applicant – triggering a new duty to disclose.

9.2.11   Advice and assistance

Public authorities are required to provide advice and assistance to applicants so far as it is reasonable to expect them to do so (reg.9(1)). For example, where the public authority considers that an applicant has formulated a request in too general a manner (so that the 'too general' exemption from disclosure may apply) the authority is required to ask the applicant for more particulars and also to assist the applicant in providing those particulars (reg.9(2)).

9.2.12   Transfers of requests

Where a public authority receives a request for environmental information which it does not hold but it believes that the information is held by another public authority, the former public authority is required either to transfer the request to the other public authority or to supply the applicant with the name and address of the transferee authority (reg.10(1)). For the purpose of the 20-day rule the transferee authority has 20 working days from the date on which it receives the transferred request. See reg.10(2).

9.2.13   Exceptions to the duty to disclose environmental information

A public authority may (i.e. there is no express duty not to disclose information just because an exception applies) refuse to disclose environmental information in circumstances where the following two conditions are satisfied:

*   the information falls within one of the categories listed below; and
*   in all the circumstances the public interest in non-disclosure outweighs the public interest in disclosing the information (reg.12(11)).

Note that both of the above conditions must be satisfied before a request for disclosure may be refused, and also that in weighing the two facets of public interest within the second bullet point the public authority must apply a presumption in favour of disclosure (reg.12(2)). In *Archer* v. *Information Commissioner and Salisbury District Council* (May 2007) the Tribunal explained, correctly, that 'the result, in short, is that the threshold to justify non-disclosure is a high one'.

A public authority may, applying the above conditions, refuse to disclose environmental information to the extent that[14] such disclosure would adversely affect:[15]

(a) international relations, defence, national security (in relation to which a ministerial certificate of adverse affect is conclusive) (reg.15(1) and (3))[16] or public safety ;

(b) the course of justice, the ability of a person to receive a fair trial or the ability of a public authority to conduct an inquiry of a criminal or disciplinary nature;

(c) intellectual property rights;

(d) the confidentiality of the proceedings of that or any other body where such confidentiality is provided by law;[17]

(e) the confidentiality of commercial or industrial information where such confidentiality is provided by law to protect a legitimate economic interest;[18]

(f) the interests of the person who provided the information[19] where that person:

(i) was not under, and could not have been put under, any legal obligation to supply it to that or any other public authority;

(ii) did not supply it in circumstances such that that or any other public authority is entitled apart from under the EIR to disclose it; and

(g) has not consented to its disclosure;[20] or

(h) the protection of the environment to which the information relates.

A special rule of some substantial potential significance applies in relation to information which relates to 'emissions'. The exemptions stated in points (d)–(g) above do not apply in relation to requests for such information (reg.12(9)). The concept of 'emissions' is not specifically defined in either the Environmental Information Directive or the EIR. Information Commissioner and DEFRA guidance suggested initially that the concept should be afforded a meaning consistent with its defined usage in other EU Environmental Directives: so that it would be construed as including both direct and indirect releases of substances, vibrations, heat or noise from individual or diffuse sources to the atmosphere, to water and on to land. This approach was, however, regarded by the Information Tribunal as perhaps being unduly cautious in *Office of Communications* v. *Information Commissioner and T-Mobile (UK) Ltd* (September 2007). The Tribunal noted that exceptions to disclosure should be narrowly interpreted, and in consequence exceptions to exceptions should be broadly interpreted. As such the word 'emissions' should bear its plain and natural meaning even if that gave it a broader meaning than that afforded by other EU Directives. In the particular case, radiation from a mobile phone base station could be properly categorised as an 'emission'. In *Decision FER0072936* (28 March 2007) the Information

Commissioner held that the concept of 'emissions' does not extend to emissions which have not yet occurred. Accordingly, in relation to a document dealing with future risks of liquid natural gas escapes, the exceptions referred to above were not excluded (see paras.32–6). In *Decisions FER0099394 and FER0099394* (14 November 2007) the Information Commissioner ruled, in relation to an application for disclosure of a PFI waste management contract, that the concept of 'emissions' included methods of dealing with bi-products of the waste management process (but information about income generated by methods of disposal of such bi-products was not information about 'emissions' and did fall within the scope of the exemption).

The ambit of certain of the exceptions within reg.12(5) has been considered by the Information Tribunal or the Information Commissioner, as follows.

International relations, defence, national security and public safety

In *Office of Communications* v. *Information Commissioner and T-Mobile (UK) Ltd* (September 2007) the Information Tribunal held that this exception applied on the basis that increased information disclosed about mobile phone network base stations could make those stations more vulnerable to criminal damage, and that this might, inter alia, lead to breakdowns in service with potential to adversely affect the operations of emergency services. The Tribunal then considered whether the public interest in the exception outweighed the public interest in disclosure – and concluded that the risks from disclosure were not large and did not outweigh the public interest in having the whole of Ofcom's data publicly available in a form which could be more readily searched and analysed than was practicable from the Sitefinder Mobile Phone Base Station Finder website database.

The Information Commissioner applied this exception in *Decision FS50102202* (30 August 2007) in upholding a decision of the Health and Safety Executive not to release information relating to computer modelling exercises carried out to examine the likely impact of a terrorist attack on a major nuclear facility in the UK. The Commissioner was satisfied that the information would be of great use to a potential attacker in choosing targets and planning an operation. In balancing the public interest in favour of and against disclosure he stated that:

> release of that information into the public domain, where it would be accessible to anybody, would be of immeasurable assistance to anyone contemplating a terrorist attack . . . Indeed, . . . the nature of the information is such that its release might in fact help to precipitate such an action, or at least help attackers to maximise their impact. He also accepts the view that it would not be possible to produce a redacted version of the information that would contain any information useful to the complainant that would not also be helpful to the potential terrorist. Taking all these factors into account, the Commissioner is therefore of the view that on this occasion – despite the presumption – the public interest in maintaining the exception clearly outweighs the public interest in disclosing the information.

The course of justice, the ability of a person to receive a fair trial or the ability of a public authority to conduct an inquiry of a criminal or disciplinary nature

This exemption has been held, notwithstanding the absence of clear words to such effect, to give some protection to legal advice which is covered by legal professional privilege.[21]

In *Kirkaldie* v. *Information Commissioner and Thanet District Council* (July 2006) the Information Tribunal stated that:

> the purpose of this exception is reasonably clear. It exists in part to ensure that here should be no disruption to the administration of justice, including the operation of the courts and no prejudice to the rights of individuals and organizations to a fair trial. In order to achieve this, it covers legal professional privilege, particularly where a public authority is, or is likely, to be involved in litigation.

In *Burgess* v. *Information Commissioner and Stafford District Council* (June 2007) the Information Tribunal held that the exception was equally applicable to advice given to a local authority even where the request was made after the legal proceedings in relation to which the advice was sought were concluded. This was the case, at any rate, where the advice was of a sufficiently general nature that it might be relevant to guide the local authority at some future juncture. In the *Burgess* case the local authority argued for non-disclosure on the grounds that disclosure would render it difficult for the local authority to maintain any other position on the particular point in future dealings with the public; and that as the advice was simply a view of the law from one lawyer, the local authority was entitled not in that way to become constrained to that interpretation. On the facts, in *Burgess*, the Information Tribunal concluded that the public interest in maintaining the exception outweighed the public interest in disclosure.

A further issue in *Burgess* related to an argument that the advice should no longer be regarded as privileged because the privilege had been waived either by disclosure of the advice by the council to council members, or by an offer of disclosure (not followed up by actual disclosure) of the advice by a council member to an individual. The Information Tribunal held that legal advice is obtained for the very purpose of helping a council to take decisions, and disclosure of the advice to members is a necessary part of that process. Such disclosure does not involve waiver of privilege. The Tribunal also held that a mere unconsummated offer of disclosure was not something which could be equated with waiver of privilege (para.24).

In an earlier decision of the Tribunal, *Kircaldie* v. *Information Commissioner and Thanet District Council* (July 2006), privilege was held on the facts to have been waived, by dint of statements indicating the tenor of that advice made by a councillor at a council meeting (paras.40–1). The Tribunal explained that for there to be waiver of privilege there must be something more than disclosure that legal advice has been taken, there must be reference to the content of that advice: the content of that advice must be summarised or quoted. See also Information Commissioner *Decision FS50097244* (10 July 2007) at para.43; *Decision FER0082136* (3 July 2007) and *Decision FER0081589* (3 July 2007).

An attempt by Milford Haven Port Authority to rely on this exception to prevent a claimant to a legal challenge to a planning permission gaining evidence which might prove useful in that case was given short shrift by the Information Commissioner in *Decision FER0072936* (28 March 2007). The Commissioner explained:

> The context of this claim is the ongoing litigation being pursued against Pembrokeshire County Council and the Pembrokeshire Coast National Park Authority, to which the Port Authority is an interested party. These two organisations are the planning authorities with the statutory responsibility for determining applications for planning permissions and hazardous substances consents relating to the development of the two LNG terminals. Such permissions have now been granted and the litigants are taking action on the basis that, in their opinion, the planning authorities did not take sufficient account of the risks posed by the terminals in reaching their decisions. As the litigation was ongoing at the time of the request (and indeed remains so), the Port Authority has argued that to release into the public domain the two documents subject to the amended request would adversely affect that litigation. The Port Authority has argued that the disclosure of the two documents would adversely affect the litigation because the documents would be used by opponents of the LNG developments to distort and magnify the risks posed by the terminals and thereby influence the outcome of the legal action. To support this assertion the Port Authority has explained that previous disclosures of information have been used by opponents of the development to support their point of view. The Commissioner has considered these arguments and has concluded that the Port Authority has not provided enough evidence to suggest that disclosure in this case 'would adversely affect' the course of justice. He believes that, in order to demonstrate adverse affect, a public authority must be able to demonstrate that it is more probable than not that harm that would be caused if the information were to be disclosed. The Port Authority has not been able to do so in this case.

The confidentiality of commercial or industrial information where such confidentiality is provided by law to protect a legitimate economic interest[22]

Information will only be protected by law for the purposes of this exception if it is not already accessible by the public. In *Office of Communications* v. *Information Commissioner and T-Mobile (UK) Ltd* (September 2007) the Information Tribunal decided, obiter, that information is in the public domain even though it may be difficult and laborious to extract that information. As such, a request for disclosure of that information in more readily accessible form was not a request for information which was protected by the law of confidentiality. See paras.63–6, following the approach adopted by Jacob J in *Mars* v. *Teknowledge* [2000] FSR 138.

A good example of the Information Commissioner's approach to this exception may be seen in Decision FER0072936 (28 March 2007), where Milford Haven Port Authority sought to justify non-disclosure of two liquid natural gas terminal risk assessments provided to it on a basis of confidentiality by promoters of the development. On the issue of 'public interest' the Information Commissioner stated:

There is an inherent public interest in individuals having access to information that helps them to understand the decisions made by public bodies. . . . In this particular case, the Commissioner believes that there is a very strong public interest in the disclosure of environmental information relating to the development of LNG terminals in Milford Haven. The LNG developments are locally controversial, with proponents arguing that the terminals will bring jobs and investment to the area and opponents arguing that the actual and potential environmental impacts are too high. Disclosure of environmental information of the type requested in this case could add significantly to public knowledge of the risks posed by the development and better inform public debate. Furthermore, the Commissioner believes that there is a public interest in ensuring that the Port Authority is undertaking its duties effectively and that it adequately assesses and manages risk within the Haven. In terms of high-profile and potentially hazardous developments such as the LNG terminals, there is a legitimate public interest in demonstrating that public safety has been fully considered by all relevant authorities, including the Port Authority, at each stage of the development process. In terms of the public interest in maintaining the exception, the Commissioner recognises that there is an inherent public interest in maintaining the confidentiality of commercial information. Commercial confidentiality exists to allow companies to develop and maintain a competitive advantage in a market economy, and in balancing the public interest the Commissioner must weigh up the extent to which the developers' interests would be adversely affected by the disclosure. The Commissioner recognises that the Port Authority, whilst it is a public authority for the purposes of the regulations and does undertake functions of public administration, operates in a largely commercial environment. The Port Authority has developed and continues to develop close working relationships with private sector partners to take forward economic development in the area. The Commissioner believes that it is important for the Port Authority and developers to share information, particularly information relating to the management of risk and, ultimately, public safety. If the disclosure of commercially confidential information would dissuade other organisations from sharing information with the Port Authority in the future, then this would have a negative impact on the Port Authority's ability to carry out its functions. It could, ultimately, impact on its ability to manage environmental and public safety in the Haven. After weighing up the competing factors, the Commissioner has concluded that the public interest in disclosure outweighs the public interest in maintaining the exception. In reaching this decision he has considered that the adverse affect to the confidentiality of commercial information would not outweigh the considerable public interest in providing information about issues of public safety and environmental concerns. The Commissioner does not believe that disclosure of the environmental information in this instance would dissuade the developers or other organisations from sharing commercial or industrial information with the Port Authority.

An equally robust approach was taken by the Information Commissioner in respect of a request for disclosure in its entirety of the waste PFI contract entered into by Onyx/Veolia and East Sussex County Council and Brighton and Hove Council: *FER 0073984* and *FER0099394* (14 November 2007). Both authorities were willing to disclose the principal clauses forming the contract, and also certain of its 43 Schedules. Certain other Schedules, some in redacted form, were also released after the applicant made initial contact with the Information Commissioner. However, other Schedules were regarded by the local authorities as falling within this exemption, and non-disclosable on balance of public interests.

The Commissioner examined in detail the provisions of the contract and its many Schedules. A two-staged analysis was conducted: (i) whether or not particular kinds of information within the contract fell within the ambit of the this exemption; and (ii) where information fell within that ambit, whether the public interest in maintaining the exemption outweighed the public interest in disclosure of the information.

The Commissioner found:

- That the Schedules did contain information which could assist competitors, and that disclosure of some of the information could adversely affect the 'legitimate economic interests' of the waste company.
- That as the contract provided that confidential information contained within it should be kept confidential by *both* parties, the exemption might also apply in respect of any adverse effect on the 'legitimate economic interests' of the local authorities (i.e. protection of their position as purchaser) which might result from disclosure.
- That the mere presence within a contract of a 'confidentiality clause' does not render all information caught by that clause confidential. The matter is one of substance and not form. For information to be 'confidential' it must (i) have been imparted in circumstances which created an obligation of confidence, and (ii) have the necessary 'quality' of confidence.
- That as regards point (i) above – the decision in the *Derry City Council* case (EA/2006/0014, on the FOIA, and holding contract provisions not to be within an FOIA exemption because not information provided to the authority 'by another party') was not applicable to this differently worded EIR exemption. The Commissioner took the view that both the contract's confidentiality clause and the circumstances surrounding the tendering process indicated that information contained within the contract had been imparted in circumstances which, subject to the information having the necessary 'quality' of being 'confidential', gave rise to obligations of confidence.
- That as regards point (ii) above – information could remain confidential even after some years have elapsed, so long as in the meantime it had not entered the public domain or ceased to be commercially significant.
- That the information in the non-disclosed Schedules could be divided for purposes of analysis into broad categories, such as: pricing, operational

information, training directory, systems and technical information, company information, personal information, planning and development information.

- That following a detailed review of each of these categories, some fell within the scope of the terms of the exemption, but others did not. For example, the Commissioner took the view that it was unlikely in this kind of contract that the competitive advantage of the contractor would be unduly prejudiced by disclosure of pricing information unaccompanied by information about how in the circumstances of the particular contract those prices were calculated. A different conclusion was reached, however, as regards information about profit margins and techniques for minimising costs in performing the contract. Much 'operational information' was held to fall within the ambit of the exemption; as also information about likely future planning applications.
- That after assessing, at some length, the competing public interests, the following information within the contested Schedules should be disclosed: (i) all information relating to pricing contained within the contract other than that highlighting specific costs or profits of the contractor; (ii) all operational information contained within the contract other than the names of preferred subcontractors for the supply of equipment and services which are not already known; (iii) all planning and development information held within the contract, other than that containing systems and technical information falling within the scope of the exception.
- In contrast, the following information could be withheld from disclosure: (i) specific systems and technical information which is not otherwise in the public domain; (ii) specific information on the costs and profits of the contractor held in the contract; (iii) specific information on the likely claw-back of costs through the sale of bi-products of the waste management system which aid in lowering the overall cost to the contractor; (iv) the contractor's Quality Management Manual.

In addition to the exceptions listed above within reg.12(5) the Regulations provide more generally that a public authority may refuse to disclose environmental information in circumstances where the public interest in non-disclosure outweighs the public interest in disclosure, and:

- it does not hold the information when the applicant's request is received (note here the duties imposed on a public authority where that body is aware that the requested information is held by another public authority: see **9.2.12**);
- the request for information is manifestly unreasonable (the Information Commissioner's advice on vexatious requests under the FOIA is likely to be a useful guide also to interpretation of this 'manifestly unreasonable' exception. See Awareness Guidance 22);

- the request is formulated in too general a manner (note here the public authority's obligation under reg.9 to assist the applicant in providing particulars which may render the request less general);
- the request relates to material which is still in the course of completion,[23] to unfinished documents or to incomplete data;[24] or
- the request involves the disclosure of internal communications, including communications between government departments.[25]

The last of these exceptions – that the request involves the disclosure of internal communications, including communications between government departments – has been considered in several cases before the Commissioner and the Tribunal.

At first glance this exception would appear to be of very wide scope. Is it not the case that a high proportion of documents sought from public authorities will fall within the general rubric 'internal communications'? The key point to note, however, is that none of these exceptions is satisfied simply because the request falls within the scope of one of the bullet-pointed expressions. The exceptions only apply where the request falls within that ambit, and in addition the public interest in non-disclosure outweighs the public interest in disclosure (with the presumption being always in favour of disclosure). In other words, taking the last example on the list, there is no blanket exception in relation to internal communications; there is simply an exception in relation to internal communications in respect of which a clear case can be made out that in the circumstances of the case the public interest in protecting the confidentiality of that disclosure outweighs the public interest in such disclosure.

The public interest in non-disclosure of such internal communication has generally been described in terms of the concept of 'private thinking space'. A typical statement may be found in the Information Commissioner *Decision FER0082566* (11 October 2007) where the applicant sought 'internal communication' documents relating to the consideration by DEFRA of responses to a consultation on pesticide crop spraying matters. The Commissioner commented:

> The Commissioner recognizes that frank and honest debate is necessary for high quality policy formulation and that there is a public interest, in certain circumstances, in maintaining private space for such discussion away from public scrutiny. That is, the EIR will protect internal communications when it is sufficiently in the public interest to do so.

On the facts of the case, however, the Commissioner held that the public interest in disclosure (allowing the public to understand the way in which government had reached decisions, and allowing more informed participation by the public in debates with government) outweighed the public interest (outlined above) which lay behind this exception.

This approach to the public interest may be seen also in Information Tribunal cases.

288

In *Friends of the Earth* v. *Information Commissioner and the Export Credits Guarantee Department* (August 2007) a request for inter-departmental correspondence in relation to an application for export credit for the 'politically sensitive' Sakhalin II oil and gas project was resisted on the grounds that reg.12(4) applied, and that there was a strong public interest in the full and frank provision and discussion of advice within government, because that makes for better quality decision making. Moreover, it was argued that such disclosure would be contrary to the public interest as undermining the convention of collective responsibility. Friends of the Earth countered, inter alia, that given the environmentally-controversial nature of the project in question (e.g. its threats to the already endangered Grey Whale species) there was a strong public interest favouring disclosure so that the reasons for any public funding support for the project could be discerned. On appeal, the Information Tribunal overturned the decision of the Information Commissioner and held that the balance of public interest lay in favour of disclosure: that on a balance of probabilities the ECGD had failed to prove a sufficiently demonstrable public interest requiring protection from disclosure, such as to overturn the clear legal presumption in favour of disclosure. The Tribunal referred to the:

> onus which clearly rests on a public authority in the context of the EIR whenever it chooses to rely on an exception . . .; that onus being to *specify clearly and precisely the harm of harms that would be caused were disclosure to be ordered* [emphasis added].

The Tribunal made clear that each case must accordingly be assessed on its own merits, and that there could be no 'immutable' principle that, for example, the convention of ministerial collective responsibility should operate in all cases as some form of 'trump card' against applications for disclosure.

Having looked at the documents in question and having weighed the controversial nature of the project against the quite ill-defined, and generic rather than specific, assertions of the harm that disclosure would entail, the Tribunal ordered disclosure.[26]

This exemption was also considered by the Information Tribunal in *Rt Hon Lord Baker of Dorking* v. *Information Commissioner and Department of Communities and Local Government* (June 2007). Lord Baker had, before the Information Commissioner, been successful in obtaining certain documents relating to a controversial decision of the Deputy Prime Minister not to follow a recommendation of a planning inspector, but rather to grant planning permission for a controversial 50-storey residential tower in the vicinity of the Palace of Westminster. In the appeal to the Tribunal, the applicant sought that there should also be disclosed the advice provided to the Minister by his civil servants prior to reaching his decision. It should be noted that the Minister's decision had been taken prior to the claim to see these documents: it was accepted by the parties to the appeal (and supported by Information Commissioner *Decisions 0071457* (4 September 2007) and *FER0070181*

(27 July 2006)) that the public interest would support non-disclosure of such information at any time prior to the planning decision having been taken. However, once the decision has been taken different considerations were held by the Tribunal to apply. Following an elaborate analysis of public interest factors weighing for and against disclosure, the Tribunal concluded that disclosure of the advice of officials after the decision in question has been taken will not undermine to any significant extent the proper and effective performance by civil servants of their duties in the future. The Tribunal uttered a plea to the media:

> We hope that we are justified in having . . . confidence in the media to deal responsibly with the information that falls into their hands as a result of government now being conducted in a more public manner. Ministers, who are responsible for their decisions, should continue to be held to account for them, and not their officials.

And then sounded a warning:

> We can envisage that a Tribunal considering a similar category of information in the future may take a more restrictive view on disclosure if it has become apparent by then that the media habitually use officials' advice, disclosed under freedom of information principles, as the basis for partial or irresponsible criticism or to justify intrusion into the private lives of the individuals who have contributed to that advice.

A further, and important, part of the Tribunal's Decision is that the key date upon which the public interest shifts in favour of disclosure is, as indicated above, the date of publication of the decision in respect of which the advice was tendered. In argument the Department had sought that the key date should be the date following which an appeal against that decision would be time-barred. The Tribunal disagreed. The key date was when the Minister's decision had been announced. (Compare Information Commissioner *Decision FER0086093* (25 June 2007).)

9.2.14 Power to neither confirm nor deny

Where a request for environmental information is for information which, if held by a public authority, might fall within one of the various exceptions referred to above, and the public authority holding such information forms the view that the information should not be disclosed under one of the exceptions, the public authority is empowered in certain situations to respond to the request by neither confirming nor denying whether such information exists and is held by the authority. The situations where the refusal to disclose will legitimately incorporate a statement neither confirming nor denying that the information exists and is held by the authority are where such confirmation or denial would itself adversely affect international relations, defence, national security or public safety, and the public interest in such confirmation and denial would be outweighed by the adverse effect in question (reg.12(6) and (7)).

9.2.15   Personal data[27]

We noted earlier that the general duty of disclosure under the EIR does not apply to the extent that the environmental information is personal data of which the applicant is the data subject (reg.5(3)). Applications for such data must instead be treated as subject access requests made under the Data Protection Act 1998 (DPA) (see, in particular, DPA, s.7).

In contrast, to the extent that the requested environmental information may comprise personal data of which the applicant is not the data subject, the information is subject to the provisions of the EIR. Although requests for this category of environmental information do not fall to be governed directly by the DPA, some of the protections afforded by that Act to personal data are replicated in the EIR.

The EIR provide that such requested personal data must not be disclosed where one or other of the two conditions laid down in reg.13(2) are satisfied (reg.12(3)).

The first of those conditions deals separately with two distinct situations depending on whether or not the information falls within the first four categories of data in s.1(1) of the DPA.[28]

Where the information falls within those categories of data the information must not be disclosed where such disclosure would either contravene one or more of the data protection principles (reg.13(2)(a)(i));[29] or would contravene s.10 of the DPA (i.e. where the data subject has given notice that disclosure would cause unwarranted substantial damage or distress to the data subject), and the public interest in not disclosing outweighs the public interest in disclosing the information (reg.13(2)(a)(ii)).[30]

Where the information does not fall within the first four categories of data in s.1(1) of the DPA (i.e. it is recorded information held by a public authority not falling within the first four categories of data listed in s.1(1) of the DPA) the information must not be disclosed where the disclosure of that information would contravene any of the data protection principles (reg.13(2)(b)).[31]

The second condition is that requested information must not be disclosed where the information is exempt from the disclosure requirements of s.7 of the DPA by virtue of any of that Act's exemptions (see DPA, Part IV) – in other words, generally speaking the non data subject cannot access information under the EIR which the data subject himself/herself could not access under the DPA –and in all the circumstances of the case the public interest in not disclosing the information outweighs the public interest in disclosing it (reg.13(3)).

9.2.16   Reasoned decisions

Decisions by public authorities to refuse to disclose information under any of the various exceptions, or under the personal data provisions, must be communicated in writing and within 20 working days of the receipt of the request (reg.14(1)). (For power to extend this period, see **9.2.10**.) The decision must indicate the particular exception(s) relied upon, and must indicate the matters the public authority took into consideration in reaching its decision that the public interest favoured non-disclosure rather than disclosure (reg.14(3)).

The written refusal must also inform the applicant of the right to make representations to the public authority under the reg.11 internal review procedure, and of the enforcement and appeal provisions applicable to the decision.

9.3   ENFORCEMENT AND APPEALS

At the outset of this chapter it was emphasised that although the new EIR came into force on the same day as the FOIA, their pedigrees are quite different: one a home-grown measure, the other a measure designed to meet requirements set at international multilateral treaty level and at EU level. As such a warning was sounded that in significant ways their substantive breadths of operation are by no means identical.

One area, however, where a close link has been achieved between the two regimes lies in the fields of enforcement and appeals. Regulation 18 provides that, subject only to certain modifications (for example, Part IV (enforcement) does not apply where a certificate has been issued by a Minister under reg.15), the enforcement and appeal provisions of the FOIA (Parts IV and V) apply also for the purposes of the EIR.

The relevant provisions of the FOIA are dealt with in **Chapter 10**. In briefest summary, a person who has made a request may make initial complaint (this should follow the internal review process provided for by reg.11) to the Information Commissioner if he considers that the request has not been handled (the complaint may for example be as regards level of fee charged, or time taken to determine the request) or determined in accordance with the EIR. The Information Commissioner has power to issue an Information Notice as a means of gaining the information the Information Commissioner will need in order to determine the complaint. The Information Commissioner also has powers of entry, search and seizure; and offences exist with respect to any obstruction of the Information Commissioner in the exercise of these functions. Given the ubiquity within the EIR of the need for the balancing of public interests it will generally be necessary for the Information Commissioner to review documents sought in order to decide whether a correct decision has been reached by the public body in question. The Information Commissioner will issue a Decision Notice giving his decision on the merits of the application.

From decisions of the Information Commissioner, appeal lies at the suit of the applicant for information or at the suit of the public authority as the case may be, to the Information Tribunal. From the Information Tribunal there lies a further right of appeal on a point of law to the High Court (and beyond).

9.3.1 Offences (reg.19)

Where a request has been made to a public authority for environmental information and that request is one which does not fall within the scope of the above-mentioned exemptions (including the provisions restricting access to personal data) an offence is committed by any person who, with the intention of preventing the disclosure of all or part of the information, alters, defaces, blocks, erases, destroys or conceals any record held by the authority. (The offence is triable summarily. The maximum penalty is a fine not exceeding level 5 on the standard scale.)

No proceedings in relation to this offence may be instituted except by the Information Commissioner, or by or with the consent of the Director of Public Prosecutions (reg.19(4)).

NOTES

1   Ratified by the UK in February 2005. For the text, see **www.unece.org/env/pp/ documents/cep43e.pdf**.
2   Compare, for example, FOIA, s.44 with reg.5(6) (contrary approaches to effect of prior legislation requiring that a public authority shall not disclose information in its possession). Note also that there is no provision in the EIR permitting non-disclosure on grounds of the cost of compliance: cf. FOIA, s.12.
3   In a case where the public authority or the Information Commissioner may have proceeded on a wrong conclusion as to whether information is or is not 'environmental information', no appeal will succeed if the same conclusion would have followed had the correct categorisation of the information been made. See *Robinson* v. *Information Commissioner and East Ridings Yorkshire Council* (October 2007).
4   For example, Milford Haven Port Authority (an 'other body . . . that carries out functions of public administration': reg.2(2)), and hence the significance of the Information Commissioner's decision that information relating to risk assessments of plans to develop liquid natural gas terminals was 'environmental information': see *Decision FER0072936* (28 March 2007) at paras.4 and 5.
5   For a good example of a context in which there might be a difference in conclusion (based on the scope of exemptions within the two regimes) see *Office of Communications* v. *Information Commissioner and T-Mobile (UK) Ltd* (September 2007) at para.30.
6   For a broad construction of the notion of information relating to the state of land see *R.* v. *British Coal Corporation, ex p. Ibstock Building Products Ltd* [1995] Env LR 277, decided under the earlier Regulations.
7   Note that where information covered by para.(b) is made available, the public authority is required, upon request, insofar as it is possible so to do, to refer the

applicant to where information can be found on the measurement procedures used in compiling that information. See reg.5(5).

8   Indeed, the Information Tribunal concluded later in its Decision that applying the tests laid down in cases such as *Parochial Church Council for the Parish of Aston Cantlow and Wilmecote and Billesley* v. *Wallbank* [2004] 1 AC 546 and *YL* v. *Birmingham City Council* [2007] UKHL 27, Network Rail should not be regarded as a 'public body'. See para.48.

9   DEFRA's original Guidance on the Environmental Information Regulations included some conclusions about the scope of these phrases which seem difficult to square with either the wording or the legislative history of the Regulations and EU Directive. For example, it was stated:

> Examples of bodies covered by EIR are private companies or Public Private Partnerships with obvious environmental functions such as waste disposal, water, energy, transport companies (such as the Civil Aviation Authority and port authorities), and environmental consultants. Public utilities, for example, are involved in the supply of essential services such as water, sewerage, electricity and gas fall within the scope of the EIR. Other bodies covered include the Ambulance Service, which carries out a public service and collects statistics in road traffic accidents, and Customs and Excise in dealing with the illegal import of endangered species.

Certain of the bodies referred to certainly do qualify as public authorities under earlier limbs of the definition than the one presently under consideration. However, as regards those bodies referred to within the paragraph which are not government bodies per se, nor are bodies exercising functions of public administration, the words quoted reach very broad conclusions which are asserted rather than explained, and in a number of instances may legitimately be doubted. In relation to certain of the examples given there may have been a confusion between notions of activities with evident environmental impacts, and activities which genuinely fall within the three phrases in the main text above. Moreover, remember that falling within one of those three phrases is only one part of the test within part (d) of the definition of public authority. Such bodies also have to fall within the control requirement before they may be regarded as public authorities. The present Guidance seems to be couched in slightly less extensive, although perhaps still potentially misleading, terms:

> Examples of bodies that may be covered by EIR limb (d) are private companies or Public Private Partnerships with obvious environmental functions such as waste disposal, water, energy, transport regulators. Public utilities, for example, are involved in the supply of essential public services such as water, sewerage, electricity and gas and may fall within the scope of the EIRs.

10 The DEFRA Guidance (para.2.4) suggests:

> Control . . . mean[s] . . . the possibility of directly or indirectly exercising a decisive influence on a body . . . Control may relate not only to the body but also to control over the services provided by the body. It covers financial, regulatory and administrative control.
>
> This suggests an interpretation of control which seems rather broader than that suggested in the text above, and for which no source of authority is provided. DEFRA's broad approach should be noted, but with the caution that ultimately it is for the courts to interpret and apply the unelaborated definitional phrase.

11 Incorporating by reference Art.7(2) of Directive 2003/4. Note that Art.7(2) also requires that such information 'shall be updated as appropriate'. This requirement does not expressly appear within the EIR.

12 In the draft Regulations put out to consultation in the summer of 2004 this phrase read 'complexity or volume'.

13 The wording of Recital (18) to the EU Directive may be instructive in interpreting notions of reasonable charge. It reads:

> Public authorities should be able to make a charge for supplying environmental information, but such charge should be reasonable. This implies that, as a general rule, charges may not exceed actual costs of producing the material in question. In limited cases where public authorities make environmental information available on a commercial basis, and where this is necessary in order to guarantee the continuation of collecting and publishing such information, a market-based charge is considered to be reasonable.

14 The phrase 'would adversely affect' seems a more onerous pre-condition than its equivalent under the FOIA: that is, 'would be likely to prejudice'.

15 A Minister may designate another person to certify such matters on his or her behalf: reg.15(2).

16 In Information Commissioner *Decision FS50094124* (22 May 2007) this exception was applied so as to uphold non-disclosure of information relating to a confidential investigation by the local government ombudsman into a complaint of maladministration made by the information request applicant. Although under the EIR the bar on disclosure of such information under the Local Government Act 1974, s.32(2) was not determinative (compare the position under the FOIA) the balance of public interest here lay in favour of non-disclosure.

17 This exception was analysed and found to apply on the facts in *Office of Communications* v. *Information Commissioner and T-Mobile (UK) Ltd* (September 2007): information on mobile phone base stations comprised confidential information.

18 In *Dainton* v. *Information Commissioner and Lincolnshire County Council* (September, 2007) the Information Tribunal adverted to the fact that where an anonymous provider of information fears that disclosure of a document will allow identification by handwriting, this exemption will not apply because the public authority should discharge its disclosure duties by way of a typed transcript: see para.36.

19 For cases where the Information Commissioner has held that the adverse affect on the party providing the information outweighed the public interest in disclosure see e.g. *Decision FER0125285* (8 October 2007); *Decision FER0066999* (17 September 2007); *Decision FER50086605* (15 February 2007) – taking into account the statutory process whereby the requested information might become available at a later juncture; *Decision FS50062329* (12 July 2005) – documents ordered to be disclosed except for parts revealing identities of those providing the information. Contrast, however, *Decision FER0072936* (28 March 2007) – no adverse affect demonstrated, and even had such adverse affect been demonstrated, the public interest in disclosure of risk assessments relating to proposed liquid natural gas terminals at Milford Haven would have lain in favour of disclosure.

20 For Information Commissioner decisions upholding the public interest in non-disclosure of privileged legal advice see, e.g: *Decision FER0155651* (2 October 2007); *Decision FER0123644* (25 July 2007); *Decision FS5012004* (11 July 2007); *Decision FS50097244* (10 July 2007); *Decision FER0131423* (21 June 2007); *Decision FS50091315* (12 February 2007); *Decision FS50078600* (5 February 2007); and *Decision FER0078604* (14 November 2007).

21 For a careful analysis of evidence in order to ascertain which parts of the information requested fell within the category of being 'confidential', and which parts of that material might if released adversely affect the interests of the supermarket businesses about which the information related, see Information Commissioner *Decision 98306/7* (24 August 2007).

22 For an Information Commissioner Decision holding a report to comprise the final stage of a distinct phase of the implementation of a scheme (and so not 'material in course of completion') rather than a document which was a mere part of an as yet incomplete wider project, see *Decision FER0069925* (2 March 2006).

23 Where this exemption is relied upon the written decision refusing disclosure must specify, if known, the estimated time in which the information will be finished or completed. See reg.14(4).

24 Reg.12(4) and (8). The intent here appears to be to provide some protection in relation to communications which do not yet constitute the settled view within government on a particular matter.

25 For an apparently rather different approach to the weighing of public interests in relation to reg.12(4)(e) compare *Benjamin Archer* v. *Information Commissioner and Salisbury District Council* (May 2007).

26 This concept is defined in DPA, s.1(1) as data which relate to a living individual who can be identified (a) from those data; or (b) from those data and other information which is in the possession of, or is likely to come into the possession of, the data controller, and includes any expression of opinion about the individual and any indication of the intentions of the data controller or any other person in respect of the individual. For a restrictive interpretation of the scope of this definition see *Durant* v. *Financial Services Authority* [2003] EWCA Civ 1746; and more recently, *Harcup* v. *Information Commissioner* (Information Tribunal, 5 February 2008). In *Dainton* v. *Information Commissioner and Lincolnshire County Council* (September 2007) the Information Tribunal has held that answers given in a local authority questionnaire by users of a disputed footpath about their use of the path, what has happened to them when using the footpath, and their opinions about its legal status, amounted to 'personal data' (see at para.19).

27 'Data' within the meaning of s.1(1) of the DPA consists of information which:

    (i)   is being processed by means of equipment operating automatically in response to instructions given for that purpose;
    (ii) is recorded with the intention that it should be processed by means of such equipment;
    (iii) is recorded as part of a relevant filing system or with the intention that it should form part of a relevant filing system;
    (iv) does not fall within paragraph (i), (ii) or (iii) but forms part of an accessible record as defined by s.68 of the DPA; or
    (v)   is recorded information held by a public authority and does not fall within any of paras.(i)–(iv).

28 The data protection principles are set out in Sched.1 to the DPA and further elaborated in Scheds.2, 3 and 4. They include the principle that 'personal data shall be obtained only for one or more specified and lawful purposes, and shall not be further processed in any manner incompatible with that purpose or those purposes'. In *Decision FER0086785* (10 October 2007) the Information Commissioner held that personal data should be released under Sched.2 Condition 6 (see at paras.47–51).

29 The public interest criterion applies only to the s.10 ground, so that where disclosure would contravene one of the data protection principles no such balancing of public interests arises.

30 For these purposes the exemptions from the data protection principles for the fifth category of data in s.1(1) of the DPA, i.e. recorded information held by public authorities, should be disregarded. The exemptions referred to, and to be disregarded, are those contained in s.33A(1) of the DPA (added by FOIA, s.70). In

Dainton v. *Information Commissioner and Lincolnshire County Council* (September 2007) the Information Tribunal held – in relation to disclosure of personal information contained in responses to a local authority questionnaire – that the first data protection principle would have been breached by disclosure of such information. The requirement of 'fairness' would not have been met because those completing the questionnaire would have anticipated that their answers would not be disclosed unless and until a later stage in the statutory 'rights of way modification' process had been reached. See para.30.

31 Strictly speaking, the offence may be committed only by the public authority, or any person who is employed by, is an officer of, or is subject to the direction of, the public authority. See reg.19(2). Moreover, where the public authority is a government department, the department shall not itself be liable to prosecution (although the offence may in that case be committed by a person in the public service of the Crown, i.e. a civil servant).

CHAPTER 10

Enforcement and appeals

Jeremy Ison, Clifford Chance LLP

10.1 INTRODUCTION

Life after FOIA has changed and had to change.

So said the Information Tribunal in August 2007 when deciding to grant an appeal brought by Friends of the Earth, which was seeking disclosure of information passing between government departments in relation to the controversial Sakhalin II oil and gas project. The panel confessed to being 'unimpressed' by the arguments that a disclosure order would create a 'chilling effect' in Whitehall such that civil servants would be fearful of documenting their views candidly and meetings would no longer be minuted.

Thus, the Information Tribunal, together with the Information Commissioner, have played a significant role in bedding down the new culture of increased openness over the last three years. Their decisions have assisted public authorities and applicants alike to better understand the practical implications of the Freedom of Information Act 2000 (FOIA). Yet the ever-expanding body of 'case law' is dynamic; markers seemingly put down are liable to change. At the time of writing, for instance, a further appeal in the Friends of the Earth case is pending before the High Court. And while all those with an interest in freedom of information scrutinise the constant stream of adjudications, the concept of 'precedent' is an elusive one. Each case is decided on its own facts, and merely because an earlier case concerned a similar situation, that does not mean that the outcome of the later case will inevitably be the same; time will have moved on and considerations as to the application of the exemptions and the public interest test may well be materially different.

Primary responsibility for enforcement of the FOIA lies with the Information Commissioner, who monitors public authorities and can issue notices directing them to take action so as to comply with their statutory obligations. Failure to comply with the Information Commissioner's notices can be punished as if it were a contempt of court. The enforcement and appeals regime under the FOIA applies also to the Environmental Information Regulations 2004, SI 2004/3391 (EIR).[1] The FOIA applies in England, Wales and Northern Ireland only. In Scotland the enforcement regime under the Freedom of Information (Scotland)

Act 2002 and the Environmental Information (Scotland) Regulations 2004, SSI 2004/520, is broadly similar but there is no equivalent of the Information Tribunal north of the border. The only appeal from the Scottish Commissioner is to the Court of Session, and only on a point of law.

At the heart of the enforcement regime lies the complaints process. This is the route (outlined in Figure 10.1) which an applicant must follow if the applicant considers that his or her request for information has been turned down or dealt with improperly.

This chapter will first review the Information Commissioner's role and the various notices he can serve, before looking in detail at the complaints process at **10.5–10.8**, including appeals to the Information Tribunal. Finally, it will turn to the position of interested third parties (such as private sector companies which do business with the public sector) and their somewhat limited opportunities to restrain disclosure of information which affects them.

10.2   THE INFORMATION COMMISSIONER'S ROLE

Although appointed by the Crown and answerable to Parliament, the Information Commissioner is independent of government. (It may be more accurate to say 'largely' independent, as his budget is set by the Ministry of Justice (MoJ), a matter which has become controversial since it became obvious to the Information Commissioner and others that he was under-resourced to deal efficiently with the high levels of work generated by the FOI legislation, which has led to a backlog of cases.)

As the regulator, he is charged with ensuring that the rights and duties contained in the FOIA and the EIR are widely known about and respected. (He has a similar role in relation to the Data Protection Act 1998 (DPA).) He investigates complaints and has the power to instruct bodies to disclose information. In practice, his primary focus in this regard is to consider whether the exemptions in Part II of the FOIA have been properly applied by public bodies and to ensure that, in doing so, those bodies have had due regard to the public interest in disclosure.

He is supported by a large staff, including two Deputy Commissioners and a legal department. The Information Commissioner's Office is based in Wilmslow, near Manchester, with satellite offices in Cardiff, Edinburgh and Belfast.

10.2.1   Duties

The Information Commissioner's duties are outlined as follows under Parts III and IV of the FOIA and under the EIR:

- to promote the following of good practice by public authorities generally, and in particular to carry out his work in such a way as to promote the

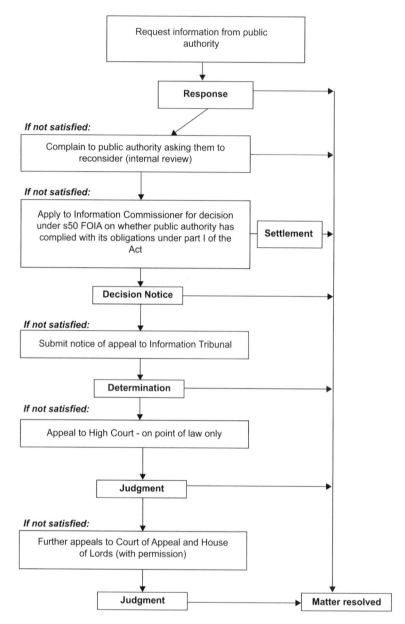

Figure 10.1 The complaints process

observance by public authorities of the requirements of the legislation and the provisions of the Codes of Practice made under the FOIA and the EIR[2] (FOIA, s.47(1); EIR, reg.16(5)) (good practice in this context is stated not to be limited to following the provisions of the FOIA and the Codes of Practice made under ss.45 and 46 of the FOIA);

- to publish information about the operation of the legislation, good practice and other matters relating to his statutory functions (FOIA, s.47(2); EIR reg.16(5));
- to lay an annual report before both Houses of Parliament containing a general report on the exercise of his statutory functions (s.49(1));
- (save in certain circumstances) to determine, when asked to do so by an applicant under s.50(1), whether or not a public authority has complied with its obligations under Part I of the FOIA, or Parts 2 and 3 of the Regulations, in responding to a request for information (FOIA, s.50(2); EIR, reg.18).

The Information Commissioner is subject, in addition, to the same public law duties of any executive decision maker, and his decisions may be challenged, where appropriate, by means of judicial review. The High Court has held expressly that the Information Commissioner is 'under a broad duty to act fairly' in his handling of complaints (*British Broadcasting Corporation* v. *Sugar* [2007] EWHC 905 (Admin), 27 April 2007, para.52).

10.2.2 Powers

In order to assist him in carrying out these duties, the legislation gives the Information Commissioner the following powers:

- to advise anyone on the operation of the legislation, good practice and other matters relating to his functions (FOIA, s.47(2); EIR, reg.16(5));[3]
- to assess whether a public authority is following good practice, subject to that authority's consent (FOIA, s.47(3); EIR, reg.16(5));
- to issue a written Practice Recommendation to a public authority, specifying the steps which it should take to remedy the situation where he considers that its practice does not conform to the Codes of Practice (FOIA, s.48; EIR, reg.16(5));
- to charge for certain of his services – those under s.47(4) of the FOIA and reg.16(5) of the EIR – subject to consent from the Secretary of State;
- to lay reports before both Houses of Parliament from time to time as he thinks fit, in addition to the obligatory annual report referred to above (FOIA, s.49(2));
- to approve a public authority's Publication Scheme, or to refuse to approve it or revoke his approval for it (giving reasons); and to approve a Model Publication Scheme, or to refuse to approve it or revoke his approval for it (again, giving reasons) (FOIA, ss.19–20);

- to issue Decision Notices, Information Notices and Enforcement Notices (FOIA, ss.50–52; EIR, reg.18);
- to obtain a warrant to enter and search premises so as to obtain evidence where he suspects a public authority of failing to comply with its obligations under the legislation or the notices referred to in the previous bullet, or where he suspects an offence under s.77 of the FOIA or reg.19 of the EIR (obstructing disclosure of requested information) (FOIA, s.55 and Sched.3; EIR, reg.18);
- to certify to the court that a public authority has failed to comply with a Decision Notice, an Information Notice or an Enforcement Notice, so that the court can investigate and punish the non-compliance as a contempt of court if appropriate (FOIA, s.54; EIR, reg.18).

It should be noted that the Information Commissioner has no power to impose fines on public authorities for a breach of their duties under the FOIA or the EIR, nor does he have the power to award compensation to complainants or to make costs orders against the parties involved in a complaint which is directed to him for determination. It is also important to be aware that the Information Commissioner is not empowered to adjudicate formally on, and issue Decision Notices about, complaints against public authorities by anyone other than a person who has sought information from them under s.1 of the FOIA or reg.5 of the EIR.

10.3   THE INFORMATION COMMISSIONER'S NOTICES IN MORE DETAIL

10.3.1   Decision Notices

Decision Notices are only issued in the context of a complaint by someone who is dissatisfied with a public authority's response to his request for information and has applied to the Information Commissioner under s.50(1) for a decision on whether the authority has met its obligations under Part I of the FOIA, or Parts 2 or 3 of the EIR. Following his determination of the matter, the Information Commissioner must either notify the complainant of his reason for not adjudicating on the complaint or serve a Decision Notice on the complainant and the public authority (s.50(3)). Where he decides that the public authority failed to comply with obligations under ss.1(1), 11 or 17 of the FOIA or regs.5(1), 6, 11 or 14 of the EIR,[4] the notice must set out the steps he requires it to take to be in compliance and by when they must be taken. There is no bar on the Decision Notice containing such steps in other cases, however. The Information Commissioner may also make reference in a Decision Notice to any provisions of the Section 45 Code of Practice which the public authority has breached and with which it is to comply (see the Foreword to the Code of Practice at para.9).

Either the complainant or the public authority may appeal to the Information Tribunal against a Decision Notice under s.57 and notices must contain details of that right of appeal (s.50(5)). The deadline for taking the steps specified in the notice cannot expire before the end of the period within which the public authority is entitled to appeal – namely 28 days from when it is served with the notice (Information Tribunal (Enforcement Appeals) Rules 2005, SI 2005/14, r.5). Further, if the authority does challenge the Information Commissioner's decision, it is not obliged to take any action affected by the appeal until the appeal's determination or withdrawal (s.50(6)). Failure to comply with a Decision Notice is ultimately punishable in the High Court as if for contempt of court (s.54). It can also lead to the Information Commissioner obtaining a warrant to search premises to find evidence of non-compliance (s.55 and Sched.3). There is no provision permitting the Information Commissioner to cancel a Decision Notice once issued, as is possible with other notices. A Decision Notice can, however, be overridden by the so-called ministerial veto (see **10.3.5**). For details of the Information Commissioner's policies regarding the issuing and publication of Decision Notices see **10.6.1**.

10.3.2 Information Notices

If the Information Commissioner has received an application for a Decision Notice or reasonably requires any information to determine whether a public authority has complied with, or is complying with, any of the requirements of Part I of the FOIA (or Parts 2 and 3 of the EIR) or the Codes of Practice under ss.45 and 46 of the FOIA and reg.16 of the EIR, he may serve an Information Notice on the authority requiring any information relevant to those matters (which, unlike with access requests, can include unrecorded information (s.51(8)) and he may specify how, and by when, he is to receive it (s.51(1)(b)). If the Information Commissioner serves the Information Notice in response to a request for a decision under s.50(1), the notice must say so. Otherwise, the notice must state that the Information Commissioner regards the information sought as relevant for the purposes mentioned above and reasons must be given (s.50(2)).

The public authority (but not a complainant) may appeal against the notice to the Information Tribunal under s.57 of the FOIA and notices must contain details of that right (s.51(3)). The deadline for providing the Information Commissioner with the information he specifies cannot expire before the end of the period within which the public authority is entitled to appeal, which is 28 days from service of the notice (Information Tribunal (Enforcement Appeals) Rules 2005, SI 2005/14, r.5). Further, if the authority does challenge the notice, it is not obliged to furnish the Information Commissioner with the information before the appeal's determination or withdrawal (s.51(4)). The Information Commissioner may cancel an Information Notice by written notice to the relevant public authority (s.51(7)). (An authority could thus seek cancellation of the notice where it was for some reason no longer appropriate but the time for appealing had expired.) Failure to comply with an Information Notice is ultimately punishable in the High Court as if it were a contempt of court. The same is true where, in purported compliance with an Information Notice, a public authority makes a statement which is false in a material respect, either with knowledge of its falsity or else recklessly (s.54), i.e. not caring whether it is true or false. Failure to comply with the notice can also lead to the Information Commissioner obtaining a warrant to search premises to find evidence of non-compliance (s.55 and Sched.3).

In responding to the notice, the public authority is under no obligation to provide the Information Commissioner with information in respect of any legally privileged communications containing legal advice on a client's rights, obligations or liabilities under the FOIA or made in connection with, or in contemplation of, proceedings arising out of the Act (s.51(5)). This provision was at the centre of an Information Tribunal case which ruled that the Information Commissioner was not permitted to issue an Information Notice requiring the Department for Constitutional Affairs to provide him with legal advice from the Attorney General regarding the public interest test and its interpretation under the FOIA (*Ministry of Justice (previously the DCA)* v. *Information Commissioner*, 6 August 2007).

The Information Commissioner's policies regarding the issuing and publication of Information Notices are discussed in **10.6.1**.

10.3.3 Enforcement Notices

If the Information Commissioner is satisfied that the public authority is in breach of any of its obligations under Part I of the FOIA or Parts 2 and 3 of the EIR, he may serve an Enforcement Notice requiring the public authority to take particular steps by a particular time to comply with those obligations. An Enforcement Notice cannot be issued purely in relation to a breach of a Code of Practice unrelated to a breach of the FOIA. Code breaches can be the subject of Practice Recommendations (see **10.3.6**).

An Enforcement Notice must specify those obligations with which the Information Commissioner is satisfied the public authority has failed to comply, and his reason for reaching that conclusion. It must also give details of the right to appeal against the notice under s.57 (s.52(2)). Only a public authority may appeal, not any complainant with an interest in the matter. As with the notices considered above, the deadline for taking the steps specified in an Enforcement Notice cannot expire before the end of the period within which the public authority is entitled to appeal – 28 days from when it is served (Information Tribunal (Enforcement Appeals) Rules 2005, SI 2005/14, r.5). Again, the authority is not obliged to comply with it pending the determination or withdrawal of any appeal (s.52(4)). The Information Commissioner may cancel an Enforcement Notice by written notice to the public authority (s.52(4)). (Again, an authority could thus ask him to cancel the notice where it was for some reason no longer appropriate but the time for appealing had expired.) An Enforcement Notice can also be overridden by ministerial veto (see **10.3.5**). Failure to comply with a notice can be punished in the High Court as a contempt of court (s.54) and can also lead to the Information Commissioner obtaining a warrant to search premises to find evidence of non-compliance (s.55 and Sched.3).

The distinction in practice between Enforcement and Decision Notices is that the latter arise in the context of specific complaints, whereas the Information Commissioner has indicated he is more likely to issue the former where there have been systemic failures or repeated non-compliance with the FOIA. Examples of where an Enforcement Notice might be issued include:

- systemic, repeated or serious non-compliance with the FOIA or the EIR (especially delay);
- where there is evidence that obligations are being deliberately or persistently ignored or not taken sufficiently seriously;
- where it is necessary to clarify an issue or set a precedent;
- as a means of grouping together several similar complaints against the same public authority;
- failure to adopt a Publication Scheme or to make information available in accordance with the scheme;
- where an authority has clearly failed to follow a Practice Recommendation and to provide proper responses to subsequent requests for information under s.1(1);
- where an authority subject to the EIR does not have an internal complaints process as the Regulations require.

Rather than rushing to issue Enforcement Notices at the earliest opportunity, the Information Commissioner aims to give public authorities ample opportunity to comply voluntarily. He has said he will not resort to formal action where he is satisfied that the risk can be addressed by negotiation or other less formal means.[5]

There is only one published Enforcement Notice to date but it is one that attracted a great deal of attention, concerning as it did several requests by different people for the Attorney General's advice to the Prime Minister in 2003 on the legality of military intervention in Iraq (Enforcement Notice dated 22 May 2006 addressed to the Legal Secretariat to the Law Officers).

10.3.4 Preliminary notices

Although there is no provision for them in the FOIA, the Information Commissioner initially adopted a policy of issuing Preliminary Decision (or Enforcement or Information) Notices where he considered it likely that this could lead to the satisfactory informal resolution of the matter. (To see how this worked see the ICO document *Regulation under the Freedom of Information Act 2000* and the Environmental Information Regulations 2004 (ICO, 2.3.05), Annex 1.) Following criticism of this procedure from the Information Tribunal, however, this policy is no longer active.

10.3.5 Ministerial veto

Under the controversial s.53 of the FOIA, a Decision Notice or an Enforcement Notice issued by the Information Commissioner (or modified on appeal by the Information Tribunal) and served on a government department, the Welsh Assembly or any public authority designated by the Secretary of State (s.53(1)(a)) can be overridden by a politician. This applies equally to such notices issued under the EIR (reg.18(6)). The notice ceases to be of effect if within 20 working days of its service (or of the withdrawal or determination of any appeal under s.57) an accountable person in relation to the authority in question gives the Information Commissioner a signed certificate stating that he has, on reasonable grounds, formed the opinion that in respect of the request(s) concerned there was no failure:

- to comply with s.1(1)(a) of the FOIA in respect of information which falls within any provision of Part II of the Act stating that the duty to confirm or deny does not arise; or
- to comply with s.1(1)(b) in respect of exempt information.

What this obscure drafting means is that where the Information Commissioner has decided that the information falls within a qualified exemption but that the public interest requires the authority to disclose the information (or at least confirm whether or not it holds such information), the accountable person can trump the Information Commissioner's view on the public interest analysis (or the Information Tribunal's view) and prevent disclosure.

As soon as practicable after delivering the certificate, the accountable person must lay a copy of it before both Houses of Parliament, and the Northern Ireland or Welsh Assembly too, if relevant to those bodies. Further, where the certificate overrides a Decision Notice, as soon as practicable after delivering the certificate, the accountable person must also inform the complainant of the reasons for their opinion but need not, in so doing, provide any exempt information.

An accountable person is in most cases a Cabinet Minister or the Attorney General, but in relation to a Northern Ireland department or public authority would be the First Minister and Deputy First Minister of Northern Ireland acting jointly, or the First Secretary of the Welsh Assembly regarding that body or any designated Welsh public authority.

There is no statutory appeal to the Information Tribunal against such a certificate. The ministerial decision would, however, be subject to judicial review on the application of a party with the requisite standing – the most obvious candidates being the complainant or the Information Commissioner. To succeed in the Administrative Court, however, would generally mean showing that the Minister had acted irrationally or in a way that no one in his position reasonably could have done, which will often be a difficult test to meet. The complainant and even the Information Commissioner may in addition be largely ignorant of the relevant detail lying behind the government's decision, as it will no doubt be kept back from them, being allegedly exempt and quite possibly made the subject of a claim to public interest immunity. There would also be the risk of being ordered to pay the government's costs if the application for review was unsuccessful.

When the Act first came into force, Lord Falconer, the then Lord Chancellor, sought to allay fears that the government would actually resort to the override by indicating that it would only be used very exceptionally and subject to the approval of the entire Cabinet.[6] For his part, the Information Commissioner expressed the view that it is desirable for the credibility of the FOIA, and indeed likely, that the veto will only be used rarely. To date, it does not appear to have been deployed.

10.3.6   Practice Recommendations

If it appears to the Information Commissioner that the practice of a public authority does not conform to provisions of the codes of practice issued under ss.45 and 46 of the FOIA and reg.16 of the EIR, he may give the authority a recommendation specifying the steps which ought in his opinion to be taken for promoting such conformity (FOIA, s.48(1); EIR, reg.16(5)). A Practice Recommendation differs from the notices discussed above as there are no sanctions for non-compliance with it, nor is there any statutory right of appeal against it. This difference is reflected by the fact that the notices are dealt with in Part IV of the FOIA (entitled 'Enforcement') and Practice Recommendations in Part III, which is concerned with the general functions of the Information Commissioner. A failure to take account of a Practice Recommendation will not be formally sanctioned, yet it could lead to an adverse comment in a report to Parliament by the Information Commissioner or other negative publicity; the Information Commissioner has altered his earlier policy and now makes Practice Recommendations public (see **10.6.1**). Also worth bearing in mind is that an authority which receives a Practice Recommendation is by definition at risk of breaching the FOIA itself, so it serves as a warning that procedures need to be addressed in order to avoid a more formal sanction. In the absence of an appeal mechanism, the Information Commissioner's decision to issue a Practice Recommendation is likely to be amenable to judicial review if one can show grounds, namely, that the decision was irrational, unlawful or procedurally unfair, or else a breach of the Human Rights Act 1998.

Practice Recommendations are more likely to be issued in response to grave breaches of the codes than minor breaches. However, repeated poor practice could also be a ground for serving a public authority with a Practice Recommendation. The ICO may become aware of poor practice when investigating complaints from requesters, when carrying out a practice assessment under s.47(3) of the FOIA, or when contacted by a public authority for assistance in carrying out its obligations under the legislation. Where the poor practice in question is also a breach of the Act or the Regulations – such as the provision of inadequate advice and assistance to requesters – the Information Commissioner is more likely to investigate using his enforcement powers and the result will be a Decision Notice or an Enforcement Notice rather than a Practice Recommendation.

The sort of issues likely to be the subject of Practice Recommendations under the Section 45 Code of Practice include the following:

- the quality of assistance given to applicants;
- shortfalls in consultation with third parties;
- a lack of, or poor, internal review procedure;
- poor records management;
- a lack of, or poor, retention and disposal policies; or
- the existence of excessive confidentiality obligations inconsistent with FOI disclosure requirements.[7]

In the case of the Section 46 Code, Practice Recommendations can only be made after consultation between the Information Commissioner and the Keeper of Public Records (or the Deputy Keeper in cases concerning Northern Ireland) (s.48(3) and (4)).

By way of example, Liverpool City Council was issued with a Practice Recommendation on 8 May 2007 as a result of its repeated failures to handle FOI requests appropriately or in a timely manner, and its failures to respond to the Information Commissioner's investigations. (This included failing to respond to an Information Notice, leading the Information Commissioner to threaten High Court proceedings.) His concerns about the Council had been sparked during his investigation of a complaint from an information seeker (and by a separate data protection prosecution) and he therefore audited all complaints which the Information Commissioner's Office (ICO) had received about the Council. These totalled 18. Among other failings, it was apparent that the Council had failed to explain in refusal notices why exemptions applied, and its responses to applicants were inadequate. Upon finding that the Council was falling short of good practice in its provision of advice and assistance to requesters (and that a 10-week internal review process was unreasonably lengthy), the Information Commissioner recommended action on various fronts, including conducting a review of the resources allocated to dealing with FOI requests, and providing all staff with relevant training (ICO case ref: FPR0152907; see also the connected Decision Notice FS50079486).

10.4 ADDITIONAL SUPPORT FOR THE INFORMATION COMMISSIONER'S ENFORCEMENT POWERS

10.4.1 Non-compliance with notices punishable as if contempt of court

A public authority which has been served with a Decision Notice, Information Notice or Enforcement Notice might, deliberately or otherwise, fail to comply with the steps specified in the notice within the required deadline.[8] Once the time for compliance has expired, and likewise the time for appealing against the notice (28 days from service), or else after an unsuccessful appeal, then assuming that the notice has not been overridden by ministerial veto (see **10.3.5**), the Information Commissioner can take further enforcement action. In many cases the prompt for him to do so will be another complaint from the applicant who is waiting to receive the requested information. The Information Commissioner can certify the non-compliance in writing to the High Court (the Court of Session in Scotland), upon which the Court may inquire into the matter and, after hearing any witness who may be produced against or on behalf of the public authority, and after hearing any statement that may be offered in defence, deal with the public authority as if it had committed a contempt of court (s.53(3)).

The principal sanctions for contempt are an unlimited fine and a fixed-term prison sentence of up to two years (Contempt of Court Act 1981, s.14) but the Court can also order sequestration of assets,[9] or issue an injunction (*Elliot* v. *Klinger* [1967] 3 All ER 141). Committal and sequestration, being drastic penalties, are only imposed in serious cases, where there is an element of fault or misconduct (*Fairclough & Sons* v. *The Manchester Ship Canal Co. (No.2)* (1897) 41 Sol Jo, 225). They will not often feature in the context of the FOIA. The amount of any fine imposed must take account of the seriousness of the contempt and the damage to the public interest.[10] Where a public authority accidentally fails to comply with the Information Commissioner's notice, the court will often simply make an order for costs against it, although this can be on the indemnity basis (e.g. *Stancomb* v. *Trowbridge Urban District Council* [1910] 2 Ch 190).

In principle, only the party bound by an order can be liable for civil contempt (breach of a court order – in this case the Information Commissioner's notice). As s.54(3) provides that the authority can be dealt with as if it had committed a contempt, it seems unlikely that the Court could sanction the individual officers and employees by whom it acts (and who were in fact responsible for breaching the notice), unless it made a further order requiring named individuals to act or refrain from acting in a certain way and they then breached that order. On an application for committal brought by the Information Commissioner over Allerdale Borough Council's failure to adopt a Publication Scheme and to respond to an Enforcement Notice, the court ruled that the contempt proceedings should have been instituted against the council rather than its CEO, as they had been (2004, Chester Crown Court, unreported).

Where the public authority is a corporate body, however, an order for sequestration or committal could possibly be made against any director or other officer aware of the terms of the notice if they wilfully fail to take adequate steps to ensure compliance, by virtue of RSC Order 45, r.5(1), contained in Sched.1 to the Civil Procedure Rules 1998 (CPR) (see *Attorney General for Tuvalu* v. *Philatelic Distribution Corp. Ltd* [1990] 2 All ER 216, CA). There is perhaps in addition a risk that any employee of a public authority who knowingly assists it in breaching a notice issued by the Information Commissioner could be liable for criminal contempt, on the basis that this constituted an interference with the administration of justice. That could certainly be the case in relation to a breach of any subsequent order from the court to comply with the notice (*Marengo* v. *Daily Sketch and Sunday Graphic Ltd* [1948] 1 All ER 406). An intention to interfere with the course of justice would need to be proved, however, with mere recklessness not sufficing (*R.* v. *Runting* (1989) 89 Cr App R 243, 247, CA, per Lord Lane LCJ). While it is not possible for the Crown to be held in contempt, a Minister can be (*M* v. *Home Office* [1994] 1 AC 377).

Procedure regarding orders for committal is dealt with in RSC Order 52 (Sched.1 to the CPR) and the accompanying Practice Direction. Even with civil contempt the criminal standard of proof applies, i.e. the case would need to be proved beyond reasonable doubt (*Dean* v. *Dean* [1987] 1 FLR 517, CA). That said, it is not necessary to prove that the authority intended to breach the Information Commissioner's notice (See *Stancomb*, above, at 194), merely that it knew of its existence (*Z Ltd* v. *A-Z and AA-LL* [1982] QB 558, 580 per Eveleigh LJ) and intended to do the acts or omissions which constituted the contempt (i.e. the failure to comply); an argument by the authority that it was simply negligent in overlooking the notice may well not suffice to avoid liability (*VDU Installations Ltd* v. *Integrated Computer Systems and Cybernetics Ltd* [1989] 1 FSR 378, 394 per Knox J). On the other hand, if breach of the notice is accidental, the authority may well face costs but no additional sanctions (see *Fairclough & Sons*, above). If the Information Commissioner's notice does not express in clear terms what steps the authority must take to comply with it, that might give the authority scope to argue against the making of an order for committal. Any order punishing a contempt, whether civil or criminal, can be appealed to the Court of Appeal (see Administration of Justice Act 1960, s.13(2)(b), as amended by Courts Act 1971, s.56(4), Sched.11 Part II, and CPR rule 52.3(1)(a)(i)).

Public authorities ought to bear in mind that even where contempt proceedings are not brought, an authority which fails to comply with a notice from the Information Commissioner opens itself up to negative publicity and reputation damage beyond that surrounding the publication of the Information Commissioner's determination, as its non-compliance is likely to be included in a report to Parliament, by way of either a special report or the Information Commissioner's regular annual report under s.49 of the FOIA, or both.

10.4.2   Prosecution of offences under s.77 (obstructing disclosure)

Where a public authority has been asked for information, it is an offence under s.77 of the FOIA for the authority or any of its officers, employees or anyone under its direction to alter, deface, block, erase, destroy or conceal any record which it holds, with the intention of preventing disclosure of any information to which the applicant would have been entitled under s.1 of the FOIA (subject to payment of any fee). The offence is punishable in the magistrates' court by a fine of up to level 5 on the standard scale (currently £5,000 (Criminal Justice Act 1982, as amended, s.37)).

The Information Commissioner is a prosecuting authority for these purposes and a prosecution under this section can only be started in England, Wales and Northern Ireland by him or by, or with the consent of, the Director of Public Prosecutions. Any investigation into a suspected offence would take place under the rules of the Police and Criminal Evidence Act 1984 and prosecutions are brought in accordance with the Code for Crown Prosecutors. Government departments are not liable to prosecution under this section but a person in the public service of the Crown can be (s.81(3)).

10.4.3   Exchange of information with other ombudsmen

Schedule 7 to the FOIA (which is given effect by s.76(2)) provides that certain ombudsmen[11] can make available to the Information Commissioner any information which they obtain in the exercise of their statutory functions if it appears to them to relate to a matter in respect of which the Information Commissioner could exercise any power conferred by Part IV of the FOIA (which includes the issuing of Enforcement, Information and Decision Notices and the powers of entry and inspection) or s.48 of the FOIA (Practice Recommendations) or the commission of a s.77 offence.[12]

10.4.4   The Information Commissioner's powers of entry and inspection

Where the Information Commissioner has reasonable grounds to suspect that a public authority has failed to comply with any requirement of Part I of the FOIA or of one of his notices (not including Practice Recommendations), or similarly where he has reasonable grounds to suspect an authority of committing an offence under s.77 of the FOIA (see **10.4.2**), he can apply to a circuit judge for a warrant authorising entry to any premises[13] and search, inspection and seizure of materials which may be evidence of such breaches. The warrant may in addition authorise the Information Commissioner to inspect, examine, operate and test any equipment found there in which information held by the public authority may be recorded. This will give the Information Commissioner access to computer files. These powers are granted under s.55 and Sched.3 to the FOIA.

Except where urgent or where a warning might prevent seizure of relevant evidence, the judge will need to be satisfied before he grants the warrant that (i) the Information Commissioner gave seven days' written notice to the occupier of the premises demanding access; (ii) either access was demanded at a reasonable hour but unreasonably refused or entry was granted but the occupier unreasonably refused to comply with a request of the Information Commissioner or his staff; and (iii) the occupier has been notified by the Information Commissioner of the application for the warrant and has had an opportunity of being heard by the judge in relation to whether it should be issued or not.

Schedule 3 contains provisions for the manner of execution of such a warrant which include the following: a person executing the warrant may use such reasonable force as may be necessary (para.4); the warrant must be executed at a reasonable hour unless the person executing it considers that he has grounds to suspect that to do so would prevent finding the evidence which is sought (para.5); the warrant must be shown to an officer or member of staff of the occupier of the premises (whether the occupier is a public authority or not), if present, and a copy must be given to them or left in a prominent place (para.6(1) and (2)); the person executing the warrant must on request give a receipt for any item seized (para.7(1)); if requested by the occupier of the premises, and if the person executing the warrant considers it is possible without causing undue delay, he must give a copy of anything seized under the warrant (para.7(2)); anything seized under the warrant can be retained for as long as is necessary in all the circumstances (para.7(2)).

Certain information is exempt from inspection or seizure under the warrant. This applies first to any national security-related information falling within the exemptions in s.23(1) or s.24(1) in Part II of the FOIA (para.8). Secondly, a warrant cannot authorise inspection or seizure of any legally privileged communication held by a client or his legal adviser which contains legal advice relating to the FOIA or is made in contemplation of proceedings under or arising out of the Act (para.9). This does not extend to any material held in furtherance of a criminal purpose or held by a third party. Where the occupier of the premises objects to inspection or seizure on the ground that some of the material contains matters which are covered by these exemptions, he must nevertheless give the person exercising the warrant a copy of the remaining material if the latter so requests (para.10).

10.4.5   Related criminal offences: obstruction of execution of a warrant

The following offences are created by para.12 of Sched.3 to the FOIA:

- intentionally obstructing a person in the execution of a warrant issued under Sched.3;

- failing without reasonable excuse to give any person executing a warrant such assistance as he may reasonably require for its execution.

10.5 INTERNAL REVIEW FOLLOWING A COMPLAINT

Where an applicant has requested information from a public authority and is dissatisfied with the result (perhaps because it has been refused or he suspects that there is additional disclosable information which has not been produced or he considers that the authority has not satisfied particular procedural requirements imposed by the FOIA), his first step must in most cases be to complain to the authority itself, asking it to reconsider its decision. The FOIA does not require authorities to have a procedure for reviewing decisions (the EIR does, by contrast: reg.11) but the guidance in the Section 45 Code of Practice is that they ought to (para.36).

Not only is a complaint to the authority in question likely to be the most straightforward way of resolving the matter but it is also virtually required by the FOIA by virtue of s.50(2)(a), which permits the Information Commissioner not to entertain a complaint where the complainant has not exhausted any internal complaints procedure which the public authority provides.

From an applicant's point of view, it is worth bearing in mind that the more wide-ranging the request (and the larger the public authority in question), the more likely it is in practice that relevant information will have been missed first time around and thus a different result might be reached when the request is looked at by a fresh pair of eyes, which will often be those of a more senior person, who may have a better or broader view of the work of the organisation.

10.5.1 The Section 45 Code of Practice

The Section 45 Code of Practice contains guidance for public authorities from the Secretary of State for Constitutional Affairs (now the Secretary of State for Justice) on practice which he thinks it desirable for them to follow in connection with the discharge of their functions under Part I of the FOIA. Breach may result in the Information Commissioner issuing a Practice Recommendation but cannot form the basis of a s.50(1) complaint by an applicant unless it also constitutes a breach of the FOIA. Paragraph 36 of the Section 45 Code of Practice suggests that in the first instance a complaint should, if possible, be resolved informally. If this cannot be achieved swiftly or satisfactorily, however, the public authority ought to give the applicant details of its internal complaints procedure, and of how to contact the Information Commissioner about the matter, should they wish to. Complaints procedures are to be as clear and simple as possible and to encourage prompt determination of complaints (para.39).

313

Similarly, when communicating a decision to refuse a request on the grounds that an exemption in Part II of the FOIA applies or that the request is vexatious or repetitious or that the estimated cost of complying with the request exceeds the free-provision ceiling, public authorities are obliged, under s.17(7) of the FOIA, to give applicants details of their internal complaints procedure, or else state that they do not have one. In doing so, para.37 of the Code of Practice says they should also inform the applicant of his or her right to complain to the Information Commissioner under s.50 if he or she is still dissatisfied following the authority's review.

Applicants wishing to submit a complaint to a public authority should therefore request details of the authority's complaints procedure, if not already provided, and follow it. Details of the complaints procedure will often be published under a public authority's Publication Scheme and may be available on its website.

Applicants should put their complaints in writing or confirm them in writing if made initially by telephone or in person. (Complaints (representations) under the EIR must be made in writing: reg.11(2).) Providing a clear, dated record of the complaint will assist its resolution by the public authority and also any subsequent complaint to the Information Commissioner. It also obliges the authority to deal with it properly because para.38 of the Code of Practice advises authorities to treat as a complaint any written communication from the applicant (which includes faxes and emails) expressing dissatisfaction with its response to a request for information, as well as any written communication from a person who considers that the authority is not complying with its Publication Scheme. Such communications are to be handled in accordance with the authority's complaints procedure, even if the applicant does not expressly state their desire for the authority to review its decision or handling of the request. Nonetheless it would be advisable to mark the envelope or entitle the email, 'Request for internal review under FOIA/EIR', to ensure it is dealt with promptly. In urgent or significant cases which are likely to be appealed to the Information Commissioner, it would also be prudent to send any letters by recorded delivery in order to have proof of posting and evidence of receipt by the authority. Similarly, to obtain a speedier result it will be worth making a telephone call to find out the name of the FOI officer or other appropriate person to direct the request to.

10.5.2 Formulating arguments for and against the complaint

Even if not required by the relevant public authority's complaints procedure, it will usually help an applicant to set out in as much detail as possible the grounds for disputing the authority's notice refusing disclosure of the requested information. Not only is a well argued case more likely to succeed in the first instance, but it may well draw out more detailed reasons for any further refusal. This would be of value to the applicant, first in evaluating whether it is worth referring the matter to the Information Commissioner, and second in knowing what issues and arguments to deal with when putting together a complaint to the Information Commissioner.

An applicant requesting an internal review would thus be well advised to consider the reasons for non-disclosure given in the authority's refusal notice against the detail of the exemption provisions in Part II of the FOIA or the exceptions in reg.12 of the EIR (both available on the internet via the ICO website (**www.ico.gov.uk**)). Helpful interpretation of how those provisions (and the public interest test) should apply in practice is provided not only in books such as this but also in a series of Awareness Guidance notes (and separate EIR guidance) available on the ICO website, and in guidance for public authorities produced by the MoJ (see **www.justice.gov.uk/whatwedo/ freedomofinformation.htm**). Similarly, the Department for Environment, Food and Rural Affairs has published guidance on the EIR (*A Guide to the Environmental Information Regulations*, available at **www.defra.gov.uk/corporate/ opengov/eir/guidance**). The applicant may be able to support the argument for disclosure further by pointing to cases where information was supplied in response to comparable requests, and should consider:

- reported rulings of the Information Tribunal (see **www.informationtribunal. gov.uk**);
- published decisions (and related guidance) of the Information Commissioner (see **www.ico.gov.uk**) – note that the site now permits searches by section number of the legislation and by public authority);
- any disclosure log published by the authority in question, which will show whether it has granted similar requests in the past (see, for example, details of information released by DEFRA at **www.defra.gov.uk/corporate/opengov/ inforelease**);
- disclosure logs kept by similar organisations; and
- public interest arguments drawn from the freedom of information case law of comparable jurisdictions, and also the decisions of the UK Parliamentary Ombudsman under the non-statutory Code of Practice on Access to Government Information, which was in force from 1994 to 2004.[14]

In addition, assistance with complaints under the EIR can sometimes be obtained from the European Directive which it sought to implement – EU Directive 2003/4/EC on public access to environmental information. The Directive has been successfully used by an applicant to challenge the reasonableness of fees charged for providing photocopies of planning documents (*Markinson* v. *Information Commissioner*, Information Tribunal, 28 March 2006).

Public authorities would of course also be well advised to have regard to such sources of guidance and authority, and they are likely to find that giving as detailed reasons as they can for turning down requests (supported by reference to any cases from the above list) is the best way of reducing the number of complaints to the Information Commissioner that they are forced to deal with. As stated in **10.1**, however, and as the Information Commissioner has underlined, 'it would be a mistake to regard one decision as setting a binding precedent in other circumstances'.[15] The Information Tribunal also frequently notes that it is free to depart from its own earlier decisions. (However, the Information Commissioner does follow the rulings of the Information Tribunal, and the Tribunal follows any FOIA-related rulings of the High Court.)

Public authorities may also wish to note the Information Commissioner's recommendation that only the strongest reasons for turning down a request should be referred to in a s.17 refusal notice (or on a request for internal review) rather than listing every single possibly relevant exemption, as this could give the impression of an over-secretive organisation. It will also potentially add delays to any subsequent investigation by the Information Commissioner or appeal to the Information Tribunal.

10.5.3   A fair, thorough and independent review

The Section 45 Code of Practice provides that an authority's complaints procedure should constitute a fair and thorough review of the handling of the request and of decisions taken pursuant to the FOIA, including decisions about where the public interest lies in respect of exempt information (para.39). There should be a full reconsideration of the case and where the complaint concerns a request for information the review should be undertaken, where reasonably practicable, by somebody senior to the person who took the original decision (para.40). The Information Commissioner has glossed this as, 'someone independent of the original decision making process'.[16]

10.5.4   Timescales

No time limit for the submission of requests for internal reviews under the FOIA is specified in the FOIA or the Code of Practice but complainants ought to consult the procedures of the relevant public authority to see what regulations it imposes in this regard. The position is different with complaints under the EIR – see **10.5.6**. If the authority refuses to accept a complaint, saying it is out of time, the applicant should apply direct to the Information Commissioner (but see **10.6.1** on time restrictions for such complaints).

As for public authorities' responses, the Code of Practice states that complaints should be acknowledged promptly and that the complainant should be informed of the authority's target date for determining the complaint. Where it is apparent to the authority that it will take longer than estimated to deal with, it should inform the applicant and explain the reason for the delay (para.41). Authorities are encouraged to set their own target times for dealing with complaints but these are required to be reasonable and subject to regular review. They must also be published, together with details of how successful the authority is in meeting them (para.42).

Following complaints that public authorities were abusing the review process to stymie the progress of complaints for weeks or months, the Commissioner introduced guidance on what he considers a reasonable period for dealing with requests for review. He advises that public authorities should respond substantively to such a request within 20 working days of the request. (That is the same period as appears in the Scottish Act, s.21(1).) The Commissioner notes that in exceptional circumstances it may be reasonable to take longer but, if so, as a matter of good practice a public authority should notify the requester and explain why more time is needed. No internal review should take longer than 40 working days according to the Commissioner, and any public authority taking that amount of time to complete the review would be expected to be able to demonstrate that it had commenced the review procedure promptly following receipt of the request for review and had actively worked on the review throughout the period. Significant or repeated unreasonable delays in dealing with internal reviews can result in monitoring by the Commissioner's Enforcement team and possibly the issuing of a Practice Recommendation (see **10.3.6**). Where a public authority does not meet these deadlines, the Commissioner is more likely to exercise his discretion under s.50(2)(a) to entertain a complaint from a requester even though the internal review has not been completed (see *Freedom of Information Good Practice Guidance No. 5 – Time limits on carrying out internal reviews following requests for information under the Freedom of Information Act 2000*, ICO, 22.2.07).

10.5.5   Outcomes

The Section 45 Code of Practice provides, naturally enough, that the complainant ought always to be informed of the outcome of the complaint (para. 40). Where the outcome of a complaint is a decision that information should be disclosed which was previously withheld, the information in question should be disclosed as soon as practicable and the applicant should be informed how soon this will be (para.44). Where the internal review reveals that the procedures within an authority have not been properly followed, the authority is to apologise to the applicant and take appropriate steps to prevent similar errors occurring in future (para.45).

Where the outcome of a complaint is that an initial decision to withhold information is upheld, or is otherwise in the authority's favour, the applicant is to be informed of the right to ask the Information Commissioner for a determination on whether the request for information has been dealt with in accordance with the requirements of Part I of the FOIA, and is to be given details of how to do so (para.46).

Public authorities are required to maintain records of all complaints and their outcome. They are also supposed to have procedures in place for

monitoring complaints and for reviewing, and, if necessary, amending, procedures for dealing with requests for information where such action is indicated
by more than occasional reversals of initial decisions (para.43).

10.5.6 EIR

The Section 45 Code of Practice does not apply to requests made for environmental information but largely similar provisions are contained in the code of
practice issued under reg.16 of the EIR. The EIR themselves provide that
applications for an internal review of decisions on requests for environmental
information must be submitted in writing within 40 working days of the date on
which the applicant believes the public authority has failed to comply with a
requirement of the EIR. In most cases this will mean within 40 working days of
receipt of the refusal notice turning down the original request. The authority
cannot charge any fee to consider the complaint and it must reply as soon as
possible, within 40 working days in any event. Notification of any revised
decision by the authority must include a statement of its failure to comply with
the EIR, the action it has decided on in order to comply with the relevant
requirement and the period within which that action is to be taken (reg.11).
Where the decision is taken to release information this should be actioned
immediately (reg.16 Code of Practice, para.65).

10.6 COMPLAINING TO THE INFORMATION COMMISSIONER

10.6.1 Complaints about individual requests for information

The term 'complaints' when used in this context is convenient shorthand for
what is in fact an application to the Information Commissioner under s.50(1)
of the FOIA, by a person who requested information from a public authority,
for a decision on whether that request was dealt with by the authority in accordance with its obligations under Part I of the FOIA (or Parts 2 and 3 of
the EIR where relevant). An application under s.50(1) cannot be made merely
because a public authority has breached a Code of Practice provision.

Those obligations include, most significantly, the obligation under s.1(1) of
the FOIA to confirm or deny whether the authority holds information requested
by the applicant and to communicate it to him or her (subject, most importantly,
to the exemptions in Part II). However, it also includes many obligations of a
more procedural nature, so that a complaint could, for instance, be made to the
Information Commissioner where the applicant believes:

- the public authority has charged excessive fees for responding to his
request (FOIA, ss.9 and 13; EIR, reg.8);
- the authority took longer to respond to the request than it should have
(FOIA, s.10; EIR, regs.5(2), 7 and 14);

- the authority was unreasonable in not complying with his preference for how he wished to receive the information (FOIA, s.11; EIR, reg.6);
- the authority was wrong to say the cost of complying with the request meant that it was not obliged to comply (FOIA, ss.12 and 13; EIR, reg.8);
- the authority was wrong to label the request vexatious or repetitious and refuse to deal with it (FOIA, s.14; EIR, reg.12(4)(b));
- the authority failed to offer him appropriate assistance in formulating and submitting his request (FOIA, s.16; EIR, reg.9);
- the authority should have given reasons for claiming that the information sought was exempt (FOIA, s.17(1), (3) and (4); EIR, reg.14(3)).

The typical stages through which a complaint to the Information Commissioner will pass are described below. Certain aspects of this procedure are set out in the FOIA but much of the detail is a matter of discretion for the Information Commissioner. This detail can be found in various ICO publications. The most significant of these are the following:

(i) Freedom of Information: ICO Enforcement Strategy (May 2007);[17] and
(ii) a memorandum of understanding between the Information Commissioner and, effectively, government departments[18] (referred to in this chapter as the MoU).

How to submit a complaint

Applications for a decision under s.50(1) should be submitted to the ICO in writing either by post to FOI/EIR Case Reception, Information Commissioner's Office, Wycliffe House, Water Lane, Wilmslow, Cheshire SK9 5AF; or by fax to 01625 524 510. A complaint can be submitted online (**www.ico.gov.uk/Global/online_enquiries.aspx**) but given the need to send accompanying documents, which an applicant may not have in electronic form, it may be easier to do so by post or fax. It would be prudent to obtain proof of posting by using the recorded delivery service. A complaint form can be printed off from the 'document library' section of the ICO website but it is not necessary to use it. Queries can be made via the telephone helpline on 01625 545 745.

The applicant must be identified, i.e. complaints submitted anonymously will not be considered. (This does not preclude the submission of requests by a named person on behalf of another, whose identity is not disclosed.) An address of course must also be provided, and it can be helpful for the applicant to give his or her telephone number and/or email address as well.

Only the person who submitted the original request (or a person acting on their behalf) may apply to the Information Commissioner under s.50(1) of the FOIA. (Third parties cannot apply: see **10.9**.)

In order to consider the complaint, the Information Commissioner will expect to receive the following, as appropriate:

- brief details of the issues the applicant wishes the Information Commissioner to consider;
- a copy of the original request for information, or in the absence of that (i) a summary of the request; and (ii) evidence that the request was submitted to the public authority (a recorded delivery receipt, for instance, or an acknowledgement from the authority);
- a copy of the refusal notice issued by the public authority;
- a copy of the applicant's complaint to the public authority concerning that initial refusal of information (i.e. the applicant's request for an internal review); or if no such complaint was made, an explanation why not;
- a copy of the public authority's response following its reconsideration of the request;
- any other information the applicant believes relevant. This could include, for example, the complainant's arguments as to why the information does not fall within the exemptions claimed by the authority, or why the public interest favours disclosure if a qualified exemption is relevant. Although there is no requirement for an applicant to set out any arguments in support of the access request, it may well be in his or her interests to do so, both in order to persuade and to make decision-making as speedy as possible, against a background of a backlog of complaints. If the applicant needs the information urgently, it would be relevant to say so and why. There is no guarantee, however, that the complaint will be expedited as a result.

Applications must be submitted without undue delay or the Information Commissioner is entitled not to consider them (s.50(2)(b)). 'Undue delay' is not defined in the FOIA but the Information Commissioner has indicated that he will normally expect complaints to be submitted within two months of receipt of the public authority's final refusal to disclose the information, i.e. following any internal review (*Regulation under the Freedom of Information Act 2000 and the Environmental Information Regulations 2004*, para.10). Complaints submitted later than this might still be considered if there is a good reason for the delay. On the other hand, the Information Commissioner will not consider complaints submitted before the end of the period which the FOIA allows the authority for complying with a request, or before the extended period (if reasonable) which the authority has said it needs, in a re-fusal notice under s.17(2), to consider the public interest position regarding the request. The Commissioner's guidance in this regard is that all requests should be decided within 20 working days, including where the public interest test is to be applied; only in exceptional complex cases may it be reasonable to take longer, up to a maximum of 40 working days in total (*Freedom of Information Good Practice Guidance No.4 – Time limits on considering the public interest following requests for information under the Freedom of Information Act 2000*, ICO, 22.2.07).

There is no fee to pay on submission and neither the applicant nor the public authority can be ordered by the Information Commissioner to pay the other's costs. In some cases, parties (especially public authorities) will want to obtain expert evidence and/or legal advice in order to argue their case before the Information Commissioner. Such costs will potentially be recoverable only if the matter goes on appeal to the Information Tribunal (see **10.7.1** and **10.7.2**).

The Information Commissioner decides whether to deal with the complaint

The Case Reception Unit will consider the case and respond within 14 days. It can deal with the most straightforward cases, or it may request more information. Often, however, further investigation is needed. If so, there will be a delay while the matter waits in a queue to be allocated to a complaint resolution team. (The delay is caused by the high number of complaints being handled by the ICO at any one time, and may be several months, especially for more complex cases.) A case officer will then get in touch with the complainant and provide a case reference number for use in correspondence. The ICO communicates with parties not only by post, but also by telephone and email.

Under s.50(2), the Information Commissioner has a duty to make a decision on all complaints about the way a public authority has handled a request for information under s.1 of the Act, except in the four specific situations listed below. The Case Reception Unit and the case officer will bear these in mind when considering whether to take up, or continue dealing with, the complaint. There is no duty to make a decision on a complaint:

1. Where the complainant has not exhausted any complaints procedure provided by the public authority in conformity with the Section 45 Code of Practice, i.e. by requesting an internal review (see **10.5.1**).
    The Information Commissioner might, however, be prepared to take on such a complaint where, for example, the public authority has simply not responded to the applicant's request for information, or where there is nobody suitable to undertake the internal review because there is no one on the authority's staff who is independent of, and more senior to, the original decision maker.
2. Where there has been undue delay in making the application (in most cases this means anything later than two months after the public authority's final decision).
3. Where the application is frivolous or vexatious.
    These terms are not defined in the FOIA but the Information Commissioner has issued guidance on his approach – see Awareness Guidance 22 (23 July 2007) and 'A Robust Approach to FOI Complaint Cases' (November 2006). He may regard a complaint as vexatious or frivolous where it meets the

criteria he has laid down by which public authorities should judge whether a request for information is vexatious or repeated under s.14 of the FOIA, and that there is little to persuade him otherwise. In terms of repeated requests, those criteria can broadly be summarised as a request that unreasonably repeats a previous request. The criteria for vexatiousness are that the complaint would impose a significant burden on the public authority in terms of expense or distraction, and, in addition, at least one of the following applies:

- it clearly has no serious purpose or value;
- it is designed to cause disruption or annoyance;
- it has the effect of harassing the public authority (or the Information Commissioner) including where it is part of a campaign conducted by different, but linked, individuals;
- it can otherwise be fairly characterised as obsessive or manifestly unreasonable.

These criteria are capable of covering a situation where the breach complained of is trivial (e.g. a complainant had received all the information requested within 21 days rather than 20) or where the public authority has already remedied the breach (e.g. by disclosing the requested information, whether during the Information Commissioner's handling of the matter of otherwise – see 'The Information Commissioner's policy on Decision Notices' below.

4. Where the application has been withdrawn or abandoned.

    An internal ICO policy paper in April 2005 suggested that the Information Commissioner will only regard a complaint as withdrawn where the ICO has received a written statement from the complainant confirming that that is the case. Similarly, the Information Commissioner is likely to regard a complaint as abandoned only where the complainant has failed to reply to a minimum of two pieces of correspondence, the latter of which will warn that this is what will happen in the absence of a response within a given period, such as 28 days.

Even where there is no duty to determine a complaint, the Commissioner may exercise his discretion to do so nonetheless. Either way, the complainant, and the public authority, will be kept informed of any decisions taken and what the next steps are, usually on a monthly basis during the lifetime of the complaint.

An applicant whose application for a decision under s.50(1) is not proceeded with on one of the four s.50(2) grounds discussed above could challenge the Information Commissioner's decision in that regard by way of judicial review – there is no appeal to the Information Tribunal in these circumstances (see *Day* v. *Information Commissioner*, Information Tribunal, 24 September 2007, para.8). The bar to success would be set high, however, as the applicant would need to show that no Information Commissioner could reasonably have come to the same decision.

Case law has established a further, implied, ground upon which the Information Commissioner can decline to entertain a complaint purportedly made under s.50(1), namely where the complaint in fact lies outside that jurisdiction. A request made to the BBC for (what was adjudged to be) journalistic information was not a request to a public authority governed by the FOIA, because such information fell outside the Act under Sched.1, Part VI (see *British Broadcasting Corporation* v. *Sugar* [2007] EWHC 905 (Admin), 27 April 2007).

The Information Commissioner investigates the complaint

In all but the clearest of cases the Information Commissioner asks the public authority for information so he can make his assessment. It is worth noting in passing that a public authority cannot refuse to disclose any information to the Information Commissioner or the Information Tribunal which is 'necessary for the discharge of their functions' on the grounds that in doing so it would be making itself civilly or criminally liable – by breaching a confidence, for example (FOIA, Sched.2, para. 18). Nor will a claim of legal privilege permit the public authority to withhold information from the Information Commissioner except where it concerns FOIA-related communications between a lawyer and client, or, where proceedings are in contemplation, a third party (s.51(5) and (6)).

The approach which the Information Commissioner takes with public authorities when requesting information is set out in the MoU (see p.319), which contains guideline procedures designed to apply in the majority of cases in relation to his functions under ss.50 and 51, which deal with Decision Notices and Information Notices. Procedures regarding Enforcement Notices are not covered by the MoU. Nor does the document apply where a government department is claiming an exemption under the national security provisions of the legislation (ss.23 and 24 of the FOIA and reg.12(5)(a) of the EIR), in which case the separate considerations discussed at Annex 2 to the MoU will apply. Although the MoU applies directly only to government departments, the same standards apply to the rest of the public sector, and all public authorities are expected to follow the principles of the MoU in their dealings with him.[19]

The Information Commissioner will initially make an informal request for information and normally only issues authorities with Information Notices (see **10.3.2**) where he believes information is being withheld or unreasonably delayed. Where possible, he will warn of his intention to serve such a notice.[20] In general the Information Commissioner does not seek information from public authorities unless necessary to determine the complaint. Specifically, he will not ask authorities to provide information where they claim exemption from the duty to confirm or deny in cases where he can see such a claim is justified without access to any further information (para.12 of the MoU). Other situations where the ICO is unlikely to request information include where a public authority is self-evidently justified in relying upon an absolute exemption or can clearly justify refusal on public interest grounds, or else where the complaint simply concerns a procedural point, such as an inadequate refusal notice.

The Information Commissioner aims to notify public authorities of the details of complaints against them as soon as practicable. He asks for all relevant information and invites the authority to comment on the case, ideally through a single channel of communication (para.7 of the MoU). The Information Commissioner expects public authorities to supply him with the information as quickly as possible and in any event within 20 working days of his request. Any follow-up requests for information are to be met within 10 days. Where authorities cannot meet these standard deadlines, they will be expected to give reasons and a date by when they aim to provide the information.

The Information Commissioner generally requests the public authority's record of how it responded to the access request and why, and he may want to see any information that was withheld from the applicant or redacted (blanked out). He is also entitled to ask for relevant unrecorded information, such as what officials know of the relevant matter beyond what is documented (FOIA, s.51(8)). He may also wish the authority to tell him any views on the access request expressed by an interested third party, such as on the potential for prejudice to arise from disclosure or the relative public interests in disclosing or withholding the information. If he judges that any such third party's views are potentially relevant but have not been provided, the Information Commissioner will in some cases approach the third party himself and in others invite the public authority to do so.

In sensitive cases and where the security of the public authority's information is a particular issue, government departments (and potentially other public authorities) can ask the Information Commissioner himself or named staff to go and inspect papers *in situ* rather than sending them to the ICO. The Information Commissioner will not refuse such requests unless they significantly obstruct the discharge of his statutory functions (MoU, paras.15 and 16). In other cases, the Information Commissioner may agree it is mutually beneficial for his staff to inspect information at the public authority rather than being provided with it, such as where the papers are voluminous or need technical explanation by officials (MoU, para.17). The Information Commissioner has agreed not to retain papers obtained from authorities for longer than necessary and will liaise over their return or disposal (MoU, para.13).

If the Information Commissioner has not received all the information he requires from a public authority after informal request and service of an Information Notice, he can seek a warrant to obtain access to any premises where he might find such information (see **10.4.4**).

The Information Commissioner contacts the complainant whenever appropriate during his consideration of the complaint. He will not, without the public authority's consent, however, disclose information to the complainant (or a third party) if the information is arguably exempt or potentially the subject of an appeal to the Information Tribunal or the courts. In addition, as the Information Commissioner is himself a public authority under Sched.1 to the FOIA, he has agreed to notify government departments (and probably any public authority) as soon as possible where he has been asked (whether under the FOIA or otherwise) to provide information supplied by a department, or he considers release of such information necessary in connection with any enactment, proceedings, EC-related obligation or otherwise. In addition, the Information Commissioner has undertaken to resist disclosure by all reasonable means, including appeals, where it is reasonable to do so (see MoU, paras.10 and 11). Indeed, he did so successfully in *Friends of the Earth* v. *Information Commissioner*, Information Tribunal, 4 April 2007.

Authorities should take up the Information Commissioner's invitation to comment on the complaint by setting out in writing their arguments against disclosure or in defence of whatever other complaint is levelled at them. In appropriate cases this might include written expert evidence showing why a particular exemption applies. For example, where a public authority is relying on the exemption under s.29(1)(a) in respect of disclosures which would be likely to prejudice the economic interests of the UK or part of it, the authority's arguments might be bolstered by presenting the Information Commissioner with a report prepared by a suitably qualified economist or industry expert. Similarly, in the context of the exemption under s.41, an authority may wish to obtain professional legal advice on whether the disclosure of requested material would breach a duty of confidence owed to a third party and whether there would be a defence of public interest or not. (The Information Commissioner may sometimes appoint his own expert to advise on the validity of the arguments presented to him in relation to the exemptions.) The costs of seeking external advice would not be recoverable from the other party by order of the Information Commissioner. Even if the case went to the Information Tribunal the recoverability of costs is limited (see **10.7.1** and **10.7.2**).

It is important to point out that there is nothing to prevent a public authority from arguing before the Information Commissioner that it is entitled to withhold information on the basis of an exemption which it did not rely on when turning down the applicant's request for information originally (*Bowbrick* v. *Information Commissioner*, Information Tribunal, 28 September 2006, paras.42–5.) In such a case, the public authority may find, however, that the Information Commissioner issues a Decision Notice ruling it in breach of the s.17 refusal notice provisions and ordering it to issue an amended refusal letter citing the relevant exemption and grounds. (As to whether the Information Commissioner has a positive duty to consider the applicability of exemptions which have not been relied upon by a public authority, see below, 'The Information Commissioner's Decision'.)

Where an authority is relying on a qualified exemption, it will clearly need to give the Information Commissioner what it thinks are the public interest arguments in favour of maintaining the exemption, but it should certainly consider commenting on the arguments in favour of disclosure as well. This is a tactical question. Instinctively one might not wish to draw attention to matters which support the opponent; but it may often be advantageous to the authority to do so, thereby showing the Information Commissioner that it has thought carefully about all the issues, and maximising the persuasiveness of its claim that the public interest arguments in favour of maintaining the exemption do indeed outweigh those supporting disclosure.

Hearings

The Information Commissioner does not hold hearings.

Burden of proof and standard of proof

There is no express burden on either the complainant or the public authority to prove their case or else know that they cannot succeed. Yet, there is in effect an underlying presumption of openness in the FOIA. The statute does not provide a 'white list' of matters which may be disclosed by contrast with all other information. Rather, it grants applicants a general right of access, subject to certain limitations – principally the exemptions, and even the majority of those are circumscribed by the public interest test. Furthermore, when applying the public interest test, it follows from the wording of s.2(2)(b) that information must be disclosed where the public interests in disclosure and maintenance of the exemption are evenly balanced. There is no burden on the applicant to show that the public interest in disclosure outweighs that in the maintenance of the exemption. This is a question for the Information Commissioner or Tribunal to determine on the basis of the evidence and the relevant circumstances of the case (*Kessler* v. *Information Commissioner*, Information Tribunal, 29 November 2007, paras.56–7). Thus, the Information Tribunal has said that while there is no express presumption in favour of disclosure:

> The default setting in the Act is in favour of disclosure. Information held by public authorities must be disclosed on request, unless the Act permits it to be withheld.
> . . .
>
> There is an *assumption* built into FOIA that disclosure of information by public authorities on request is in the public interest in order to promote transparency and accountability in relation to the activities of public authorities. The strength of that interest, and the strength of the competing interests must be assessed on a case-by-case basis and not least because section 2(2)(b) requires the balance to be considered 'in all the circumstances of the case'.
>
> (*England and London Borough of Bexley* v. *Information Commissioner*, Information Tribunal, 10 May 2007, para. 65; emphasis added)

The position differs under the EIR, as public authorities are subject to an express presumption of openness (reg.12(2)), and thus bear the burden of rebutting that presumption. Accordingly, should there be doubt as to whether an exception applies or where the greater public interest lies, there will be an order for disclosure.

Where the public authority does present evidence, it will need to come up to the normal civil standard, namely that the facts alleged are, on the balance of probabilities, true. This would be the case, for example, where an authority argues under s.38 that disclosure of the requested information would, or would be likely to, endanger someone's physical or mental health or their safety. Merely asserting harm will not suffice (*Attorney General* v. *Guardian Newspapers (No.2)* [1990] AC 109, 263, 283). Similarly, it is not enough under the EIR for a public authority merely to assert that it does not hold the information requested; it must advance adequate evidence to overturn the presumption of disclosure. This could be done by providing evidence of the search carried out, or of its document destruction policy, or of an explanation as to why the information is not (or is no longer) held (*Fowler* v. *Information Commissioner*, Information Tribunal, 6 November 2007, paras.22–4).

Exceptionally, the legislation provides five instances where a government Minister may serve a conclusive evidence certificate, which precludes the Information Commissioner from assessing the evidence himself. For example, under reg.15 of the EIR a Minister can assert conclusively that disclosure of certain information would adversely affect national security and would not be in the public interest (see **10.7.2**).

Attempt at informal resolution

In the early days of the FOI regime, applicants and public authorities alike were understandably keen to obtain rulings from the Information Commissioner (and the Information Tribunal) in order to obtain clarity on the practical application of the FOIA and establish points of principle. As time goes on, the Information Commissioner's hope is that parties will increasingly be prepared to settle complaints prior to a formal ruling, so that all involved can enjoy the savings of time, money and effort and the increased regulatory efficiency that that would bring. He has agreed to explore the scope for settlement wherever practicable (MoU, para.20). In some cases public authorities have been galvanised into responding to a previously ignored request simply as a result of the Information Commissioner's intervention. In other cases, the Information Commissioner may seek to stimulate such a change of heart by indicating to the public authority that he is minded to rule against it. Where the authority agrees as a result to provide all or at least some of the information, the complainant may then be invited to withdraw the complaint. If the complainant agrees, the Information Commissioner no longer has a duty to make a decision on the complaint by virtue of s.50(2)(d) and thus the matter can be closed. If the complainant refuses to withdraw the complaint without good reason, however, he runs the risk that the Information Commissioner will not go on to make a decision, on the grounds that the complaint is then frivolous or vexatious (see 'The Information Commissioner's policy on Decision Notices' below).

Details of informally settled complaints are in general not posted on the ICO website, thus providing an incentive to public authorities wishing to avoid the public censure of a Decision Notice. It is possible, however, that occasionally – such as where the case highlights a point of principle – the Information Commissioner might exercise his discretion to issue a Decision Notice in any event, in compliance with his s.47 duty to publish information about the operation of the FOIA and about good practice.

The Information Commissioner's decision

If the matter cannot be resolved informally, the Information Commissioner issues a Decision Notice setting out any steps required of the public authority, such as what information is to be disclosed, how soon and by what means. He might order disclosure of all or just part of the requested information or else he might uphold the authority's claim that it is exempt from disclosure.

The question arises whether the Commissioner has a duty, or a discretion, to consider complaints or arguments against disclosure which are not advanced by the parties themselves.

The Information Tribunal ruled in *Bowbrick* v. *Information Commissioner* (Information Tribunal, 28 September 2006, para.46) that the Information Commissioner has no positive duty to consider the applicability of exemptions not relied upon by the public authority. On the other hand, the Information Tribunal acknowledged that he has discretion to do so, though seemingly only 'in some exceptional cases'. Examples given (at paras.49–51) were:

- where he finds that the authority mis-identified the applicable exemption (e.g. the s.30 exemption (investigations and proceedings) instead of the closely related s.31 exemption (law enforcement));
- where he finds that the authority mistakenly identified an exemption under the FOIA in a case where the EIR apply (or vice versa) and there is a corresponding exemption (see *Kirkaldie* v. *Information Commissioner*, Information Tribunal, 4 July 2006); and
- where he believes the authority has failed to identify the applicability of the s.40 exemption (personal information) and the rights of data subjects ought to be protected.

The last situation was given in the light of the Information Commissioner's statutory responsibilities regarding data protection under the Data Protection Act 1998. The limits of this discretion are not clear but may well be tested in litigation. This is because one of the grounds of appeal to the Information Tribunal is where the Information Commissioner has exercised his discretion inappropriately.

The Information Tribunal has also indicated that, even where a complainant does not mention this in his complaint, the Information Commissioner should be ready to consider whether a public authority has breached its s.16 duty to provide the applicant with advice and assistance with their request for information (*Barber* v. *Information Commissioner*, Information Tribunal, 11 November 2005, paras.17–19).

Served with the Decision Notice there is a Statement of Reasons summarising the Information Commissioner's rationale for the decision. This provides a basis for the parties to consider an appeal. In view of the fact that public authorities may wish to appeal against the decision to the Information Tribunal and that a Statement of Reasons may include references to, or quotations from, material which an authority considers exempt, the version given to the applicant is not always identical to that given to the authority. Decision Notices and Statements of Reasons are served on parties simultaneously and they are given a few days to digest the contents before they are made public. The parties have 28 days in which to lodge an appeal. In the absence of any appeal, the deadline for taking the action ordered in the Decision Notice is often 30 days from the date of the notice but the length of time specified is a matter of the Information Commissioner's discretion.

As to the requirements in the legislation regarding the content of Decision Notices, their appealability, the potential for ministerial override, and the consequences of non-compliance, see **10.3.1** and **10.3.5**.

The Information Commissioner's policy on Decision Notices

Largely in response to the overstretch on resources at the ICO over the first 18 months of the FOIA's operation, and the consequent development of a sizeable backlog of cases, the Information Commissioner decided to alter his policy on the issuing of formal Decision Notices at the end of every case (see 'A Robust Approach to FOI Complaint Cases', ICO, November 2006).

Under this more 'robust' policy, cases are not taken up in the first place, or continued with, once it becomes clear that issuing an adverse Decision Notice against the public authority would serve no useful purpose. This would be the case where the authority had belatedly complied with the request and thus there are no actions which can be ordered of it in a Decision Notice. It would also apply where the alleged breach is trivial (such as a technical defect in a refusal notice under s.17), or some procedural failing which has since been acknowledged by the public authority, including the s.16 obligation to provide advice and assistance to information seekers. In such circumstances, the parties are informed that the case is closed, and the authority is directed to the

Information Commissioner's published guidance on the particular topic in which its response had been defective. Details of these closed cases are not published but they are recorded by the ICO in case patterns of conduct emerge suggesting the need for some future enforcement action or written guidance.

The complainant may not be happy with the decision not to proceed to a Decision Notice, yet the Information Commissioner will regard any attempt to pursue the complaint in such circumstances as rendering it 'frivolous or vexatious' – which gives him discretion not to reach a decision on it (s.50(2)(c)). There are exceptions, however, where the Commissioner considers it a justifiable use of regulatory resources to issue a Decision Notice, so a complainant can seek to argue that his case falls within such an exception. Exceptions include where the ICO has reasonable grounds for believing that:

1. the public authority has deliberately delayed its response to a request or has otherwise deliberately failed to meet its obligations;
2. the effect of delay or other non-compliance served the purposes of the public authority and requires censure in an adverse Decision Notice (e.g. avoiding disclosure at a critical time);
3. the requested information was eventually disclosed, perhaps after ICO intervention, but it would be right in the circumstances to proceed to a Decision Notice, for example to provide a formal record of the outcome;
4. the public authority has delayed responses or otherwise failed to meet its obligations in similar circumstances in previous cases;
5. there are sound reasons of principle or precedent for proceeding to a Decision Notice; or
6. it would be manifestly unreasonable in the particular circumstances not to proceed with the case.

If the Information Commissioner refuses to issue a Decision Notice, there are no grounds for appeal to the Information Tribunal and the only means for a complainant to challenge the Information Commissioner's refusal to issue a Decision Notice would be by way of judicial review or else by invoking the ICO complaints procedure and then appealing to the Parliamentary Ombudsman (see **10.6.4**).

Publicity

All Decision Notices and Enforcement Notices are publicly available and are posted on the ICO website, excluding any exempt information. Both a case summary and the full text of the decision appear. The database of decisions now has a useful function which allows you to search, inter alia, by reference to individual public authorities or section numbers of the legislation. Whereas the public authority which is the subject of a complaint will almost always be identified, complainants' names are not released.

There might be the occasional exception to this, such as where the requester is a journalist who has publicly referred to their complaint.[21] Where appropriate, parties should consider notifying the ICO of any preference they may have not to be identified in case reports. Complainants are generally named in the appeal decisions of the Information Tribunal.

The Information Commissioner has indicated[22] that he will normally make a public statement where he decides to take any 'structured or regulatory intervention'. This can include not only the formal enforcement notices but also the issuing of advice, 'exhortations', good practice assessments or Practice Recommendations. By contrast, due to the sensitive nature of their contents, Information Notices are not normally published.

Certain cases (whether resulting from complaints or the ICO's own monitoring) may receive additional publicity where this would illustrate the Information Commissioner's approach to enforcement and any lessons to be learned (e.g. Annex B of Awareness Guidance 22 on vexatious complaints). Furthermore, public authorities may find themselves criticised in a Report to Parliament, if they ignore Practice Recommendations for example.

Timescales

Whereas the Scottish Information Commissioner is required to reach a decision within four months of receiving the application, or such other period as is reasonable in the circumstances (Freedom of Information (Scotland) Act, s.49(3)(b)), no time limit is prescribed under the FOIA. The time taken to resolve complaints will obviously vary considerably from one case to another, depending on its complexity and the speed and adequacy of response of the public authority and the workload of ICO staff. Procedural cases can be dealt with relatively quickly but cases involving the application of the exemptions take longer. Workloads have been very high and the length of time taken to resolve complaints has been raised as a subject of concern before the Constitutional Affairs Select Committee (2005–6, 7th Report) and also in decisions of the Information Tribunal (e.g. *Spurgeon* v. *Information Commissioner*, Information Tribunal, 29 June 2007, paras.18 and 31). The Information Commissioner has sought to address the problem both by applying for extra funding from the government and by implementing procedural changes. In October 2007, the ICO website was reporting that 58 per cent of FOI cases were resolved within one month of receipt, 64 per cent within three months, 69 per cent within six months, and 81 per cent within a year. So far as complex cases are concerned, the backlog is still clearly a big issue.

10.6.2   Case-handling statistics

Table 10.1   Case-handling statistics for the ICO[23]

Number of complaints made to the ICO in the first three years of FOIA operation	6,000
Number of cases closed	5,000
Number of new cases received by the ICO per month	220
Number of formal Decision Notices issued by the ICO	700
Proportion of cases resolved informally	50%
Proportion of ICO Decision Notices appealed to the Information Tribunal	25%
Proportion of those appeals granted	25% (i.e. ICO decision upheld in 75% of cases).

(All figures are approximate.)

10.6.3   Complaints relating to a Publication Scheme

A person seeking to obtain information from a public authority which is supposedly available under its Publication Scheme may be concerned at the amount of money he has been asked to pay for it or at the near impossibility of obtaining access to it in practice. In another situation a company or an individual whose reputation has been damaged by information released by a public authority under its Publication Scheme may be irate that they were not consulted prior to the disclosure. An application under s.50(1) for a decision of the Information Commissioner cannot be made, however, in relation to a complaint about a public authority's Publication Scheme. Nevertheless, were these people to bring their grievances to the Information Commissioner's attention, he would be able to investigate the matter under his general duties to promote authorities' observance of the FOIA and the Codes of Practice (ss.47 and 48). The outcome may be that he issues the public authority with a Practice Recommendation or an Enforcement Notice but, unlike a Decision Notice, these are not required to be served on the person who had complained. In some circumstances, it may be open to an aggrieved party to take legal action in respect of disclosures under a Publication Scheme, such as for judicial review, breach of confidence or under the DPA (see **10.9.5**).

10.6.4   Complaints about the ICO

A party dissatisfied with the content of the Information Commissioner's ruling should appeal to the Information Tribunal. However, if a party wishes to complain about the way in which an assessment was conducted, rudeness of staff, for example, they should ask for a copy of the ICO's complaints procedure. The ICO will try to respond to complaints with their findings within 28 days. If the complainant remains dissatisfied, he or she can appeal the decision and ultimately complain to the Parliamentary Ombudsman through an MP (see **www.ombudsman.org.uk/make_a_complaint**).

10.7   APPEALS TO THE INFORMATION TRIBUNAL

Formerly known as the Data Protection Tribunal, the Information Tribunal deals primarily with appeals under the FOIA and the DPA. There are two separate regimes for appeals to the Information Tribunal under the FOIA: the first in relation to appeals brought under s.57(1) or (2) of the FOIA challenging notices issued by the Information Commissioner; the second concerns appeals brought under s.60(1) or (4) relating to ministerial certificates issued in the context of information which is allegedly exempt as it relates to national security matters. The two regimes are governed principally by procedural rules contained in two different pieces of subordinate legislation. Appeals under the EIR are subject to the same regimes by virtue of reg.18.

10.7.1   Appeals against the Information Commissioner's notices (s.57 appeals)

Under s.57 of the FOIA both the complainant and the public authority may appeal as of right to the Information Tribunal against a Decision Notice served on them by the Information Commissioner. A public authority has a similar right in respect of an Enforcement Notice or an Information Notice, as does a responsible authority in relation to certain Decision Notices or Enforcement Notices regarding materials in the National Archives (which incorporates the former Public Records Office).[24] An interested third party or a complainant without an automatic right of appeal may ask the Information Tribunal to exercise its discretion to join him to the appeal.

Curiously, perhaps, by contrast with litigation through the courts, no matter whether an appeal is brought by a complainant or by a public authority, the respondent to the appeal is the Information Commissioner rather than the other party. He is called upon to justify his Decision Notice (though there is no formal burden of proof on either party). The non-appealing party can participate in the appeal as a third party (see below).

Grounds of appeal

The grounds of appeal are contained in s.58 of the FOIA, which provides that the appeal will succeed if the Information Tribunal finds that the notice is not in accordance with the law or the Information Commissioner should have exercised his discretion differently in dealing with the complaint. In all other cases, the Information Tribunal is bound to dismiss the appeal. By virtue of s.58(2), the Information Tribunal may review any finding of fact on which the Information Commissioner's notice was based. Where the Information Tribunal considers that the grounds of appeal are made out, it 'shall allow the appeal or substitute such other notice as could have been served by the Commissioner' (s.58(1)).

In a number of cases before it, the Information Tribunal has made observations on the framing of claims under these grounds of appeal, as well as more widely on the nature of its own jurisdiction:

- The Information Tribunal is entitled to enter a merits-based judgment and is not restricted merely to a review of the lawfulness of the Information Commissioner's decision-making process, as the Administrative Court would be on a judicial review. Indeed, it regards itself as freer than the Court of Appeal to hear fresh evidence, hence the exercise is more akin to a re-hearing than an appeal, albeit that the starting point is the Information Commissioner's Decision Notice (*Guardian Newspapers and Brooke* v. *Information Commissioner*, Information Tribunal, 8 January 2007, para.14(1)–(2)).

- The Information Tribunal can consider evidence that was not before the Information Commissioner (*Bowbrick* v. *Information Commissioner*, Information Tribunal, 28 September 2006, para.27). This can be fresh evidence put forward voluntarily by the parties; but since the Information Tribunal also has an investigatory role it can also call for witnesses or particular evidence to be provided. In consequence, a decision of the Information Commissioner may be found to be unlawful not because of any error of legal reasoning on his part but because the Information Tribunal has fresh evidence before it and makes different findings of fact (*Guardian Newspapers*, above, para.14(4) and (6)). Where it transpires during the appeal that further factual investigation is required to produce relevant evidence, the Information Tribunal has been prepared to adjourn the hearing and remit the matter to the Information Commissioner to conduct that investigation by liaising with the public authority. When the Information Commissioner reports back, the hearing continues and the Information Tribunal proceeds to its ruling (e.g. *Barber* v. *Information Commissioner*, Information Tribunal, 11 November 2005, para.14; see also *Fowler* v. *Information Commissioner*, Information Tribunal, 6 November 2007).

- To determine whether the Information Commissioner's notice is 'not in accordance with the law' the Information Tribunal is required to consider whether the provisions of the FOIA were correctly applied or not (*Guardian Newspapers*, above, para.14(3)). The notice would equally be 'not in accordance with the law' if it was based on a flawed decision-making process in public law terms, for example because the Information Commissioner ignored a material fact or consideration (see e.g. *Burgess* v. *Information Commissioner*, Information Tribunal, 7 June 2007, para.49).

- The Information Commissioner's analysis of the public interest test in the context of qualified exemptions (or the EIR) is not a question of discretion but a matter of law, or mixed law and fact (*Guardian Newspapers*, above, para.14(5)). (An example of a wrong use of discretion might be where the Information Commissioner finds in favour of the complainant but allows the public authority too long a period before it has to disgorge the information in question under s.50(4).)
- Where an appeal is brought on the basis that the Information Commissioner exercised his discretion wrongly, the Information Tribunal should consider how it would exercise its discretion on the issue, taking account of any fresh evidence (*Guardian Newspapers*, above, para.14(7)).
- The Information Tribunal should not subject the Information Commissioner's Notice to a highly minute or technical analysis. 'Where the overall intent is clear, the Tribunal should interpret the notice accordingly, disregarding any minor errors or infelicities of expression or reasoning which do not affect the substance of the matter' (*Guardian Newspapers*, above, para.15).
- A public authority may be able to rely on an exemption before the Information Tribunal which it had failed to advance at any earlier stage of the dispute, though this will depend on the facts of the case, including whether any prejudice is thereby caused to the other party (and possibly other Tribunal users whose cases would be delayed), whether it would have been possible to raise the exemption earlier, and what consequences might follow if the authority is not permitted to argue the point. Public authorities will have less latitude to bring forward a new exemption on appeal where they are the appellant rather than a third party joined to an appeal brought by the information seeker (see: *Benford* v. *Information Commissioner*, Information Tribunal, 14 November 2007, para. 39; and, by analogy, *Evans* v. *Information Commissioner*, Information Tribunal, 26 October 2007, para.15; *Dainton* v. *Information Commissioner*, Information Tribunal, 10 September 2007, para.8; *Ofcom* v. *Information Commissioner*, Information Tribunal, 4 September 2007, para.18; and *Bowbrick*, above, paras.46–57).
- Similarly, in cases about environmental information, a public authority may be permitted to rely for the first time before the Information Tribunal on an exception under the EIR where the dispute had earlier been fought, mistakenly, on the basis of provisions in the FOIA. It will have a better hope of doing so where the EIR exception is similar to the FOIA exemption relied on previously (see *Archer* v. *Information Commissioner*, Information Tribunal, 9 May 2007 and *Kirkaldie* v. *Information Commissioner*, Information Tribunal, 4 July 2006).

- The Information Tribunal is under no general duty to consider whether there are any relevant exemptions not raised by a public authority in an appeal (*Bowbrick*, above, para.56).

Note also that where the Information Commissioner declines to issue a Decision Notice in relation to a complaint (or issues one without jurisdiction), the proper way of challenging the Information Commissioner is to apply to the High Court for judicial review, as no appeal lies to the Information Tribunal in such circumstances (*British Broadcasting Corporation* v. *Sugar* [2007] EWHC 905 (Admin), 27 April 2007).

It is important to bear in mind that the 'principles' set out in the bullet points above come with an inherent health warning: the FOI regime is still in its formative stage and the rules of the game are liable to be made and then remade. The Information Tribunal regards itself as bound by FOIA-related decisions of the High Court, but it frequently points out that it is at liberty to depart from its own past decisions.

As to remedies, the Information Tribunal is not able to award compensation or impose fines in connection with breaches of the FOIA. The question of costs is dealt with below. Unlike the Information Commissioner, the Information Tribunal has no power to issue recommendations to public authorities on how they might better comply with the codes of practice under ss.45 and 46 of the FOIA or reg.16 of the EIR. It has, however, been prepared to issue a Decision Notice in which it invited the Commissioner to make a Practice Recommendation under his s.48 powers, an invitation which he took up (see *Bowbrick*, above, para.1(D) and see Information Commissioner's Practice Recommendation of 13 February 2007 issued to *Nottingham City Council*).

The Information Tribunal panel

Appointment to the Information Tribunal in general is governed by s.6 of the DPA, which provides for a legally qualified chairman and one or more deputy chairmen, chosen by the Lord Chancellor, and for members appointed by the Secretary of State for Justice, who do not have to have a legal qualification but who represent the interests of either public authorities or those who make requests for information under the FOIA.

The Information Tribunal panel that hears specific appeals under s.57 of the FOIA is presided over by the chairman or a deputy chairman and an equal number of the members appointed to represent the interests of applicants and of public authorities, thus making a panel of at least (but usually) three. The individual members are nominated by the chairman, or, if he is unable to act, by a deputy chairman. There is an exception in relation to certain appeals against Information Notices, which are heard by the chairman alone (see below). The chairman may also act for the Information Tribunal on matters preliminary or incidental to an appeal under certain rules (rule 25 of the amended 2005 Rules – see below).

Procedure

The rules governing procedure in appeals under s.57 are principally contained in the Information Tribunal (Enforcement Appeals) Rules 2005, as amended ('the 2005 Rules') (see **www.informationtribunal.gov.uk** for the Rules and supplementary Practice Directions).[25] Provision is made for a wide range of procedural steps, some familiar from ordinary court-based litigation but others not. Some are of particular note.

Under rule 5, time for appeal, a written notice of appeal must be served on the Information Tribunal within 28 days of service on the appellant of the Information Commissioner's notice. This time limit can be extended if the Information Tribunal considers it just and right to do so in the circumstances.

A notice of appeal (rule 4) must: (a) identify the decision of the Information Commissioner which is being disputed and the date on which the related notice was served on the appellant; (b) state the following: the name and address of the appellant; the grounds of appeal; whether or not the appellant is likely to want a hearing; the name and address of the public authority to which the disputed decision relates; the special circumstances which justify the Information Tribunal accepting jurisdiction where the notice has not been served within the ordinary 28-day limit (see above); an address for service of documents on the appellant; and (c) be signed by or on behalf of the appellant.

An appellant may seek the early determination of the appeal by including such a request in the notice of appeal and giving reasons for it.

In an appeal against an Information Notice, the notice of appeal must include any representations the appellant wishes to make as to why it is necessary in the interests of justice for the appeal to be heard by an Information Tribunal panel rather than by the chairman sitting alone as provided by rule 21(2) (see the discussion on hearings (rules 16–24) later in this section).

A notice of appeal form and guidance is available at the Information Tribunal's website. The completed notice of appeal should be sent to: Information Tribunal, Arnhem House Support Centre, PO Box 6987, Leicester, Leicestershire, LE1 6ZX. The fax number is 0116 249 4253. The email address is: informationtribunal@dca.gsi.gov.uk and the telephone number is 0845 600 0877. Information Tribunal staff will send the appellant an acknowledgement of service and serve a copy of the notice of appeal on the Information Commissioner and any other party (rule 6(1)(b)). The Information Tribunal can decide to deal with different cases together – 'consolidation' – where a common question of law or fact arises in both or all of them, or where it is desirable for some other reason to hear them together, subject to the parties having the chance to make representations (rule 13).

(Rule 25 covers notices generally. Documents required or authorised by the 2005 Rules may be served by registered or recorded post, hand delivery or electronic communication (i.e. fax or email). Parties are, however, not obliged to accept service of documents sent electronically unless they have agreed to do so.)

Under rules 8 and 9 the Information Commissioner has 21 days to send the Information Tribunal and the appellant a written reply in which he sets out his grounds for opposing the appeal (or says he will not oppose it). The Information Tribunal may extend this period on the same basis as for the period for service of the notice of appeal. (The Information Commissioner may also seek expedition of proceedings, say whether he thinks a hearing is desirable if the appellant has indicated he will not want one, and indicate whether he thinks it might be necessary in the interests of justice for the appeal to be heard and determined otherwise than by the chairman sitting alone if it is an appeal against an Information Notice (see rule 21).)

In his reply the Information Commissioner may, giving reasons, apply to strike out the notice of appeal on the grounds that (i) an appeal does not lie to, or cannot be entertained by, the Information Tribunal; or (ii) the notice of appeal discloses no reasonable grounds of appeal. The strike out application may be heard as a preliminary issue or at the start of the substantive appeal. There is no similar express provision for the appellant to strike out the Information Commissioner's reply. An appellant aware of a fundamental flaw in the Information Commissioner's case could seek to bring it before the Information Tribunal as a preliminary issue (see the discussion about directions, rule 14, below).

Rule 7 gives the Information Tribunal power, should it judge it desirable, to order another person to be joined as a party to the appeal and it may make such an order of its own motion, or on the application of one of the parties, or where a third party has itself applied to be joined to the appeal. The most likely third parties to an appeal would be anyone affected in some way by the information whose disclosure was ordered by the Information Commissioner (such as a pressure group or the subject of the information), or either the applicant for the information or the public authority wishing to support the Information Commissioner in opposing the appeal. Practice Direction 2 makes it clear that as the case progresses Tribunal Chairmen are to keep under review whether it is desirable for any third party to be made a party to the appeal. The Information Tribunal has used this power to call its own expert witnesses to assist it in determining appeals.

Whether or not it has been contacted first by the Information Tribunal and sent a copy of the notice of appeal or the reply, any third party wishing to participate in the appeal must give notice of this fact to the Information Tribunal by way of a joinder notice. The notice must be in writing and must include: the full name and address of the person seeking to be joined to the appeal; a statement of his interest and whether or not he opposes the appeal, together with any reasons on which he relies in support of his interest; and the name and address of any representative the person appoints, and whether the Information Tribunal should send correspondence and notices concerning the appeal to the representative instead. The notice and any attachments must be provided to the Information Tribunal in triplicate to enable it to send a copy to each of the other parties. The joinder notice will be treated as the third party's reply to the notice of appeal if the Information Tribunal issues an order of joinder making him a party to the appeal. The Information Tribunal may give directions in relation to the joining of a third party to an appeal.

By rule 10, after considering the notice of appeal and the reply, the Information Tribunal may of its own motion dismiss the appeal summarily if it considers it proper to do so, but it must first notify the appellant of its intention and give him an opportunity to make written representations and request a hearing. There is no express provision for the Information Commissioner to apply for summary disposal (but we have seen above that he can apply to strike out the notice of appeal), nor for the appellant to seek summary determination in its favour.

The Information Tribunal may, of its own motion or on application by a party, give any directions which it thinks proper to enable the parties to prepare for the hearing or to assist the Information Tribunal to determine the issues (rule 14). Directions may be made in the parties' absence but a party may always apply to have a direction varied (i.e. amended) or set aside. Typical directions might cover disclosure and inspection of relevant documents (subject to the ordinary rules of privilege); the exchange of witness statements and statements of expert witnesses; the preparation of lists of agreed matters, chronologies and skeleton arguments; and a direction that a specific matter be dealt with as a preliminary issue and that there be a pre-hearing review. A pre-hearing review is not merely for administrative efficiency in preparing for the hearing but can be used as an opportunity to hear argument on a preliminary issue. The Information Tribunal is expressly permitted to treat a pre-hearing review as the hearing of the appeal, and rule accordingly, where it considers that its decision therein substantially disposes of the whole appeal. An illustrative list of possible directions is available on the Information Tribunal website, together with guidance of use in particular to non-lawyers.

The parties may ask the Information Tribunal to vary or set aside any direction, or extend any time limit. A party that fails to comply with a direction of the Information Tribunal risks having their appeal/application, or their reply, wholly or partially struck out. Any information or material provided under directions (such as in witness statements or in disclosure of documents) may only be used for the purposes of the appeal. The Information Tribunal holds preliminary hearings, such as hearings for directions, by telephone or video conference where appropriate (Practice Direction 3).

By rule 15 the Information Tribunal can make an order requiring the occupier of any premises, on seven days' notice, to permit the Information Tribunal (accompanied by the parties and Information Tribunal staff) to enter the premises at a specified time and inspect, examine, operate or test any equipment there which is used (or intended to be used) in connection with the storage or recording of information, and to inspect, examine or test any documents or other material on those premises connected with the same. Privileged documents are immune from inspection, examination or testing. The occupier can apply to have the order set aside.

The appellant must seek permission from the Information Tribunal if he or she wishes to amend the notice of appeal or deliver supplementary grounds (rule 11). If leave to amend is granted, this triggers a right for the Information Commissioner (and any other party which has been joined to the appeal) to amend their replies and serve them on the Information Tribunal and the other parties within 21 days. There is also provision for the Information Commissioner to seek the Information Tribunal's permission to amend his reply in any event, although this does not trigger an express right for the other parties to amend their notice/reply in consequence. There is no express provision for a third party to seek leave to amend its reply spontaneously. In view of the Information Tribunal's wide power to give directions, however, a party wishing to take steps which are not expressly provided for in the rules should apply to the Information Tribunal to give an appropriate direction on the grounds that it would assist that party (and the others) to prepare for the hearing or that it would assist the Information Tribunal to determine the issues.

Hearings are covered by rules 16–24. Unless the appellant or Information Commissioner requests a hearing, or the Information Tribunal orders one, the appeal will be determined without one. Where a party requests a hearing, the Information Tribunal must grant the request unless it is satisfied that the appeal can properly be determined without one (rule 16). (Simpler cases, and those where the facts are essentially agreed between the parties, and the dispute comes down to a question of law, are especially suited to paper hearings.) Oral hearings take place in public, subject to concerns of the parties or the Information Tribunal relating to the desirability of safeguarding commercially sensitive information or any allegedly exempt information (rule 22 and Practice Direction 1). For the most part, hearings are held in London but they may be held elsewhere if this is requested and clearly shown to be more suitable.

Upon the application of a government Minister, the Information Tribunal has power to exclude any party from the appeal if it is satisfied that this is necessary for reasons of substantial public interest (rule 23). Such applications are made without notice to the other parties.

In the absence of specific requirements in the 2005 Rules, the Information Tribunal is free to conduct proceedings in any way it thinks fit and is to avoid formality so far as is appropriate (rule 24(4)). (In practice, however, its proceedings tend towards the legalistic, but complainants who are representing themselves are given time and assistance to present their case.) The Information Tribunal may compel a person anywhere in the UK to appear at an appeal hearing, answer any questions and produce any relevant documents under his or her control as it specifies. Parties may appear in person or be represented by anyone they choose (legal aid is not available). Provision is made for examination and cross-examination of witnesses, followed by representations on the evidence and on the appeal generally.

Where a party fails to appear at a hearing without good reason, the Information Tribunal can simply dismiss the appeal if that party is the appellant or, in any case, hear and determine the appeal, or any particular issue, in the party's absence and may make such order as to costs as it thinks fit.

Appeals against Information Notices, and any related issues, are heard or determined by the chairman sitting alone unless it appears to him that the Information Tribunal must, in the interests of justice, sit as usual in a panel of (at least) three, taking into account any representations made by the appellant in the notice of appeal or the Information Commissioner in his reply (rule 21).

Any evidence may be adduced even if not admissible in a court (rule 27). Hearsay and documentary evidence is therefore admissible (but would potentially carry less weight than direct oral evidence). The Information Tribunal can require evidence to be given on oath or affirmation.

The Information Commissioner has the burden of satisfying the Information Tribunal that the disputed decision should be upheld in appeals by a public authority against an Information Notice or an Enforcement Notice (rule 26, as amended by rule 6 of SI 2005/450). That is not the case with appeals brought against Decision Notices under s.57(1), however, where neither one side nor the other shoulders an express burden of proof.

Rulings are covered by rule 28. Once the Information Tribunal has determined the appeal, the chairman certifies the outcome in writing, and includes, to the extent possible without disclosing exempt information, any material finding of fact and the reasons for the decision. (Decisions are taken on a majority basis: DPA, Sched.6, para.5). The Information Tribunal's determinations are published on its website, subject to any amendments necessary to safeguard commercially sensitive information and information which is exempt under the FOIA. Unlike the published decisions of the Information Commissioner, the names of individual claimants do generally appear. The Information Tribunal may, however, assent to a request for anonymity where they deem it appropriate (e.g. *S* v. *Information Commissioner*, Information Tribunal, 9 May 2007).

Whereas public authorities will have at least 28 days to comply with a disclosure order in a Decision Notice of the Information Commissioner, the Information Tribunal may require disclosure in rather less time (10 working days, for example, in *Kirkaldie* v. *Information Commissioner*, 4 July 2006). How long does it take overall for the Information Tribunal to process an appeal? Delays are now being experienced at this stage, as well as with complaints to the Information Commissioner. At the end of 2007, cases were taking up to nine months to progress from service of the appeal notice to a final decision.

Costs

The Information Tribunal rarely awards costs but it does have power to do so (rule 29) as follows:

- against the appellant and in favour of the Information Commissioner where it considers that the appeal was manifestly unreasonable;
- against the Information Commissioner and in favour of the appellant where it considers that the disputed decision was manifestly unreasonable;
- against any party, and in favour of any other, where it considers that party was responsible for frivolous, vexatious, improper or unreasonable action, or for any failure to comply with a direction or any delay which with diligence could have been avoided.

A party will not receive an adverse costs order without first having an opportunity to make representations to the Information Tribunal against the making of the order. The Information Tribunal has power to award a specific sum in respect of the costs incurred by the beneficiary in connection with the proceedings, or all or part of such costs as taxed (if not otherwise agreed) by county court taxation. A costs order can also be made in relation to appeals which are withdrawn by the appellant under rule 12.

In the rather extreme circumstances of the *Bowbrick* case, the Information Tribunal ordered the public authority to pay the whole of the applicant's costs (to be taxed). Nottingham City Council had effectively told Dr Bowbrick that it held none of the information which he had requested. The Information Tribunal concluded, however, that the Council knew all along that it did hold relevant information. Indeed, by the end of the appeal, the council had disclosed, in a piecemeal and drawn out fashion, around a thousand pages of information. Even then it was ordered to release additional information by the Information Tribunal, which declared itself 'dismayed' at the public authority's conduct, commenting that it 'appears to have misled [the applicant] and then the Information Commissioner in his investigation'. In drafting its decision, the Information Tribunal took the opportunity to assess its powers in relation to costs orders, and found that while it cannot award a punitive (rather than compensatory) sum, it may make an award in respect of costs incurred prior to the Information Tribunal proceedings, provided they were incurred 'in connection with the proceedings' (*Bowbrick* v. *Information Commissioner*, Information Tribunal, 28 September 2006, paras.71–102). Where a public authority is itself in breach of the legislation, any claim for costs against an appellant who is acting unreasonably in pursuing the appeal will be materially undermined (*Fowler* v. *Information Commissioner*, Information Tribunal, 6 November 2007, paras.42–3).

Obstruction effectively contempt

Acts or omissions of a person involved in proceedings before the Information Tribunal which would, in court, constitute a contempt can be certified to the High Court by the Information Tribunal, investigated by the High Court and then punished as if for contempt of court (DPA, Sched.6, para.8). (For the penalties the court can impose for contempt see **10.4.1**.) This would include a failure to comply with the terms of a Decision Notice issued by the Information Tribunal.

10.7.2 Appeals against national security certificates (s.60 appeals)

There is a special procedure for challenging ministerial conclusive evidence certificates issued under ss.23(2) and 24(3) of the FOIA and reg.15(1) of the EIR in relation to national security matters.[26] The Commissioner has no power to overturn these certificates, only the Information Tribunal does. Thus, an information-seeker wishing to challenge a certificate can bypass the Information Commissioner and appeal directly to the Information Tribunal. On the other hand, it is possible that a certificate will only be adduced by the public authority after the Information Commissioner has already become involved in a complaint lodged under s.50(1) of the FOIA, and he is also entitled to appeal to the Information Tribunal over the validity or applicability of the certificate. Indeed, where timing allows it may be prudent for an applicant to seek the involvement of the Information Commissioner, as a way of protecting himself against costs (see below).

There are, in fact, two categories of national security appeals under s.60.

* S.60(1) appeals
  A government Minister can issue a certificate under s.23(2) of the FOIA asserting that particular information falls within the s.23 exemption because it was directly or indirectly supplied by, or relates to, one of the bodies dealing with security matters listed in s.23(3). That list includes MI5, MI6, GCHQ and the National Criminal Intelligence Service. On an appeal brought under s.60(1), however, the Information Tribunal can quash the certificate if it finds that the Minister was wrong.

  Similarly, a Minister can issue a certificate under s.24(3) of the FOIA or reg.15(1) of the EIR asserting that particular information is exempt under s.24 of the FOIA or reg.12(5)(a) of the EIR because (broadly) its disclosure would prejudice national security and the public interest test favours non-disclosure. Again, on an appeal brought under s.60(1), the Information Tribunal may quash the certificate where it finds that there were no reasonable grounds for issuing it. The standard applied is the same as in judicial review cases, i.e. that no one standing in the Minister's shoes could reasonably have concluded that it was appropriate to issue the certificate.

- S.60(4) appeals

  It is permissible for certificates issued under FOIA, s.24(3) or EIR, reg.15(1) to be framed in general terms. Where a public authority claims that a generally worded certificate applies to the specific information requested, the Tribunal can, on an appeal under s.60(4), determine that the certificate does not in fact cover that information.

The Information Tribunal panel

Appeals relating to national security certificates can be heard only by members of the National Security Appeals Panel. This is made up of people designated for the role by the Lord Chancellor from among the Information Tribunal chairman and deputy chairmen. In most cases there must be a panel of three such people, presided over by whichever of them the Lord Chancellor designates. Certain proceedings may be heard by just one such person (or more than one), however.[27] In addition, the designated president may act alone on behalf of the Information Tribunal on certain preliminary or incidental matters (see Information Tribunal (National Security Appeals) Rules 2005, SI 2005/13, rule 26).

Procedure

The relevant procedural rules are principally contained in the Information Tribunal (National Security Appeals) Rules 2005, SI 2005/13 (the '2005 National Security Appeals Rules').[28] The provisions of the 2005 National Security Appeals Rules are largely similar to those governing appeals under s.57 (see **10.7.1**) but they have some important differences, which are now highlighted.

The respondent to s.60 appeals is the relevant Minister. Public authorities are sidelined. They are not party to the appeal, even though an appeal will generally only arise where they have refused disclosure of requested information in reliance on one of the certificates, and in spite of the fact that the appeal may result in their having to disgorge the information.

Unlike appeals against the Commissioner's notices, there is no provision for third parties to be joined to appeals against ministerial national security certificates. Hence other interested parties – such as the public authority to which the request was submitted, the security service allegedly connected with the information, or pro open government NGOs – have no means of addressing the Tribunal directly on the issues, unless called as witnesses.

Rule 6 covers time allowed for appeal. For appeals brought under s.60(1) of the FOIA (or that section as applied to the EIR by reg.18), a notice of appeal may be served on the Information Tribunal at any time during the currency of the disputed ministerial certificate to which it relates. For appeals under s.60(4) of the FOIA (or that section as applied to the EIR by reg.18), the notice must be served on the Information Tribunal within 28 days of the claim constituting the disputed certification (i.e. the disputed claim by the public authority that a generally worded ministerial certificate applies to particular information). This period may be extended if the Information Tribunal considers it just and right to do so in the circumstances. If sent in accordance with the notices provisions in rule 31 (similar to those for s.57 appeals above) a notice of appeal will be treated as having been served on the date on which it is received for dispatch by the Post Office.

The notice of appeal (rule 5) must: (a) identify the certification which is being disputed; (b) state the following: the name and address of the appellant; the grounds of appeal; the name and address of the public authority from which the disputed certification was received; the name and address of the appellant's representative, if he has appointed one; an address for the service of notices and other documents on the appellant; and (c) be signed by or on behalf of the appellant.

For appeals under s.60(4) of the FOIA (or as applied to the EIR) the notice of appeal must also state: the date on which the public authority made the claim constituting the disputed certification; an address for service of notices and other documents on the public authority; and the special circumstances which justify the Information Tribunal accepting jurisdiction where the notice has not been served within the ordinary 28-day limit.

An appellant may seek the early determination of the appeal (brought under either subsection) by including such a request in the notice of appeal and giving reasons for it. A blank notice of appeal form is available on the Information Tribunal website.

Information Tribunal staff will send the appellant an acknowledgement of service and serve a copy of the notice of appeal on the Information Commissioner (where he is not the appellant).

The Information Tribunal is placed under a general duty (rule 4) to secure that information is not disclosed contrary to the interests of national security. The point is expressly made that a disclosure which would merely indicate the existence or otherwise of any material can itself be contrary to the interests of national security.

The Minister who signed the disputed certificate has 42 days from receipt of the notice of appeal to send to the Information Tribunal the following (rule 8): a copy of the relevant certificate, and a written notice stating:

(i)   (regarding appeals under s.60(1) of the FOIA, or as applied to the EIR) whether or not he intends to oppose the appeal and, if so, a summary of the circumstances relating to the issue of the certificate, the reason for its issue, his grounds for opposing the appeal and the evidence in support of those grounds;

(ii) (regarding appeals under s.60(4) of the FOIA, or as applied to the EIR) whether or not he wishes to make representations in relation to the appeal and, if so, the extent to which he intends to support or oppose the appeal, his grounds for supporting or opposing it and his evidence in support of those grounds; and

(iii) (in either case) a request for early determination of the appeal, if he so wishes, supported by reasons.

The Minister may apply to strike out the notice of appeal either in his notice in reply or otherwise. The provisions are, *mutatis mutandis*, the same as under the 2005 Rules (see **10.7.1**).

When he submits his notice in reply the minister can enclose a written objection to his notice being copied to the other party (or the Information Commissioner) on the basis that disclosure of the information would be contrary to the interests of national security. He must give reasons and if possible supply a version of the notice which can be disclosed. The Information Tribunal must consider this application as a preliminary issue before disclosing the material in question and must consider it in the absence of the parties (but with the Minister present if he so wishes). He must be allowed to make oral representations where the Information Tribunal is minded to overrule his objection or to order him to prepare a notice of reply in a version different from that which he submitted.

The Information Tribunal will send the Minister's notice in reply to the other party and the Information Commissioner unless it decides to dismiss the appeal summarily or where the minister has objected to disclosure.

Under rule 17, the Information Tribunal must notify the relevant Minister in advance of giving (or varying) any directions, issuing a witness summons or publishing or certifying a determination, and must allow him 14 days to make an application to the Information Tribunal requesting it to reconsider, on the basis that to go ahead would result in disclosure of information which is exempt under the FOIA. Where such an application is made, the Information Tribunal may consider it as a preliminary issue or at the start of the hearing of the substantive appeal but in either case it must be in the absence of the parties (but with the Minister present if he so wishes) (rule 18).

Rules 19–25 cover hearings. An individual issue or the entire appeal can be determined without a hearing where the parties agree in writing, or the Information Tribunal considers that the issues raised on the appeal have been determined on a previous appeal brought by the appellant on the basis of facts which did not materially differ from the current case and the parties have had an opportunity of making representations to the effect that the appeal ought not to be determined without a hearing (rule 19).

Hearings are to take place as soon as practicable, on at least 14 days' notice and with due regard to the convenience of the parties and to any request for an early hearing (rule 20). Witnesses may be summoned by the Information Tribunal or at the request of the parties (in which case the summoning party must pay the witness's reasonable travel expenses and an allowance for attending the hearing) (rule 21). The Minister may attend and be represented, as can the other parties (rule 22). If the appellant or the Minister does not intend to attend or be represented at a hearing, he or she must inform the Information Tribunal and may send the Information Tribunal additional written representations in support of the appeal (rule 22(3)).

All hearings under the 2005 National Security Appeals Rules take place in private unless the Information Tribunal, with the consent of the parties and the relevant Minister, directs that the hearing or any part of it take place in public (rule 24(1)). Even where it sits in private, the Information Tribunal can admit individual non-parties to the hearing where the parties and the Minister agree. The Information Tribunal has a duty to exclude any party from some or all of the proceedings (other than the relevant Minister) where it considers this necessary to secure that information is not disclosed contrary to the interests of national security. Any person excluded in this way has the right to have the reasons explained and given to him in writing, so far as this is possible without disclosing information which would prejudice national security (rule 24(3)).

Once the Information Tribunal has determined the appeal (on a majority basis) the chairman certifies the outcome in writing, and includes, to the extent possible without disclosing exempt information, any material finding of fact and the reasons for the decision (rule 28). The Information Tribunal's determinations are published, subject to any amendments to the text which are necessary to safeguard commercially sensitive information and information which is exempt under the FOIA, and national security. No such decisions have been published to date.

Costs

The Information Tribunal can award costs (rule 29) in a wider set of circumstances in national security certificate appeals than on s.57 appeals, as follows:

(a)   in an appeal under s.60(1) of the FOIA (or as applied to the EIR):

- against the appellant and in favour of the relevant Minister where it considers that the appeal was manifestly unreasonable;
- against the Minister and in favour of the appellant where it allows the appeal and quashes the disputed certificate, or does so to any extent;
- against the Minister and in favour of the appellant where, before the Information Tribunal has made a determination, the Minister withdraws the certificate to which the appeal relates;

(b)   in an appeal under s.60(4) of the FOIA (or as applied to the EIR):

- against the appellant and in favour of any other party where it dismisses the appeal, or dismisses it to any extent;
- in favour of the appellant and against any other party where it allows the appeal, or allows it to any extent;

(c)   in an appeal under either section: against any party, and in favour of any other, where it considers that party was responsible for frivolous, vexatious, improper or unreasonable action, or for any failure to comply with a direction or any delay which with diligence could have been avoided.

A party will not receive an adverse costs order without first having an opportunity to make representations to the Information Tribunal against the making of the order. The Information Tribunal has power to award a specific sum in respect of the costs incurred by the beneficiary in connection with the proceedings, or all or part of such costs as taxed (if not otherwise agreed) by county court taxation.

Surprisingly, one might think, the rules do not require the Tribunal to send a copy of its decision to the public authority, but it has no power to order the public authority to disclose the requested information to the applicant. This means that if the Tribunal quashes the certificate or rules that it is inapplicable to the information in question, the applicant will have to resubmit his request to the public authority, enclosing a copy of the Tribunal's decision, and if he is not happy with the outcome, complain to the Commissioner under s.50(1). If such a complaint had already been made prior to the appeal, then depending on the circumstances the Commissioner will presumably direct the public authority either to reconsider the applicant's request in the light of the Tribunal's ruling or to disclose the information without further ado.

10.8   APPEALS FROM THE INFORMATION TRIBUNAL

10.8.1   Appeals to the High Court

Any party to an appeal to the Information Tribunal under s.57 (including a joined third party) may, under s.59, appeal against the Information Tribunal's decision to the High Court (the Court of Session if the public authority's address is in Scotland) – but only on a point of law. An appeal on a point of law includes an appeal on matters of legal interpretation and all judicial review grounds (*Nipa Begum* v. *Tower Hamlets London Borough Council* [2000] 1 WLR 306, CA), therefore covering situations where, for example, the Information Tribunal misunderstands or misapplies the law, makes an order which it has no power to do, comes to a conclusion which is irrational, makes findings of fact without any evidence, does not provide adequate reasons for its decision, fails to take account of a material consideration or has regard to an irrelevant one, makes a procedural error, or acts incompatibly with the European Convention on Human Rights as domesticated by the Human Rights Act 1998.

Permission to appeal is not required. An appellant's notice would need to be filed at the High Court within 28 days of the Information Tribunal's decision (or receipt of its statement of reasons, if later) and served on the other parties and the Information Tribunal chairman (CPR Part 52 PD 17.3–5) as soon as practicable and within seven days in any event (CPR rule 52.4(3)). On determining the appeal, the court has power to: affirm, set aside or vary any order or judgment of the Information Tribunal; refer any claim or issue back to the Information Tribunal; order a new trial or hearing; make orders for the payment of interest; and/or make an order for costs (CPR rule 52.10(2)).

Unlike the case of appeals to the Information Tribunal, the FOIA does not provide that the effect of the Information Commissioner's notice (as modified or substituted by the Information Tribunal) is suspended pending appeal to the High Court or above. In practice, however, it is most unlikely to be enforced until any appeal is disposed of.

In relation to national security certificate appeals brought under s.60 there is no similar provision permitting any further appeal to the courts. That being the case, however, the Information Tribunal's rulings in such appeals are likely to be subject to judicial review in the High Court. Nevertheless, the reviewing court would extend a considerable degree of deference to the Minister, as the courts regard decisions on matters of national security as largely the province of the executive rather than the judiciary (see, e.g. Lord Steyn in *Secretary of State for the Home Department* v. *Rehman* [2001] UKHL 47, [2003] 1 AC 153 at [31]).

10.8.2   Further appeals

An appeal from the High Court lies to the Court of Appeal but only with the permission of the Court of Appeal, which will not be given unless the appeal raises an important point of principle or practice or there is some other compelling reason for the Court of Appeal to hear it (CPR 52.13). A final possible appeal lies to the House of Lords, subject to leave from the Court of Appeal or the House of Lords (see s.1 of the Administration of Justice (Appeals) Act 1934 and CPR Part 52 PD 15.19).

10.9   THIRD PARTIES

10.9.1   Limited rights of intervention under the FOIA

In the context of the FOIA a third party is anyone other than the applicant requesting access under s.1(1) and the public authority to which he addresses that request. A third party might have an interest in an access request (or in information which an authority proposes to publish under its Publication Scheme) because it supplied that information, is its subject, or it would in some way be affected by its disclosure. It could be another public authority, an individual, or a private sector company providing services to the authority under contract. There are many reasons why that person or entity might be reluctant to see the information disclosed: to protect their confidential or commercially sensitive trading information or their reputation, to name but the most obvious. To an extent, their interests are protected by the exemptions under the FOIA but they are still dependent on the public authority choosing to invoke the exemption (the FOIA does not prohibit authorities from disclosing exempt material but doing so may of course bring criminal or civil consequences under other laws such as the Official Secrets Act 1989 or the law of confidence). They also face the risk that the public authority may not appreciate that the requested information is exempt, or may disclose it without meaning to. The third party will often have knowledge which puts them in a better position than the public authority to know, for example, that certain information is a trade secret or that its disclosure would prejudice their commercial interests or the national or regional economy, or to appreciate the relevant public interest arguments in favour of maintaining the exemption and withholding information. More generally, a third party may well have a stronger impulse to shield from public view information concerning it than the public authority which has been asked to disclose it.

In spite of all this, it is a notable (and in the eyes of many, lamentable) difference between the FOIA and freedom of information regimes in many other countries that in the UK (the position under the Scottish Act is the same) interested third parties have no statutory right to be notified about requests made for information which affects them, nor is there an effective procedure under the FOIA by which they can maintain an objection to its disclosure (known in the US as 'reverse FOI'). They have no standing to apply to the Information Commissioner under s.50(1) to complain about the authority's proposed or actual disclosure of information.

10.9.2   Participation in appeals before the Information Tribunal

The only legislative provision that third parties can directly make use of is their entitlement to apply to be joined as a party to an appeal to the Information Tribunal under s.57 against a notice of the Information Commissioner (rule 7 of the 2005 rules, above). It should be noted, however, that it is not open to a third party to lodge the appeal in the first place: that must be done by the applicant or the public authority. In practice, third parties may be prevented from taking advantage of this right because they will not be aware that the appeal is taking place: there is no obligation on the parties to the appeal to notify them that it is, nor to notify the Information Tribunal of the existence of an interested third party. The parties to the appeal, one of which will be the Information Commissioner, are entitled to ask the Information Tribunal to order that an interested third party be joined to the appeal, and the Information Tribunal may decide to make such an order of its own volition. The problem is that in many cases this right of participation in the complaint comes too late in the day, in that disclosure might have occurred at an earlier stage, following a decision of the public authority or the Information Commissioner.

10.9.3   Rights to be consulted when request first made

Interested third parties have a limited entitlement to be consulted by a public authority when it receives a request for information. This is provided by the non-statutory guidance in Part IV of the Section 45 Code of Practice, whose provisions are not binding obligations but constitute practice which, in the opinion of the Secretary of State, is desirable for public authorities to follow in connection with the discharge of their functions under Part I of the FOIA. Even where consultation takes place, however, ultimate responsibility for deciding whether or not to disclose the information requested lies with the public authority. An authority is thus not bound to withhold information simply because a relevant third party asks it to do so or argues that it should.

It is worth pointing out in passing that the Code of Practice provisions on consultation with affected third parties appear to be applicable also in the context of information which a public authority is proposing to release under its Publication Scheme, even though the Code makes no express reference to Publication Schemes in the section on consultation. Although the Information Commissioner encourages public authorities to devise Publication Schemes which entitle them to withhold information covered by an exemption,[29] they are not prevented by the FOIA from releasing such material if they so wish. They may also not always realise that, or be certain whether, the information in question is exempt. Consultation may well be required in such cases under the Code of Practice. There is no mechanism in the FOIA for the making of complaints about Publication Schemes, but see the comments in **10.6.3**.

The Code of Practice indicates first that consultation with an interested third party will in some cases be necessary, either for the public authority to know whether the information requested is covered by an exemption or to determine whether the obligations in s.1 of the FOIA arise in relation to it (para.27). This last phrase seems likely to mean that it may also be necessary for a public authority to consult a third party on how the public interest test should be applied where information is potentially exempt. (It could also mean such consultation may be necessary to know whether the authority is even required to confirm or deny that it holds the information requested.) However, this begs the question: when will consultation be necessary for those purposes? The word 'necessary' in this context is assumed to mean: practically needed in order for the public authority to form a view on whether an exemption applies or on the relative public interests at stake, rather than required by law. It is arguable, however, that consultation could be required in some cases because of a public authority's obligations under public law (see **10.9.5**). In addition, any contract between the authority and the third party may require consultation in certain circumstances. Some help with deciding when consultation is necessary can perhaps be drawn from what was para.37 of the original text of the Code of Practice (issued November 2002) even though it has been removed from the current edition (November 2004). The earlier edition explained that consultation would not be necessary where: (i) the authority proposes to oppose disclosure on other grounds; (ii) the third party's views could be of no effect, for instance because disclosure is required or prevented by other legislation; and (iii) where no exemption is relevant (which presumably meant, where none was even potentially relevant).

A second category of cases which the Code of Practice contemplates is those where consultation is not necessary but would still be good practice. This applies 'in a range of . . . circumstances' and it gives the example of where an authority proposes to disclose information which relates to a third party or which is likely to affect its interests. Here, though, the Code does not appear to be recommending consultation in the ordinary meaning of the word: authorities are merely to take 'reasonable steps . . . where appropriate, to give [third parties] advance notice, or failing that, to draw it to their attention afterwards' (para.28).

Thirdly, public authorities are advised that in some cases, it may also be appropriate to consult interested third parties about other sorts of question, such as whether the applicant ought to be given any explanatory material or advice, such as any copyright (or other) restrictions as there might be on the applicant's further use of the material (para.29).

The requirement to consult in all three categories of cases appears to be further qualified where the information to be disclosed relates to, or affects, a number of third parties. Where these share a representative organisation, the authority may consider whether it would be sufficient to notify or consult with that organisation or, in other cases, to notify or consult with a representative sample of the third parties (para.30).

The Section 45 Code, in addition, highly recommends that public authorities ensure that third parties are made aware of the authorities' duties of disclosure under the FOIA (para.26). An authority could comply with this, however, by making a general statement to this effect on first dealing with a particular person or entity rather than in connection with a specific request for information. In summary, the position as to when consultation is required or will take place is uncertain and third parties can take only limited comfort from the provisions of the Section 45 Code of Practice. In the context of the EIR, the Regulation 16 Code of Practice puts even less of an onus of consulting with interested third parties prior to disclosure. Interestingly, the position is made (slightly) clearer where both the public authority and the third-party information provider are government departments:

> No decision to release information which has been supplied by one government department to another should be taken without first notifying, and where appropriate consulting, the department from which the information originated (para.29).

Even where a third party is consulted, there is no provision in the Code of Practice requiring the public authority to notify it of its final decision, or of any request for internal review or of any subsequent complaint to the Information Commissioner. Further, nothing in the FOIA or the Code of Practice obliges the Information Commissioner to consult an interested third party when considering a complaint under s.50 (but see **10.9.5**).

Except in the very clearest of cases, however, where there can be no chance that the public authority has failed to take account of some relevant issue, public authorities would be well advised to do all they reasonably can to consult an interested third party in advance of disclosing information. If they do not, then not only will they risk breaching the Code of Practice (and potentially receiving a Practice Recommendation from the Information Commissioner) but they may find themselves involved in legal proceedings with financial consequences potentially far more severe than a breach of the FOIA or the Code of Practice (see **10.9.5**). Liaising cooperatively with third parties will often of course be fundamental to maintaining good relationships with important suppliers.

Under the legislation, then, interested third parties are essentially left to hope that public authorities and the Information Commissioner will consult them at each stage and that authorities will resist requests with the same zeal and effectiveness as they themselves would at the outset, on any internal review and before the Information Commissioner and that they will, if necessary, appeal to the Information Tribunal.

10.9.4 Maximising the third party's chances of being consulted

A third party can improve its position in advance of any particular request being made by its negotiations and relationship development with the public authorities it deals with. As well as ensuring it has an open channel of communication with such authorities (including their FOI officers), it should look to insert confidentiality undertakings in relevant agreements, as well as terms requiring the public authority to notify and consult with it promptly and adequately in relation to any request for information which it receives that relates to or affects the third party in any way. It might also look for a commitment to be consulted in the wake of any Decision or Enforcement Notice of the Information Commissioner requiring disclosure of information affecting the third party, so that it and the public authority could consider the scope for appealing against the notice to the Information Tribunal. Similarly, it can review any information it provides, or has in the past provided, to public authorities and draw their attention to which elements it considers as confidential or engaging any of the other exemptions under the FOIA, and it should mark the documents accordingly. With regard to a third party prompting the Information Commissioner to consult it, see **10.9.5**.

10.9.5 Are there options for direct action open to third parties?

Yes, there are but each has difficulties and limitations and although some may in theory be used to obtain an injunction to prevent the disclosure of material, the value of such a remedy is severely limited by practicalities: where a public authority has ignored the Code of Practice's provisions on consultation, the first that the third party hears of the request will be after the information has already been disclosed and they receive a call from an interested journalist, for example. Even where the third party is on notice of the request, the window for action may be very narrow because public authorities are under an obligation to respond to requests promptly and in any event within 20 working days. There is the further difficulty that if disclosure has already taken place or cannot be stopped, the right of action, or its value to the third party, may fall away because there are no quantifiable damages to be compensated. Information cases (such as breach of confidence cases) tend to be all about the injunction application, for preventing disclosure is the only valuable remedy to the claimant. Lastly, taking legal action can be costly and exposes the litigant to a court order to pay the other side's legal costs if they lose.

Contract

Where the third party had negotiated a term in an agreement that the public authority would notify and duly consult them over any request for information in which the third party had an interest, it could seek to enforce the contract by applying for an injunction prohibiting disclosure and requiring consultation, in the unlikely event that it discovered this in time.

Judicial review

Alternatively, a third party could seek to enforce consultation by looking to public law for a remedy, as it is certainly arguable that in certain circumstances public authorities will have a duty at public law to take proper account of the views of interested third parties when deciding how to respond to a request for access under s.1(1) of the FOIA. It is a fundamental principle of public law that a decision maker must have regard to all relevant considerations. Furthermore, there is an obligation on decision makers to take reasonable steps to acquaint themselves with relevant material, which can include consulting third parties (*R. v. Secretary of State for Education, ex p. London Borough of Southwark* [1995] ELR 308 at 323C). The potential relevance of third parties' views is reflected within the FOIA regime by: (i) the requirement in s.45(2)(c) for the Secretary of State's Code of Practice to include provision on public authorities consulting with interested third parties over requests for information which affect them; (ii) the resultant Section 45 Code of Practice, which makes such provision; (iii) the obligation on the Information Commissioner in s.47 of the FOIA to act in a way which promotes the observance of the Section 45 Code of Practice; and (iv) the provision for third parties to be joined to appeals before the Information Tribunal (see **10.7.1**). One could add that the essence of procedural fairness in public law is that a person who will be affected by a decision should be given prior notice of what is proposed and an effective opportunity to make representations. Consultation may be judged to be all the more important where the public authority's decision in favour of disclosure (or that of the Information Commissioner where he is considering a s.50(1) complaint, or the Information Tribunal on appeal) could affect the third party's reputation or financial interests. More generally, third parties will arguably have what public law terms a 'legitimate expectation' that public authorities will adhere to provisions of the Section 45 Code of Practice.

Failure to consult by the authority (or the Information Commissioner or the Information Tribunal) may therefore render a decision or order to disclose unlawful and liable to be quashed by the Administrative Court on the third party's application for judicial review. (Whether it does or not will of course depend on the circumstances of the case.)

It is important to add in this context that the requirements of proper consultation have been established by the courts:

- consultation must take place at a time when the proposals are still at a formative stage;
- the proposer (in this context, the public authority) must give sufficient reasons for the action it proposes to take to permit intelligent consideration and response;
- adequate time must be given for consideration and response;
- the product of consultation must be conscientiously taken into account in finalising any proposals (*R.* v. *North and East Devon Area Health Authority, ex p. Coughlan* [2001] QB 213).

The duty to consult does not imply a duty to obtain agreement before acting (*R. (on the application of Smith)* v. *East Kent Hospitals NHS Trust* [2002] EWHC 2640, LTL 9.12.2002 per Silber J at [61]), nor will a different outcome necessarily be reached where the reviewing court orders the public authority to reconsider its decision in the light of the third party's views.

Even if an interested third party has been consulted, there may be other grounds for judicial review entitling it to challenge the decision of a public authority or the Information Commissioner, including where such decisions are flawed by: errors of law or fact; substantive unfairness or unreasonableness; unjustifiable inconsistency with earlier decisions; being supported by inadequate reasons; or involving a breach of the Human Rights Act 1998.

Pre-action injunctions are available ancillary to an application for judicial review and the Administrative Court may also grant declaratory relief and award damages (Supreme Court Act 1981, s.31(2) and (4)). The procedure on judicial review applications is set out in Parts 8 and 54 of the CPR and the Pre-Action Protocol under Part 54. As a matter of discretion, the courts will not normally make the remedy of judicial review available where there is an alternative remedy by way of appeal (*R.* v. *Chief Constable of the Merseyside Police, ex p. Calveley* [1986] QB 424).

Bringing a successful judicial review will often prove a significant challenge to third parties. Indeed the only known attempt to date ended in failure. A US-based gaming company had resort to judicial review in an attempt to prevent Birmingham City Council disclosing details of commercial arrangements between the company, the Council and Birmingham City Football Club to try and bring a super-casino to Birmingham. A request for this information had been made by a local newspaper, the Birmingham Post. Although it was turned down initially, this decision was reversed on internal review on public interest grounds. The judicial review application was rejected and not appealed (*R. (Las Vegas Sands Corp.) v. Birmingham City Council*, 2006, unreported).

Protecting confidential information

A third party could apply for an injunction restraining a public authority from disclosing its confidential/private information (or to restrain an applicant who had received it from the authority, or anyone who had received it from them, from making any further disclosure).[30] Damages are available to compensate losses where disclosure has already taken place, as is an account of the profits made from the disclosure. It is a defence for the public authority to show that the material was already in the public domain or that there is a public interest in disclosure.[31]

Where a public authority discloses a third party's confidential information in compliance with a Decision Notice of the Information Commissioner or the Information Tribunal, it remains legally uncertain whether or not the public authority will thereby have a defence to a breach of confidence claim by the third party. The issue was raised but not decided in *Milford Haven Port Authority v. Information Commissioner*, Information Tribunal, 6 November 2007, at para.24. A public authority may stand a better chance of making out such a defence where it has fought against disclosure as far as is reasonable (e.g. by refusing the applicant's request and appealing against the Information Commissioner's decision) and has notified and consulted the third party throughout. Where proceedings to restrain a breach of confidence have been issued in parallel with the Information Commissioner's investigation of a complaint which concerns the s.41 confidentiality exemption, it may be that he will decide to defer his decision until after the court has determined that issue.

It is important for third parties to appreciate that although a public authority may be under a contractual duty to keep certain information confidential, that will not necessarily mean the authority can avoid disclosing it to an applicant making an access request. In view of its obligations under the FOIA, a public authority will only be able to agree to withhold information where its disclosure would constitute an actionable breach of confidence at common law (i.e. a claim to which the public authority would not have a good defence). Public authorities cannot contract out of the FOIA, since a party may not contract out of a statutory protection which is intended to serve the public interest (*Johnson* v. *Moreton* [1980] AC 37).

Copyright

A third party affected by information to which access has been requested will in some cases have provided that information to the public authority and will own the copyright in the underlying document or work. However, whether third parties are entitled to seek an injunction against public authorities on the grounds that disclosure would constitute an infringement of their copyright is also, as yet, unclear. The FOIA is silent on whether the duty of public authorities to provide access to information is subject to the laws of copyright or not. Guidance from the DCA (now the MoJ) states that a public authority will not be infringing copyright by responding to a request for information.[32] Such guidance is perhaps given in view of s.50(1) of the Copyright, Designs and Patents Act 1988 (CDPA), which provides a defence to infringement where 'the doing of a particular act is specifically authorised by an Act of Parliament . . . unless the Act provides otherwise'. The similar common law tort defence of statutory authority may also apply: no liability in tort can arise from acts done in pursuance, and within the scope, of statutory powers where the powers are exercised in good faith, reasonably, without negligence, and for the purpose for which, and in the manner in which, the statute provides (*Halsbury's Laws of England*, 4th edn reissue 1999, vol.45(2) para.365).

If these defences are available in respect of disclosures by public authorities, third parties will not be able to bring proceedings against authorities to prevent a disclosure which would otherwise constitute an infringement of copyright. The defence would only be likely to apply to disclosures of non-exempt information, however, as it would be hard to characterise the FOIA as authorising disclosure of exempt information. Yet there is uncertainty over whether these defences do apply to the FOIA, which does not expressly authorise the disclosure of copies of documents, but of information. It may often be possible (though time-consuming) for a public authority to convey information from a document to an applicant without falling foul of copyright protection of the original document, such as by summarising it in different words or simply granting applicants the right to inspect the information. (These two options are specifically referred to in s.11(1) as means by which an applicant is entitled to have information communicated to him or her as an alternative to receiving a copy of the information, if reasonably practicable.) In addition, there is a separate argument that the FOIA does in fact prohibit disclosures of material which would constitute copyright infringement, by virtue of the absolute exemption in s.44(1)(a), which applies to information whose disclosure is prohibited by or under any enactment, which could arguably apply to the CDPA. (The force of that argument may be limited, however, since the CDPA does not prohibit disclosure of information per se; rather, it prohibits copying of the form in which that information is expressed.)

Yes if third parties were able to rely on these arguments to prevent (or recover compensation for) disclosure of their copyright material, the effectiveness of the FOIA as a means of promoting freedom of information could be significantly undermined. The courts may therefore not look favourably on such arguments and rule that public authorities can indeed rely on the s.50(1) defence.[33]

Regardless of these issues, the third party would need to prove its case in the normal way, including showing that what was copied was a substantial part of the copyright work. Equally, the authority might be able to rely on any of the other normal defences to such actions, which include consent (express or implied), public interest and – of specific relevance to many public authorities – the CDPA defences in ss.47 (copying of material which is open to public inspection under statute), 48 (the issuing to the public of material communicated to the Crown in the course of public business), and 49 (copying of materials which are public records under the Public Records Act 1958).

What is not in doubt is that even assuming that a public authority is authorised to make disclosures which would otherwise infringe copyright, a third party would be entitled to prevent the applicant who receives the material from making any further infringing use of it (*Ofcom* v. *Information Commissioner*, Information Tribunal, 4 September 2007, para.51). Again, this would be subject to any defences, and where the media is concerned it might have a defence of fair dealing for the purpose of reporting current events (CDPA, s.30(2)). The public authority itself could take such action in respect of its own copyright materials, hence applicants need to obtain the consent of rights-holders before re-using material obtained under the FOIA, including from the public authority that released it. Public authorities may wish to consider protecting their position by marking disclosed third party materials with a clear warning that reproduction without appropriate consent could lead to liability in damages and that the authority is not to be taken as authorising any such further disclosure. Otherwise, the authority could potentially be liable for authorising of the applicant's subsequent infringements, by virtue of s.16(2) of the CDPA.

Data protection

Certain personal data is exempt from disclosure under s.40 of the FOIA. A third party concerned that a public authority will disclose information containing personal data about him or her (or has already done so), may serve notice on the public authority under s.10 of the DPA requiring it to stop processing such data if disclosure (which would constitute 'processing' for these purposes) is likely to cause the third party substantial and unwarranted damage or distress. Service of a valid notice would bring the information within the qualified exemption in s.40(3)(a)(ii) of the FOIA (or reg.13 of the EIR). In addition, the third party could potentially apply to court for an order:

(i)   enforcing the s.10 notice;
(ii) blocking disclosure, or correcting, erasing or destroying the data (DPA, s.14); and
(iii) awarding compensation where disclosure has taken place (DPA, s.13).

Breaches of the DPA can also be investigated by the Information Commissioner under s.42 of that Act, and may result in his issuing the public authority data controller with an Enforcement Notice under s.40, specifying similar steps in relation to the data in question, save that he cannot award compensation.

For a more detailed discussion of the workings of the DPA and the interaction between it and the FOIA, see **Chapter 8**.

Defamation

A public authority could potentially be liable to a third party for disclosing information which contained a statement that identified the third party and would have made ordinary, right-thinking people think less of that person or organisation. However, where that information was supplied to the authority by another party and the authority is required to disclose it in response to a request under s.1 of the FOIA, the third party would not succeed in an action in defamation unless the authority acted maliciously in doing so (see FOIA, s.79). An authority will be acting maliciously where it knows the defamatory information is untrue or is reckless as to whether or not it is true. Malice will be particularly difficult to prove in the context of a statutory duty to disclose the information. By contrast, where the defamatory material is exempt from disclosure but the authority releases it anyway (perhaps not realising that it is exempt), the authority will not enjoy the protection of this statutory privilege. In general where defamation is concerned an interim injunction to restrain publication is very difficult to obtain.[34]

It is worth noting, however, that the s.79 defence will not protect a public authority where the defamatory allegations were contained in papers generated internally, so authorities could be sued in defamation by third parties in respect of such material. In addition, there is no protection in the FOIA for applicants republishing (i.e. communicating to any third party) defamatory information which they have received from public authorities, and thus a third party which was the subject of such allegations could sue the applicant (and anyone else) in respect of any such re-publication. In any claim, the defendant will have various further defences open to it (such as that the third party had consented to their disclosure or that the allegations were substantially true, or amounted to fair comment, or were made on a privileged occasion), and a media defendant may be able to rely on the qualified privilege defence for responsible journalism under the *Reynolds* case (*Albert Reynolds* v. *Times*

Newspapers Ltd & Others [2001] 2 AC 127) where there is a public interest in publishing the allegations.

As a public authority could be liable for subsequent disclosures where these were reasonably foreseeable, authorities might wish to consider marking disclosed materials with a clear warning that re-publication or reproduction without appropriate consent could lead to liability in damages and that the authority is not to be taken as authorising any such further disclosure.

Negligence/breach of statutory duty

Even where a public authority is flagrantly in breach of duties imposed on it by or under the FOIA, it is not open to applicants or third parties to bring a civil action against the authority for damages or an injunction or any other remedy, as a result of the bar in s.56(1). The position is the same under the EIR (reg.18(1) and (4)(e)).

Action regarding the Information Commissioner

Where an interested third party becomes aware that an applicant is seeking an adjudication from the Information Commissioner under s.50(1) of the FOIA on whether the authority's refusal to disclose the information is justifiable, the third party could write to the Information Commissioner with its views on the questions at issue. The Information Commissioner would arguably be obliged under public law to take account of them when reaching his decision, and were he not to do so, he could be open to a challenge from the third party by way of judicial review.

As a separate possibility, where no appeal to the Information Tribunal is made by the applicant or the authority, an interested third party would potentially be able to seek judicial review to challenge a decision of the Information Commissioner's contained in a Decision Notice issued in response to a complaint under s.50(1) of the FOIA.

Lastly, if all else fails, a third party might consider drawing any failure to consult on the authority's part to the Information Commissioner's attention. (This could not be done by means of a s.50(1) complaint, which is only available to applicants for information.) The Information Commissioner might look into the matter and issue the authority with a Practice Recommendation for a breach of the Code. That will be of no immediate benefit to the third party, but it might stimulate a more cooperative response from the authority in relation to future requests.

NOTES

1   The enforcement provisions of the FOIA (contained in Part IV of the Act, including Sched.3) and its appeals provisions (contained in Part V) are applied to the

EIR (SI 2004/3391), with the necessary modifications, by reg.18 of the EIR. Similarly, the Information Commissioner's powers and duties under ss.47 and 48 (the latter dealing with Practice Recommendations) are applied, as modified, to the EIR by reg.16(5) and (6). References in this chapter to the FOIA are to be taken to include a reference to the EIR and references to exemptions include a reference to exceptions under the EIR – unless clearly inappropriate in the context. See **Chapter 9** for a full discussion of the EIR.

2   Two codes of practice have been issued under the FOIA: the code issued by the Secretary of State for Constitutional Affairs under s.45 giving guidance to public authorities on the practice which he judges it desirable they should follow in order to satisfy their obligations under Part I of the Act (sometimes referred to as the 'Access Code'), and the Lord Chancellor's code under s.46 of the FOIA containing guidance for public authorities on record management. Under reg.16 of the EIR the Secretary of State for Environment, Food and Rural Affairs issued a code of practice in February 2005 for public authorities in respect of their obligations under the EIR.

3   By virtue of this section anybody (including public authorities or applicants for information) can contact the ICO for advice on the operation of the FOIA or the EIR, including on compliance issues, such as an authority's obligations with regard to access requests or the effect of particular exemptions. They will be advised by staff in a separate section of the ICO from those dealing with enforcement or complaints handling. Advice will be generalised, however, and staff will not advise on particular cases.

4   FOIA, s.1(1) requires public authorities to provide information requested (or to confirm or deny that they hold such information), and EIR, reg.5(1) requires authorities to make environmental information available on request. FOIA, s.11 and EIR, reg.6 require an authority to give effect to an applicant's preferred means of receiving the information where reasonably practicable, or to say why it is not. FOIA, s.17 and EIR, reg.14 contain the requirements for the sending and content of refusal notices, such as explaining why an exemption applies or why the greater public interest lies in withholding the information. EIR, reg.11 requires an authority to review its decision following representations from the applicant.

5   See ICO Enforcement Strategy (ICO, May 2007) and Regulation under the Freedom of Information Act 2000 and the Environmental Information Regulations 2004 (ICO, 2.3.05), paras.14–21.

6   See Lord Falconer's comments in an interview with the *Guardian* on 1 January 2005 'Falconer rejects risk to information act' (available at **www.guardian.co.uk/ uk_news/ story/0,,1381649,00.html**).

7   The Information Commissioner's policy regarding Practice Recommendations is set out in *FOI Practice Recommendations Policy Statement*, ICO, August 2006.

8   In the case of an Information Notice, non-compliance includes cases where, in purported compliance with the notice, a public authority makes a statement which is false in a material respect either knowingly or recklessly (s.54(2)).

9   RSC Order 45, rule 5, contained in Sched.1 to the CPR.

10 *Re Agreement of The Mileage Conference Group of The Tyre Manufacturers' Conference Ltd* [1966] 2 All ER 849 at 862, [1966] 1 WLR 1137 at 1162–3, per Megaw P; *Re Supply of Ready Mixed Concrete* [1991] ICR 52 at 70–2, RPC, per Anthony Lincoln J (affirmed [1995] 1 AC 456, [1995] 1 All ER 135, HL).

11 The Parliamentary Information Commissioner for Administration, the Information Commissioners for Local Administration in England and Wales, the Health Service Information Commissioners for England and Wales, the Welsh Administration Ombudsman, the Northern Ireland Information Commissioner for Complaints and the Assembly Ombudsman for Northern Ireland.

12 Similarly, s.76 of the FOIA provides that the Information Commissioner may disclose to those same ombudsmen (plus the Scottish Parliamentary Information Commissioner for Administration, the Information Commissioner for Local Administration in Scotland and the Scottish Health Service Information Commissioner) any information which he has obtained under the FOIA or the DPA if it appears to him that it relates to matters investigable by them in accordance with their functions under the statutes tabulated in s.76 of the FOIA.

13 Not only premises owned or occupied by the public authority in question but any premises at which the Information Commissioner reasonably suspects there to be relevant evidence (FOIA, Sched.3, para.1). The term also applies to any vessel, vehicle, aircraft or hovercraft, in which case references to the occupier of the premises mean the person in charge of that vehicle (FOIA, Sched.3, para.13).

14 See for example *Balancing the public interest: applying the public interest test to exemptions in the UK Freedom of Information Act 2000*, a study carried out by the Constitution Unit at the request of the Information Commissioner. Available in hard copy, priced £15, from the Constitution Unit, University College London, 29–30 Tavistock Square, London WC1H 9QU (email: constitution@ucl.ac.uk). See also, Parliamentary Ombudsman *Access to official information: monitoring of the non-statutory codes of practice 1994–2005* available at **www.ombudsman.org.uk/ improving_services/special_reports/aoi/aoi_1994_2005**.

15 *Regulation under the Freedom of Information Act 2000 and the Environmental Information Regulations 2004* (ICO, 2.3.05), para.41.

16 *Ibid.*, para.10.

17 *ICO Enforcement Strategy* available at **www.ico.gov.uk/upload/documents/library/ freedom_of_information/detailed_specialist_guides/enforcement_strategy_including_ moj_update_30_05_07.pdf**.

18 *Memorandum of Understanding between the Secretary of State for Constitutional Affairs (on behalf of government Departments) and the Information Commissioner, on co-operation between government Departments and the Information Commissioner in relation to sections 50 and 51 of the Freedom of Information Act 2000 (including ss 50 and 51 as applied, as amended, by Regulation 18 of the Environmental Information Regulations 2004)* (2.3.05). N.B. This document was devised in the earliest days of the FOIA's operation. It is in need of updating and thus may not be an accurate guide to ICO practice in all respects.

19 See paras.24 and 38 of *Regulation under the Freedom of Information Act 2000 and the Environmental Information Regulations 2004* (ICO, 2.3.05).

20 *Ibid.*, para.25, and para.8 of the MoU.

21 Personal communication from Assistant Information Commissioner with responsibility for complaints resolution (April 2005).

22 See generally *Freedom of Information: ICO Enforcement Strategy* (ICO, May 2007).

23 Source: Generally, Richard Thomas, Information Commissioner, conference speech, 2 November 2007, at New Square Chambers, Lincoln's Inn, London. Exceptionally, the informal resolution figure is drawn from the ICO website and relates to the first half of the year 2007/8 (see: **www.ico.gov.uk/about_us/what_ we_do/corporate_information/complaints_handling_performance.aspx**).

24 Namely, any such notice which concerns (i) information which is contained in transferred public records but has not been designated open information by the responsible authority for the purposes of s.66 of the FOIA; and (ii) the issue of how the public interest test in s.2 applies to that information. Broadly, transferred public records (defined in s.15(4)) are those which have been transferred to the Public Records Office and the responsible authority in relation to them is the Minister who appears to be primarily concerned (s.15(5)).

25 The 2005 Rules, SI 2005/14, are amended by the Information Tribunal (Enforcement Appeals) (Amendment) Rules 2005, SI 2005/450. The 2005 Rules revoke the Data Protection Tribunal (Enforcement Appeals) Rules 2000, SI 2000/189 as amended, and the Information Tribunal (Enforcement Appeals) (Amendment) Rules 2002. The 2005 Rules also apply to appeals under s.48 of the DPA. Appeal proceedings are also governed by Sched.6 to the DPA as amended by Sched.4 to the FOIA.

26 By contrast, the FOIA does not provide for any appeal against the conclusive evidence certificates issued under s.34(3) in respect of parliamentary privilege or s.36(7) in respect of prejudice to effective conduct of public affairs resulting from disclosure of information held by Parliament. In the absence of a statutory appeal, the only remaining avenue of challenge to these certificates would be by way of a judicial review but the courts are most unlikely to intervene, both because of the way the clauses are drafted and out of reluctance to interfere with parliamentary privilege.

27 This applies only to a hearing of an appellant's representations against summary dismissal of the appeal under rule 12 of the Information Tribunal (National Security Appeals) Rules 2005 (see para.6(1) of Sched.6 to the DPA and rule 4(3) of the Information Tribunal (National Security Appeals) Rules 2005).

28 These rules revoke the Data Protection Information Tribunal (National Security Appeals) Rules 2000, SI 2000/206). Appeal proceedings are also governed by DPA, Sched.6 as amended by FOIA, Sched.4.

29 See paras.6.8–6.10 under the section on guidance in *Guidance and Methodology for Publication Schemes* (ICO, April 2003, ICO website) and section 4 of *Publication Schemes: A Practical Guide: Part 1 'Classes'* (ICO, April 2003, ICO website). Publication Schemes are discussed in detail in **Chapter 2**.

30 To obtain an interim injunction, a claimant may well have to show it is more likely than not to succeed at trial. This is a higher test than that ordinarily required on injunction applications, where the claimant must show it has a 'real prospect of success' or there is a 'serious question to be tried' (*American Cyanamid Co. v. Ethicon Ltd* [1975] AC 396). This is because of the effect of s.12(3) of the Human Rights Act 1998 where an injunction is sought in a claim for breach of confidence to prevent the exercise of the Art.10 (ECHR) right to freedom of expression (*Cream Holdings Ltd & Others v. Banerjee & Another* [2005] 1 AC 253). A government claimant will in addition have to show that there is a public interest in keeping the information confidential (*A G v. Jonathan Cape Ltd and others* [1976] QB 752 at 770–771). For a fuller discussion of what constitutes confidential information, see the section on the s.41 exemption in **Chapter 4**.

31 Despite the public domain defence, where there has been only a limited degree of disclosure the courts may be prepared to grant an injunction preventing further disclosure (see e.g. *Franchi v. Franchi* [1969] RPC 149). Note also that in cases involving private information of the kind protected by Art.8 of the European Convention on Human Rights, the relevant defence is that the public interest in the Art.10 right to freedom of expression outweighs the Art.8 right (see *Ash v. McKennitt*, [2006] EWCA Civ 1714).

32 See *Procedural Guidance*, Chapter 8: 'Responding to the request' DCA, October 2004 (available at **www.dca.gov.uk/foi/guidance/proguide/chap08.htm**).

33 For arguments in support of such a position, see the article, 'Could copyright be an obstacle to an efficient and effective Freedom of Information regime?' by Julia Apostle and Mark Lawry in *Freedom of Information*, Vol.1, Issue 4, March/April 2005.

34 Due to the rule against prior restraint in *Bonnard v. Perryman* [1891] 2 Ch 269 (which the Court of Appeal held in *Greene v. Associated Newspapers Ltd* [2004]

EWCA Civ 1462, [2005] 1 All ER 30, [2005] EMLR 10 remained unaffected by s.12 of the Human Rights Act 1998), under which a court will not normally grant an injunction where the defendant publisher of the allegedly defamatory statement indicates an intention to prove it is true, or would be subject to some other substantive defence, unless the claimant can clearly show that none of these defences will succeed at trial.

APPENDIX

FOI resources

For general freedom of information guidance and assistance:

The Information Commissioner's Office
Wycliffe House
Water Lane
Wilmslow
Cheshire
SK9 5AF
Tel: 08456 30 60 60; 01625 54 57 45
Fax: 01625 524510
www.ico.gov.uk

To subscribe to the *Freedom of Information* journal and for freedom of information training courses:

Freedom of Information journal
PDP Companies
16 Old Town
London
SW4 0JY
Tel: 0845 226 5723
Fax: 0870 137 7871
www.foij.com

For updates and guidance on freedom of information:

Ministry of Justice
Selborne House
54 Victoria Street
London
SW1E 6QW
Tel: 020 7210 8500
Fax: 020 7210 0647
www.justice.gov.uk

For enquiries relating to the Environmental Information Regulations:

Department for Environment, Food and Rural Affairs
Environmental Information Unit
Area 1E
Whitehall Place West
3–8 Whitehall Place
London SW1A 2HH
Tel: 020 7270 8885
Fax: 020 7270 8970
Email: environmentalinformationunit@defra.gsi.gov.uk
www.defra.gov.uk

For information on the Annual Freedom of Information Conference & Workshop Series:

Freedom of Information Conference
PDP Conferences
16 Old Town
London SW4 0JY
Tel: 0845 226 5723
Fax: 0870 137 7871
www.foiconference.com

Index